THE WHO

MAXIMUM R&B

THE WHO: MAXIMUM R & B

Written, Compiled, and Designed by
Richard Barnes

Assisted by
Roxane Streeter

Additional Research by
Ed Hanel

Many thanks to the following people for their assistance and contributions: Roger's Mum and Dad, Keith's Mum, John's Mum, Pete's Mum and Dad, Chris Chappell, Keith Altham, Chris Stamp, Dougie Sandom, Alex Kipfer, Steve Margo, Jared Hauser, Tom Wright, Hillary Stabler, Ira Robbins, Irish Jack Lyons, Max Athanase and Barbara, Robert Stolpe, Mike Shaw, Ron Nevison, Dougal Butler, Bobby Pridden, Bill Harrison, Alan Rogan, Cy Langston, Roy Carr, Bill Curbishley, Jackie Curbishley, Greg Biggs, Martin Hitchcock, Cheryl, Diane Volpe, Lisa Seckler, Tim Prior, Ena Nicholls, Billy and Annie Nicholls, Judy Waring, Carla Rankine, Russ Schlagbaum, Martine Houadec, Mike Quinn, Mike Cable, Dave King, John Schollar, Ian Sternfeld (Sage 2 Designs), Fiona Foulger and Margaret, Wendy, Cathy and Julia from NME. Rolling Stone Magazine, Circus Magazine, Creem Magazine, Melody Maker, New Musical Express, Sounds, Time Out, Record Mirror, the following record companies: Atco, Decca, Brunswick, Fontana, Reaction, MCA, Track, Polydor, Ode, and Warner Brothers.

Also special thanks to Ed Hanel for the discography, David Costa for artwork, and Nick Locke for moderately amusing jokes and varied talents. And of course, thanks to THE WHO.

Thanks to Eel Pie, without whom this wouldn't have been impossible.

THE WHO: MAXIMUM R&B

Copyright © 1982 by Richard Barnes. All rights reserved.
Printed in the United States of America. No part of this book may be used or reproduced in any manner whatsoever without written permission except in the case of brief quotations embodied in critical articles or reviews.
For information address St.Martin's Press, 175 Fifth Avenue, New York, N.Y. 10010.
An Eel Pie book.
Library of Congress Cataloging in Publication Data

Barnes, Richard.
    The Who, Maximum R&B.

    Discography: p.
    1. Who (musical quartet) 2. Rock groups-United States-Iconography.
3. Rock Music-United States-Pictorial Works.
ML421.W5B4   784.5'4'00922   82-5705
ISBN 0-312-86989-4   AACR2
10 9 8 7 6 5 4 3 2 1

Picture Credits
1 Rex Features ● 12 Courtesy of Pete's Mum and Dad ● 13 Courtesy of Roger's Mum and Dad ● 14 & 15 Courtesy of Keith's Mum ● 16 & 17 Courtesy of John's Mum ● 19 Newspaper article: Acton Gazette ● 20, 21, 22 Courtesy of John and Roger's Mums ● 23 Newspaper article: Acton Gazette ● 24 Top Left: Courtesy of Mrs. Moon, Bottom Right: Courtesy of John Schollar ● 25 Top & Bottom Left: Fabulous Magazine ● 26 & 27 Syndication International ● 28 & 29 All pics T. Spencer/Colorific ● 30 Bottom Left: Richard Barnes ● 31 All pics Trinifold ●32 All pics Trinifold except Top Right: Ricky Wisdom ● 33, 34, 35 All pics Trinifold ● 40 Disc Magazine ● 41 LFI ● 42 Colin Jones ● 43 Trinifold ● 44 & 45 Tom Wright ● 46 & 47 Chris Morphet ● 48 & 49 Tom Wright ● 51 Top Left: Eric Plunkett, Bottom Row: Fabulous Magazine ● 52 Top Left: Trinifold, Bottom Right: Dominique Tarlé ● 53 Top Right: Chris Morphet, Bottom Right: Trinifold ● 52 & 53 Centre Series: Dominique Tarlé ● 54 Top Right: Jean Louis Rancurel ● 55 Syndication International ● 56 LFI ● 57 Middle Left: French Polydor, Bottom Left: Dezo Hoffman/Rex Features ● 58 Top Right: Trinifold, Bottom Left: Trinifold/French Polydor ● 59 Top L to R: Fabulous Magazine, Trinifold, Fabulous Magazine, Trinifold, Bottom: Music Parade/Topteen Magazine ● 60 Top L & R, Bottom Right: Fabulous Magazine, Bottom Left: French Polydor ● 61 Top: Fabulous Magazine, Bottom Left: French Polydor, Bottom Right: Jean Louis Rancurel ● Top L & R: Colin Jones, Middle Left: Premier Drums, Pillow: Courtesy of Keith's Mum, Bottom Left: Chris Morphet, Bottom Right: Dominique Tarlé ● 63 Syndication International ● 65 All pics Chris Morphet ● 66 Top Left: LFI ● 67 Trinifold ● 68 Bottom L & R: Chris Morphet ● 69 Left, Top & Bottom: Chris Morphet, Right: Colin Jones ● 70 Top Middle: Rex Features, Bottom: Kink Magazine ● 71 Trinifold ● 72 Top Right: Chris Morphet ● 73 Top Left: Chris Morphet, Bottom Left: Neil Smith, Right: Colin Jones ● 74 Top Left: Pictorial Press, Top Right and Middle: Premier Drums, Bottom Right: Tom Wright ● 75 Right: David Montgomery ● 76 Top & Bottom Left: Chris Morphet ● 77 Bottom Right: Chris Morphet ● 78 Top Right & Bottom Row: Chris Morphet ● 79 Left: Chris Morphet, Right Series: Who Films Ltd. ● 80 Chris Morphet ● 82 Top Series: Who Films Ltd., Bottom: Teen Life Magazine ● 83 Top Left: Michael English/Nigel Waymouth/Hapshash & The Coloured Coat, Top Right: Disc Magazine ●84 All pics Tom Wright except Top Left: Colin Jones ● 86, 87, 88 All pics Tom Wright ● 89 Top Left: Tom Wright, Bottom Right: Chris Morphet ● 90 All pics Dominique Tarlé except Bottom Left: Ethan Russell ● 91 Top: Ethan Russell, Bottom L & R: Dominique Tarlé ● 92, 93, 94 All pics Dominique Tarlé ● 95 Top: Disc Magazine, Bottom Left: LFI ● 96 Evening Standard/Richard Barnes/Bill Fallover ● 97 LFI ● 98 Barrie Wentzell ● 100 Phase Two ● 101 Kieser/Lippmann + Rau GmbH & Co., KG ● 102 Simms-Watts ● 104 Graham Hughes ● 105 Trinifold ● 106 Dominique Tarlé ● 107 All Pics Dominique Tarlé, Art Work: David Jarvis ● 108 Left: Disc Magazine, Bottom Right: LFI ● 109 Top: Disc Magazine ● 110 Top Row: Barrie Wentzell, Middle Left: French Polydor, Bottom Left: Dominique Tarlé, Bottom Right: Robert Ellis/Trinifold ● 111 Top Left & Bottom: Barrie Wentzell, Top Middle: Peter Cook, Top Right: Paul Takakjian ● 112 Top: Trinifold, Bottom Left: Ethan Russell, Middle & Bottom Right: Claude Gassian ● 113 All pics Claude Gassian ● 114 Top Left: Eric Jelly, Top Right: Barrie Wentzell, Bottom Left & Middle: Tom Wright ● 115 Top Left: Barrie Wentzell, Top Right: Ethan Russell, Bottom Middle: Evening News/Associated News Group ● 116 LFI ● 117 Middle Left: Neil Jones, Middle Strip: RSO/Columbia Pictures, Bottom Right: Richard Barnes ● 118 Trinifold ● 119 Julien Ruthven ● 120 LFI ● 121 Lippmann + Rau GmbH & Co., KG ● 123 Bill Graham ● 124 LFI ● 125 Trinifold ● 126 All pics Robert Stolpe ● 127 Top Right: Trinifold, Centre: MCA Records, Bottom Left: National Screen Services ● 128 Bottom Left: Syndication International ● 128-129 John Collier/Detroit Free Press ● 130 Top Left & Bottom Row: Trinifold, Top Right: Barrie Wentzell ● 131 Top & Bottom Right Corner: David Hooley, Bottom Left: Trinifold, Bottom Middle: Disc Magazine ● 132 Top Left: Syndication International, Top Right: Barrie Wentzell, Middle Left: LFI, Middle Right: Red Saunders/Trinifold ● 133 Top: Graham Hughes, Bottom Left: Trinifold, Bottom Right: LFI, Bottom Extreme Right: Syndication International, Cartoon: Chris Williams/NME ● 134 Top Left: Rex Features, Top Right: Evening News/Associated News Group, Middle left: Syndication International, Middle Right: Claude Gassian, Bottom: Dougal Butler ● 135 Storm Thorenson/Trinifold ● 136 Top Left: Russ Schlagbaum, Top Right: Terry O'Neill/Trinifold, Middle Left: LFI, Bottom Series: Robert Ellis/Trinifold ● 137 Top: Rex Features, Bottom Left: Russ Schlagbaum, Bottom Right: Robert Ellis/Trinifold ● 138 Top Far Right & Bottom Left: Rex Features, Centre Pic: Graham Hughes ● 139 Top: Kevin Stein, Bottom L & R: Terry O'Neill/Trinifold ● 140 Left Top to Bottom: MPL, Right Middle & Bottom: Syndication International ● 141 Bristol United Press ● 144, 145, 146 Polydor ● 147 Graham Wiltshire ● 148 Richard Barnes ● 149 Kid pics: Courtesy of Kenney Jones, Middle Right: Fabulous Magazine, Bottom Left: Michael Zagaris/Trinifold, Bottom Right: Rex Features ● 150 Top Right: Gavin Cochrane/Trinifold, Middle Right: David Harte/Trinifold, Bottom Right: Lippmann + Rau + Scheller ● 151 Top L & R: Claude Gassian Bottom L & R: Neal Preston/LFI ● 152 Top Left: LFI, Centre Pic: Gus Christie/Trinifold, Bottom Left: Robert Ellis, Bottom Right: Virginia Turbett ● 153 Top: Cincinnati Enquirer, Middle Left: Evening News, UK, Middle Centre: Buffalo Evening News, Bottom Left: Rex Features, Bottom Right: Gamma/John Spooner ● 154 Left: Claude Gassian, Top Right: Time Magazine, Bottom Right: Richard Evans/Trinifold ● 155 Right: Claude Gassian, Bottom Left: Richard Evans/Trinifold ● 156 All Pics Richard Barnes except Bottom Left Corner: Pennie Smith/Trinifold ● 157 All pics Richard Barnes ● 158 Top Row L to R: Tom Wright, LFI, Rex Features, Middle Right: Richard Barnes, Bottom Row L to R: Atco, Richard Barnes, Tom Wright ● 159 Top Row L to R: Pennie Smith/Trinifold, Ross Halfin, Pennie Smith/Trinifold, Middle Row L to R: Richard Barnes, Richard Barnes, Rolling Stone Magazine, Bottom Row L to R: Richard Barnes/Trinifold, Pennie Smith/Trinifold ● 160 All pics Richard Barnes ● 161 All pics Richard Barnes except Bottom Row, 2nd from Left: Pennie Smith/Trinifold ● 162 Top Row: Richard Barnes, Middle Left: Richard Barnes, Middle Right: Pennie Smith/Trinifold, Bottom Middle: Richard Barnes, Bottom Right: Pennie Smith/Trinifold ● 163 Top Two Rows of Pics: Richard Barnes, Top Right Corner: Warner Brothers, Bottom Middle: WDR, Bottom Right Corner: Claude Gassian ● 164 Top Left: Robert Ellis/Trinifold, Middle Left & Centre: Tom Wright, Bottom Left & Three on Right: Richard Barnes ● 165 Right middle: Russ Schlagbaum, Bottom strip: Graham Hughes. All other pics Richard Barnes ● 166 Top Left: Gered Mankowitz, Top Right: Chalkie Davies, Bottom L & R: Richard Barnes ● 167 Top Left: Graham Hughes, Top Right: Chalkie Davies, Bottom L & R: Gered Mankowitz ●

THE WHO
MAXIMUM R&B

by Richard Barnes

**ST. MARTIN'S PRESS
NEW YORK**

1962-1964

Detours/Club circuit/Art school/Moon joins/Meaden/Mods/High Numbers

Pete Townshend and John Entwistle formed their first group, the Confederates, when they were about 14 and both attending Acton Grammar School in West London. "The central part of it all then was the Congo Club in Acton," remembers Pete. The Congo Club was a youth club in the Acton Congregational Church.

The Confederates never played in front of an audience except at the club and were really just four schoolboys practising together. John played trumpet, Pete played banjo, another school friend Chris Sherwin played drums and Phil Rhodes played clarinet. "When Phil and John asked me to join them I had to rush out and get a chord book," explains Pete. "As I'd been buggering about playing guitar for nearly two years I wasn't getting anywhere. They expected me to play and were fairly impressed, which I couldn't work out. Perhaps they thought that if you could play three chords you could play the rest." John was quite an accomplished musician having studied piano till he was eleven and played french horn in the Middlesex Youth Orchestra.

John was playing in two bands, the one with Pete and another, bigger, Trad Jazz outfit, eventually dropping out of the Confederates to concentrate on the other band. "We had a guy who used to hum through the tuba because he couldn't play it," recollected John. "But he could hum right and it sounded just as if he was playing it properly. We also had a trombone player who couldn't play too well either."

Phil Rhodes, the Confederates' clarinet player, and Pete both eventually joined the exodus. At one time there were three banjo players recalls Pete. "This guy Alf Maynard had a Vega banjo and was very much the central figure of the band, so I got edged out. I was a better player than him but I didn't really fit and didn't push myself too much."

John continued with the bigger band. "We never had a name and the only gigs we did were at the Ealing club and at an interval session at the Corgi books factory dinner and dance. We were really just learning to play. I could play the trumpet and I used to make up most of the songs. I used to go upstairs while they were rehearsing downstairs and write a new Trad song. We did Kenny Ball and Acker Bilk stuff mainly. The most money we ever earned was when we went busking in the street in Hammersmith. Pete came along and it was New Year's Eve. We went from pub to pub playing and then collecting money." Pete remembers "I got £8 which was half what my share would have been had I been a full member of the band. So they must have really collected a lot of money."

John recounts one incident from that night. "In one pub my mother and step-father came into the pub while we were playing. I found it extremely embarrassing. I was only fifteen and I shouldn't have been in a pub. My step-father gave me five minutes to get out – he didn't want his evening's drinking disturbed by a rather loud and not very good trad band."

Pete had an unhappy last year at school. "I got into a row with the Confederates drummer, Chris Sherwin. I used to hang around with him a lot and once we got into a fight and I hit him over the head with a bag and he had concussion which I didn't realise. As a result I was sort of ignored by our little school playground clique. They gave me the cold shoulder. I was a little disturbed by it and went more into my shell in a way and transferred it to the guitar. I just decided to use what was really a pretty bleak period for that."

So Pete bought a £3 Czechoslovakian guitar from his mother's antique shop, and gave up his mandolin banjo. (This was Pete's second guitar. The first was bought for him by his grandmother when he was twelve. "I fought tooth and nail with it for a year and finally gave up because it was such a

bad instrument.") Pete still saw a lot of John and they formed another band with the kid that sat next to John at school, Mick Brown, and another schoolchum, Pete Wilson. Pete played guitar and John now had a bass guitar. We used to do Shadows' numbers" Pete recalled. "I was terribly happy with it and people quite liked us. It gave me a new confidence. I hadn't made it very well with chicks, and at the time when my mates started to get it together with chicks I was getting into the guitar. It became quite an obsession." The group were first called the Aristocrats, and then the Scorpions. According to John the Scorpions only played

once and that was at the Congo Club. "And we were terrible. We were just sort of ill-prepared."

Pete considered the Congo club quite instrumental in his development. "It was when I came closest to being part of a gang. I got caught up with a guy called Stewart Dodd. He and I both had big noses at school and he was nicknamed Oscar after some cartoon character with a big nose. He went through an incredible metamorphosis. We didn't see him for some time and I saw him rolling down the street drunk one day. I said, hallo Oscar and he smacked me in the teeth and threw a bottle at me. He had turned into a petty villain overnight and was caught up with a local bunch of hardnuts, and just hated being called by his school nickname. I started to live in the real world after that. I had shut myself away plunking away on the banjo at home and suddenly realised that the Congo wasn't just a place where we got together and entertained the troops, as it were. There was a lot of violence and sex and stuff going on."

One day after a rehearsal with the Scorpions John was walking back when he met Roger Daltrey in the street.

"I hear you play bass guitar", said Roger.

As John was carrying his bass under one arm and an amplifier under the other he laughed, "Yeah."

"Do you want to try in my group?" asked Roger.

"I'm already in a group," John replied.

"Well, mine's earning money," said Roger.

John arranged to go to the drummer's house in Shepherd's Bush for an audition the following week. He wasn't sure who was auditioning who though. "I sat in with them for a couple of numbers, then Roger came up to me and said, 'Now you've heard us, do you still want to join?' I laughed and said 'Yeah,' and so I was in."

Roger had also been at Acton County Grammer School, in the year ahead of John and Pete, but the headmaster had written to his parents suggesting that they take him out of the school when he was only fifteen, because of his rebellious attitude. "I wouldn't wear their silly uniform," remembers Roger, "I didn't like it. I could've been quite academic I think. I just didn't want to know. From the time I heard Elvis Presley and Lonnie Donegan I didn't want to be anything else." Roger's problems started when his parents moved from Shepherd's Bush to Bedford Park, a better part of Acton. "I'm the only one of the band that really came from Shepherd's Bush. It was real working class. Street community working class. The areas where Pete and John lived were quite middle class. After passing the eleven plus I was top of the class, so if I'd have gone to the grammar school in Shepherd's Bush I might have been alright. When I got to school, I was used to talking to people who talk like I do, but there were all of these galloping 'hoorays'. I just could not identify. I thought this is what the school's gonna do to me, it's gonna make me like them. They were totally foreign to me. They didn't even know what playing in the street was. There was a group of about ten of us – we all felt the same way. We all ended up Teddy Boys. We were the worst lot at school. I remember Townshend, although I was in a different year from him, and I know he used to have a hard time, but we never gave him a hard time. We were yobs but we weren't bullies."

He got a job as a sheet metal worker. His band, the Detours, were making money, although not much. They played a few firm's outings, some weddings and barmitzvahs, and such. They used to rehearse regularly at Reg Bowen's house. Reg was the rhythm guitarist. John remembers, "We brought in this guy on rhythm guitar because he'd come into a little bit of money and bought himself a Vox amp and a guitar. We figured like if we had him in the group we'd be able to use his amplifier. He could sing a bit as well. The poor guy went on holiday with his fiancé and drowned, so we took over his amplifier. We figured he didn't need it any more. We still had this other rhythm guitarist called Reg Bowen, but he only knew about five chords so eventually we started looking for a new rhythm guitarist and that's when I managed to persuade Pete to join. He didn't, however, want to join at first but I told him we had a real Vox amplifier, so he thought 'A Vox amplifier . . . well . . . ' and he joined."

"The Detours became a good social thing," remembers Pete. "The drummer's father sort of managed us and drove us around in his Dormobile van." The drummer and his father went off for two weeks holiday and while they were away another drummer, Dougie Sandom, who Roger had just met in the street a week earlier, sat in. He was so much better that they asked him to stay and threw out the original drummer although this left them without transport. Doug was about seven years older than the rest and had five years experience. He gave them a new confidence and was a stabilising influence. Roger's father felt better knowing that Doug was around – "He was a sensible chap."

The five-piece Detours were Colin Dawson; singer Roger Daltrey; lead guitar, Pete Townshend; rhythm guitar,

John Entwistle; bass guitar and Doug Sandom; drums.

The leadership then was shared between Roger and Colin Dawson. Dawson being the singer had a lot of say about which material they played. "Roger regarded it as his band but I think that it was just because he was like the biggest mouth really", Pete thought. John remembered, "Roger would punctuate his decisions with punches." John and Pete were still thinking of forming a band of their own but never actually broke away from the original five-piece Detours.

"When we first started, I used to *make* all the bloody guitars. We used to make our amplifiers as well, used to make these huge boxes," Roger remembers. "In them days it was all psychological warfare being in a group, so we hit on the idea of having the biggest cabinets you've ever seen in your life – yet inside we'd have this little 12-inch speaker. It looked like a bloody sideboard. It looked like me mum's front room on stage. People would come and see us and say 'Hey, they must be good, look at the size of their gear.'"

Roger's first guitar was one he made himself out of ply-wood, based on an acoustic he borrowed. "I made several and they were quite good except that the necks used to fold up. The last one I made was actually a good guitar because my uncle, who was a carpenter, made the neck for me. I used that on stage up until about 1962 and then my dad bought me an Epiphone."

Pete also cut a guitar body from a block of wood and Roger helped file the edges down for him. Pete then unscrewed the neck of his Harmony guitar, transferred it to his new solid guitar body and added some pickups.

John's first guitar was also made on the cheap. There was a guitar factory near his house and he was able to buy the body of a Fenton Weill, which had been smuggled out, for £5. He then made a deal with one of the employees at the factory to restring it and make it up for him, "He did it all for three quid, so the whole thing only cost £8."

A little later John bought himself a Goodman's 18″ speaker and had the front covered with a red, green, turquoise and yellow curtain fabric. "The rest of the band refused to carry it into gigs because it was so heavy," John remembers. The PA was a Decca mono HiFi valve amplifier. "We used to call it the valve sandwich because the tops of the valves were so near the casing that if any of the audience leant on it, it would blow the valves up. We had to carry spare sets of valves everywhere," recalls John. "It came in very useful though because it got so hot that we could use it to dry out the tiny little Grampian microphones we used. They were great mikes but the more you slobbered into them as you sang the wetter and quieter they got. We'd always have a couple of spare mikes drying out on the valve sandwich at gigs."

Signing for Commercial Entertainments

John recalls some of the early gigs. "We'd like go out on a firm's outing – put all the equipment in the back of their coach and go somewhere like Bognor. On the way back the firm would have already hired a Church or a pub hall. We'd stop and do a dance and they would all get pissed out of their minds and have a bit of a dance and then we would load all the equipment back into the coach again and go home. But our first fairly regular gig was in Ealing at a place called the Jewish Club. We did it four or five times. It was a big house in Ealing and they used to hold dances in a big room for the Jewish kids."

After leaving school Entwistle got a job at the local tax office and Pete went to Ealing Art School which wasn't far from where he lived, Roger continued to work as a sheet metal worker, Dougie as a bricklayer and Colin Dawson as a sales rep.

While he was employed at the tax office John used to go to day school once a week. He had a friend there who got the band a gig in a place called the Paradise Club in Peckham. "We used to get paid six pounds for the night. The van which we hired from Wilments cost us three pounds ten shillings, and we used to get ten shillings each which would usually disappear in food and drink while we were there." The Paradise Club had a rival club in Peckham. John remembers, "We'd get this rival gang come in and start to smash everything up every other week. We'd stand in front of our equipment as they were trying to wreck the place and try to ward them off but in the end something got damaged quite badly

and it became too risky so we had to pull out of it, which was a drag because it was a good regular gig."

The band were really helped to their feet by Pete's mother, Betty. Pete's parents were both in the music business when they met. His dad, Cliff Townshend used to play in the famous RAF dance band, the Squadronaires and Betty was a singer before she married, known as Betty Dennis with the Sidney Torch Orchestra. They therefore had contacts with people in the business. Betty was also very capable and industrious. She drove around finding out where dances were being held and who was running them. She set up four auditions for the band, one of which gave them their first big break.

They passed their first audition at the Castle Hotel in Richmond but turned down the gig to try for something better. The biggest promoter in that area was Bob Druce. Betty had somehow got them an audition for Bob Druce's circuit of dance halls. Dougie Sandom remembers that night. "I've never seen anyone so nervous as Roger that night. Pete was white as a sheet too." The audition was at the Oldfield Hotel in Greenford, a suburb in West London. Betty drove them there. Playing that night were the Bel-Airs, Bob Druce's top band and very popular in that area. The Detours did their audition in the interval using the Bel-Airs' equipment, playing three or four numbers. According to Doug Sandom

TO MARK RE-OPENING OF
ACTON TOWN HALL

A
GALA
BALL

will be held

SATURDAY NEXT. 1st SEPTEMBER
7.45 to 11.30 p.m.

THE RON CAVENDISH ORCHESTRA
and
THE DETOURS' JAZZ GROUP

Demonstration by

PETER EGGLETON and
BRENDA WINSLADE

International Professional Champions 1962

the compere at the Oldfield asked the audience "What do you think of the lads. Do you want them back?" The audience cheered so they had passed the audition. Druce gave them a contract saying that they would work exclusively for him after that.

One of the first gigs that Bob Druce got for the Detours was at a new promotion he was doing by the coast at Broadstairs. John remembers, "Broadstairs was an old people's seaside resort with only about sixteen young kids. We used to get the same sixteen every week. The place was a miserable failure but Bob Druce sent us there every week for ages." Since the equipment was kept at Pete's house, his mother Betty would take it in her little Ford van, while the group travelled to the gig with one of Druce's bouncers in his van. "At first it used to be a bloody nightmare," Roger says, "John, Pete and I used to go with Betty. Pete used to sit in front with her and we used to lay on top of the gear in the back of a five hundred-weight van with the roof about three inches from our heads all the way to Broadstairs."

"We went whatever the weather," said John. "Once I remember going down in a ridiculous snow blizzard. My speaker cabinet, which was on top of Betty's van, had about a foot of snow on it when we arrived. When I started playing it was so soggy that the cone shot straight out on to the floor."

They couldn't make any money because the cost of hiring

vans was usually more than their earnings for the night. They soon bought a secondhand van for £40. Bob Druce paid for it and stopped it out of their money every week. It was an Austin 15cwt ex-Post Office van with sliding doors but no side windows. They painted the van maroon and black with DETOURS and a long arrow painted down the side in white. To cover up dents in the back of the van it had a series of footprints painted in red. Roger had welded a black pipe with a witches hat cover to the back like a chimney sticking out of the van. Roger drove the van despite being only a learner driver. On one trip back from Broadstairs he crashed the van into a bridge and dented the side in, putting the passenger door out of action. It stayed like that all the time they had it and everybody had to get in through the driver's door. Having the van meant they could handle as many bookings as they could find.

Colin Dawson modelled himself on Cliff Richard and they did a number of Cliff Richard songs as well as Shadows intrumentals. The line up was very much a singer with a backing band, and after a while the others got fed up with this. Dawson, however, got engaged and was devoting more time to his fiancée and his job as a Danish bacon rep and spending less time playing with the band. He also was a bit too clean cut and respectable. "He used to wear navy blue blazers and light grey slacks and was just a bit too dapper" recalls John.

Pete points out, "He was a nice enough bloke but at that time he was such an opposite of Roger, who by then really was the balls in the band and ran things the way he wanted them. If you argued with him you usually got a bunch of fives. It was good in a way because every band needs someone in that strong pushy role."

Dougie remembers, "The band had lost faith in him anyway, they'd be joking about him behind his back on stage." A new singer, Gabby, joined them. He had been the bass player for the Bel-Airs. Pete remembers. "We had a period when we went kind of nuts. We started experimenting a lot with the line-up. For a while we had a guy called Peter Vernon Kell join the band. He played lead guitar very badly, and occasionally claviolene."

Being signed up by Bob Druce's company, Commercial Entertainments Ltd. meant that the Detours were guaranteed regular work in his clubs. Commercial Entertainments ran weekly dances at various pubs and halls around London, mostly in Acton, Ealing and the Greenford area. Druce would take out of their weekly pay cheques 10% for management and a further 10% for agency commission. But the band were in the healthy position of having constant work and regular money. His venues consisted of a number of halls attached to pubs and three or four licensed clubs. He would try other one-off promotions now and again to test out an area. The main circuit was the White Hart Hotel in Acton, The White Hart in Southall, the Fox and Goose Hotel in Ealing, the Oldfield Hotel in Greenford, the Goldhawk Rd. Social Club in Shepherd's Bush and the Glenlyn Ballroom in Forest Hill. These six places were to become the mainstay of the Detours stage act for the next year or two. "Doing our National Service" said Doug.

Druce's stable of bands consisted of the Bel-Airs, the Detours, the Riversiders, the Corvettes, the Beachcombers, the Federals and the Macabre. He would juggle the bands around his clubs and ran a thriving and profitable business. "We used to supplement our regular money from the Druce gigs by doing weddings and things like that," recalls Pete. "At the end of the evening you'd get some bloke come up and he'd be pissed as a rat, determined to spend as much money as possible on his daughter's wedding and he'd say 'You were great lads, here's fifty quid'."

The biggest fee they got was from playing at an American Servicemen's club in London called Douglas House. Betty had got them the gig which paid a staggering £75 for a Sunday afternoon. Gabby used to sing lots of Johnny Cash and C & W songs that the Americans loved. Roger, although still lead guitarist, used to alternate on vocals with Gabby so that Gabby could go and get a drink or Roger could leave the stage to take one of the girls outside. Occasionally Gabby would play bass guitar when John played trumpet, and Roger attempted trombone for their Trad jazz spot. Pete recalls, "At that time we did a bit of everything; the top ten, Cliff Richard, Telstar, some Country and Western and a Trad jazz medley. That was the thing we were well known for – 'the Detours are a very versatile band' and all that."

"Bob Druce thought we were a bit scruffy," said Doug Sandom, "So we had some suits made up by a Hammersmith tailor that were designed by Pete. They had maroon jackets with no lapels, which we wore with white shirts and black bow ties. After about six months we got fed up with them and Roger lent them to another band and we never saw them again."

The next major change in the line-up came as a result of them playing support for Johnny Kidd and the Pirates. They had played support to many bands, notably Shane Fenton and the Fentones and Cliff Bennett and the Rebel Rousers, both of whom influenced the Detours' style. They were so impressed with Johnny Kidd and the Pirates that they decided to copy their line-up and sound – a four piece band with a vocalist, lead guitar, bass and drums, with no rhythm guitar.

Gabby, who'd only been with the band for a few months, was dropped, and Roger became the vocalist. Pete moved from rhythm guitar to lead guitar. "For a long time I was playing so-called lead guitar, but really I was still the rhythm player."

They played at the tiny Ealing Club in West London where the Stones had started out. "The Ealing Club was one of the first R & B clubs. Every time the owner made his announcements the sweat on the wall used to become live because this lousy amp that he used was so dangerous," remembers John. "If you were leaning against the wall at the same time as holding your guitar you'd get a terrible electric shock. It happened to me loads of times and was so dangerous that once we kicked the shit out of it, so he couldn't use it again. While he wasn't looking we all ganged up and just stomped on it. He never knew it was us."

The Detours were building up a good following around their area. They were working regularly four or five nights a week, doing the Oldfield Hotel three nights a week at one point. They would get a sheet from Druce each month with the next four weeks gigs listed. Doug Sandom remembers, "The young girls used to put presents for you in the van, little dolls and things. My wife refused to go out shopping with me because I'd be recognised and fans would talk to me. After we did a big promotion at Acton Town Hall once, lots of girls chased us up the alley screaming and we had to sign their arms and stuff."

Art School and Rhythm & Blues

Things weren't all roses with the band. The arguments between Pete and Roger had started. "When we were practising sometimes, it was nothing to see Roger smack Pete in the nose or something. They were always at each other's throats." Doug remembers an important audition they did in a pub in Willesden. "We were packing the gear up and the promoter said 'come into the bar and have a drink.' Pete stayed in the hall still putting gear away and the guy said to Doug, Roger and John, "Get rid of him and I'll sign you." Roger seemed interested but Doug Sandom insisted, "Either you have us as we are, or you can get stuffed."

Much of the ingredients of the Who's later success can be directly attributed to specific incidents experienced by Pete at Ealing Art School. The destruction of the equipment, although initially the result of an accident on stage, was developed and legitimized because of Pete's exposure to 'auto-destructive art' at Ealing Art School. The 'pop-art' period was obviously influenced by Art School, where what used to be called 'commercial art' became 'graphics' and merged with 'fine art' to become 'pop-art'. However, the real influence on Pete and consequently on the Detours (and the High Numbers and the Who) came, not just through specific incidents, but through the general day-to-day awareness of art school life.

"I couldn't believe it" said Pete. "It was such a great period for me. I had a natural artistic bend which was why I ended up at art school, but basically I should have done something to do with writing I suppose, but if I had I probably wouldn't have ended up sort of so open-endedly creative as I later became. The art side did get my brain going creatively and started me thinking.

Pete was still withdrawn when he arrived at art school. "For me, it was a revelation because of the fact that it was so different from my last year at Grammar school, being ostracised and stuff like that just because of the first fight I'd got into and half won. I couldn't understand that everyone else who won fights had become heroes."

Pete was quite reserved and hung up about his nose when he first arrived. "I soon decided that I was going to get nowhere as an introvert and that I'd become an extrovert – and that's what I did."

I first met Pete at Ealing art school and we soon became friends. Pete also struck up a friendship with an American student in the photography section of the college, Tom Wright. One day Pete had asked if he could play a guitar belonging to a student called Tim Bartlett in the student's common room. The following day this guy told his friend Tom Wright how well this new student could play and Tom approached Pete the next day to ask if he could teach him some of the 'fancy guitar licks' he'd played. Pete told Tom years later that Tom had been the first person to come up and speak to him at art college. In return for Pete teaching Tom some guitar licks at Tom's flat in Sunnyside Road opposite

---

WHITE HART HOTEL

ACTON

264, HIGH STREET, ACTON, W.3

JIVING & TWISTING

MONDAY

AND THURSDAY

ALSO

EXCLUSIVE SUNDAY CLUB

FEATURING

BEL-AIRS   RIVERSIDERS

FEDERALS   DETOURS   CORVETTES

7.30—11.0 p.m.   LICENSED BALLROOM BARS

Admission 3/6 (Members)   Girls 2/- before 8 p.m.

Enquiries : 3, Thorney Hedge Road, Chiswick W.4 (Taylor Entertainments)

---

the college, Tom introduced Pete to two things that were probably more crucial to his life than the rest of art school put together. Tom had an absolutely amazing collection of blues, R & B and jazz albums that he'd brought over from the States. Tom also had a stash of pot which was in 1962 relatively unknown in Britain outside of the West Indian community and merchant seamen.

Tom recalls, "We put in a lot of research into rhythm 'n' blues in that small flat in Sunnyside Road – most of it flat on our backs."

The main focal point of the college life was the café 'over the road'. Tom had secured half the spaces on the juke box for the student's use, the rest were for the lorry drivers that used the cafe too. So on this juke box Frank Ifield's *I Remember You*, Pat Boone's *Speedy Gonzales* and Cliff Richard's *Batchelor Boy* would exist alongside Jimmy Reed's *Shame, Shame, Shame,* Booker T's *Green Onions* and Slim Harpo's *King Bee*.

Art schools produced many British rock musicians in the sixties, such as John Lennon and Keith Richard, and Ealing

Art School at that time also had Ronnie Wood, Roger Ruskin Spear and Freddie Mercury as students.

By some fluke, Tom was busted for possessing pot and ordered to be deported. He asked Pete and myself who were in the process of trying to find a flat to rent near the college whether we would take over his place and look after the contents. We, of course, jumped at the chance.

Pete could now immerse himself in Tom's 150 or so high calibre album collection and Sunnyside Road became a focal point for him for a couple of important years. The albums in Tom's collection included all of Jimmy Reed's albums, all of Chuck Berry's, all of James Brown's, Bo Diddley, John Lee Hooker, Snooks Eaglin, Mose Allison, all of Jimmy Smith's, Muddy Waters, Lightnin' Hopkins, Howling Wolf, Slim Harpo, Buddy Guy, Big Bill Broonzy, Sonny Terry and Brownie McGhee, Joe Turner, Nina Simone, Booker T, Little Richard, Jerry Lee Lewis, Carl Perkins, The Isley Brothers, Fats Domino, The Coasters, Ray Charles, Jimmy McGriff, Brother Jack McDuff, John Patton, Bobby Bland, The Drifters, The Miracles, The Shirelles, The Impressions, and many jazz albums including Charlie Parker, Mingus, Coltrane, Miles Davis, Milt Jackson, Wes Montgomery, Jimmy Guiffre, Dave Brubeck, plus albums by Jonathon Winters, Mort Sahl, Shelly Burman and particularly Lord Buckley. There were also about thirty classical albums.

Pete told Zig-Zag magazine some years later, "When I first got into pot I was involved in the environment more; there was a newness about art college, having beautiful girls around for the first time in my life, having all that music around me for the first time, and it was such a great period – with the Beatles exploding and all that all over the place. So it was very exciting, but although pot was important to me, it wasn't the biggest thing: the biggest thing was the fact that pot helped to make incredible things even more incredible."

None of the other members of the band were interested in smoking marijuana and they rarely came back to his flat. Pete's life revolved around art school, playing four or five nights a week, getting stoned and absorbing his new treasure trove of American blues and jazz. He went to sleep to music and woke up to music, usually the slow lazy rhythm of Jimmy Reed. Art school also gave a sense of self-confidence to go with his new musical inspiration.

Ealing Art School was a very unusual art school. This normally staid and conservative institution had, in the same year that Pete enrolled, acquired a new head tutor, Roy Ascot. He had replaced most of the staff with young fresh sixties designers and artists and was to begin a revolutionary experiment in art tuition based on the science of cybernetics. Cybernetics is the study of systems of control and communication in such things as diverse as animals, calculating machines and economics. Just what such an obscure science had to do with art and design was a bit of a mystery. Roy Ascot maintained that "Art is more than just 'old apples on tables' ". This truism might have been an effective dig at the 'old guard' of the art school but it was never really helpful to the excited but fairly confused students. However, Pete got caught up in this daring experiment. Cybernetics, the 'science of sciences', the theory of computer thinking, became the watch word. Printmaking, basic design, sculpture and colour theory were all intermingled with feedback, noise-interference and automation principles. There is no doubt that confusing as the course appeared and, to a certain extent, was, it was the most exciting and aware and radical at that time. Nevertheless, unless involved with the day-to-day evolution of the project, any comprehension of what was happening was practically impossible.

For instance, one day a visiting group of educationalists from Sierra Leone or Canada or somewhere were looking in bewilderment at the polythene and perspex 'artificial environments' that the students had built into the college classrooms. They were further perplexed to see Pete push himself along the corridor on a kids trolley cart made out of old orange boxes and pram wheels. The other students didn't give him a second glance as they had become quite used to seeing him like that. Pete had been using his trolley-cart for several weeks as part of a serious college project where students were given different characteristics to the ones they had. It was part of a process of breaking down their preconceived ideas about art, design, life and themselves. Pete had been given as one of his characteristics, the physical

6

disability of having no legs. So as a way round this particular problem he and his group of students had made him the trolley-cart to get around on. "Not only did I have to push myself about on this cart, but I also had to communicate in a phonetic alphabet that my group had to think up", remembers Pete. "In a way it was like fucking acting school. The lecturers always expected something incredible to happen. I think I started to confuse them because I found that by acting impulsively you could come up with some good creative ideas but that you couldn't always explain them. And they wanted explanations for everything. They were very academic."

Apart from the actual daily courses at Art school, there were a number of lunchtime lectures and concerts that were particularly significant to Pete. The Jewish radical playwright, David Mercer, gave a devastating speech which epitomised the early sixties British working class cultural explosion and cleverly exposed the 'Ford Anglia outside — but expecting a Ford Consul' mentality of the narrow-minded suburban middle classes.

Both Larry Rivers, the American pop art painter and Robert Brownjohn, an American London-based graphic designer (who designed the credits for the early James Bond films and did the sleeve for the Stones *Let it Bleed*), impressed the students by their 'hipness' and casual but outrageous manner, to the disgust of the 'old guard' ladies from the plant-drawing and pen-lettering departments.

Pete, of course, was to have no idea how valuable to him in later years would be the lecture and slide show given by Gustav Metzke on autodestructive art. He showed slides of paintings done in acid on sheets of metal showing the stages of 'beauty' as the acid slowly destroyed the metal and was later publicly acknowledged by Pete for his inspiration on autodestruction. "Metzke turned up at some of our shows when we were smashing stuff up. He really got into it," said Pete.

A student friend of Pete's called Dick Seamen used to go on about this mysterious person that he knew who was a post office engineer by day and some sort of lonely undiscovered genius musician at night. Dick arranged for him to play at the Art School in the lecture theatre one lunchtime. The resulting concert by Thunderclap Newman (real name Andy Newman) on piano and kazoo was an incredible experience. He was a very strange and mysterious person who had never played to an audience before and he played and sung mostly his own weird compositions. He set a metronome going on top of the grand piano and just played for over an hour until he was stopped. He never looked at the audience once. The students went wild at the end.

Pete became slightly obsessed with him and regarded him as a sort of undiscovered genius. He got from Dick an album by Thunderclap Newman and Richard Cardboard called *Ice and Essence*. There were only two copies of this album which were cut from a tape recording of some of Thunderclap's numbers performed by himself and Dick (Richard Cardboard) in a church hall and it was an amazingly inventive album with all sorts of convoluted time changes. It had an eerie, delicate, echoey quality about it and Pete played it constantly.

One day Pete and I saw Thunderclap Newman coming along the opposite side of the street. We were both very stoned and totally in awe of this mysterious figure. He was shaped like a barrel, chinless, and he walked along with his hands behind his back and looked like some mysterious, eccentric professor out of a Rupert annual. We followed him, hiding behind cars, totally struck by fear, wonder and reverence for this odd genius. Some days later he visited Sunnyside Road and held forth about the valuable contribution Bix Beiderbecke made to jazz before he died. Pete went through a Bix Beiderbecke period for the next three or four weeks.

Years later Pete produced Thunderclap Newman in a group of that name along with drummer Speedy Keene and guitarist Jimmy McCulloch. Their single, *Something in the Air*, was a big hit in the States and got to number one in England. Pete also financed Thunderclap Newman to do his own solo album produced by Dick Seaman called *Rainbow* and he himself produced the group's album *Hollywood Dream* in 1969. "I think he's a genius . . . Andy's new solo record is like a work of art" Pete said at the time.

Perhaps the most significant impact Thunderclap Newman's music had on Pete was in getting him interested in taping and tape multi-tracking. "Before I even knew what tape recording was he was into it. Multi-tracking bird songs and locomotive recordings . . . special effects, echoes", Pete told Zig-Zag magazine. After *Ice and Essence* (which wasn't multi-tracked) Thunderclap played us more of his recordings. Some had over twenty multi-tracked instruments. All done with two mono single track tape recorders in his bedroom at his parents' house.

The regularity of working Bob Druce's club circuit, apart from freeing the band from the problems of constantly looking for work, also imposed a heavy discipline on them. That such a demand was made of them, and kept, at such an early stage in their musical lives partly explains why they went on to be such a professional and hard-working band. It was also one of the contributing factors to their longevity.

I was amazed at how uncomplaining they were at having to perform their nightly stints. Not that belonging to a band and playing at dances was in any sense unpleasant. They enjoyed it – they loved it. They weren't just doing it as a job for financial reward. They did it out of choice, like most kids in groups at the time. But when, for instance, the Art School was having some kind of dance, or there was a party planned, Pete would always have to decline the invitation. Often, there would be a number of friends from college round at Sunnyside Road, pretty girls smoking pot, somebody strumming a guitar or listening through headphones to Lord Buckley or Jimmy Reed. Everybody having a really great time and at about 5.30 Pete would have to tear himself away and pick up his guitar case and leave in the group van for another night's gig. I had to admire his self-discipline because it certainly wasn't easy to depart from these very pleasant occasions.

The band's work would have first priority over girlfriends, birthdays, cup finals on TV, or friends' weddings. True, when Pete returned from the gig at about midnight, it wasn't unusual to find the same friends still sitting around drawing doodles and listening to records and he would carry on where he'd left off. The demands of the band also meant that they didn't get to see too many other bands. They would get

HIPPODROME · BRIGHTON
Manager: J. A. FRANKLIN   Telephone: 26126
6-0 — SUNDAY, 23rd AUGUST — 8-30
ONE NIGHT ONLY

ARTHUR HOWES presents
THE FABULOUS

DUSTY
SPRINGFIELD
EDEN KANE
with the DOWNBEATS
VAL McCULLAM
SENSATIONAL NEW R & B STAR

THE HIGH NUMBERS | JON BEST AND HIS CHALLENGERS | YOUR COMPERE DAVE REID

THE INTERNS
"CRY TO ME"

PRICES : 10/6   9/6   8/6   5/-

to know the other bands on their dance hall circuit – very often they'd spend fifteen minutes joking and talking shop. They'd even try to catch the other band's show some night that they had off, to see what the competition was up to. But the very fact they were a hard working band and so committed, meant that they couldn't get to see other bands outside their own set-up. It was ironic that because they were so closely involved in music, they were missing out on what was happening musically. And what was happening was that the Beatles and the Merseysound had 'ignited the powder keg of British pop.'

The London scene was surfacing and growing as a response to Merseysound. Another West London group, the Rolling Stones, were filling the Station Hotel in Richmond on Sunday nights, and also getting a big following and reputation at Eel Pie Island. The Detours hadn't seen the Rolling Stones. How could they? Every Sunday they were themselves playing the Oldfield Hotel in Greenford. When the Cyril Davies Allstars with Long John Baldry were playing the Harrow and Wealdstone Railway Hotel on Fridays, the Detours were playing the Glenlyn Ballroom the other side of London in Forest Hill. At the same moment the Yardbirds were playing the Crawdaddy Club at Richmond Athletic ground, the Detours were playing the Goldhawk Club at Shepherd's Bush.

The band relied on reports from their friends. People like myself were in a unique position. I went along to most of the Detours gigs but I also queued every week for the Crawdaddy and rarely missed Cyril Davies at the Railway Hotel. The Detours were playing much better material thanks mostly to the record collection Pete now had in his possession. They were introducing more and more R & B and blues numbers, but what struck me as a mere punter and one of the very few of my generation that didn't play an instrument, was that they performed a number exactly like the original record. A three and a half minute song would last three and a half minutes. They played it very well and very competently, they were by then a lot better than most bands, but they didn't do anything with it. When the Yardbirds played, for instance *Smokestack Lightning*, it lasted for at least fifteen minutes. I suggested to Pete that they should extend numbers and build up guitar riffs to make them different to the originals.

Supporting the Rolling Stones

The Detours did start working on a few numbers. Roger played more harmonica and Pete and John would 'jam' a bit together. They also began seeing more bands play because they were playing the same bills with them. Bob Druce needed one of his bands that could play a first set for an hour or so, then after the main band had played their set, return and play for the rest of the evening. The Detours were the obvious band for this task. They had supported Shane Fenton and the Fentones and Johnny Kidd and the Pirates a number of times. Also people like Wee Willie Harris, Screaming Lord Such, Dave Berry and the Cruisers. But this was before the merging rhythm and blues scene and these groups were rocker outfits.

I remember them doing a whole series of support shows for fairly big name bands at the Glenlyn Ballroom in Forest Hill in South London and the St. Mary's Ballroom in Putney. These support concerts consolidated the Detours as the top band at these ballrooms and after a while they were as much of a draw as the named attraction.

Not only did they learn a lot about what other bands were playing, but they could see the various stage acts and promotional gimmicks employed to plug current releases. At St. Mary's in Putney, they played with Brian Poole and the Tremeloes. Each member of the audience was given a stick of rock with the words, 'Candy Man' running through the middle to plug their latest single.

At the Glenlyn they supported the Undertakers, a much under-rated Liverpool group, who turned up in a hearse, dressed in black mourning suits and top hats and played with a very ornate coffin on stage all the time. They were already familiar with the antics of Screaming Lord Sutch and Wee Willie Harris.

Each week they would support a different name band from different parts of the country. They played with The Big Three and the Searchers from Liverpool, Wayne Fontana and the Mindbenders, and the Hollies from Manchester, Lulu and the Lovers from Glasgow, and the Rolling Stones from London.

The first time they played with the Rolling Stones was at St. Mary's Ballroom in Putney. "It was a revelation to me," remembers Pete, "When I first saw the Stones I was amazed that they were so scruffy, so organic, and they were still stars. Glyn Johns was then a singer in a band called the Presidents and he seemed to like our band a lot and was always very kind to us. He knew the Stones and got me into their dressing room, it was like going into a sacred place after the gig. Mick Jagger was very polite and so was Brian Jones, who was very complimentary about the Detours, and I just found what he was like, it was like God touching me on the head." Brian Jones offered to help the band if he could and encouraged Pete. But Keith Richard was "completely sardonic and arrogant and unapproachable, basically."

It was at this concert that Pete first got the inspiration for his 'windmill' guitar playing from Richard. "He just swung his arm up in an up motion before the curtain opened, and the crowd didn't actually see. And as the curtain opened, he just sort of brushed the curtain away and they went in to *Come On!* I just started to do it after that. It was a real heartfelt tribute, and then it developed from there. There was only one person who ever mentioned it, a girl at the Glenlyn Ballroom. 'You're copying Keith Richard' she said. And it was somebody who'd been backstage and seen it. When I later talked to Keith Richard about it he couldn't even remember doing it, and basically he didn't give a shit."

John remembered after a gig with the Undertakers, "As we were both leaving they threw this tear gas cannister into our van which made us all cry and we had to get out of the van. When we'd got rid of it, they threw another one but it didn't smash, so we got hold of it and threw it back into their van just as they were driving off. They went off careering all over the place down the road."

The Detours had introduced into their set by now, numbers like Jimmy Reed's *Big Boss Man*, James Brown's *Please, Please, Please* and *I Don't Mind*, and a lot more blues like, *Smokestack Lightning, I'm a Man* and *Spoonful, I Just Wanna Make Love to You* and numbers by Bo Diddley, Slim Harpo etc. Probably the most unique new song they did was Mose Allison's *Young Man Blues*. Originally they had been introducing more R & B material gradually, while still playing what was expected, the Top Ten. However, one evening Bob Druce asked them to step in at the last moment on their night off for another band that hadn't turned up at the Oldfield. They rushed to the gig, and without time to change, went on in what they were wearing. As they were doing Bob Druce a favour they decided to play whatever they wanted. The set went down exceptionally well, so as John put it "We thought, fuck this, we're not gonna play chart stuff any more. We're gonna play what we think is good."

Pete heard Bob Dylan's first two albums *Bob Dylan* and *Freewheelin'* at the flat of one of the girl students. He returned to Sunnyside Road raving about them. He bought both albums the next day. When *Another Side of Bob Dylan* was released Pete played it endlessly, especially the track *All I Really Want To Do*. Dylan and particularly this track spurred him on with his own song writing. After this he would sit down with a guitar and a notepad and play around with a few lines he'd written. He kept a book of odd bits of writing, possible lyrics, scribbles and doodles and general plans and ideas.

The band didn't play any of their own material at this time. The first song Pete wrote when he was sixteen, *It Was You*, was also the first song that they ever recorded and the only recording they did with Dougie Sandom on drums. Pete's dad was a session musician and knew Barry Gray, who was the music director for a successful TV show of the time called 'Thunderbirds', a space adventure for children. He had his own recording studio built into his house and they recorded *It Was You* there one Sunday evening with Barry Gray as engineer. It was very powerful for a first recording, but sounded too much like a Beatles song. They never released it, but a version by the Naturals was later released in the US and it flopped. The English group, the Fourmost, also did it as a B-side.

Pete's rough designs for a Detours logo were to be of no use as one day another band called the Detours appeared on the TV show 'Thank Your Lucky Stars'. "The other Detours were a nine-piece outfit and we thought, they're on TV, they're more well-known than us so we can't call ourselves the Detours any longer," John recalled.

The following Friday, after a gig, Roger drove to Sunnyside Road to drop Pete off. "We sat outside in the van for ages trying to think up a new name," remembers Roger. Pete suggested they come into the flat and ask me for some ideas. The five of us sat around drinking coffee and suggesting new names. Pete and I smoked some pot, but the others declined. I wanted a name that would make people stop and think and thus remember the group. The first two names that I thought of were 'the Group' and 'the Name'. Pete came up with 'The Hair'. Another contender was 'No-One'. We kept imagining the compere at the Oldfield, Lou, who was a bit of an old-time spiv and liked to act a little flash by making a joke out of his announcements. We would imagine him announcing "And now I'd like to present 'No-One'," or "Ladies and Gentlemen, the next group is called 'The Group'." But I finally thought 'The Who' worked best for many reasons. It made people think twice when they saw it and it worked well on posters because it was so short and therefore would print up so big. Lou would have a field day with it, or a lot of problems. We didn't come to a decision but it narrowed down to a choice between either 'The Who' or 'The Hair'. Pete suggested 'The Hair and the Who' and seemed really keen on it, but it sounded too much like the name of a pub. Hair was a very topical and controversial subject. The Beatles' hair had caused uproar with the older generation and the Rolling Stones' hair was considered positively filthy and obscene.

SHEPHERDS BUSH 4400

H. GORDEN
MANAGER

"THE WHO"

14, WENDELL ROAD,
SHEPHERDS BUSH,
LONDON, W.12.

Long hair on boys was the number one concern of letters to The Times. So the choice lay between these two names. I got more and more stoned and was finally convinced that the band should rename themselves British European Airways. This was too much for the rest, and as it was about two in the morning they left.

The indecision was resolved by Roger who came round to the flat the next morning to pick Pete up and visit Jim Marshall's music store in Hanwell to borrow some equipment, a regular Saturday event. As he passed me to go upstairs he said 'It's the Who, innit?" So that was that and a new name had been born.

Dougie Sandom remembers the next time they played at the Oldfield Hotel, "We finished our set and Lou took the mike and said 'Who's up here next week?' and they're all going "The Detours". And he's going "The Who", and they're all going "The Detours" and he's going "The Who" you know, and it was ridiculous. It went on and on and on and in the end he got it through to everyone, but they couldn't make it out, it was such a strange name."

The new name passed its poster test immediately. I had just started promoting the Tuesday nights at the Railway Hotel. After trying out a number of bands including the Who (who were by far the best) it soon became obvious that it would be better for the club and the group to have the Who as resident group. So we designed and printed our own rather crude posters at art school. The words, The Who were in huge letters and we fly-posted about 50 around the area. We had also printed some cards to hand out and put a small ad in the Melody Maker.

The Who were paid £20 at the start (it then went up to £25) and they built up the club from around 60 people on the first night to over 600 at the height of their residency. There was a new kind of audience in places like the Railway. They were younger than the normal pub audiences although the Railway was in the basement of a pub. And they knew what they wanted. Unlike the slightly older and more conventional audience from the Royal Oldfield Hotel, where there were still traces of the fifties tradition of the boys drinking together and the girls dancing together, until the final number when the boys would condescend to have a jive with the particular girl they wanted to go home with. At the Railway, the boys danced with girls all night. In fact the boys often danced on their own or with each other. The band was still being held together by Roger. He drove the van, picked everyone up for the gigs, dealt with the gear, and liaised with Bob Druce and Commercial Entertainments on behalf of the band.

The Railway Hotel (later to be renamed the Railway Tavern) was a Who stronghold. They had a number of very loyal new fans at places like the Railway, the Goldhawk Club, the Trade Union Hall at Watford, and the Assembly Rooms at Carpenters Park as well as their usual places.

The change of name for the group seemed to be the start of lots of other changes. The group was now getting to the stage where it needed to expand out of the Bob Druce circuit. Druce wasn't capable of taking them any further and they'd really outgrown the local scene. They needed something to happen. They needed a manager or a backer.

At last a financial backer

Dougie Sandom's sister-in-law worked for a little foundry in Shepherd's Bush that made doorknobs, and got along well with the owner, Helmut Gorden. "He used to come round my house to see my wife and would hear us talking about the band, and Gorden said once 'Are they any good?' so I said 'Of course they're good, I play with 'em' and he said 'Well, I might be interested in them'." He told Dougie he'd like to come and hear them and Dougie invited him along to the White Hart, Acton one night. "And all the little girls were hanging around screaming and all that lark, and I'm sure he saw nothing but pound notes, you know." The band had a meeting with Helmut. He suggested that he manage them, and was prepared to invest some money in them. The band were delighted – at last they'd found a backer. They felt that if they just stayed with the Commercial Entertainments set-up they would never be able to break out of it to make a record. Bob Druce heard through the grapevine what was going on. According to Roger, "We were playing at the Oldfield that Thursday night and old Lou said to us 'I want to see you boys. Come and have a drink afterwards'. We were all giggling, because we knew Bob wanted to sign us before Helmut. Bob had told Lou to sign us for him. Lou grovelled and grovelled and grovelled and we let him go on and on and on and let him build right up to it and then he came out with it, 'I'm going to sign you up boys' and someone said 'Sorry mate, we've already signed'." Doug remembers Helmut Gorden promising them the earth. Helmut was a short, balding, fortyish Jewish businessman who lived with his mother, and, as it turned out later, knew very little about the current music scene. However he was one of many aspiring businessmen of that time who thought they could be Brian Epsteins, and that managing a pop group would be much easier and vastly more lucrative than working for a living. It was almost like a hobby for Gorden. He referred to the band as "my little diamonds."

A meeting was arranged at his factory soon after they had signed with him. I went along with the group, as I was a sort of unofficial 'mother' in those days. Roger picked everyone up in turn and we drove to an untidy factory in the backstreets of Shepherd's Bush. We were directed through the works to the back, to Helmut Gorden's office. We walked through the factory which seemed very Dickensian and squalid. There was a large black man stripped to the waist, sweating from the heat of a forge as he ladled liquid metal into a casting mould.

In his office the five of us lined up one side of his desk while he outlined some plans he had for the group. On his desk he had a typewritten sheet of paper listing various influential people in the music industry. Helmut's hope was that by him going to the top and dealing with important people the group would achieve a breakthrough. Despite his inexperience of the music industry, Helmut was an astute and successful businessman, and reasoned that he could apply the same logic that he had in his other enterprises. A lot of the names on his list, which I was attempting to read, were names of the people who used to run the 'biz when it was a good old schmaltzy Tin Pan Alley music 'biz. The old Denmark Street stronghold on the music business had been, to a certain extent, usurped by the arrival of the Beatles and the British group phenomenon. However, a great many were still very influential and had names like Arthur Howes, Harold Davidson and Dick James, who were undoubtedly Big Time entrepreneurs.

The group had driven to their first long distance gig in Derby and their van had blown up on the way back. At this meeting Helmut agreed to buy the group a new van, some new clothes and pay for some odds and ends. They were to have some new stage outfits made up that Pete had designed. These were long light tan coloured leather waistcoats that came down to the knees. They looked like waisted three-quarter length overcoats but had no sleeves, collars or buttons. These would flair out when one swung around. At the end of this meeting John asked if he could have some of Helmut's fancy gold-coloured handles for his wardrobe and chest of drawers at home. "There were thousands of them all piled up in a corner and many many more in boxes. He said 'Take some' so I did and as we went to leave he made me pay six shillings for them."

Roger chose a newer van. It was a Commer diesel. It was a very smart and modern looking light blue job with comfortable seats and a heater. The only trouble was that this particular van had no power. When loaded up with all the gear and the group it would get slower and slower as they tried to climb any steep hill. Roger would change down through the gears until he was back in first gear and it still wouldn't have any power. "If the wind was against you – you'd be going backwards." At first when the lack of power was noticed Roger put it down to the well known fact that diesels didn't have a lot of acceleration but it soon became obvious that this particular engine didn't have a lot of anything. Not long after they'd bought it they broke down on their way to a gig on the A1. They telephoned Helmut who came out in his car with some money to rescue them. He took a photograph of them and the van supposedly to show people that he had rescued them.

The band bought themselves new stage gear. The Beatles wore a certain kind of black ankle boot with a two-inch Cuban heel that they bought at Anello and Davide, an old-established ballet shoe and riding boot shop in Covent Garden. They soon became an almost compulsory item for pop groups and we all trooped down to Anello and Davide to get our 'Beatle boots'. As Helmut was paying for them the band got two pairs each, (I managed one pair), with the exception of John, who had to have one of each colour and ended up with about fourteen pairs.

Helmut Gorden had a meeting with Bob Druce as the band still needed their regular Bob Druce gigs and he needed them, it was agreed that, although no longer their manager he would still be their agent. They were getting more and better outside bookings. The band had got much raunchier and aggressive and were playing mostly blues. Roger had developed a very low gravely voice similar to Howling Wolf and Pete had started to smack the guitar strings instead of picking or plucking them.

A sign of the progress the group were making came in the development of one of their new bookings. They were booked to play as support band to Chris Farlowe and the Thunderbirds at the Watford Trade Union Hall. This was a large venue, holding over a thousand. After a few weeks it was noticed that although the hall was fairly packed for the first half of the show when the Who, the support band were on, it thinned out considerably after the interval when the main band were on. The promoter eventually put the main band on first and the Who on second but the first half was now near-empty and the place filled up for the second half. Soon after this the promoter dropped Chris Farlowe and the Thunderbirds and booked the Who as the main group, although not with a backing group, so that they had to do the whole gig themselves.

Helmut Gorden got the Who a series of bookings in the Stork Club, a sort of very straight businessmen's club in central London. It was to the Stork Club that he brought people to see the band. Arthur Howes was one of his guests at the Stork Club and the band were signed to the Arthur Howes agency soon after.

Helmut used to have his haircut in the West End by a barber called Jack who was a close friend of his. As he was having his hair cut he told Jack all about the group. Another customer of Jack's worked on and off in the pop business and he too used to unwind to Jack as he had his haircut. He was Peter Meaden and he'd been involved with the early Rolling Stones career through his association with Andrew Oldham. He was a freelance publicist and picked up commissions when he could. He did Georgie Fame's publicity. Jack the barber told Pete Meaden about Helmut Gorden the manager and Helmut Gorden about Pete Meaden the publicist.

Meaden got in touch with Gorden and went to see the group at a rehearsal in Shepherd's Bush. Meaden realised that the Who could be really big. He also had a secret dream that one day he would develop a band that could play for and be accepted by the select number of elitist fashion heads that frequented the West End – the mods. Meaden saw the potential for using the Who to fulfil his dream. Helmut Gorden knew nothing about music or image or style, but he realised that Pete Meaden did. Pete Meaden was very intense. The band were quite overawed by him. He would talk all the time calling everyone 'Baby'. "This is what we gonna do John Baby. We're gonna hit the scene and be real cool." It was hard to believe he was real. His fast talking American DJesque jargon was really impressive. He seemed to know where the group should go and what it should wear.

He introduced the group to the mysterious world of mods. It was his religion and he was very devout. The boys were hooked – well, Pete and Roger were. Pete got especially interested. He could identify with what he could understand of the mod cult, and also realised that if the band could become a mod band, then it could have its own identity and direction and not have to follow in the shadow of the Stones or Merseybeat.

Helmut was a bit mistrustful of Pete Meaden and in a way jealous of him. We all took to Meaden and found him exciting. He used to namedrop and visit clubs and knew writers from the music press and so on. He was part of the scene. He knew what was happening, or at least made out that he did. Although Helmut had plans for the group and had invested some money, the boys found him difficult to identify with. The band really wanted to have Pete Meaden as manager, but he had no money. If Helmut would be the silent backer and leave the running of the band up to the band and Meaden then it would be fine, but it was clear that Helmut wouldn't be interested in that set-up. He wanted to be Brian Epstein. "I used to see him as a cash register. Simple as that," Roger recalls, "A way for us to get some money to get better gear. Our gear used to hold us back a lot. We were always sticking things together with cellotape and string."

Helmut Gordon arranged for an audition with a record producer and hired a restaurant-cum-club that was not used during the daytime called the Zanzibar in Edgware Road for the occasion. The whole place was covered in bamboo. The band set up and played through a couple of numbers for the record producer, Chris Parmienter. He made a few comments, at first quite favourable but he wasn't too happy about the drumming. He kept criticising it. "He seemed to start picking on me as soon as I walked through the door," says Dougie, "He wouldn't let me set up my own kit and insisted I use this other one there. He was saying things like, 'Doesn't he ever let himself go?' and then Pete would say 'Sometimes. Ha ha ha', – that sort of thing. I felt really terrible."

Chris Parmienter was giving general advice. He said Pete would look good on television because he was long and thin. Of the three numbers The Who were auditioning for a possible single, he preferred their version of Bo Diddley's *Here 'Tis* and spoke of filling out their sound by clanking chains in the background. However he finally said "If you wanna make a record, you'll have to get the drumming sorted out."

Pete turned around to Dougie and snarled something to the effect "Get it together. What's wrong with you? If you can't get it right then you're out of the group." The others were a little bit stunned by this outburst. Pete realised that unless the matter was brought to a head, they would lose their chance of making a record. What he did was necessary but the way he did it left a lot to be desired. There was one other person who also realised the problem – Dougie himself. Dougie was a very quiet, unassuming person and afterwards when Roger and John both said to him that there was no way they would drop him from the band, he told them that he knew he was standing in their way and that he would drop out. "It was the worst day of my life," he said, "I felt so humiliated that I wouldn't have played with them again anyway." Dougie had been thinking of leaving the band before this incident because he didn't like the new numbers they were playing. "They started doing all this out and out blues, and I hated it. I liked the Johnny Kidd stuff, but playing *Dimples* and all that was boring. It was all building up because my missus was sick of me being out playing six or seven nights a week."

Keith Moon's grand entrance

The band were looking for a new drummer, but Dougie offered to do a month's work until they got somebody and when he left he lent them his drumkit for several weeks.

Helmut Gorden booked the Zanzibar again the following week and the band auditioned a new drummer he'd come up with. He was from Liverpool and had previously played with the Fourmost. However the band didn't think he was right and an embarrassing scene occurred when Helmut began to argue and try to assert his authority as manager. The poor drummer was sitting there while his suitability, or lack of it, was debated. The band told Gorden that he just didn't look right. "Vot is wrong with him, he looks fine to me" snapped Helmut. "He just isn't right and he's got a rocker haircut and wears glasses" put in Roger and Pete. That was the end of it.

The drummer was sheepishly trying to make the point that he thought looks were important too and agreed with the band. But Helmut would have none of it. "Ve can buy a wig and get contact lenses and even plastic surgery." The drummer who was quite good looking but just wouldn't have fitted in with the Who was looking even more worried at the suggestion of plastic surgery. Helmut realised he had lost and paid the drummer £40 for his troubles, much to the astonishment of the band. This was one of the many trials of strength between the band and Helmut. Helmut would really have been better off with a group of young immature kids that did as they were told. The Who, however, although very young kids, had been around and had a few years experience and were not going to let someone like Helmut mould them into a middle of the road novelty act.

Another time the group were in the West End with

The No. 1 Hip Record in Town . . .

"ZOOT SUIT"

By the

HIGH-NUMBERS

ON FONTANA TF480

Release date

JULY 3rd 1964

Order your copy of this Record
NOW from your Record Shop

Helmut after seeing some impressario that Helmut had lined up. The others were still in his office and I was waiting with Helmut in his car in the street. The Beatles came on the car radio and I asked if he liked them. He said that he didn't like the Beatles or the Stones. He couldn't stand them. He said his favourite band was the Batchelors. We went on to talk about hair length and he said if he had his way we would have the band's heads shaved bald and dress them in kilts. He was quite serious.

Dougie dropped out of playing with the band and they used a session drummer from Jim Marshall's music shop for a few weeks. They auditioned a few more drummers including Mitch Mitchell who later went on to be drummer with the Jimi Hendrix Experience. One night while at the Oldfield one of the audience came up to the stage. He was very drunk and couldn't stand up too well. He said "My mate can play a lot better than your drummer." Then somebody said "Well, if he can and he's here get him to come up in the interval because we're looking for a drummer." During the interval, while the band were having a drink by the bar, the drunk's friend came over to talk to the group. He was all dressed in ginger. Ginger suede jacket, suede trousers and as John said "A Wayne Fontana haircut." They arranged for him to sit in. "Have you ever played *Roadrunner*?" Pete asked this fringed gentleman. "Oh sure" he said. So they began their second half of the set playing *Roadrunner* with him on drums. He was very good. His drumming was very heavy and had tremendous drive. "He played about three numbers and mucked up the drummer's hi-hat. He also damaged the foot pedal" remembers John. The group went into a huddle after the end of the gig and then Roger came over to him and said "What are you doing Saturday? We'll pick you up at 6 o'clock."

Keith Moon was the new drummer for the Who. The band wanted him to join straight away as the session drummer they were using was costing them a fortune. Keith Moon strung them along for a couple of weeks until his position was really settled. He had been playing with a band on the Bob Druce circuit called the Beachcombers. They played mostly surfing music and for about two weeks Keith played in both bands. "He knew the Who were a better band. We were the top group on Druce's circuit then, but we had a nasty reputation" says John, "He was wondering whether to join the nasty people and leave his nice surfing group." Some years later Pete said, "From the time we found Keith it was a complete turning point. He was so assertive and confident. Before then we had just been foolin' about."

John remembers the first time Keith did a gig with the Who, "He came in with his drum kit and about twenty yards of rope. I asked him what he wanted it for and he just said 'Oh I need it'. He lashed his bass drum to two pillars and halfway through the gig the mains went and there was no power. Someone said, 'Drum solo' and he started whacking away at his drums. When we looked his drums were going up and down and backwards and forwards and we realised he'd tied it all down."

Dougie was so shattered by the day he was slung out of the band, that he lost his confidence and didn't play drums regularly for three years. However, one night shortly after he'd left Bob Druce turned up at his door. "He asked me 'Dougie, could you help us out? We got a band up at the Oldfield and their drummer hasn't turned up and the kids are getting a bit rowdy.' So I said 'Alright, I'll help you out' and went up to play with this band and it turned out to be the Beachcombers." Their drummer Keith Moon was obviously elsewhere.

Helmut eventually gave Meaden £50 to buy some clothes for the group. Pete was 100% for Pete Meaden's ideas and Roger and Keith were prepared to go along with them. But John had a few reservations. "I liked his plans and ideas for the group but I didn't like the clothes. I had my own way of dressing, a bit like the Stones, high-heeled leather boots and leather waistcoats. I didn't want to dress like a little ticket."

The original idea was for Roger to dress up as a sharp top mod; a face, and the rest of the band to be in T-shirts and Levi's, boxing boots and the current 'in' clothes of a typical street mod; a ticket.

Roger was kitted out with a white seersucker jacket with two 4-inch long side vents (correct at the time) and black hipster parallel trousers. He got a pair of white and black two-

tone shoes. He had a blue button-down collar shirt and a black knitted tie. Meaden knew what was the right look. They all went off with Helmut Gorden to have mod haircuts from Jack the barber. As soon as Entwistle left the shop he got his comb out and re-styled his hair. Nevertheless they were to attempt to be a mod group. The idea of being accepted by mods was very exciting and emotional and challenging.

The mod lifestyle was a subtle and near-secretive set of styles, fashion and attitudes. It wasn't something that you could simply buy your way into by wearing the correct clothes. The Who were simply trying to do that at the time, but they were also beginning to get the same obsessions and fascinations as the mods and began to adopt more and more of their ways. Instead of simply being four people in mods clothes with mods haircuts, they slowly, under Meaden's influence and guidance began to turn themselves into real mods. Pete especially threw himself into all things mod. He was fascinated by this almost invisible sect. He was the first of the group to start taking pills – mod fuel. The band had soon realised that Pete Meaden's strange behaviour, his never-ending fast slick talking and his constant energy, were down to pills. Quite often when the band were walking around the West End with him, he would stop and try to

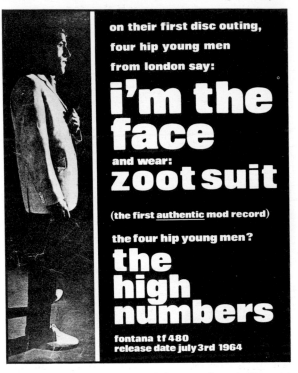

on their first disc outing,
four hip young men
from london say:

i'm the face

and wear:

zoot suit

(the first <u>authentic</u> mod record)

the four hip young men?

the high numbers

fontana tf 480
release date july 3rd 1964

vomit violently in the gutter. Unfortunately as 'pill-heads' hardly ever ate (the pills took away their appetites), there was nothing in his stomach for him to bring up, and after a short time he would continue his journey practically blue with the straining. Meaden took far too many pills.

Shortly after the first meeting with Meaden, Pete and I went to see the 1964 Chuck Berry tour of England at Hammersmith Odeon. This was the first large gathering of mods that we'd seen. Although Chuck Berry might seem like a rocker hero, many of the mods also held him in high esteem as one of the originals. The support bands included the Animals, who had just released their first single *Baby Let Me Take You Home* and who the mod's seemed to approve of, giving particular applause to their stage version of Bob Dylan's *House of the Rising Sun*. When the Swinging Blue Jeans came on they were booed, howled at, slow handclapped and had things thrown at them. The mods didn't like them, because they were a bit rocker-looking and not playing R & B. They had to leave the stage. Chuck Berry too had to leave the stage but for a different reason. About twenty mods were actually on stage in a long line on their knees bowing down as though praying to Mecca, as an incredulous Chuck Berry did his famous duck-walk guitar solo across the stage before them.

The mod phenomenon had begun a couple of years before

in a very small way as a movement among a few middle class kids who were clothes-obsessed to the point of being 20th century Dandies. It grew and spread to the young working class who had a new found affluence. It was a predominantly masculine cult and to a certain extent it was a peacocking of the young English male. They had their own dances, which were continually evolving and changing. They were very intense about their particular taste in music.

The mods were mysterious. The media didn't know they existed for a long time. They were subtle. Being short haired, smart and neat, they could just pass for a clean-cut office boy. But in the clubs, dance halls and coffee bars, minute details of clothing were very important. The changes in fashion details among the top mods were frequent and imitated all the way down the chain from the top 'face' to the humblest little 'ticket' or 'number'. What mattered was outposing your peers.

Pete Meaden introduced the Who to the very hub of this exclusive group. He took them to the Scene Club in Ham Yard in London's Soho. This dark, dirty, dingy basement not far from Piccadilly Circus was the 'in' place. Top mods would check each other out and dance or stand around looking cool until about 4 o'clock in the morning. The DJ, Guy Stevens, had the most amazing collection of records. Having direct access to most minor record companies in the States, he would have obscure R & B records from obscure black record companies that wouldn't normally be available to whites in the States, let alone in Britain.

Pete practised complicated steps to the two main mod dances, the 'block' and the 'bang'. He rehearsed the mod way of walking and tried to pick up the correct mod way of standing around.

Pete even went to the Roaring Twenties, a West Indian Blue-beat club. The club was actually in a basement in Carnaby Street when Carnaby Street was still a dreary no-where backstreet of London with a few as yet undiscovered men's clothes shops. The Roaring Twenties was dark, full of pot smoke and extremely loud. The West Indian dances and Blue-beat music were adopted by mods as their own.

The mod cult gave Pete something he could identify with and fired him with a new passion. He also took a lot more pills and they fired him with even more. Mods used to take handfulls of purple hearts (drynamil) to get the artificial energy to dance all night or, at weekends, to stay up from when 'Ready Steady Go' would finished on TV at 7 o'clock on Friday evenings until late Sunday night.

Pete Meaden and other mods that the group met through him were constantly influencing the group now. The boys bought more clothes and even John, once he could drop his 'ticket' look and get some better tailored suits and well-cut jackets and trousers, accepted the mod look and began to enjoy it.

Pete and I eventually made our first visit to Carnaby Street. It was a shabby little place. About two-thirds of one side was taken up by a big Electricity Board warehouse. The street was practically deserted on this rainy Wednesday. Carnaby Street hadn't been mentioned in any newspapers yet. The clothes were incredible. French cut hipster matelot trousers, waisted jackets with centre vents, three-buttoned jackets with five inch side vents, button down shirts, roll collar shirts, elephant collar shirts. Many were the sort of thing that only homosexuals and camp theatricals would have had the nerve to wear a year before.

Having initiated the group into mod clothes, hairstyles, music and dances, Meaden proposed that now they were mods they should change their name to a mod name. They had only been the Who for a short period and the name was very successful and it seemed unwise to change it again so soon. However, the group were so caught up with the whole momentum of the mod movement and Meaden's enthusiasm that they agreed to change from 'the Who' to 'the High Numbers'. A 'Number' was a mod that wore a T-shirt with a number printed on the front. And 'High' presumably because they were high on hearts or high up in mod status.

The band had further improved their live act. Keith Moon's drumming had added a whole new dimension to their sound. His intensity and drive gave them a fantastic extra edginess. John had earlier bought a large 4 × 12 bass cabinet that Jim Marshall's had started to manufacture. He liked the sound so much that he bought another one and doubled in volume. With John's bass speakers and Keith's drumming, they were beginning to become known for being loud. Pete followed John's example and he bought a large Marshall speaker cabinet and his volume increased. Pete first experienced feedback at the Oldfield Hotel. "Where I stood on stage was a piano and I stuck my cabinet on it and it was dead level with the guitar and I started to get these feedback effects that I really liked. When I went to other gigs and put the speakers on the floor it wouldn't happen. So I started to put it up on a chair and then I decided to stack the thing so that I could *induce* feedback."

Pete was also quite aware that he was not a great solo lead guitar player at that time and seized at the chance of using feedback as one of his trademarks as did Ray Davies and Jeff Beck. Rather than try to compete with better guitarists on their terms he would try to perfect feedback and express himself physically.

With their mod image, their loudness, Roger's aggressive voice, Pete's feedback and the unusually high number of Tamla-oriented songs in their set, they were truly unique. Meaden successfully got them a residency down the Scene Club. A major coup, although John only remembers playing there a couple of times. It was the big credibility test. If the ultra-cool, ultra-critical top mods from the Scene would accept the High Numbers, then they had won half the battle. There was always a danger that the suspicious and sceptical mods would see through the High Numbers and reject them for being manufactured, which to a certain extent they were. They were an incredible success. All the more remarkable because the Scene didn't usually have live bands, the kids came to listen to rare R & B records and to dance and check each other out on a diet of fruit juice and pills. There was at the time no performing mod group with which to identify. The mods were a difficult audience to satisfy and the cardinal sin was for a group to start massacring their R & B favourites. They took few homegrown groups to their hearts.

I'm the Face - the first mod single

Meaden prepared a large four-page press hand-out for the High Numbers. It stated: "The important thing about the High Numbers which is immediately noted on meeting them is that nothing is contrived or prefabricated about them and this can be said particularly in the field of clothes. The clothes they wear bear the hallmark of the much maligned 'mod' cycling jackets, tee shirts, turned up Levi jeans, long white jackets, boxing boots, black and white brogues and all the rest; but these are also worn by thousands of other young people of today. The Number, the Face, the Ticket, or to use the generalisation, the Mod, is a product of this day and age . . . It is a way of life, and for them, an exciting way of life. And the fact that the High Numbers are drawn from this facet of society in which they are totally immersed makes them about the most potentially exciting and powerful group in the field of beat music today . . . In a nutshell they are *of* the people."

Dramatic stuff. It was introducing to the national press not just the High Numbers, but also the fact that kids existed called mods. The claims that they weren't contrived or prefabricated weren't quite accurate. However, although they might not have been 'drawn from the facet of society', there was no doubt that they were 'about the most potentially exciting and powerful group' around.

Helmut Gorden had seen Harold Davidson, one of the biggest agents at the time, and invited him along to see the band play at the Stork Club. Gorden subsequently made an agreement with the Harold Davidson agency and the group looked forward to getting some big bookings. After a few dates Helmut Gorden objected to the way the group seemed to be getting ripped off by the agency. There was a practise in those days of agencies doing deals between one another at the expense of the group. If an agency was looking for a band for £15, another agency would come along and say 'You can have this band for £12 and we'll split the difference.' It was called being 'bought and sold' and was quite widespread. Helmut Gorden suspected that maybe something like that was going on with the Harold Davidson agency because he wasn't happy with the fees they were getting for their bookings of the High Numbers. According to John he eventually declared, "Zis Harold Davidson, he is a shit. We are not

staying with him any longer." He left the Harold Davidson organisation and went with the other biggest outfit, the Arthur Howes agency. After some time Helmut also suspected them and was not happy and pulled out of Arthur Howes too. The band, although not too happy with the way big agencies treated small bands realised that for Helmut to have gone through the two most important agencies in the business, indicated something was wrong. Disillusioned anyway with him as a manager they sided increasingly with Meaden. Meaden was only the publicist but the group were turning to him for creative management as well as publicity. The group finally realised that they would have to try to leave Helmut Gorden when he asked them to play at a party he was giving at his house to which he had invited a lot of influential people to see the band. He told the band that as he didn't want the music to be too loud, he didn't want them to bring their amplifiers, just their guitars. That was the last straw.

Meaden realised that they must make a record. He wanted them to make the first mod single. He took two current records liked by the mods and wrote new words to them. The songs were Slim Harpo's *Got Love If You Want It* and a number by the Showmen. He wrote two sets of lyrics to fit the tunes and came up with *I'm The Face* and *Zoot Suit*. "I

didn't like the principle of *I'm The Face*" claimed Roger. "It was just plagiarising Slim Harpo." Pete himself was writing a lot more but he hadn't shown anything to the other members of the band.

Pete and I had moved from Sunnyside Road to a not particularly pleasant room in the next street. We soon moved out of that and lived in our van. Our van was an old ambulance that we bought from the father of one of the college students. He had cleverly fitted it out for long distance touring and it had seats that folded down into two single beds and one double bed. It had lights inside and sockets for shavers and was a very strange vehicle. We had a lot of fun with it. On lots of occasions we would be waved through traffic lights by policemen or waved down at accidents because despite the fact that it was fairly dirty and had YARDBIRDS written across the back in lipstick, they thought it was still an ambulance in service. For about three weeks we lived in this ambulance, parking it outside Sid's cafe opposite the college so that we could get up and go straight to the door and have breakfast.

After this we took the flat above Pete's parents' flat in Ealing Common. This was a great big place of seven rooms. We packed everything in the largest room, mattresses on the floor, red light bulb *à la* Sunnyside Road. Pete decided that he would turn one of the other rooms into a studio and

decided to try and soundproof it. A friend of ours from Art School, Des Donnellan, who was always anxious to help out undertook the task of laying down a 1-inch thick cement floor all over the existing floorboards of this room. It had a layer of chicken wire in to strengthen it. We bought some very expensive sheets of sound-proofing material. These were 8 × 4' sheets of about 3" thick compressed straw or something. Each sheet weighed about a ton. We had to get six volunteers from Art school to help lift each one. This was to be Pete's studio but it was perpetually in the process of being built depending on when we could find the time and money. In another room I set up a silkscreen printing table for producing the posters for the High Numbers and the Railway. The Railway was so successful that I was going to begin a company to promote dances and look for another place to run a club. I planned to call the company Fabulous Entertainments or Fabulous Promotions. I never did get past the idea stage and later Pete used the name for his music publishing company, Fabulous Music Ltd.

One day the band turned up for their first commercial recording session. The producer was Jack Bavistock. Chris Parmienter, A & R man for Fontana records, arranged it and was also present. Jack Bavistock was a successful producer at the time having produced the Merseybeats among others. Pete Meaden was at the session and everyone was roped in to help out on clapping on *I'm The Face* including Helmut Gorden and Jack the barber. Various other acquaintances joined in on backing vocals. At this session they did *I'm The Face, Zoot Suit* and *Here T'is*, the Bo Diddley number and Holland Dozier Holland's *Leaving Here* they had auditioned at the Zanzibar with Dougie Sandom for Chris Parmienter. I played maracas on *Here 'Tis* which went on for several takes and I suffered severely blistered hands and fingers for weeks afterwards.

Pete played a jazzy little guitar solo in *Zoot Suit*. The words to both songs were possibly a bit too contrived to appeal to mods. Pete Meaden went round all the shops ordering it and tried to whip up enthusiasm.

At the time of the record's release they got a big article in Fab magazine under the heading 'How High Will These Numbers Go?' along with a full page colour picture. Also planned was a spot on the bill of an Arthur Howes tour of Britain that was planned for late summer and early autumn. Pete Meaden tried to generate interest and used every contact he had to get publicity.

A lot of business was conducted in certain known pubs and Meaden, Pete and myself would hang about making a scotch and coke last as long as we could while we tried to plug the record and the band to anyone he vaguely knew was connected with the music business. We had heard that the bottom positions of the top fifty singles charts for certain music papers could be bought for something like £25 per week for position 49 and that it was in De-Hems Oyster Bar that these deals were struck.

The record never took off. It was never given a chance. Fontana only pressed 1,000 copies and never got behind it at all. Meaden went around lots of shops asking for it and ordering it. He is alleged to have bought 250 copies although I believe at the time it was only 50. Some people at art school bought copies and so did John's grandmother.

The group had taken so much time off work to attend meetings at Helmut's factory and rehearsals during the daytime that they had used up all their sick days and holidays and were losing money. Helmut was forced to reimburse them and eventually, in order to help make his contract with them legal as they were all under 21, he put them on a wage of £20 a week. After some consideration they took the risk and John, Roger and Keith left their jobs to become full-time musicians. £20 a week was a very good salary in 1964 and when Pete approached the head of the graphic department at Ealing Art school to discuss his future and get his advice, Robin Ray was amazed and told him "If you can get twenty pounds a week playing guitar, then I'd take it and leave straightaway."

Pete left and signed Helmut's contract, however his music business parents refused to countersign. (This later affected the legality of the contract when the band came to break away from Gorden.) Although Helmut paid them good wages and put up money for equipment and clothes, he received all their earnings from gigs.

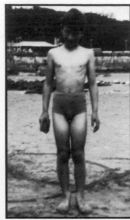

Peter Dennis Blandford Townshend was born on May 19, 1945 and was brought up in Ealing, West London. His Mum recalls "although Pete was in the choir I never thought he was talented musically, otherwise I would have bought him a piano". Pete's Dad was a member of the Squadronaires and consequently there was a constant musical influence in the Townshend household. The family spent every summer either in Clacton or the Isle of Man at Butlins, where the Squadronaires were in residence. It was in the Isle of Man that Peter was taken to see Bill Haley's 'Rock Around the Clock'. He saw the film four times in a week. On their return to London his Granny, Denny, bought him a guitar.

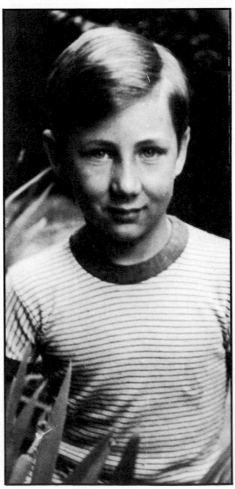

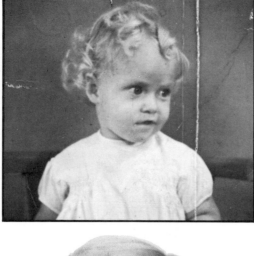

Roger Harry Daltrey was born on March 1, 1944 and was brought up in Shepherd's Bush, W. London. At age 13 his mum discovered his musical talent on holiday, finding him playing guitar to a crowd. Above: "I was good at school until I heard Lonnie Donegan and Elvis Presley; then I didn't want to know".

Wembley Portraits, 29 Central Parade, Wembley.

ALPERTON SECONDARY SCHOOL FOR BOYS

REPORT FOR *Autumn* **TERM, 1959**

Name of Pupil *Keith Moon* Form *3a*

ASSESSMENTS:— A—Excellent; B—Good; C—Fair; D—Weak; E—Very Weak

SUBJECT	MARKS: EXAM.	TERM	COMMENT	INITIALS
ENGLISH	70%	B	His recent improvement will have to continue. Showing a genuine interest.	
ENGLISH LITERATURE	49%	B	Keen & alert.	
FRENCH				
GEOGRAPHY	11%	C	Very slow progress	
HISTORY	5%	D	Tries to get by by putting on an act.	
MATHEMATICS	8%	B	slow progress	
SCIENCE	28%	C-	Work poor - much greater effort needed	
TECHNICAL DRAWING	28%	C-	Very little to show for this term	
METALWORK	7	C	Does his best, a cheerful polite boy.	
WOODWORK				
ART	3/10	D	Retarded artistically. Idiotic in other respects.	
MUSIC		B	Great ability, but must guard against tendency to "show off"	
PHYSICAL EDUCATION		C+	Keen at times but "goonery" seems to come before everything.	

Attendance *V. good.*

General Remarks:— *Must direct his talents to his school work. He has shown how he can improve when he determines to do so. Cheerful, but occasionally silly.*

L. J. Irving. — Headmaster

Form Master

NEXT TERM BEGINS 6 JAN 1960

Attendance .... Good

General Remarks :— *His behaviour is rather young for his age. His air of perky spriteliness while refreshing for a time, is, I feel, largely put on for effect. It is time he adopted a different line.*

Form Master .... *R. W. Parkinson* Headmaster ....

NEXT TERM BEGINS .... *Wed 7th Jan*

Keith John Moon (Born August 23rd, 1947 in Wembley, NW London) was an extrovert from an early age. His mum recalls his part in a school dancing display. "Keith was about seven and a half. When it came his turn to skip around his little group, he decided to skip round the whole playground, round the back of the school back to the circle. He had a cheeky grin on his face and just loved all the attention. Everyone thought it was hilarious". Below left: His first group, The Beachcombers. "Even then his drumming was fantastic. He was very young but we had to let him play."

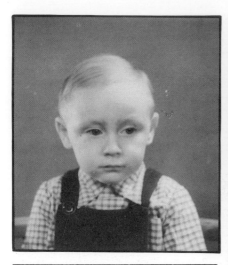

John Alec Entwistle was born on October 9, 1944 and was brought up in Acton, West London. John showed an interest in music from the age of two, as his mum recalls, ''He used to listen to the wireless and knew the words to all the songs. Later, I made him learn the piano, which he did only on condition that he also learn to play the trumpet''. His estranged father taught him to play the trumpet. ''He used to practice in the loo, where it was best for echo, and the neighbours would complain''. He played bugle in the Boys Brigade, joined the school band and then the Middlesex Youth Orchestra. He won a place at the Royal Academy of Music, ''but we couldn't afford for him to go''.

John's Mum remembers seeing him play with 'The Detours', ''I thought they were great, but when he gave up his job with the Inland Revenue, I moaned like hell''.

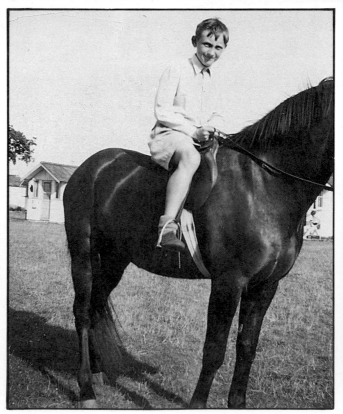

The Boys' Brigade

Discharge Certificate

This is to Certify that

JOHN ENTWISTLE

has served with Good Conduct in

the 1ST SOUTH MIDDX. Company

from 1958 till 1962

W. E. Hewlett Captain

Date SEPT. 1962

WEST END JIVING

STARRING

THE FEDERALS THE BEL-AIRS THE DETOURS

AT

5, LEICESTER PLACE, LEICESTER SQ., LONDON, W.C.2

LUXURIOUS BALLROOM

8—11.30 ADMISSION 4/6

TAYLOR ENTERTAINMENTS IN C

As schoolboys John and Pete were in a number of short-lived bands. From the Confederates, a trad jazz outfit, they 'progressed' to the Aristocats, who became the Scorpions ("we were terrible"), before John teamed up with Roger Daltrey and a group called The Detours. After hearing them play, Pete was persuaded by Roger to join as well. "I told him we had a real Vox amplifier, so he thought 'A Vox amplifier... well' and he joined". Pete remembers, "Roger regarded it as his band, but that was like he was the biggest mouth". And John recalls, "he would punctuate his decisions with punches". When they started, Roger used to make all the guitars and amps. "In them days it was all psychological warfare being in a group, so we hit on the idea of having the biggest cabinets you've ever

 C.A.V APPRENTI

presents

A

NEW YEARS R

to be held

THE SPORTS GROUND

on

SATURDAY, 19th JANU.

7-30 to 12 Midnight

FEATURING

THE DETOUR

Ticket 4/- Lic

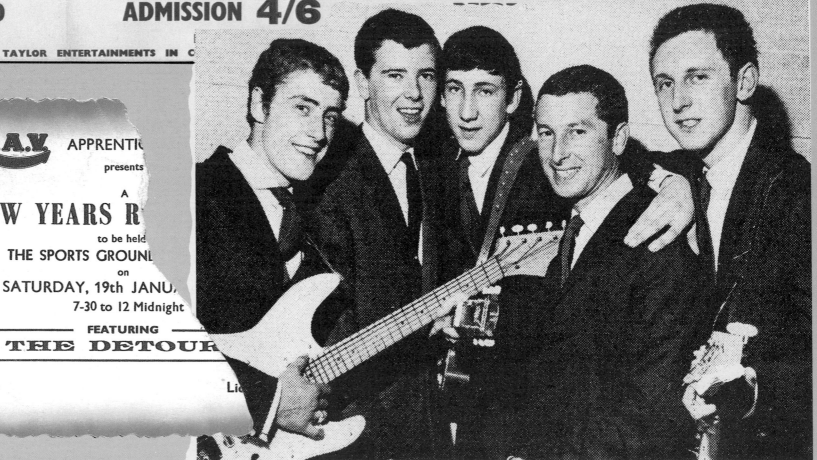

Acton jazz and jive group, the "Detours, at last found their way to a local booking on Saturday when they were the second band at Saturday's Gala Ball at the Town Hall. Left to right : Roger Daltrey (18), Colin Dawson (19), Peter Townsend (17), Doug Sandon (18), and John Johns (17)

seen ...yet inside we'd have this 12-inch speaker. It looked like a bloody side board... people would come and see us and say, 'Hey they must be good, look at the size of their gear'." The Detours would gig occasionally, often at company outings. As John remembers, they would, "put all the equipment in the back of their coach and go somewhere like Bognor. On the way back, the firm would have hired a church hall. We'd stop and do a dance and they would all get pissed out of their minds... and then we would load all the equipment back into the coach and go home". As part-timers (leaving school, Pete went to art school, John worked in a tax office, and Roger was already a sheet metal worker) they got their first chance to make decent money. After Pete's mum got them an audition, Bob Druce of Commercial Entertainments signed them with the prospect of regular gigs.

Posters: Two Bob Druce promotions. Roger's mum remembers seeing the band: "I thought they were bloody loud. I said, 'You mean people actually *pay* to see that'?"

Below: Detours' Dougie Sandom.

FOX & GOOSE HOTEL
HANGER LANE, EALING, W.5

JIVING & TWISTING
FRIDAYS
FEATURING THE DYNAMIC
"DETOURS"

7.30-11.00 P.M.   **4/- ADMISSION**
LICENSED BALLROOM BAR
BUSES—83, 187 TO DOOR   112, 105 TWO MINUTES   TRAINS—HANGER LANE, PARK ROYAL

COMMENCING FRIDAY, 11TH JAN.

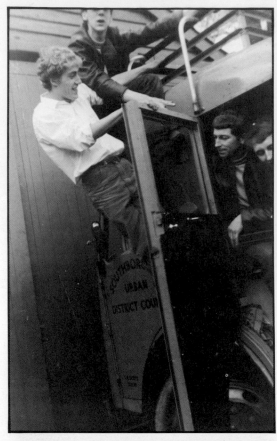

During 1963 The Detours played the Druce club circuit around London. Singer Colin Dawson was ousted, and finally replaced by Roger, until then on guitar. As a four piece with a regular following they dropped their C & W and trad jazz material and added *Shot of Rhythm & Blues* and *Shakin' All Over* and other blues to the Top 10 and Beatles numbers – "Sometimes boys would request *Twist & Shout* just to clear the bar for them". Art School for Pete was a revelation. Apart from discovering 'pop art', "The art side did get my brain going creatively and started me thinking". He also inherited a vast blues and jazz collection, and as the band graduated to gigs round the UK, supporting such acts as Johnny Kidd and The Pirates, Wee Willy Harris, and, eventually, the Stones (Where Pete got his windmill action from Keith Richards) so they did versions of Jimmy Reed's *Big Boss Man*, James Brown's *Please, Please, Please, Smokestack Lightning*, and others similar. Looking for a punchier name, 'The Detours' changed to 'the Who' and got a backer in Helmut Gorden, who called them "my little diamonds."

Centre Left: The group van with Detours' logo.

22

THE DETOURS ARE FINDING A WAY TO FAME

● **ARE YOU** getting fed-up with the Beatles? Then try screaming for a homegrown group: The Detours. I'm sure they would appreciate it.

Twenty - year - old Angela Dives, of Gibbon-road, East Acton, is the girl to contact for information about the Detours. She is the President of their fan club (over 30 members and growing fast).

And she has no doubts about the top-pop quality of her favourite group, though she wasn't quite sure what made them so special.

"They have a good sense of humour," she said after a little thought. "They laugh and crack jokes on the stage. And they can play very good harmonies."

The Detours are apparently a versatile group, too. They all sing, they all play the harmonica, one of their guitarists plays the trumpet as well and the vocalist plays the trombone.

The founders of the group got their experience years ago in the dark days of skiffle Then they formed the Detours guitar group in the summer, 1961 — and went steadily from success to success. Now the group, originally a five-man organization, consists of two guitarists, a drummer and a singer: Peter Townsend (19), John Entwistle (20), Doug Sandom (25) and Roger Daultry (21).

Roger, the vocalist, and John, the bass guitarist, were with the group when it was founded. The others have joined since.

What happens when you join the Detours' fan club, I asked?

"We send you a photograph of the group and a letter of welcome," said blonde Angela, who operates an accounting machine when she's not dealing with the Detours' fan mail. "And we're planning to send out a news letter as well, though nothing has come of that yet."

Applications for membership are, I'm told, coming in fairly steadily. The average is three a day.

"And nearly all of them are from outside Acton," said Angela jubilantly. "We have members in Tunbridge Wells in Kent, in East London — all over the place!"

That's nice. But the time to start really celebrating will be when the fan mail starts pouring in from Liverpool!

The swinging Detours from Acton (left to right): Ro[...] Daultry, Peter Townsend, John Entwistle and Doug [...]

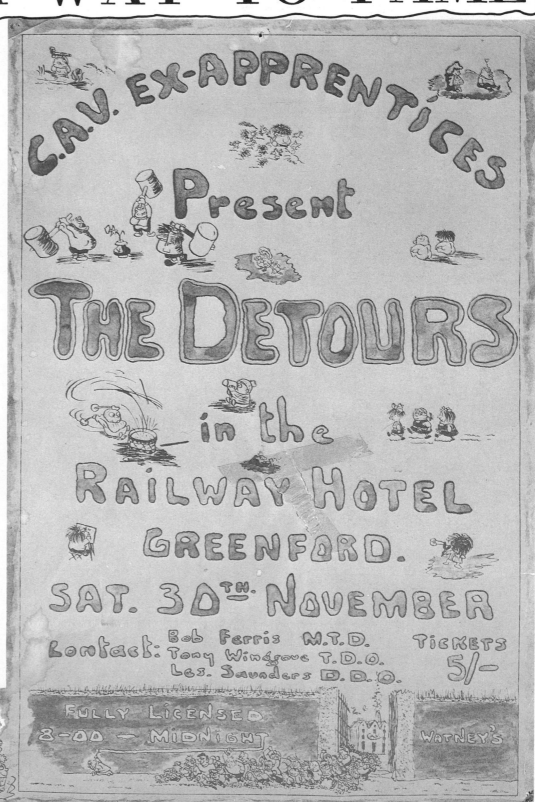

HOW HIGH WILL THESE NUMBERS GO?

HAILED as "the first authentic mod record," four hip young men called the High Numbers are out right now with "I'm the Face," backed with "Zoot Suit" — a Fontana disc. Two numbers penned by co-manager Peter Meaden.

How mod are this mod-mad mob? VERY mod. Their clothes are the hallmark of the much-criticised typical mod. Cycling jackets, tee-shirts, turned-up Levi jeans, long white jackets, boxing boots, black and white brogues and so on to the mod-est limits.

Says Peter Meaden: "After all, the Mod scene is a way of life. An exciting, quick-changing, way of life. The boys are totally immersed in this atmosphere. So they have this direct contact with thousands of potential disc-buyers.

SWITCHED

"And the reaction is already very strong indeed. Take places like the Scene Club in London. The fans are mad about the disc — both sides of it!" In fact, "Zoot Suit" was originally planned as the "A" side, being switched only at the last moment.

In a way, the High Numbers sound swivels directly round the vocals and harmonica-wailing of Roger Daltry. His blonde hair is styled in a longish French crew-cut and he buys clothes in the very latest styles. Currently he's modelling zoot-suit jackets. He digs the blues and Buddy Guy . . . and is glad he no longer has to work as a sheet metal worker.

Lead guitarist Peter Townsed originally wanted to be a graphic designer, having been to Ealing Art School. A near six-footer, he has cropped dark hair, piercing blue eyes — and says: "I admit to spending a fortune on bright and in-vogue clothes. I go for the 'West Side Story' look and the Ivy League gear." Musically, he's for Bob Dylan and the Tamla-Motown-Gordy label.

AMBITION

On bass is John Allison. He went to school with Roger at Acton County Grammar School. "I used to be in an income tax office. This gave me an ambition: to get OUT of the tax office." John is certainly the most conservative of the group, really preferring classical music to most other kinds. He is an accomplished musician.

Come in, now, drummer Keith Moon. He's the youngest of the group — only seventeen. A Wembly resident, he went to Wembley Technical College and was a trainee representative before turning professional musician. Is the smallest of the group, too, has black hair and brown eyes — and says: "I spend all my free time listening to the music in various West End of London clubs."

Record Mirror colleagues are convinced the boys stand a good chance of getting away with "I'm The Face." And one thing is for sure: the phraseology is good and authentic. Mod, in fact.

Interesting to see how the disc sells.

ZOOT SUIT
(P. Meaden)
THE HIGH NUMBERS

I'M THE FACE
(P. Meaden)
THE HIGH NUMBERS

Pete Meaden, a top name in the growing mod movement, muscled in as co-manager and started to change their image. They had drumming problems, so when at a gig one of the audience said "My mate can play a lot better than your drummer," the mystery person was asked to audition in the interval. He played three furious numbers and "mucked up the drummer's hi-hat. He also damaged the foot pedal," recalls John. Keith Moon had joined. Playing much Tamla-oriented music, Meaden turned 'The Detours' into the new and mod 'High Numbers.'
Left & Top left: Keith with his first band, the Beachcombers. Far left: The High Numbers first single (released July 3rd, 1964).

JOHN

ER

ROGER

KEITH

UNDISCOVERED BRITISH GROUPS

They're part of the new wave in raves!

THE HIGH NUMBERS

EVERY TUESDAY 3/6

RAILWAY HOTEL HARROW & WEALDSTONE !

the high numbers

The important thing about the HIGH NUMBERS which is immediately noted on meeting them is that nothing is contrived or prefabricated about them and this can be said particularly in the field of clothes.

The clothes they wear have the hallmark of the much maligned 'mod' - cycling jackets, tee shirts, turned up levi jeans, long white jackets, boxing boots, black and white brogues and all the rest; but these are also worn by thousands of other young people of today. The Number, the Face, the Ticket, or to use the generalisation, the Mod, is a product of this day and age. They can be seen in force, particularly any Saturday night in the clubs and on the streets of London's West End, and in nearly every large city in Great Britain.

It is a way of life and for them, an exciting way of life. And the fact that the HIGH NUMBERS are drawn from this facet of society in which they are totally immersed makes them about the most potentially exciting and powerful group in the field of beat music today. The things expressed on this, their first record, cause an immediate rapport between them and thousands of young people like themselves.

In a nutshell - they are of the people.

Pete Meaden (picture page 11) introduced the band to the hub of the clothes - obsessed, discriminating mod way of life in the Scene Club and along Carnaby Street in London. They found a world of pills and rare R&B but most of all "it gave us an identity". The High Numbers became the first performing mod group. Though *I'm The Face/Zoot Suit* was hardly a success, in 1964 the band became full-time musicians at £20 a week.

Previous spread: (pages 28 & 29) The High Numbers at the mod mecca, The Scene Club. (Top right: Note the author, between Keith and Pete, and Pete Meaden between Pete and Roger).
(Pages 31 & 32): Early Who.
(Page 33): The Marquee, Maximum R&B poster was taken from this series.

1965-1968

Lambert & Stamp/The Who–Maximum R & B/'My Generation'/USA/The 'Brain Opera'

Soon after the record had been issued I was at the front desk of the Railway Hotel helping take the money and issue tickets and membership cards, when I saw this straight-looking figure hovering around outside and looking decidedly shifty. A capacity was fixed at 180 but there had been occasions when we had issued tickets for as many as 1,000, though a couple of hundred of those would have to content themselves with checking out the scooters in the courtyard. That night we had an 'average' crowd of 700. I was worried that this posh-looking guy in a dark grey suit was some sort of official, either from the local council or from the brewery that owned the pub who was spying on how we ran the place. The six bouncers were alerted to try and keep this strange bird out. Eventually I approached him and announced to him that I ran the club and wondered whether I could be of any assistance. When he asked me in his upper class accent "Is it always like this?" I was decidedly worried. Then he asked "What's the name of the group?" I told him they were the High Numbers and when he said he was looking for a group to hire I was greatly relieved and of course interested. I invited him in.

He stood just inside the hall and surveyed the scene. The Railway was a very hot, sweaty and very dark place. We deliberately made it so. We turned off all the lights except two in which we had put pink bulbs. The radiators were deliberately turned up and all the windows blacked out. This and the fact we had a very good group was why it had such atmosphere. The grey suit was taking in the whole thing very attentively, the group, the kids, the dancing.

I suggested he talked to their manager and went in and found Pete Meaden and we went out into the courtyard to talk. He turned out to be a film director who was looking for a pop group to appear in a film he was going to shoot. His name was Kit Lambert and he wanted to arrange for his partner to see the band.

That evening Kit Lambert telephoned his partner in Ireland. His partner was Chris Stamp, brother of actor Terence Stamp. He and Kit Lambert had both met up at Shepperton studios whilst working as assistant directors in the film business. They formed a friendship and ended up sharing a flat together near Baker Street. They decided to make a film of their own and wanted to make a decent pop film unlike the pap that was made at the time. Chris had a friend from his school days, Mike Shaw, who was working in the theatre in Bristol. Chris suggested he came to London where Chris Stamp would try to get him a union ticket to get into the film business.

The Who wasn't the first band they'd seen, in fact they'd been searching for four months. Chris Stamp had taken a job as an assistant director on the film 'Young Cassidy' and had gone to Ireland to do it. This provided the finance for Kit Lambert and Mike Shaw to continue their hunt for the right pop group for their project. Mike Shaw remembers, "I had a scooter and I used to ride around the different areas and copy down all the info from posters and the local press – what groups were on and so on. Then I'd go along and see them and make a report back to Kit." Kit Lambert himself would also drive around and check out gigs in his Volkswagon Beetle. That was how he came to the Railway Hotel in the summer of 1964.

Chris Stamp, after receiving Kit's phone call, flew back to London the next weekend to see the band at the Trade Union Hall in Watford. He only arrived in time to see the last 15 minutes of their act but it was enough to get him excited. "They were extraordinary, very surreal, just right for our purposes. We weren't looking for a blatantly commercial band, we were looking for something, you know, quite odd. The High Numbers were immediately attractive and the whole thing that was going on was very interesting from a film point of view."

After the Watford gig, Kit and Chris arranged an audition the following Sunday at a school they'd hired in Holland Park that had a rehearsal room. Mike Shaw recalls "It really was amazing. They were even better than we'd heard already. I mean, Peter was fantastic, the guitar sound the feedback, and that."

Kit and Chris's appearance on the scene was almost uncannily timed. The band had reached an impasse. They had grown increasingly disenchanted with Helmut Gorden. The single that Meaden had pinned all his hopes on was out and not going anywhere. They hadn't considered the possibility of the record not catching on. Perhaps they hadn't thought that it would necessarily be a great hit, but they had thought that when finally had managed to release a record, *something*

**SOUTHBANK ARTISTES
PRESENT AT**

EEL PIE ISLAND
TWICKENHAM, MIDDX.

WEDNESDAY, 30th OCTOBER

THE WHO

EAST OF EDEN

PROTEUS   •   DAVID BOOTH

SUNDAY — BLUES NIGHT

---

would happen. Meaden *did* get two pieces of very valuable national publicity in Fabulous magazine and Disc and they were steadily building up their following managing to secure a spot on a national tour, including one show with the Beatles. So some things *were* looking up, but they still hadn't got the kind of feedback they had expected from releasing the record. Meaden was a bit lost as to what to do next. The boys wanted to get rid of Helmut Gorden and get a backer for Meaden to manage them, but how, why and where they didn't know.

However Meaden's main problem was, like all heavy pep pill users, his speeded-up brain, which was so good for snappy quick ideas and endless enthusiasm, wasn't any use for coping with more fundamental and down-to-earth problems.

Kit Lambert and Chris Stamp soon realised the situation the band was in and agreed amongst themselves that instead of simply using the band in a film, they would try to take over their management. Chris Stamp remembered the difficulty in trying to negotiate with Meaden. "He'd be talking away and then suddenly would start muttering. We didn't know whether he was interested in us making a film or not. He'd switch into this speeded up muttering so after a while we couldn't understand what the guy was talking about. And he definitely had that chalky thing around his mouth, you know the sugar-coated mouth."

Lambert and Stamp soon found out that they had to negotiate with Helmut Gorden and Bob Druce and not Pete Meaden. They also had to persuade the band that they would be a better bet as managers than anyone else. The band were really torn. They didn't want to stay with Helmut Gorden or Bob Druce who they were contracted to, yet they still felt close to Pete Meaden. Kit and Chris had a sort of

---

infectious enthusiasm and seemed more worldly-wise. Kit's confidence and his persuasive upper class accent were very appealing. We knew nothing about Kit. However, Roger's girlfriend at that time, a West-Indian actress called Cleo, had come across Kit previously and urged Roger and the band to go with him. Then Chris and Kit offered a contract that guaranteed to continue the boys £1,000 a year each.

Lambert and Stamp had to deal with the legal contract first, before they were free to act. They knew absolutely nothing about the pop business. They had been bluffing their way along and now they had the band ready to sign a contract and be managed. Stamp remembers "All we knew, we got from the newspapers. We were just gathering facts from the press and we read that David Jacobs was the Beatles lawyer. He was *the* rock and roll lawyer, so we went to see him." They took him the agreement that had been drawn up between Helmut Gorden and the band. "We went into his office and gave him the papers. He picked them up, glanced at them and then with a big camp mannerism he turned his head away to one side and inclined it to the ceiling and said 'You haven't seen me.' We had to creep out of the door. Legally you see, as we were taking over the management, if we bought the management contract that they had signed he could not act for us." It turned out that the contract that Helmut Gorden had had drawn up wasn't valid mainly because the boys were under age and they had not all had their parents sign it.

Stamp continues, "Now if we were going to take over this thing and because they were all under 21, we had to sort of guarantee them salaries. And they all had to get OK's from their parents to do the whole thing right. So, we were really out there on a limb. We sure didn't have a lot of bread."

They had about £1,300 between them which was not anywhere near enough. The first thing that they did was to make a 16mm promotional film of the group at the Railway Hotel. Kit hired the equipment and he and Mike Shaw together shot a lot of footage of the gig. Kit held the camera and Mike held the light. It was very crude as it was all lit by one hand-held light and Kit would be all over the place, on chairs, on the floor and up on stage with the hand-held camera. They taped the gig for a soundtrack on a mono tape recorder. As the group were playing they filmed the audience dancing and kids hanging around on scooters outside as well. The film was to be the main vehicle for promoting the band. They were going to show it to the agents and promoters and record companies. They later shot more footage of mods dancing in the Scene club and hanging around Soho and Carnaby Street. This was all edited together and used as a sort of introduction at gigs before the group came on. It was very crude but no other group or management had such originality and determination. This short intro film often worked at gigs because of its sheer nerve.

Kit and Chris thrived on sheer nerve. Chris would go round all the mod areas that the group hadn't yet been booked in to find more gigs. "I went to places like Tottenham, Leytonstone, Wanstead, Stratford, all over the East End of London. I'd go straight into a gig and find the promoter and say 'I've got this group that you wouldn't believe!' And I'd offer to show them the promotion film and show them the write-ups in Disc and Fabulous."

We got a few new venues. However, money was getting tight and so Chris took a job on the filming of 'The Heroes of Telemark', starring Kirk Douglas in Norway and sent over most of his salary every week to Kit to finance the group.

The High Numbers had been booked to do a series of

weekend shows all over the country headlined by different artists. They were to be the backing band for a new girl singer called Val McCallum. They would also get their own fifteen minute spot on the bill. The tour consisted of about half a dozen shows with different artists at the top of the bill. There was a concert in the Calvin Halls, Glasgow with Lulu and the Luvvers, Dusty Springfield at the Hippodrome, Brighton, P. J. Proby at the New Theatre, Oxford, Tom Jones and Marianne Faithful at the Demontfort Hall in Leicester and, the most important of all, the Beatles at the Opera House in Blackpool.

The latter was a memorable concert. Kit had bought a much bigger van to take the extra gear they now used. It was like a small lorry with a luton over the cab. Roger was still the driver. Typically, Kit Lambert wanted to put on as good a show as possible and make as much as he could out of these Sunday shows. He insisted that the High Numbers handle their own lighting for each show of the tour. Mike Shaw had worked at the Blackpool Opera House during the previous summer season and knew the set-up. He was familiar with the lighting board and Kit said to the theatre management that they would handle their own lighting. The management at first refused. "Well, Kit just forced his way and shouted the man down. He couldn't stop us. We had every right to do our own lighting." None of the other bands were interested in doing their own lighting, they just left it up to the theatre or stage director to work out, even the Beatles. Although the High Numbers were bottom of the bill, Kit insisted on controlling their stage image. "We wanted to put on a show rather than just be another band following on from everybody else. It was meant to be a show in itself." Mike Shaw recalls, "I knew the lighting man there. He was ex-army and he did the same set lighting for every act. I'd gone up there and changed a few colours on the lighting board because by that time we had our own lighting plot. It caused a hell of a row."

On the bill with the Beatles were, amongst others, the Kinks. They had recently released *You Really Got Me* and it was heading up the charts. Their act was very impressive and the simplicity and effectiveness of the guitar riff in *You Really Got Me* was not lost on the group, particularly Pete. They played again with the Kinks in Blackpool, this time at the Queen's Theatre a few weeks later when *You Really Got Me* had been a No. 1 hit.

The Beatles were phenomenal and so were the audience. After the fifth bar of their first number nobody in the audience could hear anything other than the massed screams of teenage girls. As soon as they'd played the last song they dropped their instruments and ran with an escort of about a dozen policemen down into a tunnel that led under the street to a building across the road where they escaped unnoticed.

The High Numbers were not so lucky. They had to take their gear out through the stage door and load it into the van. Roger bravely fought his way through the crowd of Beatle fans that surrounded the theatre and backed the van dangerously through the mob. He made his way back to the stage door and then the group, Kit Lambert, Mike Shaw and myself set off through the crowd, who by now they had probably realised that they were not going to see the Beatles. So they settled for this other group and the High Numbers were mobbed. The police at the stage door could do nothing. We wore identical seersucker madras cotton jackets – I'd swopped jackets with Moon – and they tore off the collars and Roger's sleeve. We eventually clambered over the back of the lorry and Roger pushed his way round to the driving cab and we set off. We drove a part of the way back again once safely in the truck to watch the crowd from a sensible distance. The High Numbers hadn't yet had a hit record but they *had* been mobbed by hundreds of teenage girls. Usually it happens the other way round. Pete was convinced that the crowd mistook Kit Lambert for Brian Epstein and that is why they reacted that way.

Lambert and Stamp take over

They weren't happy at backing Val McCallum, who they didn't rate at all, and Keith brought a small 5″ wide toy cymbal, which he played on the off-beat during her version of *Let the Good Times Roll*. Apparently, it sounded so tinny and empty that she said that she didn't want them to back her anymore and they got thrown off the tour, which the boys didn't mind at all. After playing at the Railway Hotel for about six months they were getting fed up with the temporary stage extension that they had to set up out of beer crates and table tops every time they played. So the Who themselves paid for a proper wooden stage to be built by some carpenters. This stage gave them a more solid and secure feeling for their increasingly physical stage act and also had a bit more room.

However, it was higher than the original stage and the ceiling at the Railway was particularly low. "I started to knock the guitar about a lot, hitting it on the amps to get banging noises and things like that and it had started to crack" remembers Pete. "It banged against the ceiling and smashed a hole in the plaster and the guitar head actually poked through the ceiling plaster. When I brought it out the top of the neck was left behind. I couldn't believe what had happened. There were a couple of people from art school I knew at the front of the stage and they were laughing their heads off. One of them was literally rolling about on the floor laughing and his girl friend was kind of looking at me smirking, you know, going 'flash cunt and all that'. So I just got really angry and got what was left of the guitar and smashed it to smithereens. About a month earlier I'd managed to scrape together enough for a 12-string Rickenbacker, which I only used on two or three numbers. It was lying at the side of the stage so I just picked ip up, plugged it in and gave them a sort of look and carried on playing, as if I'd meant to do it.

"The next day I was miserable about having lost my guitar. Roger said 'You shouldn't have smashed it up, I could have got it repaired for you.' Anyway I'd obliterated

it." Pete turned the 12-string Rickenbacker into a 6-string to continue working. "The next week I went back there and there was a whole crowd waiting to see this lunatic break his guitar."

Pete didn't break his guitar that show but after the gig was finished when they were off stage getting ready to leave, Keith went back on stage and smashed up his drumkit. There were only about fifteen of us present to witness it. "He'd done it more as a kind of act of faith," said Pete. "The next week we went to the Railway, I thought this is great, this time I've got Moon behind me, and at the end of the show destroyed his drumkit completely and I smashed up my other guitar." Pete had been very surprised when his guitar neck had first broken off but found out later that Rickenbackers were very weak at that point. "After a while I had a whole collection of them all broken at the same point." Keith managed to repair his drumkit but Pete now was without a guitar. "I had to almost start stealing guitars. I went to Jim Marshall's music store in Hanwell and said, 'Can I have a guitar?' But they had heard of me breaking up guitars and would not let me. They wouldn't do it. They thought that I wouldn't keep up the payments if I broke it. So I just grabbed a Rickenbacker off the wall and ran out. Eventually they sent me hire purchase papers for it."

Kit was against breaking guitars at the beginning because of the cost. However, he thought it should be done on special occasions. He hadn't witnessed the act at the Railway because he'd been busy editing the film he'd shot. Kit had told reporter Virginia Ironside that the group broke their equipment onstage. She had come to a gig in Reading to see it. Kit wanted the publicity and told them to smash up their instruments that night. "I said listen Kit, I've only just managed to scrape this instrument together" recalls Pete, "And he said 'Don't worry, I'll pay for it'!"

At the end of the show at Reading Pete and Keith both smashed up their gear but Kit and Virginia Ironside had missed it because they were still in the bar. Kit came up to Pete afterwards and said, "You mean you really broke it?" and went into shock when Pete opened the guitar case to show him the smashed guitar bits. "He said, 'But you've smashed it to bits', and I said. 'But that's what you told me to do. That's what I've been doing.' And he's going, 'You're crazy, how are we going to be able to afford this?' And then Keith says, 'Oh by the way, I've smashed me drum kit up as well.' And Roger was in shock too, and John thought we were bananas because he worships the instrument and even a tiny scratch makes him feel sick. It just seemed to go from there. Virginia Irronside wrote her article anyway about the group that smashes up their instruments. After that I would only do it when I could afford it or when there was time to get it repaired, or get another instrument for the next day. At one time I was making payments on eight guitars."

With all the panache of a man who confessed to having been the worst officer in the British army, Kit decided to try to promote the band himself. He wanted to expose the band to the South East and East End of London. He decided to put on his own dances at Greenwich and Lewisham. Very strong working class areas with a lot of mod kids.

Kit's flat in Ivor Court was a hive of chaos. It was in a block much favoured by the latest wave of pop stars. He had an Irish woman that came in to clean up and do some cooking and she used to look around at all the mess that there was around what was effectively the Who's headquarters. Kit had papers all over the place, maps pinned on the wall and over the floor. I had posters drying on every available surface, as well as a couple of washing lines strung across the main room, which had about fifty shiny wet posters pegged to them to dry. Mike Shaw and Kit would be coming and going constantly on various errands. Kit when in the flat would always be planning things. He would never relax. He was always worrying about everything. We printed nearly 500 posters and set out to really make a splash in Greenwich. On the day before we set out to stick up the posters Kit had driven around the area with me in his Beetle car to spot good sites for pasting up the posters. Over the next three nights we went out and pasted up rows and rows of them. Instead of just putting up one or two on an empty shop front and then moving on, we were determined to make a big display and were sticking up twenty at a time. It looked very impressive, The High Numbers, The High Numbers, The High Numbers repeated in two-tone blue all over the area. We were so pleased with the result and convinced that the amount of publicity would make the Greenwich gig an absolute sell-out. Kit had printed up some hand-outs and we gave out hundreds around Greenwich and all over Lewisham. Unfortunately, these great efforts didn't pay off. When I proudly took Kit round Greenwich a few days later to show off our impressive poster coverage we were amazed to see most of the posters covered up.

They weren't covered up with other posters necessarily, which is the usual practise for rival promoters, but they had been deliberately covered over with plain brown wrapping paper. We were amazed that somebody would go to all that trouble of pasting over our posters with blank paper, especially as there were so many of them. We were to discover the world of the professional fly-posterer.

Later when Kit put up fly-posters for the Marquee he realised that it was better to pay these men though they didn't put any of your posters up. It was a sort of protection racket. If you employed them they made sure that a certain number stayed up whether they had put them up or not. As the whole thing was mildly illegal anyway they had no right to claim various sites as theirs, but it was easier to pay them off than to be in conflict with them. For the Marquee Kit paid them £10 to leave the maximum R & B posters alone – that was 1/– per poster for 200 posters. Actually, he put up nearer 2,000 posters, so he came out of it well.

Kit had been worried that the name, the High Numbers might be interpreted as a Bingo game and attract housewives instead of kids. Mike Shaw remembers the handouts being a disaster: "The thousands of tickets we gave away at

Lewisham killed it because Kit had this brilliant idea that because people would think the High Numbers was something to do with bingo, he'd put on the tickets 'The Worst in Family Entertainment' or something. He had this strange logic that that would draw the kids in. But it really killed it, because nobody came."

The gig was a flop. Greenwich Town Hall held well over 1,000 but fewer than 100 turned up. He'd even hired the compere that was on the Summer tour and a first half support band, the Boys, who were another semi-mod band (they later changed their name to the Action). He'd bought crates of Coca-Cola to sell, which had to be returned to the factory. After a couple of weeks it was clearly not going to be successful and Greenwich was abandoned. Kit then tried to promote dances using the High Numbers in the Red Lion, Leytonstone but that wasn't a success either and ran for about five weeks.

Mike Shaw went off to the North to try to promote *I'm The Face* and use it to secure some more bookings. "We knew we were going to Blackpool so I went up to Liverpool to the Cavern to try and get a gig for them. While they were going that far I'd try and get some other gigs in the area. I took *I'm The Face* to Nems in Liverpool to see if they would order it. I went in and played it to them but they weren't interested. Then I tried all around Blackpool, as far as Bradford and Bolton to make it worthwhile travelling all the way up there instead of just doing the one night. But I couldn't get bookings because it was too short notice." The band started rehearsing at the Wandsworth Granada cinema, where Kit was working out a lighting display. They were taken to Max Factor in Bond Street to get stage make-up and be taught how to use it. "They gave us little make-up bags and little charts" remembers John "I had to stick this white stuff under the bottom of my eyelid and it was real painful. I always used to end up with my eyes watering and it running down my face." The colour they gave us was called 'light Egyptian'. It was water-based stuff and you had to put it on real fast, or else it went patchy." Then they went down to Carnaby Street and Kit provided the money for them to buy lots of new clothes, not just for stage wear but for maintaining their clothes-conscious mod image off stage as well.

The Bob Druce bookings were falling off now that the band was no longer part of Commercial Entertainments. Druce was pushing his latest group The Clique as heir to the High Numbers position as top band of his circuit. Kit and Chris had to get new bookings for the band to keep them working and building up a reputation and also to keep the money from live gigs coming in. They didn't have a clue how to go about it.

Their weakness was also their strength. Mike Shaw recalls "They really were great days because we knew nothing in effect about the music business, yet we knew the band would do it because they were such a great band. It was such good talent to work with. But we were doing everything in a sense wrong. You know, we were steaming into offices where normally you got an appointment first, except of course you could never get an appointment." The management's complete ignorance of music business procedure enabled them to bypass the usual obstacles. "I had to pretend that I was a manager of a group that was playing in Essex or Somerset or somewhere. We made up a name, the Ramrods, I think it was, and I went to the Arthur Howes agency and asked them what I should do. You know, we had to find out. How did we get a contract – what did we do? What was the normal sort of deal we could get? How did one get gigs? How did you get an agent? Then I reported back to Chris and Kit. We needed some idea of how much to ask for and so on."

After hearing the tape of *It Was You* Kit had bought Pete two vortexian tape recorders for him to use for writing and producing demos. Pete's set up had been very crude up till then. I remember him making up a metronome to keep time by fixing a pencil to a record deck turntable with sticky tape and adjusting the variable speed turntable, so that the pencil hit a piece of card and made a noise. This gave him a constant beat that was also variable.

Kit and Chris set themselves up as a limited company called New Action and had a go-ahead letterhead designed and printed with an arrow pointing forward. Kit got a secretary, a friend of his called Anya. New Action consisted of Kit, Chris, Mike and Anya.

The band had become *the* mods' band in all the places they played. The High Numbers could see from the stage what the top faces were wearing in various areas and could pick up local fashions and be themselves copied in other areas. One night Pete said he'd seen two kids wearing diamonds on their jumpers and he thought that was going to be the next big thing. He made a big black diamond on his jumper and wore it for a couple of weeks. He probably helped cause a trend in that way.

Chris Stamp had persuaded Ziggy Jackson, who ran the new Marquee club which had just moved from Oxford Street to Wardour Street, to let them put on the group one night a week. He agreed to let them try Tuesday nights, his least successful night. The Marquee had been a trad jazz club but let the more purist R & B groups play some nights. Tuesday was still one of the jazz nights and lost money. Kit had earlier decided to drop the name the High Numbers and go back to the name of the Who again. The Who appealed to him. It was very catchy and intriguing and more importantly, the Who had the essential quality of being simply unforgettable. With the change of name any suspicion that Kit and Chris were simply taking over Meaden's ideas and putting them into practice was refuted. It was strange how Pete Meaden had come and changed the group, renamed them, written their first record, then gone,

and the group, much refreshed by his involvement, reverted back to their former name and carried on. They had only been called the High Numbers for about five hectic months.

Getting a venue in the centre of town was a breakthrough for Kit and Chris. If they could successfully establish the band at the Marquee (they'd already played the 100 Club), it would be ideal for media exploitation, particularly when they released their next single. One of the reasons that the name the Who was so successful was, as I have stated earlier, it was short and appeared large on posters. Kit now decided that it needed to be longer for the very reason that he now wanted it to appear more substantial on posters. That was one of his reasons behind the decisions to add the words Maximum R & B after their name. It was a brilliant piece of pop-marketing and image building. He had a graphic artist draw up a logo for the Who with an arrow coming out of the last letter of the name like the medical symbol for male. The group had posed for some black and white pictures and from the series taken of Pete playing his guitar, a frame of him swinging his arm was chosen to be included with the new logo and slogan for a poster campaign to launch the band initially at the Marquee, but eventually all over. THE WHO, MAXIMUM R & B black and white posters were fly-posted all over London. Thousands of publicity cards were printed and given out at clubs and hundreds of free tickets given away for the first gig. Despite the campaign, the first night was sparsely attended. The band, however, were in fine form and the next week there were twice as many in the audience and the third week the Marquee was crowded. Soon, they had broken the house box-office records. Tuesday night, the worst night of the week became the most successful.

Pete had perfected his feedback guitar technique and often ended the set by smashing his guitar into an amp. Their act was aggressive, punchy and very loud. The Marquee on Tuesday night became almost as important for mods as the Scene Club or La Discotheque. Because of the success of their regular central London gig, it gave the Who an added aura at other gigs. 'The Who?, I've heard of them, aren't they that group from the Marquee?'

"On the brink of a breakthrough"

Pete was taking purple hearts more often but was still mainly a dope smoker. None of the others in the group yet smoked dope or took pills, although everybody drank quite a lot. The fact that he smoked pot put him in a different league to most of the mod fans. Mods weren't interested in dope smoking or booze. There were definitely into pills. Mostly pills that would give them non-stop energy to see them through a night or through the weekend. They took most available amphetamines, purple hearts, black bombers, french blues, dexies and also sometimes tranquilisers like librium. Pot smoking was very 'Art School and middle class'. Marijuana was an inactive drug. Stoned people just lay down and listened to music. Pilled people danced and walked and twitched and talked (and talked and talked).

Mods were very friendly and gentle kids on the whole, not like the memory of them as gang fighters and rocker bashers. The Who were making lots and lots of mod friends. Sometimes they were a little too friendly. Often they would offer to help out with the gear after gigs. One night at the Marquee a few were carrying some of the gear out and one little mod carried Pete's tape recorder out – we never saw it again.

Mods would travel around to various gigs wherever the Who were playing. They were unofficially led by a couple of Mods called Willy and H. H had a Vespa but Willy, unusually for a mod, drove a Vauxhall Wyvern. Kit Lambert later capitalised on this dedicated unofficial fan-club and developed it into a group known as the Hundred Faces. They could always be relied upon whenever the Who needed extra fan support and for spreading news and last minute changes of venues and such like.

Kit, as well as using posters and the press as much as possible had an ace up his sleeve when it came to publicity and mobilizing the kids. It was called WOMP. It stood for Word Of Mouth Publicity. The Hundred Faces were his troops and he used them to the full. If a booking came in on a Monday for a gig on the Thursday, although there was no time to place an ad in the music press, Kit could still fill it by getting the 100 Faces to go into action with WOMP. And simply by spreading the news by this grapevine through friends and kids at the Wednesday night clubs and dances, Kit could ensure a promoter that an extra 150 to 250 kids would arrive from all over London to help pack the gigs.

The most significant event in the evolution of the Who came in late '64 and early '65; their guitarist wrote a song that was to be their next single.

Their stage act had become unbeatable, but Pete knew that if he could come up with a commercial song to record, it would solve all their worries. Kit too was anxious for the band to originate their own material. Pete's demo of *I Can't Explain* was the first step in their subsequent breakthrough into the charts. The second step came when Kit's secretary, Anya, played the demo to a friend of hers, who was the wife of Kinks' record producer, Shel Talmy. Talmy liked the demo and was interested in producing it for the Who. The Kinks *You Really Got Me* with its distinctive heavy, fuzzy guitar riff, which was produced by Shel Talmy, had got to No. 2 in the English charts and had launched the Kinks as a successful singles group. Shel Talmy remembers: "I first saw them at some church in Shepherds Bush. They were loud, raw, funky and superballsy. I liked their concept and their sound. I liked everything." Kit and Chris eagerly signed a deal with Talmy, who quickly got them a deal with American Decca and then a deal with English Decca.

They went into Pye studios in London to record *I Can't Explain*. The first rough mixes were much like a sixties Bob Dylan record. Shel Talmy called in a session guitarist called

Jimmy Page to put on the lead guitar. This was a fairly usual practise at that time. Probably about 50% of all pop singles released in the early sixties had session men playing them and a good many guitar solos were by the same handful of session guitarists like Jimmy Page. Pete got annoyed at this and demanded that he put down the lead guitar as he was the lead guitarist. Both he and Jimmy Page played versions of the guitar line for *I Can't Explain* and they were almost identical. Pete thinks that in the end it was his guitar and not Page's that was used on the final mix. Shel Talmy also had The Ivy League group singing the high backing voices. They recorded it in two hours flat.

The B-side was *Bald Headed Woman*, a song written by Talmy. Jimmy Page did play the guitar on this track; it needed a fuzzbox and Page wouldn't let Pete use his for it, so he played the guitar solo.

The record was released in Britain in January 1965 to fairly favourable if low-key reviews in the music press. It immediately sold well, particularly in London, but not well enough to get into the charts. However the success of the Marquee's Tuesday nights was becoming known to the producers of pop shows on radio and television partly because Kit and Chris were bombarding them with phone calls about it. Soon Vicki Wyckham, the producer of television's most important pop show 'Ready Steady Go' was among the lucky 600 that were allowed into the Marquee and she immediately booked the Who for a coming programme. When Kit heard that the resident 'crowd arranger' for the show was unavailable he pulled a brilliant stunt. He gave out 150 tickets to the 100 Faces, so when *I Can't Explain* went on air, the nation was duped by a sensational 'staged' euphoria. The group couldn't have made a better impact. The record entered the British charts at No. 28, but then dropped out the following week. However, a second stroke of luck came their way. A group had dropped out of that week's 'Top of the Pops', BBC TV's main pop show. The Who stepped in at the last moment as the 'Tip For The Top' and that appearance, coupled with the heavy airplay the illegal 'Pirate radio stations' Radio Caroline and Radio London were giving it, put it back into the charts, where it climbed to the No. 10 position.

The band had a hit record. Immediately their fee went up threefold and they were getting bookings from all over England. They were working harder than ever. The group had never been close and always had their disagreements but since turning professional their disagreements had become very bitter and turned to fights. They simply didn't get on with each other. Roger, in particular, was very aggressive and always ready to pick a fight. He was very insecure and could see his influence being drained away, particularly by Pete. Kit soon saw that the former art student was the most creative and intelligent of the four and seemed to nurture Pete and spend more time with him, encouraging and coaxing him with his song-writing. In fact Kit did more than that, he took Pete and Keith under his wing and started to introduce them to good restaurants and coach them in what wines to order and how to behave. The real creative force of the Who in the early days was a combination of Pete and Kit. Kit knew nothing about the business, but he had a lot of common sense and a burning ambition to prove himself creatively. Roger resented Kit's preferential treatment of Pete and also disliked intensely the increasing use of amphetamines by the other three in the group.

Kit persuaded Pete to move into the flat above their new offices in Eaton Place, situated in posh Belgravia. Kit wanted Pete to live in Central London and concentrate on songwriting and not be sidetracked by his old Art school dope-smoking habits. Kit was grooming him for the big time and he wanted him where he could best influence him.

"Kit dragged me out of that environment because he thought it was decadent," Pete once told me. "He took me away from the decadence that was ours to the decadence that was his." Pete lived at Kit and Chris' flat for about four months while Chris was away. "I didn't like it much. I used to adore Kit but I could sense a tension. Apart from anything else he was worried because he was lying to me about his homosexuality. He was bringing boys back and stuff and the next day he'd introduce them at the breakfast table saying 'This unfortunate boy had a terrible accident last night and hurt his foot and I had to put him up for the night.'

We used to eat at all the gay restaurants anyway and dine out with Quentin Crisp and all that. I didn't care." Looking back Roger thinks it was right for Kit to nurture Pete. "I think Kit recognised his potential. You have to be really honest and say that without Pete Townshend the band would've been nothing."

While Pete was living in luxury, Roger had taken to living in the back of the group van. Earlier he had married in great secrecy his pregnant girlfriend. According to Roger's mother, he only lived with Jackie his wife for about six months. "Kit said that Roger shouldn't let anyone know he was married and suggested he get a flat himself away from Jackie and the baby." Roger remembers, "I had to get married, didn't I? And I couldn't stand it. It wasn't Jackie, I just didn't want to be married. So the van was wonderful. It was my house. I did 9 months in the van. Pete was in Belgravia and I lived in the van."

Pete's style of playing was formed very much by the musical influences Kit provided him with. "Kit's grooming started with etiquette and showing Keith and I the right wines and so on – up to the last years of his life Keith was still ordering the vintage of Dom Perignon that Kit had said was the best. But it went on, and with me it was more a sense of pushing me forward. I've since discovered that it had a lot to do with echoes of his relationship with his own father. He wasn't very close to him but he studied his father's life a lot, and was very impressed with it." Kit's father was com-

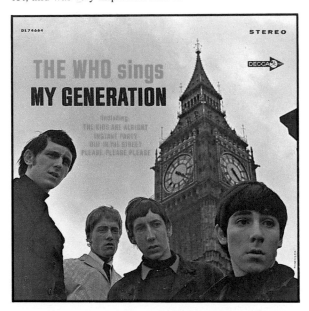

poser and arranger, Constant Lambert. "He played me a lot of music that his father had sort of unearthed. I listened to people like Purcell, Corelli, William Walton, and Darius Milhouse and lots of Baroque stuff. Kit would buy me the records and I would listen to them and they were harmonically very influencing on the way I wrote. I think the first manifestation of it was on the song *The Kids Are Alright*, where I actually started to use baroque chords, suspended chords. It did a lot to create that churchy feel and had a lot to do with the way I play."

Kit exchanged Pete's Vortexian recorders for two better Revox models. Pete spent practically every spare minute he had playing into the two tape recorders. The demos Pete produced by reel-to-reel multi-tracking would be firstly played to Kit for his reaction and suggestions. "Kit actually had something, a language, you know. He had a great grasp of musical terms and was able to make a critique. He used to throw in a lot of ideas and make suggestions that seemed to be completely inappropriate, but whenever I tried them they used to work."

Kit groomed and instructed the whole band to a certain extent. He tutored them in the art of interview bullshit. They were always to say something outrageous and make out things were better than they were, anything to get a headline. Invent any old lie if it would get in the papers. The first little article about the group in NME said that *I Can't Explain* was already selling in America. In fact it hadn't even been

released in the States and when it did it only broke in one place. This was Detroit. Radio stations in Detroit really picked up on the record and plugged it. It became a local hit but never broke out anywhere else in the States.

The group were playing bigger dates and Kit had signed an agency agreement with the Malcolm Rose Agency. They did a short tour of Scotland. Kit still attempted his own promotions of the group, this time at the Florida Rooms in Brighton, known as the Brighton Aquarium. Of the four promotions these were the most successful ever put on by Kit and Chris, not counting the Marquee. They were particularly significant on Bank Holidays when hundreds of mods on scooters used to 'invade' the various coastal towns like Brighton to wander along the front looking for rockers to fight, get 'blocked' on amphetemines and generally to create havoc.

The Who's next single epitomised part of the state of mind of the pilled-up mod. They wanted to release a single that sounded more like they sounded on stage. Although Kit and Chris were anxious to record more of Pete's own material, the rest weren't so sure. Roger in particular wanted the band to be a blues based band and thought that *I Can't Explain* was too pop sounding. He wanted to do a James Brown number for a follow up. *Anyhow, Anyway, Anywhere* was written at the Marquee just before going into the recording session. Kit made Pete and Roger stay up writing it all night so that they would have something to record the next day when they had a session booked. It is credited to both Pete and Roger although Chris Stamp says that was just to placate Roger. "Pete was saying 'What about this Roger?' It was nearly all Pete and he just gave it to Daltrey just to keep him happy."

The record incorporated much of the Who's sound and live gimmicks. "We initially set up to do something different; nobody had ever done feedback before," recalls Shel Talmy. "I set the mikes up the way I thought it would work and it worked perfectly the first time. I think the feedback was a few months ahead of its time, but it caught on eventually." US Decca sent the tape back, thinking the feedback was a technical fault, and, according to Talmy, UK Decca also rejected the record. "I don't think anything ever pissed Decca England more than they had to release this record, which had become a huge hit, because they distributed Brunswick." In the Melody Maker, Nick Jones reviewing the record wrote "Newcomers to the 'mod' style of the Who Who might well be put off by weird sounds – namely feedback and the wild friction of a microphone against a cymbal. They are sounds of the Who, NOT studio engineering." He also called the track " . . . one of the most controversial records of 1965. Either a giant hit or a terrible flop."

It was a hit – not a giant one though – it got to No. 13 in the NME charts. The record began with what was to become a feature on many Who singles; a sort of introductory guitar fanfare. *Anyway, Anyhow, Anywhere* started off with an almost flamenco like guitar introduction, which stops and pauses and then Roger launches straight into the vocal. The aggressive live Who sound is all the time offset by sweet-sounding high backing vocals, once again provided by the Ivy League. I've always thought that the lyrics reflect the feeling of euphoria and limitless energy of pilled-up mods. Pete insists it was about jazz musician Charlie Parker. The Who played 'Ready Steady Go' on the day it was released and one of the greatest boosts to their career came later when 'Ready Steady Go' picked *Anyway, Anyhow, Anywhere* as it's signature tune. Every Friday night nearly every kid in the land including every mod (this was the only TV mods would bother about) would be waiting to hear the announcer say "It's seven minutes past six – the weekend starts here!" Then hear the Who's *Anyway* play over the 'RSG' pop art credits.

The Melody Maker on June 5th, the week *Anyway* entered the Top 30, headlined an article about the group 'EVERY SO OFTEN, A GROUP IS POISED ON THE BRINK OF A BREAKTHROUGH. WORD HAS IT IT'S . . . THE WHO." The article went on to say "Their music is defiant and so is their attitude. Their sound is vicious. This is no note-perfect 'showbiz' group singing in harmony and playing clean guitar runs . . . There's sadism in their characters and in their music . . . " The article ends " . . . They are undoubtedly the most emergent young group on the scene.

And with the legions of fans shouting them on, they could well be tomorrow's big stars."

Pop art and *My Generation*

The Who moved away from their strictly mod image. They were now into 'Pop Art'. "I dreamed up the idea of Pop Art Music, which Kit then jumped on, and I explained it to him, and he thought that whatever I'd explained to him didn't necessarily make sense, but it was good enough," Pete said later. "When I had my flat in Chesham Place, I decorated it with a lot of pop art pictures I'd taken out of a book, which I'd pinched from art college. Kit kept coming in and saying 'These images are very good – the targets, the arrows, the chevrons, and all that sort of stuff.' As far as I was concerned they were little throwbacks from art school obsessions."

Pete had long been draping a Union Jack flag over his speaker cabinet, and someone thought of actually making up a jacket out of the British flag. Kit Lambert bought a large Union Jack from a flagmaker and he and Pete went to Carnaby Cavern where Pete was measured up. The Union Jacket was a much simpler, more identifiable image than the Mod look, and quite controversial. After a while, it was stolen from a dressing room and a second one was made up. However, it didn't fit Pete very well, and so John wore it, until it too was stolen. John then had two jackets made up from flags, one from the Union Jack and the other from the Royal Standard plus a Welsh flag waistcoat.

Pete's idea for wearing medals came from the Peter Blake pop art painting called the Female Wrestler. They were now the most outstanding looking British group since the mop-top Beatles.

They described *Anyway* as the first pop art single. It wasn't as great a hit as *I Can't Explain*, but it received more attention and established the Who as highly innovative pop art group. The second record any group did was always considered the most crucial; it determined whether you were a hit-making group or a one-hit wonder.

There was no doubt that the Who were 'the up-and-coming band'. Paul McCartney told an interviewer "The Who are the most exciting thing around." They were being talked about and getting more TV and radio work. They were rebooked on RSG and also did the TV shows 'Disc A Gogo' and 'Gadzooks'. However despite the success and publicity the group were not earning enough to keep them going. Kit Lambert and Chris Stamp were playing a double game and bluffing their way along. Really their whole gamble was getting bigger and bigger without any sign of it paying off. Chris Stamp recalls: "When we started we took an office and flat in Eaton Place. We bought clothes and equipment, had photographs taken. All the money went and then we were pulling every scam in the book. In those days there were still the old-fashioned credit cards, particularly if you had a Belgravia address. We had a Harrods card and Christopher Wine Company – we had some very good wines. We had several bank accounts. Kit had the Royal Bank of Scotland in Knightsbridge and I had the Midland in Sloane Square. We moved into what was then called the National Provincial Bank. We got about four or five hundred out of each of them. And it was just because of the address. We went in and had 84 Eaton Place and we had headed notepaper, three telephone lines, right, and, I mean, it was this new rock thing and we'd give the manager a load of old bollocks and they had to let us run. We'd creep up, there would be twenty or thirty cheques you're writing and it got to about £112, and then we'd do a rush, right. And suddenly there would be nine cheques to get into as heavy as we can before suddenly the man would say 'Oh' and it had gone. And then we would be next door right? And that's the way it would be, borrowing money from anywhere and anybody."

By sheer cunning and using their Belgravia address and Kit's upper class accent to the full they just about kept things going. Often when things got very desperate Kit would go gambling at the Casanova Club and miraculously win enough to pay off the creditors. Chris explained "Any stroke, any stroke we could pull. There were like two gambling clubs – it was like whether they would take a cheque. So Kit used to go in and give them a cheque for £100, and then, if he won £300, it would be alright and he'd cash it in. If he didn't the cheque would just go bump – another Bank of

Scotland job. It was Kit's voice and everything. One club in the Fulham Road, he even used to keep coming back, somehow he even planned the whole thing, and he would get away with it."

The band were very expensive anyway. Roger told in an interview in NME how they'd wanted a new amp and gone out and got themselves up to our necks in hire purchase. "We spent £2,000 on equipment that day, but our stuff is the best in the world. We have to get new guitars or drums every month or so. They just get smashed up and it's costing us a fortune."

Pete announced that he was spending over £60 a week on new clothes. He wasn't – it was all part of Kit's plan to feed outrageous headline grabbing quotes to the press. But they were regularly spending a small fortune on new clothes as they had to keep up with the momentum they'd set as fashion leaders.

The band were getting better and better bookings as they got more and more exposure through the press, radio and television since they'd had two hit singles. Their fees were

getting bigger too, but they were still spending much more than they were earning. At gigs now they would get a deal where if they pulled in a big crowd they would get a share of the gate. A typical fee would be £200 against 60% of the gate money. If they attracted 900 kids at 10/– each then of the total £450 they'd get 60% which would be £270. So they would usually get a lot more than their guaranteed fee. In order to keep a check on the promoter, Mike Shaw would stand on the door with a little clicker counter machine clicking up the number of people buying a ticket. At the end of the evening (in theory) his figure and the promoters would almost tally. Promoters who entered these deals with a knowing grin thinking the group were going to take their word for the attendance figure were often shocked when they realised the band were stationing their own man at the door to count the punters.

They went to Paris in the summer and Kit Lambert's film of the Who with London mods was shown on French TV. The French TV producer described the Who as ' . . . a logical

musical expression of the bewilderment and anarchy of London's teenagers.' In June the French magazine, International Des Rockers, described the group as 'une groupe inquietant . . . ' which roughly translated means 'a cause for anxiety.'

Pete had said in an interview soon after *I Can't Explain* had entered the charts, "I figure that we will probably have about a year as a popular group. Could be less. Maybe more. But we want to make the most of the time we have." Although *Anyway, Anyhow, Anywhere* hadn't got to No. 1 as they had hoped, its unusualness, boldness and impact had put them in the position of the most exciting new group around. Pete could now surely have looked forward to more than a year as part of a popular group. However, the rows among the group had grown into a major factor. The four of them violently disagreed with and disliked each other. Roger was bitter and argumentative about almost everything and almost everybody. Pete and Roger fought over group direction and policy. Keith and John got on alright together but they both, Keith in particular, fell out with Roger and Pete.

Roger was totally opposed to the group releasing Pete's compositions as he thought they were copying the 'pop' elements of the Kinks, which as a blues purist he didn't like. He wanted the group to be an R & B group and thought that *I Can't Explain* was just 'pop'. Kit and Chris were anxious to release Pete's latest composition *My Generation*, but met solid resistance from Roger. Stamp remembers that particular fight, "Pete wanted to record his stuff, of course, but he couldn't push it, so it was down to me and Kit. The only block, basically, was Roger. We might get a bit of blocking from Entwistle or he might get Entwistle on his side or Moonie on his side – but really it was basically Roger. The group was moving out of Roger's grasp and he wanted to do this heavy R & B thing so that songs like *I Can't Explain* and *My Generation* and later *Substitute* were like pop to him. He wanted to do the James Brown stuff and all. But *My Generation* was a heavy block. It really took a lot of persuading to actually get it going."

Originally Pete's first demo was much slower and based on a typical Jimmy Reed riff. Chris Stamp spotted the potential for Pete's demo of *My Generation*. Chris remembers "It really took a lot of convincing to actually get it going. It took me at least two months to persuade Roger and everybody that they should record it." According to Pete, "I was surprised at Chris Stamp's initial interest in *My Generation* – it was so lightweight. Kit couldn't understand what he was talking about either, and asked me to do another demo of it. He said "Make it sound beefier." It became a political and sociological song – Pete's Bob Dylan political poem and his Mose Allison *Young Man Blues* copy. *My Generation* was Britain's most serious and subversive song. Bob Dylan had showed that popular songs could be an excellent vehicle for serious subjects. The Who turned the Jimmy Reed-like *My Generation* into this spittingly caustic anthem of youth with lines like "Hope I die before I get old." It was well balanced – not too preachy or too arty. It was the stuttering statements of a pilled-up mod telling the older generation to 'fuck-off' because they were a drag and didn't know what was going on. "I knew immediately we started doing that thing that it was going to be a No. 1 record." Explains Talmy. "It was one of those things that sounded like a natural to me. We were all sky high by the time we were finished because it had everything, and it initially got banned on the BBC because Daltrey was doing his strammering bit."

My Generation was recorded first without stuttering, but the third version with the stuttering lyrics was released and entered the NME charts the week it was released at No. 16. The next week it had shot up to No. 3. It never got to No. 1, but it established the Who as the most original and articulate pop group on the scene. Brian Jones said of the Who after the release of *My Generation*: "They are the only young group doing something new both visually and musically. Originality usually means success."

My Generation became the final number of their stage act. It was the climax of a powerful, loud, uncompromising set and it was at the end of *My Generation* that Pete would start hitting his Rickenbacker on the floor to get strange electronic noises and effects from it. He would set up a feedback pattern and then run the mike stand down the strings to get a screeching loud electronic scraping noise. He'd then play the guitar with the mike stand like a violin. Then, with a mean look he'd start poking the speaker cabinet with the guitar and ripping holes in the fabric covering. The tension and drama of their act was intense. Snarling and scowling, Townshend would unleash his fury on his equipment. He would attack the speaker cabinets with the guitar, swinging it above his head and smashing the cabinet, using the guitar as an axe. Meanwhile Roger would be scraping the mike over the cymbals which created a tearing and wrenching sound. He would swing the mike by the cable and let it crash into the cymbals or onto the floor. Keith would smash away at his drums and anything else in sight. He would push the drums over, kick them across the stage and then set about the cymbals, mike and amps. John kept as still as a statue providing an anchor to the others destruction. He would keep up a constant bass to hold all the weird and strange sounds together. Now and again, if it looked like a piece of flying equipment or Keith's boot was heading for his part of the stage he would turn his back on the mayhem in a protective way in case his guitar got a scratch.

The Who were the most outrageous and stunning live act to hit the British scene. They were sheer violence and frustration set to music. Their main feature was their stage act rather than their records. Their live act was staggering and unbeatable. Roy Carr of the NME was in a band called the Executives in 1966 and remembers seeing the Who for the first time. "It was in a dance hall at the end of the pier at Morecambe, one of those places that was all wood and cavernous and echoed, there was a lot of echo even with two thousand people in and the band was so loud that my bass player with me stood there and was physically sick."

The Who's live act was like a total no-holds-barred assault on the senses. There were no half measures; they threw everything they had at the audience, ending with a blitz on their own equipment, which they would systematically destroy, and, in a cloud of smoke and fused smouldering amps and other debris, simply walk off stage. As Roy Carr puts it, "It was like seeing a piece of pure energy, pure raw energy. If you could possibly get just pure energy and put it in a form and operate it – that was the Who."

Their first album called *My Generation*, and recorded by Shel Talmy, was released in England at the end of 1965 and included eight of Pete's compositions, two James Brown numbers and *I'm a Man* by Sonny Boy Williamson. As soon as the album was released the group started publicly squabbling over it. Pete said he didn't like it because the drumming drowned Roger's voice. Roger said he liked the album but didn't like the group's singles.

Interviewed at the 'Ready Steady Go' studios for NME Keith was asked whether the reports that there were arguments and fights within the group were true. "Yes" said Keith, wide-eyed and innocent – "It's Roger – he hates me!" "Why?" asked the NME reporter. "Because I told him he can't sing . . . I don't like half of our records and Roger is the reason" Keith went on to explain. "It's not true to say we do not like the LP. There are some old tracks which we did not want released, but Pete has written some great songs for the album. I particularly like *Kids, The Good's Gone, It's Not True* and *La, La, La, Lies*. Some of the old tracks are disgusting though."

In late '65, during their first European tour, the arguing amongst group members became so bad that on their return the group broke up. Roger and Keith never got on in those days, and in the interval between two shows one night in Denmark, Roger knocked Keith out. Keith, Pete and John had been taking pills throughout the whole tour, but Roger hadn't. "I couldn't do speed 'cos I couldn't sing when I did it. Sometimes after we'd finished a gig I might take some blues and stuff with the rest of them, but if we were gigging I couldn't 'cos it would affect my voice," Roger explained later. According to Pete, Keith got obnoxious when Roger started having a go at him about taking pills. "I'm sure we were behaving really peculiarly – you know what people were like on pills."

Roger remembers, "The band was playing fucking terrible. I had a big flare-up with Moon in the dressing room, and in the flare-up I got hold of his box of pills and tipped them down the loo. And that's when he started, like a fool,

trying to beat me up." Roger badly beat Keith up, knocking him out. When Keith was revived, they had to go on and do their second show of the evening, which was understandably tense. On their return to England the other three insisted that Roger be thrown out of the group. "He was thrown out really for interfering with our lifestyles" remembers Pete, "Keith, John and I really liked drugs and he didn't."

Roger didn't leave the band straight away. "We had commitments anyway," Roger said later, "so we decided to promote *My Generation* and see if we could get a hit, and then leave while it was at the top, which I agreed to. I *was* a bastard up till then, but I had to be with that lot, 'cos before we had roadies I used to get the gear together, get them out of bed to get them to gigs, set the gear up. And there's no way you could've treated them any other way. 'Cos they were . . . Townshend was fucking 'orrible too. It's great Moon being a funny man when you're really rich and can afford it, but *then* if we were gonna get anywhere, we still had lots of responsibilities."

Roger was supposed to be replaced by Boz of Boz's People, although Boz wasn't too pleased about the idea when he heard, and commented, "The Who are children playing with electronic toys." There was talk in the music press of another drummer being brought in and Moon's "exploring other fields of expression." Keith and John were also going to break away to try and form their own group. Chris Stamp's response publicly to all the rumours was

"This is absolute c-c-crap."

However, the dissension got them their first ever front page article; on November 20th, 1965 the Melody Maker ran the headline "THE WHO SPLIT MYSTERY". According to Chris Stamp "After the incident, the other three were adamant that Roger was out of the group. There was a total ultimatum and Roger simply wasn't in the group. Kit and I were going to keep the Who as a three-piece, right, Pete singing. We really fancied Pete's voice anyway. He didn't have a strong voice but it was an interesting voice. And we were going to form another group around Roger to keep everything happy. Roger could do all these R & B things that he always wanted to do, because a lot of the arguments were about the fact that we kept shoving Pete's stuff in and Roger wanted to stay strictly with the R & B thing."

John and Keith weren't too sure about working with Pete and wanted to form a group of their own without either Pete *or* Roger. "Kit was also trying to form a double group" remembers Pete, "Keith on drums, John on bass, me on guitar, together with the group Paddy, Klaus and Gibson, also on drums, bass and guitar – like a double group that would be used in all different kinds of ways. That was Kit and I just groping for something that might keep the band together, and the idea only lasted about a week."

"Eventually", says Stamp, "Kit and I talked the other three into taking Roger back, which is ironic as things

worked out later. It was no easy thing, because they were adamant about breaking up the group." Roger rejoined the group and promised to cut his violence and try to work more harmoniously with the rest of the band. "I'll be Peaceful Perce, from now on" he declared. "It was an amazing sort of transformation he went through", Pete says, "from being one of the most aggressive, violent people I knew, to being one of the most peaceful. He had to learn to live with a lot of things he didn't like, and what I always admired about him was the fact that he managed to do it, because knowing the kind of power he had as a young man that he gave up in a sense, for the sake of the group, took a lot of guts."

Keith's large appetite for amphetamines became apparent to me at the earlier Windsor Jazz Festival. Before the show he asked me "Got anything in the upward direction, Barney?" I held out about eighteen 'leapers' which were supposed to last me for the next couple of months. I was going to just give him a couple, but now that he was Keith Moon, the Successful Pop Star, I thought he might want five or six. In one fell swoop, Keith scooped up the lot. "Ta, Barn", he said, and swallowed them all at once.

About the same time I also encountered Pete's pill-popping flash. In the late seventies Pete himself said "We were four 'orrible unpleasant little bastards." The wiry, highly-strung, and anxious nature induced by taking pills made them very touchy. Anything could spark them off and usually did.

I met up with Pete and a group of people from art school in a rented attic studio in Wardour Street to listen to records, drink some beer and reminisce about art school. Someone noticed that we were out of Pepsi-Colas and beers. "I'll get some", I said.

"I'll get them", said Pete resignedly, as though we were all expecting him to pay.

"No, it's all right, I'll get them," I said, although I really could only just afford to.

Pete, who had been showing off and trying to belittle the others all evening, said in his mocking nasally tones "Sure you can afford it", he held out a five pound note, "Here you are."

I said that I could afford the beers and got up to go. "Don't spend your bus fare home, will you," he continued in a sneering put-down. "Sure you don't want this?" He continued waving the fiver in front of me. I was very hard up at that time and I *did* want the £5 and I wasn't sure I had enough money to actually pay for the crate of drinks and pay for the train ride home, but I certainly wasn't going to let him have the pleasure of splashing his money around. When Pete realised he wasn't making his point he said, "Now are you certain that you don't want it?" and slowly began to tear the five pound note into small pieces in front of me. There was little doubt that Pete, at least, was an " 'orrible little bastard."

After *My Generation* their fee for live shows increased. Chris Stamp remembers "We even got £500 at one time. None of the promoters would believe that we'd actually got it that high. But we always had Mike Shaw on the door and we knew that state of the market pretty well and we just knew that we could get it. The top price up to that point had been £300."

However, they were still constantly battling through money crises. "I mean there was still this heavy high fashion thing – the actual clothes changes were tremendous. Then there was the equipment. That cost a fortune. Then there was Townshend's recording studio stuff, all their personal stuff, Roger's wife and so on. The thing was that if they were doing well, had a good gig or a successful record, they expected like the rock and roll rewards – right. No point in having the sort of hit record and not being able to buy the flash car. And there were these sort of celebrations, just to make the hit record seem real. Although we really all owed fortunes – real fortunes. It was incredibly dicey."

New Action moved out of Ivor Court to where they had returned after losing the Eaton Place address, into new offices that they were sharing with Robert Stigwood. Stigwood had taken a big apartment on a low rent in New Cavendish Street. "It wasn't meant to be used as an office. It had one sort of big flash room and then there were two other rooms and a kitchen. New Action and Stigwood each had one of the smaller rooms and the large room was shared.

"We used to share this flash office if any of us had a big deal. If we had an important appointment, Stigwood would have to be thrown out and we would be in there. In and out, it was like a French farce and almost everyday there would be the furniture van outside with the bailiffs. We knew all the bailiffs and they would be waiting for us and say 'the usual' and that would be like a fiver for all the furniture guys to go round the pub and the bailiffs would give us until 2 o'clock to come up with the amount of money in the injunction in cash. We'd then run around and beg, steal and borrow to get it. One time the bailiffs just had not stood for it and there were like four heavies taking over this big flash desk that we had between us. And Stigwood had this important deal lined up. The big one, he was going to make his quarter of a million or something, and as he comes up the stairs with this VIP, there's the desk going down." Stigwood had taken over the agency business for the Who, for which he paid £2,000. He was to be of major significance in the next move in their hectic career.

The group were in a very volatile position. They had released a major single which was to make them cult heroes, yet they were arguing and fighting and on the verge of breaking up. Despite the fact that *My Generation* was climbing into the Top 10, the group was practically bankrupt. The true extent of Kit and Chris's financial juggling was still being kept from the band. They were also unhappy with their position of being tied to Shel Talmy.

Shel Talmy was an independent record producer. He usually owned the acts he recorded and released finished tapes to the record companies. Kit and Chris had thought it a stroke of amazing good fortune when Shel Talmy had signed the group up. Chris and Kit hadn't any idea how to get a record deal and signing with Shel Talmy meant that they didn't have to.

Shortly after the deal had been signed with Talmy, Chris and Kit decided that Kit would look after the group in England and Europe and that Chris would handle the American side of things. Chris's brother, Terence Stamp, the film actor, had just got a part in the film 'The Collector' and been sent a first class air ticket to fly to the States to begin shooting. Chris explained that he had to go the States, so Terry swopped his first class ticket for two economy tickets and they flew to the States together. Terry also put Chris up in his suite, which the film company had provided for him in New York. Chris went to American Decca and had a shock. It was a totally different company to English Decca, which was one of the major companies and had many pop acts, including the Rolling Stones. US Decca was mainly a C&W label and was ultra conservative. "American Decca was sort of archaic" remembered Chris. "I mean they didn't even know about Elvis Presley, let alone the Who. I realised that we would never break the Who with this company."

There were three reasons why they wanted to break their contract with Shel Talmy. Firstly, it wasn't a very good contract for them financially. Kit and Chris regretted signing it. Although Talmy had been instrumental in the groups break through they were on a very small percentage. Stamp remembers "Although we didn't think it was such a bad deal at the time of signing, we then learned about the other deals. Then we thought, ' "Oh fucking hell!" ' "

Secondly, they realised that breaking into the lucrative American market would be difficult with dreary old U.S. Decca and thirdly they wanted creative freedom in the studios. Chris remembers, "We had to have it all worked out how we were going to do numbers before we went to the studio, otherwise he'd try to bring in the Ivy League and Jimmy Page and another drummer and you know what I mean. It would be nothing to do with the Who. So we used to have to work it all out in front and then go into the studio with him and say 'No, this is the way it is.' We used to get into terrible arguments with the guy." Apparently, it was Kit and Chris that had the terrible arguments and not the group. "I never had any problems with the Who in the studio," recalls Talmy. "I always thought them excellent musicians. They took suggestions, they made a few, we had a great time. The only fly in the ointment was Kit." Roger also recalls that period. "It was terrible. I stayed out of it, and I think all the band did, even Pete. All I did was sing. Kit really wanted to be the producer and he'd be telling him what to do."

Pete remembers that time as being very "miserable". "Shel was partially sighted so he couldn't move around very much. He never used to get involved in the band's rehearsals or anything like that, he'd just show up at IBC, the band would walk in and he would run the tape machine and never used to say anything. And Kit was always getting angry with him. That was really the period when the warfare between Glyn Johns, who was the engineer, and Kit started because Glyn used to side with Talmy, who was paying his wages. Kit never forgave him and Glyn never forgave Kit, and it caused problems years later. From my point of view that first album was just miserable. There was no fun at all, there was only one track that I liked and that was *the Ox*, the free-for-all instrumental. The rest was really disciplined and I thought the demos were better. It was only when we started doing albums with Kit that we realised recording could be fun . . . " Talmy adamantly refused to let the Who out of the five-year contract he had with them. After, as Chris puts it, "We did all the polite things." Chris, Kit and the group decided to sue him on the advice of their new lawyer Ted Oldman. "He was the first one to say to us, 'You can break the contract'."

What they did eventually was to issue their next single on the Reaction label which had just been set up by their agent,

Robert Stigwood. Stigwood was the only person they knew who was big enough to enable them to break the contract with Shel Talmy and not get hurt in the process.

Substitute was recorded without Shel Talmy at Olympic studios off Baker Street. Pete produced it himself. The *Substitute* single has about the most intense bass sound ever, almost 'mugging for the ears' (lost on later album versions). Although very successful, it wasn't intentional. John Entwistle explains: "In those days in the studio, if you turned your guitar up halfway through a backing track there wasn't too much anyone could do about it afterwards. During this instrumental break in *Substitute* I thought to myself 'Sod this, I'm gonna make this into another bass solo like *My Generation*,' and so I turned up the volume. When they eventually started mixing it they couldn't reduce the bass." While they were recording it Stigwood came to the studio and they played it to him. "Sounds all right," he said.

Their next single was to have been *Circles* released on Brunswick as usual and various papers carried items about this forthcoming release in early 1966. A second version of *Circles* recorded by the Who and renamed *Instant Party* was used for the B-side of *Substitute*. Chris Stamp points out, "That was a political move. 'Cause then Shel Talmy had to injunct the record. And by stopping that record he had to go

to court. He had to face us."

The record went straight in at No. 19 in the charts. Five days after its release an injunction was served by Decca on Polydor who pressed and marketed the records for Stigwood's Reaction label. They had already pressed 50,000 copies but stopped pressing any more. Polydor went to court that same afternoon to try to get the court injunction lifted but despite their counsel saying that the ban might kill the chances of the record which was expected to get to number one, the judge extended the injunction for a further eight days.

The next week Brunswick issued their version of the Who playing *Circles* and also called it *Instant Party*. It was on the B-side of *A Legal Matter* which had Townshend on vocals. It was taken from their first LP. So two Who singles had been released within a week of each other but by two different record labels.

Pete was quoted in the Melody Maker under a large picture on the front page "I don't really mind what they do. I feel that *Substitute* is a blatantly commercial number and certainly an easy hit. It's had two weeks more sales time than *Legal Matter*. So I don't think it will make much difference." Apart from anything else, the affair was great publicity for the group and got lots of coverage in the music press.

Reaction beat the ban on *Substitute* and its disputed B-side by pressing more copies with a different B-side. The new B-side was an instrumental called *Waltz For A Pig*. (The pig was supposed to be Shel Talmy.) The musicians on *Waltz For A Pig* were called the Who's Orchestra. The Who had agreed not to record until April 4th under a friendly agreement with Shel Talmy when Shel Talmy's case was to be heard in court. The Who Orchestra was in fact the Graham Bond Organization but that was not made public at the time. So the record was back on the streets the following week and moved up four places in the NME charts to number 15. *A Legal Matter* had not yet entered the charts.

On April 4th the High Court was due to hear Talmy's claim that the Who were signed to record exclusively with him, and should not record for Polydor's new Reaction label. In the States the Who put out *Substitute* on Atlantic's ATCO label. US Decca didn't bother to issue *A Legal Matter*.

The Who played *Substitute* on 'Ready Steady Go's' special edition which was broadcast live from Paris and on other Independent TV stations. The BBC had unofficially banned it although they denied it. They soon lifted the ban, however, and it got a number of plays on BBC radio. The offshore pirate's were divided. Radio Caroline played both *Substitute* and *Legal Matter* whilst Radio London only played *Legal Matter*.

In court Shel Talmy was represented by the former Lord Hailsham, Quentin Hogg QC. Chris Stamp remembers, "In the court room it just looked like the judge was going to go with Quentin Hogg because he was making him laugh and all that. You suddenly saw British justice. So when the court adjourned, we made a deal on the steps of the court."

The new deal was going to be expensive for the Who, but they had at least managed to get rid of Shel Talmy and give themselves creative freedom. Chris Stamp recalls, "Well we knew it was going to cost us, but at least it would give us the freedom. The deal was that Shel Talmy would go along with the break provided that the new deal was negotiated by Alan Klein."

Pete and Chris and Kit and Ted Oldman, their then lawyer, flew to New York to see Alan Klein on his yacht. Andrew Oldham, then manager of the Stones, had told Klein that the Who were going to be the next biggest thing in pop. Chris Stamp recalled, "We didn't know but Alan Klein was looking to take over the Who totally from Kit and I. Andrew Oldham had said to him 'It's the new big group'. And Kit and I pulled our first really sharp move – I mean we actually topped Klein you know. Because we got Klein to sign this piece of paper saying that we had given him the Who, but he had to pull the deal together in twenty days. If in those twenty days the deal wasn't completed and all that shit, etc., etc. Well we managed to hold it in abeyance for twenty days and at the end of it we were free." Kit and Chris started confusing and complicating the negotiations and causing delays. "We just sort of started mad phone calls to him, you know what I mean and mixed the whole thing up. Just very clever bullshit. He never realised what was going on and ran out of time."

Shel Talmy was given an over-ride on all Who records from then on. He took a percentage of everything they released including *Tommy*. "We were left with Shel Talmy on paper, but we were not left with Shel Talmy in the studio," remembers Chris. It was a victory for the group despite the cost. "As we were only getting like 3% on his deal, so to get out of the deal we paid him 5%, but we made a new deal for 10% so we were like 5% in front from where we actually started – and we were creatively free."

The attempt to rid themselves of Decca US didn't work. The deal meant that US Decca would retain the group for the American market but they would be free from their contracts for the rest of the world. "We went on his yacht, drank his brandy, ate his food, smoked his cigars, shat in his toilet and then flew home," Pete said.

The Who's equipment had grown to become the biggest array of amps and gear of any group. "We've got 48 12″ speakers which is about 600 watts worth of power and with my drums it makes about £3,000 worth of equipment on stage every night," said Keith. "That's why we have three road managers to get the stuff erected. In some clubs we have to turn the speakers sideways on to get them all on stage."

The injunction restraining Polydor from selling the original *Substitute* was removed by a High Court Judge on March 25th, and the stock of over 40,000 original pressings went back on sale.

The settlement meant that as long as they stayed with Decca in the US they would be free to renegotiate their record deals for the rest of the world. They also got an advance from Decca of $50,000 and had their percentage of retail earnings. As Stamp tells it, "I then had to go in there and change the company around. I had to get them to hire young guys – young commercial men to do our bidding. We had a whole revolution within US Decca." In Britain Kit and Chris signed with Polydor and were given an advance of £50,000.

"I suppose it's just animal instinct"

Kit and Chris pulled off a major publicity coup when they not only got an article about the group in one of the respectable Sunday Newspaper colour supplements, but also managed to get a picture on the cover. The picture, by Colin Jones, was a classic Who shot with them in their pop-art clothes in front of a big Union Jack flag. Chris Stamp remembers, "Getting the Observer cover took a lot of graft – about four or five months' work. The picture was mine. I placed everything and set it up. I mean, I thought, 'What can you do with Townshend's hooter and all that?' I just did the obvious thing." The reasoning behind all the effort that went into getting the Observer colour supplement cover was that it would give them more credibility and status in the record industry, as well as general publicity. "There were a number of things like that and they were designed to give us clout with the record company rather than to sell records. I mean we went for the Daily Mirror just as hard to sell records but like, the managing director's wife would see the Observer it was based on that level – industrial publicity. In those days, unless you were the Beatles or the Stones, you had a hell of a job to get your art work for ads accepted."

As well as giving the management more leverage to negotiate with the industry, it did set the seal on the Who. John Entwistle was voted into an imaginary British 'group's group' that was elected by the current top groups in a Melody Maker poll. The imaginary greatest group consisted of Eric Clapton on lead guitar, Bruce Welch on rhythm, Brian Auger on organ, Ginger Baker on drums, Stevie Winwood as vocalist and John Entwistle on bass.

The Who were included in the pop event of 1966. This was the NME poll-winner's poll; a concert including lots of the groups that had featured in the NME poll of 1965. The line-up in alphabetical order went: Beatles, Spencer Davis Group, Dave, Dee, Dozy, Beaky, Mick and Tich, Fortunes, Herman's Hermits, Roy Orbison, Overlanders, Alan Price Set, Cliff Richard, Rolling Stones, Seekers, Shadows, Small Faces, Sounds Incorporated, Dusty Springfield, Crispian St. Peters, Walker Brothers, the Who, and the Yardbirds. The NME's own review of the concert said, the Who were even more remarkable than the Beatles and the Stones.

The Who had been due to play a gig at Newbury Ricky Tick Club. The first-half band had finished their set but Keith and John still hadn't turned up. They had been to 'Ready Steady Go!' and eventually arrived at 10.10 p.m. and joined Roger and Pete on stage, where they had been playing a few numbers with the first-half group to appease the restless crowd. They did a really good show but during *My Generation* one of Keith's drums fell forward and a cymbal hit Pete in the leg. Pete told MM, "I wasn't hurt, just annoyed and upset. Keith and John had been over two hours late. Then I swung out with my guitar not really meaning to hit Keith. I lost my grip on the instrument and it just caught him on the head."

Keith had a badly bruised face and black eye and needed three stitches in his leg. He threatened to leave the group, saying on Radio Caroline "After all, who needs it?" Pete went to Keith's parents' house in Wembley, London, where Keith lived the next day to apologize but as Pete said, "... he wouldn't answer the door."

The group continued with a stand-in drummer for a few gigs, and once again it looked as if the Who's shaky structure had disintegrated. Two months earlier Pete had said in the Melody Maker, "Keith Moon used to be lots of fun, unfortunately he's turning into a little old man. It's a shame. He used to be young and unaffected by pop music, but now he is obsessed with money. I still like him and I don't really care what he thinks of me. He's the only drummer in England I really want to play with."

Keith eventually returned to play a gig at Lincoln City Football ground. However, things were not well within the group and several fights and arguments later there was a possible breakaway from the group by Keith and John, who were planning to combine with two members of the Yardbirds to form a new group to be called Led Zeppelin – a name invented by John.

The Who went on a tour of Sweden at the beginning of June and attracted 11,000 fans to Stockholm Stadium. It was in Europe that they made really big money in those days. Pete remembers that the feedback and smashing guitars and equipment stage act helped them enormously in Europe, where they didn't understand English and the lyrics were meaningless. They could still relate to the power and loudness of the sound and the physical showmanship.

During 1966 Radio Holland and several German and French radio stations announced on the news bulletins that Roger Daltrey had died. Kit Lambert characteristically exploited the situation for all it was worth, squeezing every drop of publicity he could, and said afterwards that it was probably some sort of mix-up with Pete's car smash. Pete was involved in a car crash on the M1 when his Lincoln Continental was part of a six-car pile up.

The group still were not able to issue any records but were in the ludicrous position of not having any say in what Decca released. Decaa rush-released another track from the *My Generation* LP *The Kids Are Alright* on August 12th.

Because of complaints about the noise, the Richmond Jazz and Blues Festival had been moved from Richmond to Windsor and renamed the Windsor Jazz and Blues Festival. I went along with Pete who was dressed in a dinner suit with a black bow tie, and Karen Astley his girlfriend from Art School. Pete and Karen had started dating during the year after Karen had left. Karen was a dress design student. As the Who were waiting at the side of the stage to go on, Pete began strumming the opening bars to *Batman*, their first number. Prompted by the daringness of them doing the Batman theme, pop art music if ever I'd heard it, I suggested to Roger that they play some jingles from TV commercials. Thinking it a good idea he turned to Pete and suggested it. "What like this?" Pete sneered back at Roger with contempt and sung a current nauseating TV jingle, 'Drinkapintamilkaday'.

They opened their set with a very powerful version of *Batman* and included *Barbara Ann, I Can't Explain, Anyway, Anyhow, Anywhere, Heatwave, Substitute, Dancing in the Street, See See Rider, Legal Matter* and then introduced *I'm a Boy*, which they said would be released in three weeks time as their new single. However, they thought that they weren't getting across very well and so finished with *My Generation* where Pete smashed his guitar into his amps and ripped all the fabric off the front and started laying into the speakers inside. The guitar split and then split again, the head was ripped off and then the neck snapped. He continued until the guitar was smashed to small pieces. Keith kicked all his drums over and they were rolling around the stage while Roger smashed the cymbals with his fists, hurled mikes at the back of the stage. Not content with this, Roger then started to kick out all the footlights at the front of the stage. Keith then got a bucket of water and threw it into the audience. The whole stage was covered in yellow smoke from smoke bombs which were being hurled onstage by Kit Lambert and Chris Stamp as they encouraged the onstage demolition. The crowd went absolutely wild and, according to the pop press, the act caused damage costing thousands of pounds. Keith said, "After that show, the roadies came on in little white coats and shovelled the equipment into buckets. The audience had smashed up all their seats and the whole place looked like Attila the Hun had ridden through it." But on a slightly more serious note, "this being angry at the adult world bit is not all of us. It's not me and it's not John. It's only half Roger, but it *is* Pete."

Afterwards, I suddenly realized how much more famous and controversial the group had become since last time I had seen them. The five of us were standing in a circle talking for about 25 minutes and during the whole time there was a succession of photographers' flashbulbs going off, and autograph hunters.

Once again the Who were in the situation of having two singles out at the same time. Decca had released *The Kids Are Alright* taken from the *My Generation* LP, as was the B-side, *The Ox*. Kit Lambert was furious as Decca had agreed with him to release *La La La Lies* as a single.

Released two weeks after *The Kids*, Reaction put out, *I'm a Boy*, the first single to be produced by Kit Lambert. Kit placed some very effective ads in the press to promote it. It was a story about a boy born to a mother that wanted a girl, so she keeps dressing him up in little girl's clothes, an idea Pete was working on for a futuristic opera set in 1999, when you had the freedom to choose the sex of your child.

Whatever damage the release by Brunswick of their single did to *I'm a Boy* didn't stop it from getting to No. 1 in the Melody Maker charts and to No. 2 to Jim Reeves in the NME charts. *The Kids* only got up to No. 45 in the MM chart. This was the Who's first No. 1 single. The B-side was a number called *In the City*, which was credited to Moon and Entwistle. Keith and John are the only two playing on it as on the day of the session, both Roger and Pete were unaware of the session and missed it.

The Who were recording whenever they could for their next album. They had already completed *Heatwave*, the Martha and the Vandellas number which was a part of their stage show and had been such a big hit with mods, *Barbara Ann*, to appease Keith as he was such a fan of the early Beach Boys sound, and *Man With The Money*, an Everly Brothers song. As it turned out, *Barbara Ann* was released on their next EP and *Heatwave* was included on the next album, but dropped from the US version. *Man With The Money* was released about two months after these tracks were made public by the group, *A Wild Uncertainty*, produced by Shel Talmy on his new Planet Records label.

In September they announced that the next album would be ready in October. Then it was announced that it would be released in November; it finally came out in December.

The group had pulled itself back together in the last few months of 1966. The year began with them all at each others' throats and not particularly interested in the future of the group or working with each other any more, but after a lot of hassles and legal complications they were once again in a tight working unit looking forward to their next big challenge, which was to break into the American market. Pete observed to Nick Jones of the MM, "Basically there are four soloists in this group. On our own we'd all fly off at tangents but now we've rehearsed carefully, are singing in harmony and unison, and there is a kind of orderly disorder." John said in the NME "The trouble was we used to play much too urgently, everybody did their best to outplay each other. Just play their best at all times. Now the sound isn't so messy. I prefer a clean sound to the loose raving thing actually. We went through the loose phase last year."

After the *I'm a Boy* chart success, 'Ready, Steady, Go!', realizing that the Who should really be seen doing their stage act to be really appreciated, devoted half of one of their shows exclusively to the Who. Usually on 'RSG', each artist played one number, or occasionally did two or three spots throughout the show. Kit Lambert promised that their appearance would constitute their new stage act, which was based on the theatre of the absurd. They did four new numbers for the show which was filmed at a live gig. They released the EP of the show called 'Ready Steady Who' which contained five numbers. They were *Batman, Bucket T, Barbara Ann* and two Townshend compositions, *Disguises* and their version of *Circles*, which appeared on the B-side of *Substitute*. The EP was recorded in a studio and wasn't taken from the 'RSG' show soundtrack, as most people thought.

Decca released *La La La Lies* with *The Good's Gone* on the B-side on the same day as *Ready Steady Who* was issued on the Reaction label. This was the third single they had issued using material that Shel Talmy had recorded for the *My Generation* album. The material sounded decidedly dated, as the Who had changed and developed drastically since those songs had been recorded. It only reached No. 45 in the charts. As the legal situation had now been resolved and Brunswick didn't have any fresh material, this was the last time they tried to cash in on the Who's career by issuing old material.

A month later the band's second album (which they ininsisted on calling their first album having disowned the *My Generation* LP) was issued on Reaction. Simultaneously they released their next single, *Happy Jack*.

Asked about their stage destruction, Keith commented "I don't know why we do it, we enjoy it – the fans enjoy it. I suppose it's just animal instinct"

Reactions to the Who's stage act varied from complete and utter awe and disbelief, through total excitement to outright anger and contempt. Experiencing the Who live never left anyone indifferent. A letter from someone who saw the Who at a gig at a place called Hassocks near Brighton sent to the MM summed up one such reaction. The writer talked of 'the most horrid scenes ever witnessed at Hassocks'. Pete Townshend was criticized for 'splintering his guitar against an amp' and Keith Moon for 'savaging his drum kit with a hammer'. The letter ended, quite rightly, with the demand 'It's about time these people were exposed'.

Album sales were less important in the sixties than singles sales. Although pop fans all waited eagerly for the next Beatle LP, generally mainstream pop culture was made up from singles and the singles charts. People bought Long Players at Christmas.

The Who were definitely a singles band and one of the most revolutionary. However their album, *A Quick One*, also broke ground. They were each offered £500 to come up with two numbers for the album by their new publishing company Essex Music. They all wrote their two numbers (although one of Keith's was an instrumental) except Roger, who only produced one. The story goes that in order to fill up the second side, Kit suggested to Pete that he write a 10 minute song, or string together a number of songs with some linking theme to produce something more substantial. This was quite a new approach to songwriting because of the universal unwritten law that pop songs were 2 minutes 38 seconds long, or whatever. Townshend linked together a number of tunes he had written into a little musical story. It was called *A Quick One While He's Away* and labelled the *Mini-Opera*. In a way it is quite naïve and amateurish, but at the time it was a totally new concept. It was in places very light-opera sounding. High, harmonious backing voices repeating "cello, cello, cello, cello, cello, cello, cello." Later on there is a lazy Country and Western cowboy number. "The 'cello cello' backing harmony came about because Kit didn't want to pay out for real cellos, so I suggested they sing them instead", said John Entwistle.

The MM talked of the Who being bedevilled by ideas that hadn't quite come off, by schemes that hadn't quite worked out and by a confused battle for real acceptance. It claimed that at last the album fulfilled the promise of the Who.

Earlier that year, Keith West had released two singles called *Excerpts from a Teenage Opera* about characters called 'Grocer Jack' and 'Sam'. They included orchestras and choirs of schoolchildren and were a little over-produced – *Sam* took 80 hours to record – but were very beautiful and interesting and successful, *Sam* got to No. 3 and *Grocer Jack* to No. 15. The actual *Teenage Opera*, that these two singles were selections from, never appeared.

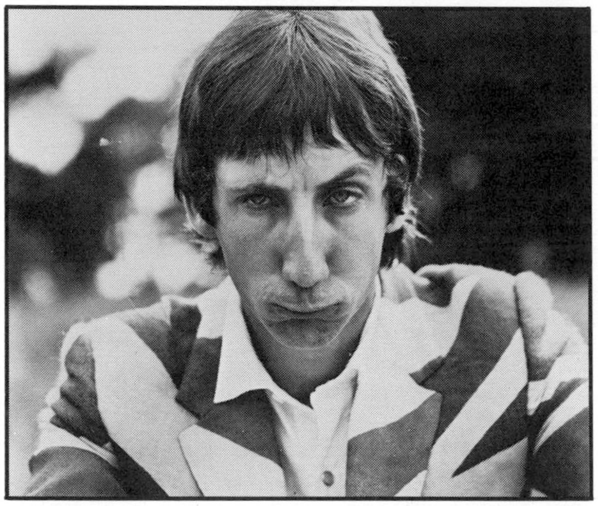

Quick One rose to No. 4 in the Charts. *Boris the Spider*, written by John Entwistle, became one of the fans' favourite numbers on stage and was requested at shows for years to come.

The change from small clubs and pubs to major ballrooms and theatres had been taking place very gradually over the previous eighteen months. The Who had had a number of Top 10 hits and were attracting screaming young teenage girls into their predominantly male audience. "We wanted to be appreciated for our music instead of screaming girls", claimed John. "Sometimes we'd do things to put off the 'screamers' from coming to see us. We'd occasionally sing 'Talking 'bout my Masturbation' and 'Prostitute' instead of 'Substitute'. On one occasion we all walked onstage smoking tampons and throwing tampons at the audience with the string alight, and I actually led Keith on with a sanitary towel over each eye as though he was blind. I led him up on stage and sat him at the drums."

Kit Lambert drove home the fact that the Who had 'arrived' when he told the pop press that they were not going to do any TV spots to plug *Happy Jack*, because they didn't want to overexpose themselves. Kit Lambert, who would have done anything, who would have pestered, bribed, bullied, promised and pleaded for any TV spot or press story, Kit, whose famous catchphrase in the trade was, "If you print a picture you can have the story exclusive," was actually keeping his carefully nurtured creation off the nation's TV screens.

The Who started 1967 with the feeling that they had conquered Britain and determined to break into the lucrative US market.

One of their first shows of the new year was a disaster. The 'Psychedeliamania' at the Roundhouse in London's Chalk Farm started out great for the Who but the power was cut three times and it turned into a fiasco. However, they talked of a completely new act. The act they had been doing for the last 18 months would be entirely changed. What was described as the biggest smash up of all time would be revealed at the new Saville Theatre. This new London venue was to be opened by the Who and Hendrix on January 29th.

The Who played better than they had done for months. The group whose trademark was their destruction of their instruments had stopped smashing up their gear. There was no ritualistic guitar and drum obliteration in this show. No smoke bombs. The Who had replaced these ingredients with even better playing and singing. It was the only way to drop part of their act and improve their show.

USA and the 'Murray the K' show

An interesting insight into the state of Pete's mind was glimpsed by the weekly Melody Maker column headlined POP THINK IN, where a famous musician is asked his or her thoughts on various topics that are relevant. Of Auto Destruction Pete said, "People probably think that auto-destruction has got very little to do with pop, but in a way the Who have been auto-destructive. We have used ideas to destroy ourselves – especially in the economic sense. We've got to the stage where we end the night by destroying everything – which is expensive. I think in pop though, it's good because it has big impact and personally we find it a great laugh. I've often felt like writing to those little drips, those little people who are nowhere, who think they can tell me what I ought to do . . . They should come up here and I could teach them a thing or two about any kind of music. I smash guitars because I like them. I usually smash a guitar when it's at its best."

And on security, Pete said, "I need it, unfortunately. I need it to work and I need it to be happy. I'm like most people, I work to be secure. I never am, so I have to go on working."

Townshend was called a morose man, the Kingpin who dominates the Who. As early as February 1967, Pete was talking of his plans for a big pop opera. It was to have 25 acts and be a double LP if recorded. "This experiment in sound presentation", he told Disc magazine, "tells the story of a man whose wife dies and he leaves his home and travels and becomes involved in wars, revolutions and gets killed."

Pete was now living in a very big room with a kitchen attached on the top fifth floor of a building on the corner of Wardour Street and Brewer Street, in the heart of London's Soho. He'd got a carpenter to build a whole wooden environment into the room. There was a raised platform and a sort of wooden DJ's booth, where he could sit and play records and tapes surrounded by electronic toys and gadgets. His bed was raised up 7ft from the ground and the underneath was used for seating. The whole thing was built as one continuous structure from the same wood, even the floor. It was very strange and looked like it was moulded. Little steps led up to the raised stage area and built-up seats. It looked very strange – something like a modern lecture theatre. Not particularly homely.

In the centre of Pete's pad was a large stone garden pedestal about 3 ft. in diameter for holding a small shrub or bush. This served as Pete's rubbish bin and ash-tray. One day as we were sitting there he suddenly realised that it was getting quite full. He picked it up – it was quite heavy – and simply tossed the contents out of the window on to busy Wardour Street five floors below. He didn't even look to see where it had all gone.

There were constant rumours and denials in the press about Keith having got married. Several fans had got it into their heads that he had married a model from Bournemouth. Kit Lambert explained once that this was just another of his little publicity stunts, but it had failed and backfired. However, Kit was being doubly devious because Keith had in fact married the model from Bournemouth very early on in his career. They had managed to keep it a secret for a long time, but in the middle of 1966 the truth came out. They also had a baby girl called Mandy. They were living together in a flat in Highgate. Keith had met his model when the Who had played Bournemouth. Her real name was Patsy Kerrigan, but the model agency had given her the name Kim Kerrigan, as it suited her better and remained. After first meeting her he decided to go to Bournemouth to see her on his own. He caught the train and was making his way to the buffet car when he spotted a fellow musician, 'Rod the Mod' Stewart from Long John Baldry's Hootchie Coochie Men. They sat together on the train and got talking. When Keith asked him why he was going to Bournemouth he was told he was going to look up this girl he fancied. It turned out to be a Miss Kim Kerrigan. Both Rod Stewart and Keith Moon were sitting on the same train going to see the same girl. Anyway Keith won her because he and Kim had married in secret.

The Who toured Germany, France and much of Europe where both *Happy Jack* and the album were selling well. They had a No. 1 single in Sweden at this time and re-scheduled their tour to play there. They also did many dates around the UK with their new act.

The big advance came in March when they flew to the States to appear in the 'Murray the K show'. It was at the RKO 58th Street Theatre. There were six shows each day starting at ten in the morning. Chris Stamp remembers, "There was something like about fourteen acts and each one would just do two numbers, or just play their hit record like bebop groups, six times a day, seven days a week. It was a hangover from that. The star had about an eighteen minute spot." Also Murray the K's wife, Jackie the K, would host a fashion show.

According to the Who's American agent Frank Barcelona of Premier Talent, their appearance on the show was accidental. Barcelona hadn't even wanted the Who on his agency. He passed them up as they were unknown in the US but someone else in his office had unknowingly signed them up. Murray the K was desperate to get another of Frank Barcelona's acts, Mitch Ryder and the Detroit Wheels, for his show. Mitch Ryder didn't want to do it so Barcelona kept asking ridiculous prices and putting outrageous conditions on the deal, Mitch had to have his dressing room all done out in blue and had to have this new English group called the Who on the act. Surprisingly Murray the K agreed to the price, the colour and the inclusion of the Who. Barcelona still tried to get out of it by calling Stigwood and telling him to ask for $5,000 when Murray the K called up to book the Who. Stigwood knew that Kit and Chris would have even paid for the Who to go on the show for nothing but Frank Barcelona insisted he ask $5,000 hoping that Murray would not pay and therefore Mitch Ryder wouldn't have to do the show. Stigwood settled for about $3,000 and the Who were booked for their first engagement in the US.

Also on the bill were the Cream. So Murray could announce as part of his Easter show two new English groups; quite a draw in New York. Also on the bill were Wilson Pickett, the Chicago Loop, Jim and Jean, Mandala, Smokey Robinson and the Miracles and the Blues Project. After each show another audience would come in and the whole thing would repeat throughout the day. The Who had to revert to their pop art, equipment smashing act specially for the States.

Chris Stamp remembers, "If you went in for the first show, the 10 o'clock ticket, you could stay for the rest of the day. Not too many people want to see a show that early. So every day I was shoving these kids, the Who freaks, right in the front . . . It was the same thing as the 100 faces at the Marquee, they became the fanatics and they were there every day." The Who appeared last on the bill and did their three numbers ending inevitably with *My Generation*. "When Frank Barcelona saw their act Pete was wearing his electric suit, covered in flashing lights and there were smoke bombs going off and feedback and they started to demolish the gear. Frank was a huge man, Frank the Tank we called him, he was shocked, he grabbed my arm and said 'What's going on? What the hell is this?' he thought that the whole thing had gone wrong. I had to explain to him that that was the act. That was it. It means this and so on. And then the kids were all standing on their seats cheering and going wild and he realized and said, 'Ah that's great man'."

At the same time as they were doing their Murray the K shows, Decca released *Happy Jack* in the US. Decca, who

had been quite impressed at seeing their name in the pop charts with *My Generation*, and who had subsequently paid a large advance to the Who, weren't going to just leave *Happy Jack* to die like the previous Who singles. Chris Stamp had been in, re-organizing the company. Frank Barcelona had called Decca, suggesting that they listen to what that Englishman Chris Stamp had to say, and, as a result, Chris had got Decca to hire three top independent promotion men. As a result the Who were getting more and more radio plays. *Happy Jack*, a completely untypical Who record, caught on with the radio stations and then the record buyers – it was the single that broke through into the American charts.

The strain of the pace demanded by doing five shows a day was beginning to tell. Especially on the Who, who did such an exhausting set and damaged equipment each show. Stamp told them to smash up the gear and not worry about the cost, but at the same time he was going frantic trying to keep coming up with new equipment. "They finished *My Generation* by smashing all their gear up. That's what I wanted them to do. And I was going out signing these bits of paper saying, you know, the Who would be the exclusive user of Vox, right. And I mean I went to every maker of equipment in New York, signing bits of paper, just to get the

equipment shipped to the theatre." The group had to be looked after as well. "The group were living in quite a nice hotel and had a limo to take them to the gigs. I had a doctor coming round with huge speed balls that he was going bump into their bums. Speed and penicillin, just in case they caught clap."

According to Stamp, the Who were the only ones on the show to get paid, as the Murray the K organisation had sprung some financial problems and folded up. "I was so skint that every day I had to go and see Murray the K and get another advance from him. I had to practically drag it out of his pockets. We got paid because we needed to eat."

Keith and John had no trouble about eating. They were staying together in a suite in the expensive Drake hotel. "We had a two day party. We kept bringing loads of people back from the shows", remembers John. Bobby Pridden saw Keith and John's party. "It was like a medieval pageant. Waiters were wheeling in trolley-loads of stuffed duck, lobsters, turkeys, oysters, racks of lamb. They were giving them marks for presentation as each one came in."

When Stamp realized what was happening, he quickly took them out of the hotel to a cheaper one. "It was a ridiculous thing to do", John now admits, "God knows what got into us. The bill was something like $4,000."

The first two days after they arrived in New York were for publicity and press interviews. Pete had been given two stock quotes which he got the reporters to write down. They were typically Lambertian: one was, "We want to leave a wound" and the other, "We won't let our music stand in the way of our visual act." Pete wore the flashing lights jacket at their main press conference. But, as he explained to the NME's Keith Altham afterwards in England, "It was a bit of an anti-climax because a girl had appeared on TV recently with a dress on the same principle." Their appearance on the Ed Sullivan Show was foiled because there was a newsreaders' strike, and as artists they were expected to support their action.

All in all there were 22 mikes destroyed during the 'Murray the K Show', five guitars completely wrecked, four speaker cabinets, a 16-piece drum kit annihilated and Pete had to have several stitches after one particularly violent show. Roger remembers "Murray had his own special gold mike. After his announcements he used to hide it. And I watched were he put it one day." Roger said he smashed Murray's gold mike against a cymbal in one show. "His wig went grey." They were nearly thrown off the show for this.

After their success in New York, they flew straight to Germany for a two-week tour. When they returned their next single, *Pictures of Lily*, was released in England. It was their first release on the new Track Records label which Polydor had set up for Kit Lambert and Chris Stamp to run. It was Track's second record release, their first being Hendrix's *Purple Haze* a month before.

There was a row about *Pictures of Lily* in the press, as some people thought it was about masturbation. Pete told the NME, "Really it's just a look back to that period in every boy's life when he has pin-ups. The idea was inspired by a picture my girlfiriend had on her wall of an old Vaudeville star – Lily Bayliss. It was an old 1920's postcard and someone had written on it – 'Here's another picture of Lily'. It made me think that everyone has a pin-up period."

Chris Stamp had picked up some old 'twenties pin-up postcards in Portobello Road for the press ad for the record. Although harmless looking, it caused quite a few people to write protesting letters.

By the end of April Pete was talking about the Who getting on together much better. Everyone in the group was now more involved with the direction and it wasn't simply a partnership of Pete Townshend and Kit Lambert churning out ideas. All the group were writing songs for the new album. Pete said, "It will be an absolute knockout to make."

The band were working harder than ever. *Pictures of Lily* received ecstatic acclaim from the pop press and other musicians. It was felt that the Who had consolidated their position at the top. Nick Jones wrote in Melody Maker, "The Who are becoming one of Britain's great pop products." Penny Valentine had earlier in the same paper declared, "*Pictures of Lily* is the best the Who have ever done." Pete said *Pictures of Lily*, *I'm a Boy* and *Happy Jack* were a novelty in England having the strange attraction of being 'sweet' songs sung by a violent group.

With Hendrix at Monterey

They were doing extensive touring, getting to such corners of the earth as Germany, Paris, Northern and Southern Ireland and the Isle of Man. At the end of May they did a show at Oxford University at a college garden party in a marquee. The undergraduates, mostly upper middle class and upper class students, were just standing in their dinner suits and summer ball gowns watching in awe as the Who went through their paces. "We were getting very effed-up with them", said John. "They were real prannies, some of them were trying to dance. I mean, dancing to the Who. They didn't clap or anything. So Moon got up and went and threw his drums into the audience. Then he went to introduce the next number standing like a letter X with his arms out and his legs apart. Next thing he falls onto the stage holding himself in pain."

Keith had strained his stomach muscles. He'd wrenched them as he violently threw all his drums off stage. He was rushed to hospital. They were out at that time in the middle of recording their next album, *Who Sell Out*. Keith was too injured to play. The next gig they did in Glasgow, a friend of the group, Julian Covey, leader of Machine played with the band in Keith's place at the Locarno. Chris Townsen from John's Children was also brought in to help out. This was a serious blow to Kit Lambert's plan to finalise their recording for the next album before their forthcoming tour of the States on the Herman's Hermits tour. A week earlier, John had broken his finger when he punched the dressing room wall at a gig in Stevenage. The recording had to be cancelled. The group tried to continue recording, intending to add Keith's drum part later, but after several attempts the recording was stopped as it didn't work out. Kit reluctantly accepted that the album wouldn't be finished before the group left for the States.

The Who flew to the States for the Monterey pop festival. Chris Stamp explains, "I had to book in five other gigs to get the Who to Detroit. This was to pay for Monterey because they had to do it for free. I booked the opening show in Detroit, then two shows in Chicago and two in San Francisco. This helped towards our air fare and equipment."

In San Francisco they realized to their horror that their act wasn't long enough for the Fillmore. They did about a 40 minute set. At the Fillmore, they were expected to do an hour and a half. They realized that if they could make an impact there and at Monterey they would find breaking the American market much easier.

They weren't familiar with enough of their new material to be able to play it, as Stamp recalls: "We really had to do an incredible act for Monterey. We had to change it totally. I had to go out and buy a cheap little record player and the Who records so they could learn stuff like the mini-opera. It was the first time they'd learnt a long piece." So the Who spent all their spare time learning how to play their own songs by listening to their own records.

Pete said afterwards, "We were immediately thrown into panic by not having enough numbers but we got by. We ended up rehearsing in our hotel. The Fillmore was a gas, we did two 45-minute spots each night. It was like going back to the Marquee club."

Pete was knocked out by the San Francisco flower-power scene.

At Monterey, Eric Burdon came on to announce the Who. "I promise you this group will destroy you in more ways than one", he told the largely unsuspecting crowd.

The Who, Pete dressed in lace ruffles, Roger in pink silk poncho and fringed cape, Keith in a red mandarin jacket and an Indian shirt and John in a yellow and red 'British Lion' jacket, had once again reverted to their auto-destruction set and proceeded to destroy the audience and their instruments. They began with *Summertime Blues*, ran through their numbers and included the mini-opera. They got applause for *Happy Jack*, which had only recently been released in the States and was climbing up the US singles charts. Greater applause greeted the opening bars of *My Generation*. Pete smashed his guitar by banging it on the stage. Roger attacked the cymbals with his mike, and Keith destroyed the drum kit. An article in the NME adds, "...and even John knocked a mike or two over as a concession."

The Who had heard that Jimi Hendrix, also making his American debut at Monterey, had intended to steal their guitar-breaking act. The Who insisted that Hendrix went on after them. Pete went to see him in his dressing room. "I had it out with him. I said 'You're not going to go out there and smash your guitar, are you?' He got very nasty about it and started to get very flashy. He varied between being very nice to me and being a bit arrogant." Jimi Hendrix, the Who's stable-mate at Track Records, usually ended his act by pouring lighter fuel over his guitar and setting light to it. At Monterey, for the first time, he broke his guitar before setting light to it. "I was sitting next to Mama Cass and she turned to me and said, 'Isn't this guy stealing your act?'," recalls Pete, "and I said, 'Yeah, but, you see, he's so fucking great, who cares.' It was all peace and love at that time and I was very magnanimous and I said to him afterwards 'Is there any chance of gettin' a piece of your guitar?' because he was my hero. He said, 'Yeah, and I'll fuckin' autograph it for you, honky', or something like that."

John thought Kit Lambert was penny-pinching at Monterey because Kit didn't want to pay to bring their own equipment over. "It sounded absolutely crummy. When we did Holland, Sweden, 'Murray the K' and our first American tour, we had to use borrowed equipment. Hendrix had big

Marshall stacks, so he sounded great."

He also remembers, "By the time we got to the dressing room we'd been given about twenty pills and capsules by various people. I took mescaline by mistake and I remember I ate about half a pound of cherries and threw them up in this toilet, and the toilet seemed to be miles away. I thought I was throwing my lungs up. I was real worried 'cause it was all red. When I finally come round I realized why, 'cause it was a real little low toilet for kids."

John has had a number of bad experiences on drugs. "We were at a party once and someone had spiked the whisky, but I also had my own half-bottle of whisky and decided that I'd drink it all to get myself pissed enough to pass out and avoid the trip. I went to sleep with my head on the window sill so that if I threw up the head would be there and I would get the fresh air and everything. I woke up the next morning with pigeon shit all over me. My hair was absolutely black and white or grey or something."

"One night, me, Pete, and Keith were returning from some gig in the back of a limo, and Keith was so out of it on pills that he thought he was in an airplane and he was reaching for the top of the car trying to adjust the air thing. Then

he thought that Pete was Kim and started massaging his leg, creeping up his leg. We got down the motorway at 80 miles an hour and he suddenly said, 'Oh great to see you', and opened the door. We grabbed him and pulled him back in just in time. When we pulled up outside my house, he thought it was a club in Ealing and stood on the doorstep, persuading my mother to let us into the club..."

After Monterey, the group went onto a seven-week tour of the States playing on the Herman's Hermits tour. They all travelled in a rickety old plane from date to date and did High Schools and 2,000 to 3,000 seater theatres. Herman had had a lot of big hits in the States. The Blues Magoos were the other support band.

Tom Wright who was on most of that tour remembers, "These young kids would be yelling, 'Where's Herman, we want Herman!' and then the Who would start playing before the curtain came up. And when the curtain came up they would be really rocking and everybody was just moving about, like Roger would be running around and Pete would be swinging his arm and hammering the guitar and Moonie would be just kicking ass. And people were in shock, they were in shock. The band just didn't stop between numbers or

maybe sometimes they'd just stop and they'd quit playing for a couple of seconds, just a couple of seconds, but it would be just long enough and BOOM into the next number."

The act was only about 25 minutes long and they would finish by obliterating their equipment. Pete would shatter the amp with his guitar and Keith and Roger would set about the drum kit and the whole stage would be covered in smoke and flash powder, and they'd just walk off. "It was spellbinding", says Tom Wright. "A lot of times there was no clapping whatsoever, just dead silence. People in the front rows were just sitting there with their mouths open – stunned."

Havoc on tour with Hermans Hermits

It was a strange combination, Herman and the Who. Herman would have to come on every night to a stage with bits of broken equipment about and discarded guitar strings and such. "I often thought I'd hate to have to walk out there like Noone did, after all that damage and have to sing. Because invariably there would be a bad sulphur smell from the smoke bombs and a lot of smoke about. He'd come out in his spotlessly clean white shirt and tie and do his sing-song routine."

Roger thought the tour was a managerial mistake. "It got us around America but it did us no good at all. The audiences didn't mix. However once we'd made that mistake the only way we were going to take America was to slog it out on the road. Although I thought it was a waste of time and we could've done it quicker without that tour, it did bring the group closer together. We had no responsibilities; we weren't headlining and we could just roll up and do our bit in half an hour, it was like having a holiday and I could be like everyone else and have a good laugh after the shows."

Stamp tried to work out with Pete a way that he could smash his guitar but not quite ruin it, as the cost of replacing and repairing them was so high. "We were getting hardly anything for the tour and in every town I had to go out first and find the local musical equipment store, right. I used to hit every local sort of cheap factory that made stuff and blag them for stuff or to get it repaired. I used to sign away anything, promise the Who would endorse them, use the Decca name, anything. I had this account in an American bank – I'd put in 50 bucks and they'd given me these two big cheque books called 'Chris Stamp Management Account One'. I was signing any fucking thing, any document – giving over the Who or anything. Just give me that amp, you know, it went day by day."

The problem was that Pete didn't like to fake smashing a guitar and he also got into it because as Stamp explains, "He'd hate the fucking audience, I mean, screaming, 'Herman, Herman'. So he was very uptight and would really get into it." He was right too. They were a much better band and having to support Herman was faintly insulting.

The fact that they were on a Herman's Hermits tour and playing to a very un-Who-like audience also had some advantages. Tom Wright met kids afterwards on the tour and it seemed that after getting over the initial shock of seeing these aggressive English boys, they would think about it and talk about it to their friends and that after a couple of weeks they would realize what they saw. They were laying the foundations for future Who fans.

Kit Lambert and Chris Stamp were always flying in and out, leaving and rejoining the tour. There would always be one of them there. One of the legendary Keith Moon stories occurred on this tour.

Keith's 21st birthday was due and Decca planned a special birthday party for him. They had sent out special cakes in the shape of drums to various DJ's around the country as a promotional gimmick. They had a big five-tier cake baked and iced specially for Keith and arranged a reception at the Holiday Inn at Flint where the tour had reached. It wasn't actually Keith's 21st, it was only his 20th, but he'd told everyone that it was his 21st so that it would come out in the papers and he would be able to drink in every State. Tom Wright remembers the occasion vividly, "How could I forget, it was one of the weirdest nights ever. We rented the conference room at the Holiday Inn in Flint, Michigan, which is not too exciting a place to be in. Nancy Lewis, their publicist, flew in and she got the cake and everything together. Kit and Chris were there and a whole bunch of friends, some people from Decca, a bunch of chicks and a lot of record promoters in the area and disc jockeys and stuff. Everything was going along fine until it got close to midnight. They've got the Who album on full blast and it's real loud and it's distorting terribly. Anyway this guy, the manager, comes running in and he says, 'OK, you've got this room till twelve o'clock. That's eight minutes from now and I expect everybody to be out of here at twelve sharp.' Well I knew that that wasn't gonna sit well with *anybody*. I told him we'd wind it down and so on and he left. At like one minute after twelve he comes running in and says, 'Godammit this sounds more like a revolution than a birthday party. We're having complaints and you can't do this and can't do that' and was just about to go into a big deal when Keith just picked up what was left of the five-tiered cake and just shoved it into the guy's face. Everybody in the room just went silent including this guy. All this stuff like, just drips. And you couldn't even laugh because it was just so shocking. The guy in his smart manager's suit and everything. I thought, 'Jesus Christ, it's gonna be the cops and everything.' And this guy just turned around real quietly and walked out of the room to the front desk and sat down at a teletype machine and puts out on all points a Holiday Inn bulletin banning us from every Holiday Inn on the planet. He then proceeded to call the cops. As soon as the guy had left the room and the silence was turning into 'Oh my God, what have we done?' Keith runs out of the room. Bobby Pridden, myself and another guy take off after him. Just on general principal. 'The cat's out of the bag, this guy is not gonna let it go at this'. Keith grabs a fire extinguisher off the wall and races outside and starts shooting foam into any cars that had open windows. You know, SWOOSH and these Cadillacs and that were filled with foam. He was going from one to the other. We spotted him and chased him and eventually I got him in somebody's room and said, 'Keith we've got to talk'. And he said, 'Yeah, you're right', and then leaned down and picked up a lamp and threw it at me. That broke and smashed. I never seen stuff like this even in the movies. I was thinking, 'They are gonna shoot somebody here for this shit'. This non-stop catastrophe in this American Hotel. He ran off and now three more of us were chasing him. We eventually got him cornered by the swimming pool and he backed on to the diving board, yelling and shouting, 'That was a lousy birthday party, I've had enough', and then he just turned around and dived into the pool, only there wasn't any water in it at the time and he landed on his face. Thump. Blood all over. Knocked his front tooth out. Just right off. Clunk.

"The police arrived and Kit and Chris were talking to the manager and writing cheques and pulling out endless credit cards. And guys are coming down from being with their secretaries and stuff and their whole car's full of fire extinguisher foam. There were mini-disasters all around. He'd woken up the whole hotel."

While Tom Wright, Bobby Pridden and the posse were chasing after Keith, Nancy Lewis and some of the others were quickly clearing up the remains of any joints and throwing them away. Paranoia was spreading fast. The police were actually very nice about it and escorted them to a dentist. They'd had to raise a dentist at three-thirty in the morning, to fix Keith's broken tooth.

The whole entourage had to be away early in the morning on their rickety charter plane. A special private plane had to be hired to take Keith later to the gig which was in Philadelphia.

The damages to the hotel and the cars with ruined upholstery came to tens of thousands of dollars and the whole affair took years to finally settle. "We had to switch to all Ramada Inns or something afterwards", concludes Tom.

The next day everybody was 'wrecked' from the night before. Keith apparently turned up just in time to go on with his new false tooth and plate and his face a bit scarred but in a great mood and excited about doing the gig. "God, he's normal again."

Apparently everyone on the tour, the Blues Magoos and Herman's Hermits all made a contribution towards the damages that Keith had to pay to the Holiday Inn.

The *Happy Jack* single had been a big hit, selling 300,000 copies in the US and reaching No. 24 in Billboard charts.

Atco re-released *Substitute* halfway through the Herman's Hermits tour. The words of which had been changed for the sensitive American market. The lines, 'I look all white, but my Dad was black' were considered a bit provocative for some reason and the Who had to record a version where these lines were replaced by 'I try walking forward, but my feet walk back'.

Later in the year the Who were booked for an appearance on the coast-to-coast Smothers Brothers TV show. They'd seen the Who at Monterey. They were anxious to go down with a bang, and they did. Part of the act involved an explosion with flash powder when they were destroying their equipment. Bobby Pridden had set the allowed amount of flash powder and carefully checked it out before the show. Unbeknown to him and the rest of the Who, Keith had used the dressing room bottle of whisky as a bribe to get some of the stage hands to help him load up his drum kit with flash powder. At the end of the number the 'official' flash powder was ignited and the ensuing flash was quite effective visually and drew applause from the studio audience. Then, however, Moon's flash powder went off and he had used far too much of course and a terrific explosion shook the set. Pete's hair

was singed and he damaged his ears. "I couldn't hear for a week afterwards." Keith's leg was cut by a flying piece of broken cymbal. Bette Davis, who was also on the show, fainted into Mickey Rooney's arms.

In between the Herman dates, the Who recorded six new tracks in the US including their next single. However, they shelved it, and released instead *I Can See For Miles*. About a year earlier I'd been at Pete's flat when he asked me if I'd like to hear his next single. He played me *I Can See For Miles*, which I thought was great, very psychedelic and just right for the times. I was amazed when they released *Happy Jack* instead. I'd thought how the Who would have had an early psychedelic record and been ahead of the growing trend. When it didn't come out until late '67 I was surprised. It was as though they had followed the movement in Britain for psychedelic sounding singles. Apparently Pete wanted to to keep it on ice until he ran out of singles to release. "It was my Ace-in-the-Hole", he said.

I Can See For Miles might not be considered a truly psychedelic single but I always considered it the Who's psychedelic record. The Who, it seemed, missed out on Psychedelia. They had run down publicly the Beach Boys'

Pet Sounds album and *Good Vibrations* single, especially Keith who saw them both as a sort of betrayal of his beloved surfing music. Pete had criticized the Beatles for recording *Strawberry Fields*, saying they were losing touch with the kids.

In particular, their new album *The Who Sell Out*, which was released shortly after the single, brilliant though it is, has a lot of the sounds of '65 and '66 rather than the acid-inspired lyrics of '67. If in some senses *The Who Sell Out* was old fashioned, it was at least fun. Pete explained, "We wanted to lighten the load of the pressures which are facing people. On the one side there's the psychedelia and on the other there's the boredom of the ballad singers. So we come out with an absurd album of melody and humour. Pop music should, we think, be understandable and entertaining." Pete thought the Who suffered by being thought a bit intellectual by the fans. "My interviews were always sort of arty and intense, and I was saying things that the rest of the band didn't give a shit about."

More than a year after the group had disowned pop art, they produced a truly pop art album. The rest of the songs, eight of Pete's, another of John's and one by Speedy Keene are all linked together by jingles used by the pirate commercial radio station, Radio London. They, along with the famous Radio Caroline, and the half-a-dozen lesser-known pirate stations had recently been outlawed by the Government. The album was a tribute to them from the Who. They had broadcast pop to Britain from ships anchored just outside the legal limit. The Who had returned to the States to promote *I Can See For Miles* and Kit Lambert was still finishing off the mix for the album and adding the jingles up to the last moment. The group didn't hear the finished version until it was released. Pete told Paul Nelson in the American Hullabaloo magazine, " . . . *Sell Out* is not meant in the usual terms of 'selling out' or sales. It refers to the fact that we've 'sold out' to a concept of advertising. We've got commercials on the album." Pete continued, "We wanted to do *The Who Sell Out* just to make fun of ourselves to a degree. We wanted as I said to take away some of the gravity which seems to be weighing the group down in this country (America). We wanted to change the fact that so many fans take us so seriously."

"I won't even let my children see the cover"

The group were obviously spurred on to make this album when they did a commercial for Coca-Cola in the States earlier in March. The praise for the album was almost universal. Nic Cohn writing 'Pop Scene' for England's Queen Magazine hit the nail on the head by stating that " . . . the whole production is roughly a pop parallel to, say, Oldenburg's hamburgers or Andy Warhol's Campbell soup cans." The real Pop Art nitty gritty at last, in fact. Cohn sympathises with their approach, " . . . being an obvious reaction against the fashionable psychedelic solemnity, against the idea of pop as capital-letter Art, . . . It is mainline pop, bright and funny and blatantly commercial . . . I think it is relevant to the way that people really live in this time much more so than *Sgt. Pepper*, for example – if Pete Townshend could get himself together one time and set himself to put down all of his potential on record, he would do things that would make the Beatles, Stones, Beach Boys, Bob Dylan, Donovan . . . and all the other obvious progressives look downright silly . . . In my estimation he could be *the* writer of the next ten years." However, in his next paragraph he continued, "Considering what it could have been, *The Who Sell Out* is a failure."

Cohn explains that the album contains a traditional Who fault, which is that the ideas have been carried out half-heartedly. "In a way it's an attractive fault, it shows a nice lack of intensity towards success." This the traditional Who fault goes "Pete Townshend works something out, the group half completes it and then everyone sits back until another group walks in and steals the whole thing. *The Who Sell Out* irritates me more than any album I can remember, just because it could have been pop's first ever masterpiece and simply isn't. What this album really should have been", Cohn declares, "is a total ad-explosion, incredibly fast, loud, brash and vulgar, stuffed full of the wildest jingles, insane commercials, snippets from your man Rosko, plus anything else that came to hand – a holocaust, an utter wipe-out, a monster rotor whirl of everything that pop and advertising really are."

The album concept came according to Pete after he had just written a number called, *Jaguar*. Pete told Melody Maker, "*Jaguar* . . . was a really powerful and loose thing, something like *The Ox* from our first album, with Keith thrashing away like hell and us all pumping out 'Jag-u-a-r' like the Batman theme tune. Of course, with Jaguar cars you have this suggestion of speed and power. At this time we were working on new ideas for our album. As it stood I could see that we just had an album of fairly good songs but there was nothing really to differentiate it from our last LP, *A Quick One*. It needed something to make it stand out." At one stage Pete had the idea of selling advertising space on a record and Chris Stamp approached a few people about it, but only Coca-Cola seemed interested. "We thought of using the powerful instrumental number that we made for Coca-Cola and then I linked it up with the number *Jaguar* and then, of course, we thought 'Why not do a whole side of adverts'?''.

Also they wanted to give the album the feel of a British pirate commercial radio station. The Government had recently passed an Act of Parliament banning the pirate stations and enforcing the BBC on the nation. The Who, and Pete in particular, resented the forced closure of the pirate stations and the BBC pop straightjacket. Although the pirates were really rather shoddy, and many of the actual ads rather amateurish and crude, their news bulletins blatantly right wing, and many of the records simply paid to be played by the big record companies, they were, compared to the archaic BBC light programme, bright, full of fun, unpompous, and gave airtime to lots of new sounds. The Who owed pirate radio a lot. It was Radio's Caroline and London that were instrumental in breaking their first four singles. Kit Lambert and Chris Stamp also moved offices from those they shared with Stigwood to set up in Caroline House, the headquarters of Radio Caroline in Mayfair. Also Rohan O'Riley, who started the whole pirate radio thing when he set up Radio Caroline on board the MV Mi Amigo, used to be part-owner of the Scene Club and became friendly with the Who.

Shortly after its release, the Who were sued by a jingle company over the use of the Radio London jingles.

The cover of *The Who Sell Out* also caused a stir. The photographs of them in mock ads were taken by David Montgomery. Roger, who had to sit in a bath full of 100 large catering sized tins of cold baked beans, caught mild pneumonia at the photo session. The LA Times said that in the year of good album covers started by the Beatles and taken up by the Stones, the Jefferson Airplane, and others, "all their elaborate efforts have just been paled by the Who." It headed its article, BIGGEST HAPPENING IN ALBUM COVERS.

US Decca had not been the most enlightened of record companies when it came to artwork on album sleeves. They changed the David Wedgebury picture on the front of the English *My Generation* to one of the group standing by Big Ben and called it *The Who Sing My Generation*. On the back they put, 'If you've enjoyed this recording . . . you're sure to like these other great Decca albums.' They then listed albums by the Kingston Trio, Brenda Lee and Ricky Nelson. On their second album which they called *Happy Jack*, after the single's success (they dropped *Heatwave* from the English original and included *Happy Jack*) they changed the back cover, spelling John's name wrongly and claiming that Keith Moon had a passion for breeding chickens and that Roger was the symbol of the mod cult. In Rolling Stone Magazine, Greil Marcus commented, "Decca had also gained special fame for the inattention they have lavished on the Who, such as their forgetting to send review copies of some of the group's singles to Billboard and Cashbox." "There are over a dozen fantastic cuts by the Who that have never been released on American LPs . . . The Who deserve better and so do we . . ." In the SF Express Times (Nov. 4 '68), Paul Williams wrote, "Imagine what these boys could do if they ever get themselves together enough to record a full-scale album. Incredible. And Decca Records would probably refuse to put it out." Still they kept the artwork of *Sell Out* practically intact after a bit of a fright from Kit and Chris. They even spelt John's name right although this time they

mis-spelt Roger's.

The musical director of New York's leading AM radio station, Joe Bogart of radio WMCA called the album, 'Disgusting'. WMCA banned it and Mr Bogart said, "I won't even let my children see the cover."

In 1967/68 the Who were still basically a live group. They had to be seen to be really experienced. They were still mainly a singles band, their albums being less important although *The Who Sell Out* was making an incredible impact on the public. But whether they are singles or albums, records are secondary to the Who's stage act. Pete said in America in early '68 "We don't concentrate as much in the studio as on live performances. We try to put a good record at a session but we don't enjoy it as much. We believe that our record success is secondary to what we've achieved on our personal appearances. We are definitely an 'in person' act, and we are always working on new ways to present ourselves in a different light. That means that the next time you see us there will be something new mixed in with the old . . . we like to think that by a gradual building-up process we can continue towards our goal – being an act that can please an audience, without having to rely on a hit record."

Just as *I Can See For Miles* entered the charts in late

October of 1967, the Who did a two-week tour headlining a package including Traffic, the Tremeloes and the Herd. Pete had talked of it being the most professional act they'd ever done. They rehearsed for a week at the Saville Theatre and Pete predicted, "This tour will blow your bloody heads off! . . . It'll be the most professional act we've done in the UK".

A Saville Sunday Show just before the tour was hailed by the pop press critics even though they had dropped their legendary smashing up routine. They blasted through *Substitute, I'm a Boy, Pictures of Lily, I Can See For Miles, Happy Jack, My Generation, Relax, Summertime Blues, Shakin' All Over,* and finished with *A Quick One*. Pete played his double-necked guitar and everything looked fine for their tour. However, on the first night of the tour in Sheffield, Roger and Pete argued and scuffled on stage. Next night in Lowerby the house manager dropped the curtain while they were still playing leaving Pete and Roger in front and Keith and John behind while the National Anthem played. Apparently, a very angry Pete pushed a couple of speaker cabinets over on to the tour manager and then proceeded to strangle him in front of the audience. Even without their destructive finale they were aggressive on stage.

They were at two different stages with their two major markets. In England they were dropping the heavy pop-art auto-destruction act and introducing more harmony and better all-round performance. Pete no longer had to use feedback and violence to cover up deficiencies in his guitar playing. They had been doing it for three years in England and wanted to move on. They felt that it was about time they were known for other things besides simply smashing up their guitars and drums. However, in the States, they were still breaking in their act. Their records hadn't sold in the States until they played live, although despite Decca Records, *My Generation* had got to No. 74.

"For God's sake don't get us all shot"

They returned to the States in 1968 for two extensive tours to consolidate their position and reverted to the smashing-up stage act. Pete explained to astonished American observers about the stage act, "I don't smash my guitar as a gimmick, but in the fit of wild abandon that comes after a frenzied performance – where we really get into our music, finally reaching a crescendo – well, the smashing scene that follows is absolutely genuine . . . For years now our act has been based upon steadily working up to a climax. My adrenalin level peaks, and I'm in such a state of high nervous tension that, when something snaps my concentration, I go absolutely stark raving mad." They had won over audiences in America almost immediately whereas it had taken three long hard years to achieve the same thing in England. The Who were very different to the current American West Coast acts and like Hendrix and Cream who were also both breaking into the US market they retained their English attitude. "We're not going to tell people, 'Well, this is us, and we're part of what's happening,' or 'we're leading the scene so you have to listen and like us!' We use a different approach. Give them what they came to see and hear . . . don't confuse them with anything they don't understand just because it happens to be hip at the moment and is therefore part of a cult."

They had now put England second and were concentrating on the US. For most of the Summer of 1967, they were in the States. They had also run out of material for singles, *I Can See For Miles* having been written over a year earlier and kept for emergencies. Kit had planned in his inimitable way that the next album would be released about the same time as Wimbledon and would be called 'Who's For Tennis'. Pete had written a song about an airline crash called *Glow Girl* which was to be their next single. It included the lines, 'It's a girl Mrs. Walker, it's a girl. It's a girl Mrs. Walker, it's a girl' and was part of the rock opera idea that he had been talking about for some time. In the summer of 1967 Pete had dabbled with LSD and started planning an opera, an idea suggested by Kit, about vibrations.

Early on in the tour they spent a week in LA where they finished off the tapes of *Call Me Lightning* at Hollywood's Gold Star studio. Pete explained to Hit Parader in 1968, "Gold Star must have an echo-chamber there which must be the cleanest, deepest sounding in the world – like the Grand Canyon or something."

Decca threw a lavishly expensive press reception for the group at the expensive Beverly Hills Hilton. "Decca never let us forget it", reports Pete and they also shot a wacky film as a promotion for *Call Me Lightning* in a deserted warehouse in Hollywood.

Pete also somehow ended up making a commercial for the US Airforce. After completing the single they recorded *Little Billy* which was an anti-smoking song to be used by the American Anti-Cancer Society and played on 4,000 radio stations all over the States. After a few bars of *Happy Jack*, Pete says, "Hi, this is Pete Townshend of the Who, I just want to say the United States Airforce is a great place to be . . ." Keith did one for the US Navy too. They also sang a jingle for Great Shakes Milkshakes.

They released *Call Me Lightning* as a single in the States, thinking it too dated for the UK market. The US tour which was originally going to be three weeks had been extended to nine weeks. This time it was their tour and they were the headline band.

Tom Wright was roped in by Kit and Chris to be tour manager. They travelled in a bus equipped with beds, a bar, a TV and showers. There were eight on the tour; the group, the driver, Bobby Pridden, Tom, and Tom's cousin to help Bobby out. Kit and Chris would join them at various spots on the way. All the time they were on this tour, Pete was writing and formulating ideas for his rock opera. The tour was a fantastic success. Townshend was getting so carried away smashing up his guitars and amps that Tom and Bobby Pridden had major problems keeping the show on the road. Bobby had a big box full of parts from broken guitars and could usually fix them together unless they were too far gone. Pete talking about his guitar-smashing around that time said, "In the last three years, I've wrecked about ninety guitars, it's a lot of money, but it's been well worth spending. There's been a lot of talk about my using a breakaway guitar. I don't, but usually, even after a super fantastic wrecking job, we're able to pick up the splinters and stick them all back together again. The only problem is that sometimes the result doesn't play too well the next day. And there's always the possibility of people in the audience keeping the pieces of flying wood."

Tom remembers, "Sometimes you'd have to sweep the guitar into a bag and get it all glued back together again and be playing it the next night. Pete would glue it back together in his room. He had this great glue. It was English and like powdered milk. He'd mix it up with water and glue the parts together and put thick rubber rings around to hold it in place. It was real quick-drying and hard as a motherfucker. When they got smashed again they'd never go in the places where they'd been glued. Once Pete had the basic guitar glued again, Bob would take over. And from that point on he was a genius at the work. He'd get the pick-ups going and such. Parts could be interchanged. Fenders seemed best, like if you had the neck you could always repair it. It was either broken or not, there might be big gashes out of it, but that just made it more fun. But one neck would fit on another. Rickenbackers often only lasted once and seemed a lot weaker. Sometimes Pete would start smashing a Rickenbacker and it would go off like a light bulb into a thousand pieces. This could spoil the effect because it broke too soon. See, the shows weren't choreographed – whatever happened, happened."

The speaker cabinets were easier to repair and they carried spares. But things rarely worked out. Tom remembers one night when they were down to the minimum number of working speaker cabinets. "It was a real inconvenience, Bob got them all together before the show and said, 'Look, tomorrow's Sunday and we're playing Sunday night and there's nowhere we can get any more speakers and we're flat out. There's no way that we can lose any speakers tonight, so we're gonna put a couple of cabinets on stage that have already got broken speakers and re-cover them with new cloth. Make sure that you get those and not the good ones'. And they'd say 'OK man, I understand'. And then, shit, as soon as it was *My Generation* they'd go straight for the good one that was working and wreck it."

Chris Stamp would show up every now and then on this tour and try to 'blag' some equipment from the stores and manufacturers and Bobby and Tom would buy stuff on the road. "We'd get great deals from them. We'd say we'll take all the Fender Stratocasters or whatever it was for fifty bucks each and buy out his entire stock."

However, the money they were getting from the shows was not enough to pay for the scale of equipment damage. They would have to have meetings about the cost of breaking the guitars and amps and drums and all agree to keep it down but the next night would destroy even more. It was a very expensive way to win over America.

Afterwards there would be a row about the destruction. Bobby and Tom would say, "There's no more speakers and they cost over two hundred dollars apiece and the drum kit will have to be fixed again and that'll cost 450 dollars" and Tom would add "We just had to pay the bus company another 1,000 dollars and that last hotel where Keith broke the TV was very expensive." It often got to the point of not having enough for clothes, beer and food because of the money spent on repairs. Kit would get Pete on the phone from England and complain bitterly about the destruction, but was always fobbed off with some excuse – "It was a shitty guitar, anyway", or "I didn't mean to."

"However," remembers Tom, "It always just about worked out financially. I kept our takings in a briefcase and

I told them, 'The bus costs, the hotels, your laundry bills, your telephone calls, your beer bills and your eating money are all coming out of the same case that is paying for all the gear.' But it always seemed, somehow, to just about even out."

There were a few concert halls that didn't care for the Who's violent stage act. Tom remembers one particularly frightening night in New Jersey: "This dance hall was on the boardwalk and there were these particularly heavy guys around and they just said to the band, 'Well, we don't want any kind of trouble here in terms of you guys scarring that brand new oak stage floor out there.' These were heavy dudes with Mafia connections and very serious. They got me to promise that their new floor wouldn't get scratched. I went back to the group and we all had this conference. 'Now look', I was saying, 'This is a very heavy concern, the mob's involved, and for God's sake don't get us all shot. I've given my word there'll be no damage.' So we were all a bit worried and they all agreed that just for this one night they'd cool it. 'We wouldn't put you in jeopardy, Tom.' Well the act went really well but at the end I can't believe it, Pete is just smashing his guitar repeatedly on their new stage. I can see chips

coming off and I felt sick. Then Keith goes and kicks the drumkit and throws it along the floor and Roger kicks the music stands around. It was just damage . . . damage . . . damage. Well I mean, these guys were just bristling. Really angry and mean and putting their hands in their pockets for guns and so on. They couldn't wait to get their hands on the band. They all came to the wings and stood there waiting. I was lost – just scared and bewildered. Next thing Keith just runs past them out onto the boardwalk and dives straight into the water. Everyone was taken completely by surprise and then we realise he can't swim. It had everybody in shock, you know, 'My God, he's suicidal, no wonder he broke up all the instruments.' So everybody just switched over from, 'We're gonna shoot ya!' to 'We're all gonna be heroes and save this guy.' So guys are leaping in all over the place. I couldn't cope. Five minutes ago I'd been ready to be shot and now all this. Anyway they dived in and hauled him up the beach and he was all right, he wasn't unconscious or anything but he looked a mess. They never bothered about the damage after that."

The group were in good spirits on this tour. John and Roger were happy, Pete was ensuring a very busy time for

the media, Keith was keeping everyone in hysterics and getting up to all sorts of trademarked Moon antics. Tom said Keith had the weirdest luggage. "He'd sort of have a suitcase with a pair of purple velvet trousers, half-a-dozen T-shirts and twenty pairs of shoes. We'd be going through some town and he'd say 'Stop the bus!' and jump out and go into a clothes store and come out with a pair of bright green trousers and three identical atrocious pink satin jackets. Once we were rolling around the back streets of Alabama and he's wearing a pink sequined jumpsuit or something with a pair of orange shoes and no socks. Every time we walked into a hotel lobby we had a 50-50 chance of getting in even if our reservations were made ages ago. We looked so bizarre."

The group somehow escaped being thrown out of the Gorham, but Kit and Chris were summoned and had the riot act read to them and had to stand large amounts of cash as securities.

While on this tour they recorded their shows at the Fillmore West to release as a live album later in the year. They returned to England to do two weeks recording. "Pete talked about his forthcoming rock opera to be called 'The Amazing Journey' and played a track from it called *Now I'm a Farmer* to MM journalist Chris Welch.

Working towards the 'rock opera'

The group and especially Pete were caught in a dilemma. Their success in America had brought a great demand for touring there but this left little or no time for Pete to write songs and record demos for the group. Usually he did these in his home studio, now moved from his flat on Wardour Street to a tall house in Ebury Street, Victoria, round the corner from his girlfriend's flat in Eccleston Square. He'd been talking about and working towards the rock opera on and off for the last eighteen months. Pete said at the time that he had been disappointed by the image of pop opera created by Keith West's Teenage Opera. His opera was really a collection of half-finished songs, very ambitious ideas and complex and sprawling notes on structure and underlying meanings. It was completely untogether. Originally, it was called 'Deaf Dumb and Blind Boy' then he wanted to call it 'Journey Into Space' but there had already been a famous radio show in the fifties of that name. So the provisional title became 'The Amazing Journey'. Later this was changed to the 'Brain Opera'.

Pete married Karen Astley his girl friend from Art School at Didcot in Berkshire on 20th May.

The constant touring of the States was affecting their British career. They were becoming out of touch with the British market. Releasing *Dogs* which they thought just right for England was a major mistake. The record wasn't funny enough to be picked up as a comedy pop record. It wasn't pop enough to stand on its own. It was in fact pretty dire and died a death. "It was a very strange in-joke phase that I hated," said Roger. "A real self-indulgent wanking off period that didn't work." They were running out of new material to release. The 'Who's for Tennis?' idea never materialised and the live recordings from the Fillmore weren't considered good enough to release. They took the decision to hold off and try to complete the 'Brain Opera' before Christmas. The group were once more in a fairly depressed state and couldn't see much hope for the future. Still they continued with their outstanding touring success of the States. The next tour was to have been a three-week tour but would have to be a nine-week tour. As Kit Lambert said "Three weeks to pay the air fares and hotels. Two for my commission and four to pay you."

About this time I'd gone to see Pete in his new house that he and Karen had bought by the Thames at Twickenham. I was very surprised by them. They were both incredibly warm and genuine and down-to-earth. Pete had lost all his sneering unpleasantness and the 'I'm a Big Shot Pop Star' ego trip had disappeared. I was profoundly impressed. It was like talking to a different person; like talking to the old Pete of Art School days. He was relaxed, interesting and for the first time in years, very very happy. I said to both of them that I couldn't believe the change in them. I didn't know what to put it down to. I thought that it must have been a combination of being married and fairly wealthy and successful. And more importantly their new found relationship with

Meher Baba, pictures of whose smiling face with twinkling eyes were hanging around the house. I was astonished that in mid 1968, long after everybody had sought out their Eastern Gurus and it was a little passé, that Pete of all people should suddenly devote himself to this strange looking Indian geezer that never said anything.

Pete's new stance on life was what he was now trying to translate into musical terms for his rock opera. When he first had his LSD experiences, his opera was to be basically about vibrations. He was trying to show what it would be like to experience vibrations without having the usual human organism and its pre-conceived ways of experiencing each vibration. He thought of writing about an animal's experiences, or someone from outer space, and then of somebody devoid of the usual channels for receiving life's vibrations, somebody who was deaf, dumb, and blind.

Pete had taken a number of LSD trips. He used to get Swiss Sandoz LSD 25 at the UFO club in London's Tottenham Court Road. However at the Monterey Pop Festival he was given some STP by its creator, Owsley. He and his girlfriend Karen took it on their plane journey back to England. Pete experienced one of the worst times in his life. He told me the only way he could cope was to leave his body. "I couldn't stand any more of it and I was in mid-air just hovering; floating about looking at myself sitting in my seat. This went on for about an hour and a half. And then I would test myself and I would go back in and it would be the same. As far as the outside world was concerned I was completely unconscious, but really I was very much alive."

The result of his horrendous STP experience made him decide to give up psychedelics completely.

Pete now attempted to translate what he understood of Baba's explanation of creation into musical terms and introduce it into his opera. It was not simply to do with vibrations now. Pete says that he dithered a lot with the very first opera he tried to write which was called 'Rael'. It was to be a genuine opera for a full orchestra with Arthur Brown as the hero. 'Rael' was to be political, about the Red Chinese (The Redchins). Pete says in a book which he and I compiled for the Ken Russell 'Tommy' film, 'The Story of Tommy', "basically the story ('Rael') was running into about twenty scenes when Kit Lambert reminded me . . . the Who need a new single. Thus 'Rael' was edited down to about four minutes and recorded in New York." It was never released as a single, and was squeezed up too tightly to make sense. 'Rael' contained the theme for *Sparks* and the *Underture* of the later *Tommy*.

Tommy, originally, was supposed to be a "series of songs that flashed between the point of view of reality and the point of view of illusion seen through the eyes of someone on the spiritual path, a young boy." Later Pete realized that having to have one song about what was really happening was too cumbersome. He had some of the songs written already before the idea had fully taken shape, notably *Welcome, Not Gonna Take It, Sensation* (written about a girl with the chorus 'She's a Sensation', later changed to 'I'm a Sensation') and the *Underture*. Much of the rest was written as poetry and roughed out structures. The lyrics had to have music. Talking through the proposed idea with Jan Wenner the editor of Rolling Stone Magazine after a Who concert at the Fillmore West, Pete said, "It's a story about a kid that's born deaf, dumb and blind . . . he's seeing things basically as vibrations, which we translate into music . . . he is touched from the outside and he feels his mother's touch, he feels his father's touch, but he just interprets them as music . . . Lyrically it's quite easy to do it, I've written it out several times and it makes great poetry, but so much depends on the music. The lyrics are going to be okay, but every pitfall of what we're trying to say lies in the music, lies in the way we play the music, the way we interpret, the way things are going during the opera . . ."

Pete was enormously ambitious with his ideas. Previously written songs were dug out and somehow made to fit in with the plot. Much of the material miraculously slotted into the story easily, with only minor modifications. Pete explained the fact that so many songs written earlier just fell into place. "This was something, if you like, that serves as an example of my thinking in spiritual terms, rather than the frustrated adolescent terms I had been thinking in up to that point." Keith thought up the idea of a Holiday Camp and said he'd

write a song for it but Pete who loved the idea was dubious about Keith's songwriting ability and told him he'd already done it, however he gave Keith the credit. *Pinball Wizard* was written much later because of and for Nic Cohn, who was obsessed with pinball.

Pete was bouncing ideas off various people including Mike McInnerney, who was designing the artwork for the cover, and Richard Stanley, a film student friend of Pete's. But the main sounding board and inspiration for the rock opera was Kit Lambert. He and Pete together talked through the project and the structure. "Pete used to come in some days with just half a demo," Roger remembers, "We used to talk for hours, literally. We probably did as much talking as we did recording. Sorting out arrangements and things." Originally, they were going to use Mose Allison's *Young Man Blues* and *Country Shack* as well as *Eyesight To The Blind*. Chris Stamp remembers, when they were in the studio, " . . . it was falling all over the place, it was just not coming together and that's when Kit wrote a script." "He was working all through the night on the script and when it was finished we went straight round to the printers. We had

it printed up as a script to impress the group and had twenty copies made up. It was going to be the first Lambert/Stamp production."

Kit's script written in 1968 brought the Tommy rock opera project together. They realized that they couldn't get it all on one album, they had about three sides of material, so they decided to make it a double album which greatly helped to clarify the plot. Kit was the producer of the album as he had been on all their records since their split with Shel Talmy, (with the exception of *Substitute* which Pete had produced). But *Tommy* was his most ambitious production and the one he most personally identified with.

They had released *Magic Bus*, which had been recorded way back in early 1966. (An American group called The Pudding had released it in 1966). It had been a chart success in the States reaching No. 10 in Billboard, but in Britain it surprisingly did as badly as *Dogs*, despite various publicity gimmicks to promote the record – including driving a French bus around London covered with streamers and posters and filled with pretty models, an elephant, circus animals, clowns and fire-eaters plus of course the Who. As *I Can See For Miles* didn't do as well as expected in Britain, this was their

third single failure there. And, there were no more in the can. They thought of doing one written by someone else. All their time had been taken up with either touring or working on the *Tommy* project. To attempt something as bold, ambitious and downright risky as a double album, a Rock Opera about a deaf, dumb and blind boy who becomes a pinball champ and then spiritual leader was, given the circumstances they were in, " . . . one fucking huge great once-and-for-all gamble", as Stamp put it. Pete explains, "I was petrified that the band was going to finish. When I wrote *Pictures of Lily* I thought it wouldn't be a hit and although I was getting better at it all the time, I thought I can't write this shit any more. I'd got to come up with something of substance and I didn't believe I could do it in the framework of the Who. I'd had the idea of rock opera way before, but when I met Arthur Brown, I was convinced that he was the perfect foil for it, he was a great rock singer with an operatic range and all that. I thought about writing an opera for him, but it was something outside of the Who – I was hedging my bets. It was Kit that kept pushing me back to the band. He seemed to have greater foresight than we did as to the level that the Who would reach."

According to Chris Stamp, "During the recording of *Tommy*, the group still had to leave the studio every Friday afternoon to go and do gigs because there was no money." Part of the reason why the record sounded so good was that they'd try out some of the numbers onstage. Then they'd go back to IBC Studios on Monday and record the numbers they'd rehearsed at the gigs. IBC was only eight-track, but the gigs had to be done to pay the studio bills as they went along. "You know, we'd spent all the advances from the record companies and we had to pull off this one to get anywhere near to making big money." The *Tommy* album was the zenith of Kit Lambert's type of production, where the technical quality took second place to capturing the musical essence. John Entwistle had always been critical of Kit's production anyway; "The drums always seemed to sound like biscuit tins", and thought that Kit had hurried them through the *Tommy* sessions. "We didn't get a chance to put on any of the overdubs that we'd planned."

Pete thinks this was because Kit wanted to put an orchestra over it. "I insisted that we did it all ourselves and Kit kept putting me off overdubs because I think he was going to try and persuade me later." The first time Pete heard the whole record was after it was actually pressed and he had the album cover in his hand. He thought the sound quality 'passable'. "There was a certain innocence to the sound which I quite liked. And I felt at the time whatever kind of spiritual input had gone into the thing from my end in the writing was somehow coming through. I couldn't work out why, but I felt the album had a kind of light to it."

Meanwhile, Track Records released *Direct Hits* in the UK, a collection of their singles and better album tracks, but out of touch as usual, Decca U.S. released *Magic Bus – The Who on Tour*. The album wasn't 'live' as the title implied. The quality of the pressings was poor but most important of all the choice of material was to say the least uninspired. The Who had suggested Decca release an album called 'The Who's Greatest Flops' and include all the singles that were released in the States before the band broke there and hadn't been hits. This would include *I Can't Explain, Anyway Anyhow, Anywhere, Substitute, I'm a Boy, The Kids are Alright* and probably *Pictures of Lily*. The woefully inept Decca only included the last of these.

The Who did a short tour at the end of 1968 with Joe Cocker, the Small Faces and Arthur Brown, and soon after took part in the Rolling Stones 'Rock and Roll Circus' that was being filmed by the Stones. The finished film was never released as apparently Mick Jagger wasn't pleased with his or the Stones' performance. Allen Klein reportedly tried to sell the finished film to the Who to be released as 'The Who's Rock 'n' Roll Circus' as their performance was so good.

The filming went so slowly that the Stones section didn't take place until about one in the morning, by which time the audience was tired and listless. But Keith, Pete and Bobby Pridden saved the day much to Jagger's relief by dressing up with seat cushions on their heads and tying themselves to each other with sheets, and brought the audience back to life with their antics. One eyewitness described them as 'very, very strange'.

1965—The band first appeared on TV's top pop show, 'Ready, Steady, Go!' after being spotted playing at the Marquee club. When the guy who usually searched the clubs, looking for cool mods and dancers to appear in the audience, became ill, Kit Lambert took over. He gave out 150 tickets to the 100 Faces and their friends and packed the studio with ardent Who fans, all dressed in the same long scarves as the group. So when *I Can't Explain* went on air, their 'staged' reaction of pure ecstasy made it look like this new group were the latest 'happening' in mod London. After charting briefly, a second chance appearance, on BBC's 'Top of the Pops' as the week's 'Tip for the Top', helped send the record to No. 10.

Right: Breakthrough in the USA. The Who have had an affection for the Detroit area, where the single entered the local charts, though it didn't spread nationwide.
Below and far right: Shopping for clothes in Carnaby Street. At one time it claimed that Pete was spending as much as £60 a week on clothes. It wasn't true – just more Lambert hype.

A BREAKOUT *in* FLINT · DETROIT LANSING PONTIAC TOLEDO *now* SPREADING FOR A NATIONAL HIT!

I CAN'T EXPLAIN

31725

BY

THE WHO

DECCA RECORDS

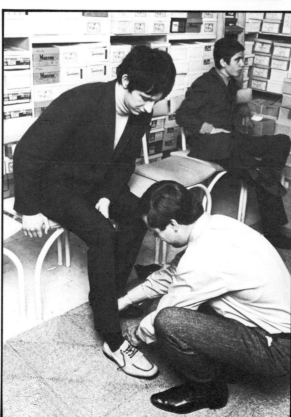

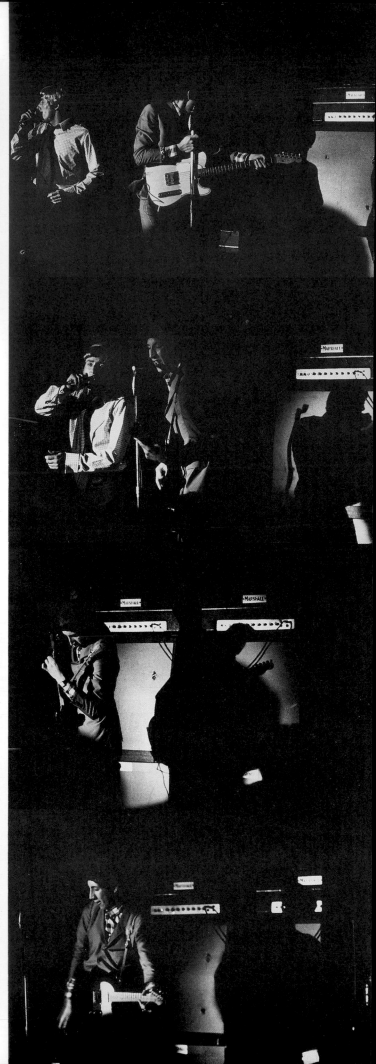

NME TOP THIRTY
FIRST-EVER CHART IN BRITAIN
—AND STILL THE **FIRST** TODAY!

Last This
Week   (Week ending Wednesday, February 24, 1965)

Last	This			Highest Position	Weeks in Chart
1	1	I'LL NEVER FIND ANOTHER YOU ... Seekers (Columbia)		6-	1
10	2	IT'S NOT UNUSUAL .... Tom Jones (Decca)		3-	2
4	3	GAME OF LOVE ... Wayne Fontana and the Mindbenders		4-	3
		(Fontana)			
6	4	DON'T LET ME BE MISUNDERSTOOD Animals (Columbia)		4-	4
2	5	TIRED OF WAITING FOR YOU .... Kinks (Pye)		6-	1
8	6	FUNNY HOW LOVE CAN BE ... Ivy League (Piccadilly)		4-	6
7	7	THE SPECIAL YEARS .... Val Doonican (Decca)		6-	7
15	8	I MUST BE SEEING THINGS ... Gene Pitney (Stateside)		3-	8
3	9	YOU'VE LOST THAT LOVIN' FEELIN' ... Righteous Brothers		7-	1
		(London)			
22	10	SILHOUETTES .... Herman's Hermits (Columbia)		2-10	
5	11	KEEP SEARCHIN' .... Del Shannon (Stateside)		7- 4	
21	12	COME AND STAY WITH ME ... Marianne Faithfull (Decca)		2-12	
9	13	IT HURTS SO MUCH .... Jim Reeves (RCA)		4- 9	
23	14	I'LL STOP AT NOTHING .... Sandie Shaw (Pye)		2-14	
13	15	GOODNIGHT .... Roy Orbison (London)		3-13	
16	16	YES I WILL .... Hollies (Parlophone)		5-16	
11	17	COME TOMORROW .... Manfred Mann (HMV)		7-14	
25	18	HONEY I NEED .... Pretty Things (Fontana)		2-18	
17	19	MARY ANNE .... Shadows (Columbia)		3-17	
12	20	GO NOW .... Moody Blues (Decca)		11- 1	
14	21	CAST YOUR FATE TO THE WIND ..... Sounds Orchestral		12- 5	
		(Piccadilly)			
18	22	LEADER OF THE PACK .... Shangri-Las (Red Bird)		7-15	
—	23	I APOLOGISE .... P.J. Proby (Liberty)		1-22	
30	24	GOLDEN LIGHTS .... Twinkle (Decca)		2-24	
—	24	STOP FEELING SORRY FOR YOURSELF ... Adam Faith (Parlophone)		1-24	
—	26	YOUR HURTIN' KINDA LOVE .... Dusty Springfield		1-26	
		(Philips)			
—	27	THE "IN" CROWD .... Dobie Gray (London)		1-27	
—	28	I CAN'T EXPLAIN .... The Who (Brunswick)		1-28	
—	29	CAN'T YOU HEAR MY HEARTBEAT .... Goldie and		1-29	
		the Gingerbreads (Decca)			
—	30	PAPER TIGER .... Sue Thompson (Hickory)		1-30	

Kit Lambert said on seeing the band for the first time at the Railway Hotel: "There seemed to be a satanic quality to them; with Keith at the back, on a rostrum of stacked beer crates, the most evil of all. For me it was a moment of certainty."

Top left: The Marquee club — A regular Tuesday night spot, which eventually broke house attendance records. It was helped by a fly-posting scheme, that included an arrow on the 'o' of 'Who' and the words 'Maximum R&B'
Above and left: The NME Top 30 No. 28 on Feb. 24th, 1965.

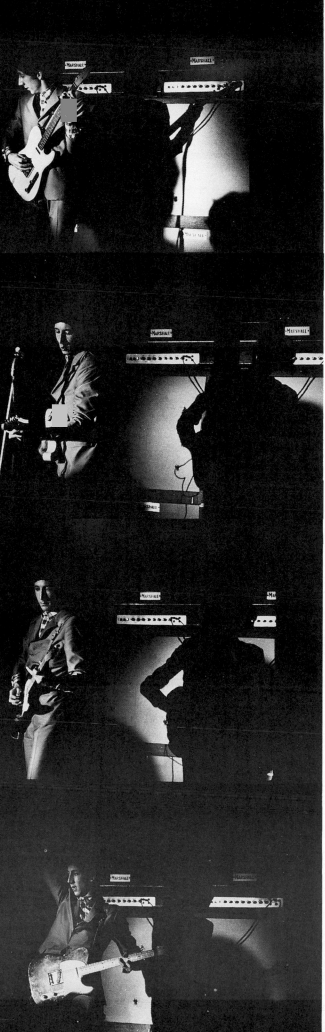

NEW ACTION LTD

KIT LAMBERT · CHRISTOPHER STAMP

84, EATON PLACE
LONDON, S.W.1
BELGRAVIA 8989

CALL SHEET

SUNDAY, 14th March

    Date: Starlite Ballroom,
          Wembley.

    Arrive: 7.00p.m. Playing Time - 1½ hrs.

MONDAY, 15th March

    GADZOOKS - Television Theatre,
          Shepherd's Bush.

    Arrive: 10.30 a.m. for Rehearsals.

TUESDAY, 16th March

    Marquee rehearsal - 12.00 - 6.00

    2.00 p.m. Shel Talmy at Marquee for L.P.
routining.
    Date: Marquee

WEDNESDAY, 17th March

    Decca photograph session (colour for American
Decca) to be arranged.

    Possible appointment with Insurance doctor
for Life Insurance medical.

THURSDAY, 18th March

    Date: Civic Hall,
          Crawley,
          Sussex.

    Arrive: 7.00 p.m. - playing time to be confirmed.

FRIDAY, 19th March

    2.00 - 5.00 p.m. Recording for L.P.

    I.B.C. Studios,
    Portland Place.

SUNDAY, 21st March

    Date: Watford Trade

    Union Bros.

Forthcoming Dates

Monday 22nd Warrington, Lancs (Manchester)
Tuesday 23rd Marquee
Wednesday 24th Ealing Club
Thursday 25th Blue Opera Club, Cook's Ferry Inn.
Friday 26th Railway, Harrow
Saturday 27th Rhodes Centre, Bishops Stortford.
Sunday 28th Ritz and Kavern Clubs, Birmingham.

Centre sequence: La Locomotive Club, Paris, in the basement of Le Moulin Rouge. Left. A 1965 call sheet—a hectic week.

THE WHO
Anyway, anyhow, anywhere

Brunswick 05935

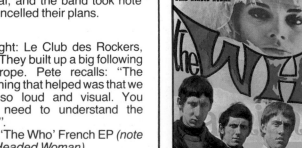

ALL NITE RAVE
MIDNIGHT TO 6 a.m.
CLUB NOREIK
HIGH ROAD TOTTENHAM, N.15
PRESENTING—
SATURDAY, JUNE 26th
THE WHO
PLUS! THE MEADYEVILS
SATURDAY, JULY 10th
THE 'IN' CROWD

Anyway, Anyhow, Anywhere incorporated much of the Who's live sound and gimmicks. So much so that the deliberate feedback on the record, caused the engineers at US Decca to send the master tape back, thinking it was a major technical fault.

Before *My Generation* came out at the end of 1965 (see right), Beat Instrumental talked of a forthcoming album from the Who, which was to contain eight cover versions (including Martha and the Vandellas' *Motoring* and *Heatwave,* James Brown's *I Don't Mind* and *Please Please Please* also Bo Diddley's *I'm A Man*), plus one Townshend track *You're Going to Know Me.* The article criticised the unoriginality of the material, and the band took note and cancelled their plans.

Top right: Le Club des Rockers, Paris. They built up a big following in Europe. Pete recalls: "The main thing that helped was that we were so loud and visual. You didn't need to understand the words".
Right: 'The Who' French EP *(note Blad Headed Woman).*

WHOOOOO!
ça fait mal...

the WHO

45 tours 10668
disques *Brunswick*

**I CAN'T EXPLAIN
E ALD HEADED WOMAN
ANYWAY ANYHOW ANYWHERE
DADDY ROLLING STONE**

ORIGINAL RECORDING IN ENGLAND BY DECCA RECORDS INC NEW YORK

NEW MUSICAL EXPRESS

The WHO (l. to r.): ROGER DALTREY, JOHN BROWNE, KEITH MOON and PETER TOWNSHEND.

THE WHO USE FORCE TO GET SOUND THEY WANT!!

HE sat tensed against a hard-backed chair, dressed in a Carnaby Street blue jacket and with a blond, Mod hairstyle that showed dark at the back. And he spoke slowly and uncertainly. "I never want to grow old," he said. "I want to stay young for ever."

This was my introduction—via vocalist Roger Daltrey—to the weird and way-out group called the Who who are climbing the NME Chart with their current disc, "Anyway, Anyhow, Anywhere."

There's a strangeness, a sort of vicious strangeness, about these four beatsters from Shepherds Bush. And they admit it.

They talk quite happily about the way lead guitarist Pete Townshend

handles his guitar, smashing it hard against an amplifier when the mood takes him. Pete says it produces an unusual sound; and I can well believe him.

They've already had a taste of chart success with "I Can't Explain," but the Who weren't particularly happy about that record.

Says Roger: "We just did it to get known. As time goes by we'll do the kind of thing we really like, really way-out."

"Arguments? Sure, we have 'em all the time. That's why we get on so well. It kind of sharpens us up. We've all got kind of—well, explosive temperaments—and it's like waitin' for a bomb to go off.

"If it wasn't like this we'd be nothin'. I mean it. If we were always

friendly and matey . . . well, we'd all be a bit soft. We're not mates at all. When we've finished a show and we've got time off, that's it. We go our own ways.

"We've done all kinds of stuff since we started. Skiffle, trad, blue beat, pop. We got sick of pop and we went over to r-and-b and long hair, then the Stones came along, so we changed.

"With the Stones around, people were beginning to say we were copying them. But we don't copy anyone. We play the way we feel."

The James Brown style is going to be the next big thing, according to the Who. They've been playing his material for some time and they think it will catch on quicker than people think.

Mind you, it wasn't so long ago that it looked as if they might have to give

up the beat scene altogether Times were hard, and they weren't made any easier by the Who's liking for the very best guitars and equipment.

"We'd be having a lean time," says Roger, "but we'd go out and get ourselves up to the neck in hire purchase debts because we wanted a new amp. We spent 2,000 quid that way. But our stuff is the best in the world."

That "Anyway, Anyhow, Anywhere," hit disc was composed at 3 am, he adds, when he and Pete were locked in a room to make them concentrate on songwriting. The recording session was due the day after.

For once, Pete forgot his other interests ("he's very political, a right Bob Dylan") and the job was finished as dawn broke over Shepherds Bush.

As Roger Daltrey was leaving: "If I wasn't with a group I don't know what I'd do. It means everything to me. I think I'd do myself in."

ALAN SMITH.

★★★★ THE WHO : MY GENE-RATION (Brunswick).
Earthy r-and-b sounds emerge as Roger Daltrey wails over his messages, aided by the others vocally and instrumentally. The two guitarists get a full sound, and drummer Townshend, who has eight composing credits, really beats out a compelling rhythm. There may be disagreement within the group, but when they get together they put on a united performance!

**I CAN'T EXPLAIN
BLAD HEADED WOMAN
ANYWAY ANYHOW ANYWHERE
DADDY ROLLING STONE**

The WHO

THE WHO
MY GENERATION LA-LA-LA-LIES THE OX
MUCH TOO MUCH

DECCA
60 002 M

...TREMENDOUS LPs

**POW!!
The WHO
LP
My generation**

LAT 8616 13" mono LP

OUT NOW!

Brunswick

Life-lines of THE WHO

	KEITH MOON	ROGER DALTREY	PETER TOWNSHEND	JOHN BROWNE
Real name:	Keith Moon	Roger Daltrey	Peter Dennis Blandford Townshend	John Alec Entwistle
Birthdate: Birthplace:	August 23, 1947 Wembley	March 1, 1945 Hammersmith, London	May 19, 1945 Central Middlesex Hospital Annexe, Chiswick	October 9, 1945 Chiswick
Personal points:	5ft. 9ins.; 10st. 7lb.; brown eyes; black hair	5ft. 7ins.; 9st.; blue eyes; assorted hair	6ft.; 10st.; blue eyes; brown/black hair	5ft. 11½ins.; 11st. 7lb.; sparkling blue eyes; green to black hair
Parents' names:	Mum and Dad	Irene and Harry	Betty and Clifford	Queenie Maud and Herbert
Brothers and sisters:	Linda and Leslie	Jill and Carol	Paul and Simon	
Present home:	Wembley	Shepherd's Bush, London	Belgravia, London	Shepherd's Bush
Instruments played:	Drums	Guitar and harp	12-string guitar	Bass guitar, trumpet, French horn, piano
Where educated:	Harrow	Victoria Primary and Acton County Grammar	Acton County Grammar School; Ealing Art School	Southfield Road School; Acton City Grammar School
Musical education:	None	None	Interesting talks with father. Listening to music	Piano from age of 9-12, studied French horn and trumpet at school
Age entered show business:	16	6 months	14	
First public appearance:	Carroll Levis Junior Discoveries	Hammersmith Hospital, March 1, 1945	Goodness knows!	Hendon Town Hall, second trumpet at 11
Biggest break in career:	3,000 pairs of sticks	Crashing group van on bridge	Meeting Kit Lambert	My little toe, rushing to answer phone
Compositions:			"I Can't Explain," "Anyway," etc.	
Biggest influence on career:	Jim Marshall	Whisky	Time, it's always behind, pushing	Lack of money, Duane Eddy, Beatles
Former occupations:	Trainee manager	Con. man	Butcher's boy, milkman, bouncer	Tax officer in Acton, Ealing and Slough
Hobbies:	—	Fishing	Scalextric car racing, painting, making pop art montages	Buying and selling bass guitars
Favourite colour:	Blue	Dark black	Any that shouts!	Any dark shades; blue and green
Favourite singers:	Cyrano, Sammy Payne	Elvis Presley, Nina Simone, Buddy Guy	Ray Charles, Sam Cooke, Bobby Bland, Baez, Dylan	Buddy Guy, Beach Boys (Brian Wilson), Everlys
Favourite actors/ actresses:	Terence Stamp, Sybil Burton and Sandie Shaw	Mitch	Keith Moon (straight up!)	Vincent Price, Steve McQueen, Jess Conrad
Favourite food:	French blues	Chinese	Bircher Muesli (slushy Swiss cereal)	Chinese, fried scampi, chicken
Favourite drink:	Bacardi, coke, Elderberry wine	—	Good wine or brandy	Scotch and coke, tomato juice, and milk
Favourite clothes:	White	Anything that fits me	New or very old	I change my mind all the time
Favourite composers:	Pete Townshend, Lennon / McCartney, Brian Wilson	—	Beatles, Stockhausen, Prokofiev, Bach	Lennon / McCartney, Peter Townshend
Favourite groups:	Beach Boys, Donovan	The Who	Vagabonds, Stones, Beatles	Beatles, Cliff Bennett and Rebel Rousers, Beach Boys
Miscellaneous likes:	Birds	See Keith Moon	Composing, recording, being with hip people, going home	Peace and quiet, playing to big audiences, easygoing people
Miscellaneous dislikes:	Shiny paper	Filling in forms	Hangovers, subtlety, King's Road, having to justify friendship	My equipment when it goes wrong; taxis in rush-hour
Most thrilling experience:	Big dipper at Belle Vue	See Keith Moon	Big dipper at Belle Vue	Falling from top of Blackpool Tower
Tastes in music:	All rubbish	Varied	Anything currently recognised as being liked	Anything except light orchestral, any kind of jazz and poor pop music
Personal ambition:	To stay young for ever	To live well	Just not to let what happens to me get me down	To make a lot of money
Professional ambition:	To smash 100 drum kits	To have group of harpists	To be a recognised composer / arranger. Die young	To make a lot of money; be best bass guitarist in country (next week as well)

★ Common To All ★

TV debut: " Beat Room," BBC-2	Recording manager: Shel Talmy
Radio debut: " Joe Loss Pop Show "	Personal managers: Kit Lambert and Chris Stamp
Current hit: " Anyway, Anyhow, Anywhere "	Musical director: Kit Lambert and group
Other disc in NME Chart: " I Can't Explain "	Album: " The Who," issued in U.S.A.
Present disc label: Brunswick	EP: " The Who," issued in France
Label in past: Fontana	Origin of stage name: We were desperate !

WHO ARE THE WHO? WELL, THEY'RE MODS WHO PLAY FOR MODS, AND, MOST IMPORTANT, HAVEN'T GONE NICE AT THE EDGES

On the day *Anyway, Anyhow, Anywhere* was released (May 21, 1965), The Who played on 'Ready Steady Go!'. Later the song was chosen as its signature tune. Every Friday night, nearly every kid in the UK would be waiting for the words, "It's seven minutes past six, the weekend starts here!" then listen to the Who's *Anyway* play over the pop art credits.
Centre Left: Offering opinions on a French radio show. Left: British TV's 'Thank Your Lucky Stars'.

THE WHO stand firmly for pop art. By their terms, pop art means how they behave and dress both on and off stage. On stage, an ordinary performance can end with guitarist Peter Townshend smashing a £150 guitar on an amplifier. Off stage, it means adopting pop art techniques into the design of their clothes . . . and spending what to most pop fans is a small fortune every week to maintain this image. The fantastic extremes to which the four musicians have gone to foster the image of violent emotional reaction, the closest ever pop music has got to a "happening", is expensive. Here, the Who count the cost . . .

THE price OF pop art
the Who count the cost

ITEM ONE: £100 A WEEK ON CLOTHES . . .

PETE TOWNSHEND   **KEITH MOON**   **ROGER DALTREY**   **JOHN ENTWISTLE**

RUE DAMRÉMONT

The Who
MAXIMUM R&B

all enquiries PAD. 5344

The Who at this time were looked upon as bold leaders of fashion, particularly during their pop art period. Although they spent a good deal of money on clothes, they also extemporised cheap ways to find a new look; often they would cut out shapes and tape them onto an ordinary pullover. (see right). Their passion for flag jackets once nearly badly backfired on a trip to Ireland, after they planned to wear an Eire tricolour flag jacket in Northern Ireland and a Union Jack, south of the border, they received a call from the IRA, threatening to kill them. They dropped the scheme.

This page, top right: Posing for a fashion promotion. Right: Music Parade Magazine – some of their original designs.

"One bank holiday we walked the length of Brighton Beach in the day, watching the first confrontations between huge gangs of mods and rockers. Some kid approached us on the beach with a shoe box full of about ten thousand pills. We swallowed some called horse pills which we were told were fantastic. They were one 1/- each. Within an hour we were 'blocked'." (the mod term for being high on amphetamines) – the author.
Top left & right; facing page, top right: Brighton.
Below left & facing page, bottom left: Paris.

We × × × Love ×
X
You
Love KeiTh (THE REST OF THE & Whô)
From × × × × × × ×
X
JiLL & Sylvie
STEVENAGE
× ×

Mod fashions became as important as music to the group and their audience. They would chronicle and reflect local fashions and bring new ideas they copied from kids on the dance floors. The audience for the Who was predominantly male, just in front of the stage rows of 16 to 19 year old mods stood and stared at the group. At the back of the hall a few kids would dance. Mods often danced alone or boys with boys and girls with girls. The girls had a pretty bad deal, often being ignored most of the time, while the guys checked each others clothes and shoes and so on. Some weeks girls were 'out', it was cissy to be seen with them.

Melody Maker
March 12, 1966 9d weekly

WHO IN RECORD RUMPUS

PETE TOWNSHEND: 'I don't really mind what they do.'

COLEMAN TRIO FOR 4 WEEKS

ORNETTE COLEMAN, voted Musician of The Year by Britain's jazz critics in the Melody Maker Poll last month, will appear...

THE Who, currently at 24 in the Pop Fifty with "Substitute" are involved in a record rumpus. They have TWO singles now in the shops at the same time, "Substitute" —two new singles now in the shops...

JUDGE PUTS TEN-DAY BAN ON WHO RECORD

A BAN was clamped on the Who's new hit this week. After... copies of the disc, Polydor Records was...

THE WHO 'Substitute' on reaction Here Now!

RECORD RETAILER & MUSIC INDUSTRY NEWS MARCH 31st, 1966

591001

March 1966: Following a legal wrangle over *Substitute,* the matter went to court. Talmy's counsel opened the case: "Your honour, this is the case of Shel Talmy versus the Who." The judge replied, "The Who?" "Yes, your honour", replied the barrister, "The Who." To which the judge replied, "Ah, yes, the World Health Organisation." Talmy admits, "That's when I knew I had my case won."

1966 SERA L'ANNÉE DES WHO

NEWSQUIZ

ON THE WHO

1. WHERE do The Who come from?
2. WHAT is the group's line-up?
3. WHO wrote their current hit?
4. WHAT was the boys' name originally?
5. WHO signed the group?
6. WHICH three have known each other since schooldays?
7. WHEN was the record released?
8. WHEN did it enter DISC WEEKLY's Top Thirty?
9. WHAT is the group's favourite musical sound?
10. WHICH member of The Who plays in a peculiar manner?
11. WHICH American artist did they appear with on their first television programme?

The answers

1. Shepherds Bush. West London. 2. Roger Daltrey (vocals), John Entwhistle (bass guitar), Keith Moon (drums), Pete Townshend (lead guitar). 3. Pete Townshend. 4. The High Numbers. 5. Shel Talmy — The Kinks' A & R man. 6. Roger, John and Pete. 7. January 15. 8. February 27 at No. 26. 9. The "Surfing" sound. 10. Pete — he crashes his guitar against his amplifiers to obtain a feed-back sound. 11. Brenda Lee —on BBC-2's "Beat Room."

Disc producer fights Who label switch

INDEPENDENT record producer ... the Who's ...

Who's record row still rages

THE pop world is evenly split over the promotion of the two Who singles presently on the market, "Substitute", ... Polydor's Reaction label ... this week's MM chart.

WHO COURT MOVE

Ban on Who record has been beaten

A BAN on the Who's latest record— containing their new hit "Substitute"— has been beaten. Last week a High Court ... action prevented Polydor ... selling the ...

Who disc row ends; LP and single on new label soon

Who original back on sale

THE Who's current hit "Substitute" ... on sale in its ...

NEXT WEEK———THE FIRST RELEASE FROM

THE WHO reaction

591001

'SUBSTITUTE'

WRITTEN BY **PETE TOWNSHEND**
Published By **FABULOUS MUSIC LTD. (ESSEX)**
A **NEW ACTION PRODUCTION**
MANAGED & DISTRIBUTED BY
POLYDOR RECORDS LIMITED

FOR **RSR** THE **ROBERT STIGWOOD ORGANISATION** LTD.

Who's club dates

April dates for the Who—at No. 14 in this week's charts are (this Sunday, 4th), Newbury Plaza, followed by Hendon Lakeside (5th), Hemel Hempstead Dacorum College (7th), Reading Olympia (8th), Altrincham Stamford Hall (9th), London Cavern Club (10th), Leicester Al Rondo (14th), Brighton Florida (17th) and Crawley Civic (18th).

The group then plays Hayes Botwell House (19th), Southampton Waterfront Club (22nd) Manchester Oasis (23rd), Boreham Wood Lynx Club (24th) Bromley Bromel (28th), and Trowbridge Town Hall (30th)

Top: the mod look has gone — note the eye make up and the new hairstyles; Roger's, created with the help of 'Dippidy-Doo' hair gel, soon earned him the title of 'Duchess'. Right: Recording the vocals for *Substitute*.

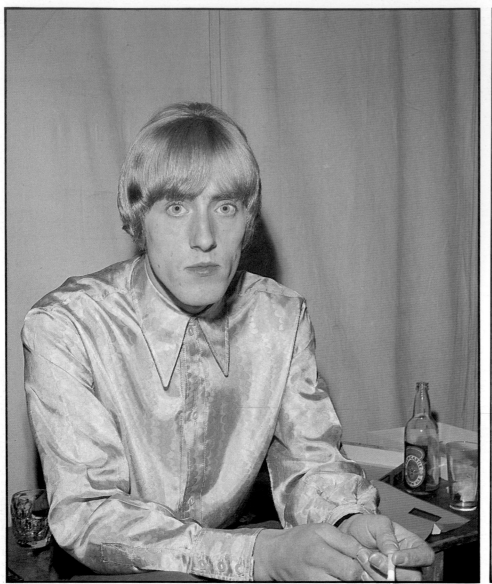

Released in 1966, I'm A Boy was the Who's first number one hit in Great Britain.
It was also Kit Lambert's first production. Only John and Keith played on the B side, *In the City*, as Pete and Roger missed the session.
Right: The band took space in the music papers to thank the illegal pirate radio stations for their heavy airplay.

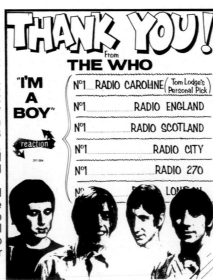

Lambert and Stamp realised that they had to invest heavily in their protegés, even if they had to secretly borrow and scrounge to raise the capital. As Chris Stamp said, "We wanted them to think they were 100% stars. They were going to the best shirtmakers to have all these shirts made, and the best tailors to get suits made. If Pete wanted another tape recorder to develop as a song writer he'd get it. We kept up our front, but there was all this other deadly mud in the background".

Sleeves.
Top - Bottom: Two US Decca sleeves, French Polydor, Reaction.
Left: In Amsterdam.

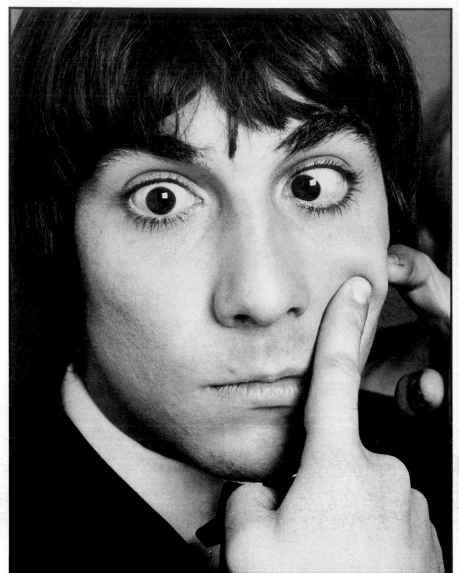

The band were very expensive to maintain. Roger told in an interview in NME how they'd wanted a new amp and gone out and got themselves up to their necks in hire purchase. "We spent £2,000 on equipment that day, but our stuff is the best in the world. We have to get new guitars or drums every month or so. They just get smashed up and it's costing us a fortune".

At the same time Keith described the mastermind Kit Lambert as "a sincere, intelligent nervo". "He'd never produce another group like us, because he'd never go though with what we've put him through again. We could never have achieved what we have with anyone else, no one else could have held us, and he possesses one important quality we all seem to lack — diplomacy".

Facing Page, far right: Kit Lambert always breakfasted at the Ritz in Piccadilly.
Top: Chris Stamp with Townshend.
This page, left: In December 1966, *A Quick One (Happy Jack in the USA)* was released. It was Lambert's first album production.

The WHO by Neil Smith

Another satirical cartoon of popland by NME's Neil who turns his attention to the WHO and their managers, KIT LAMBERT (top centre) and CHRIS STAMP.

73

Left: The ad for *Pictures of Lily* (released April 1967) caused some controversy. Top right: Keith's *Pictures of Lily* drum kit, designed by Premier — "Keith is our best customer". Centre right: Moon with a Premier rep. Below right: Destroying the said kit.

Who disc salute to Jagger and Richard

The WHO, minus bass guitarist John Entwistle, recording their Jagger-Richard tribute last Friday.

AT an emergency meeting last Thursday the Who decided to record immediately two Mick Jagger-Keith Richard compositions as a tribute to the two Rolling Stones. Co-manager Chris Stamp flew back from New York to join Kit Lambert in producing the session, which took place on Friday afternoon. Copies of the disc, which couples "The Last Time" and "Under My Thumb," are already in the shops. As group member John Entwistle was honeymooning on the Queen Elizabeth at the time, the bass guitar part was over-dubbed by Pete Townshend.

Above: The protest recording in June 1967 of *Under My Thumb* was the first of a planned series while Jagger and Richards were 'inside'.
Right: Roger poses for the infamous *Who Sell Out* album sleeve. The beans were cold and Daltrey caught mild pneumonia as a result. WMCA Radio in New York City banned the album.

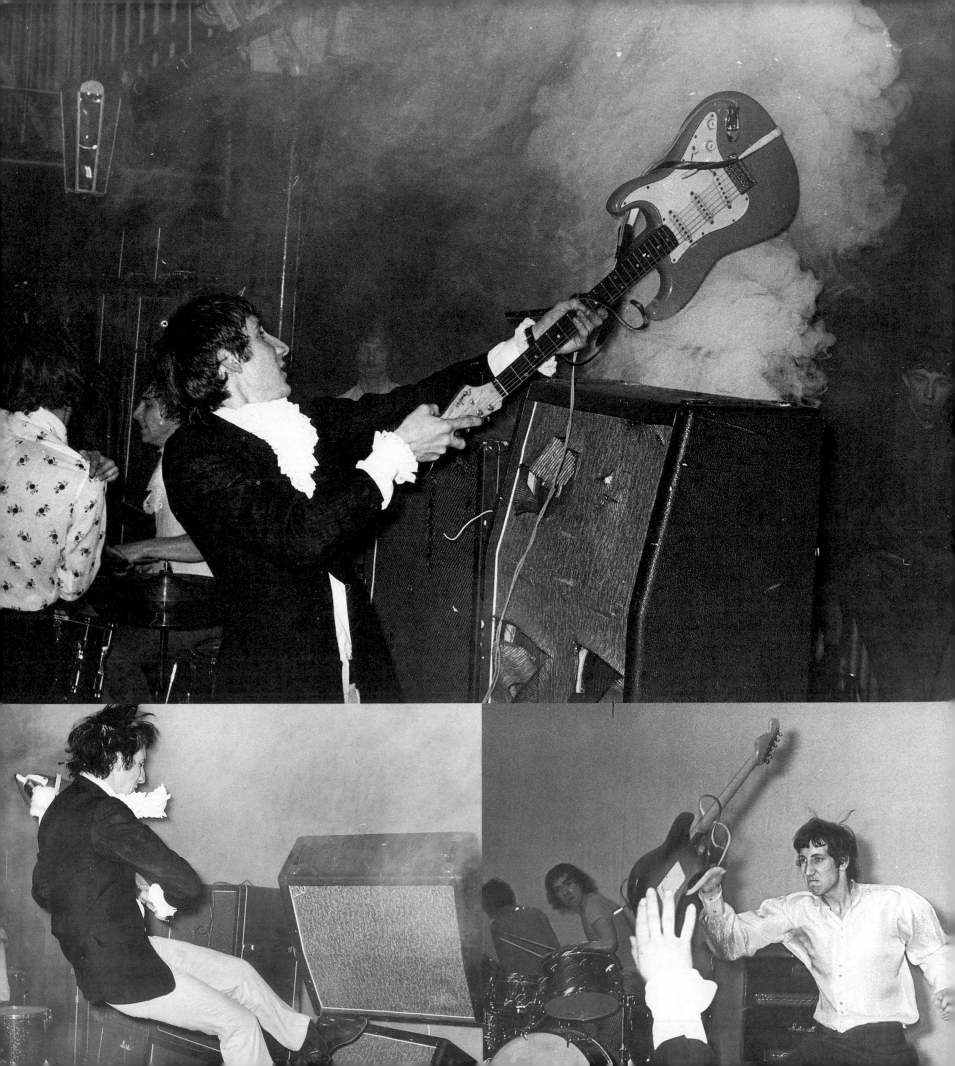

Smashing time costs WHO fortune!

WHO at National Jazz and Blues Festival, Windsor, last weekend—prior to wrecking their equipment!—(l to r) JOHN ENTWISTLE, KEITH MOON, ROGER DALTREY and PETE TOWNSHEND. NME picture by Napier Russell.

Who 'wreck' festival

IKE four raving dervishes the Who succeeded in wrecking most of their equipment as they closed Saturday night's performance the National Jazz and Blues Festival held last weekend at Windsor acecourse.

In a cloud of yellow smoke and tificial mist, Pete Townshend mashed his guitar to fragments by mming it into his amplifier. Keith oon

Herman

WHO CAUSE THOUSANDS OF POUNDS OF DAMAGE AT FESTIVAL

I became a hero— smashing guitars!

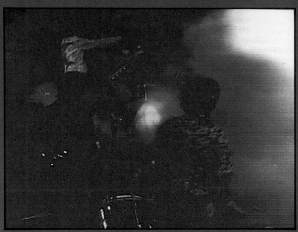

Pete Townshend

Keith Moon

Roger Daltrey

John Entwistle

The things I LOVE about KEITH:

1. He's a wonderful drinking companion. Generous.
2. He's never moody.
3. The way he grows old backwards.
4. His inbuilt, inborn showmanship.
5. His sheer stamina.

The things I HATE about KEITH:

1. His eating habits.
2. His taste in socks.
3. He's trying too hard to please!
4. Always late.
5. I'm always later!

The things I LOVE about ROGER:

1. His wonderful, devil-may-care disposition.
2. Lovely smile.
3. Always has lots of nice friends.
4. Generous.
5. And completely insecure.

The things I HATE about ROGER:

1. Always having to reassure him.
2. His guitar playing!
3. Lovely smile.
4. His Volvo (Swedish) car.
5. He's money-conscious!

The things I LOVE about JOHN:

1. His zany humour.
2. His absolute calmness.
3. His musical solidity.
4. His taste in magazines.
5. His understanding, guiding hand for Keith.

The things I HATE about JOHN:

1. Occasional thoughtlessness.
2. He's always calm when I'm panicking.
3. His red shoes.
4. The Sound Of Music!
5. He has too many suit cases.

The things I LOVE about JOHN:

1. His kidneys!
2. His songs.
3. The way he plays cards.
4. He goes along with my insane ideas and ventures.
5. He shares my taste in horror movies and comics.

The things I HATE about JOHN:

1. His tendency to talk your ears off!
2. He won't eat the wild dishes I cook up.
3. He always manages to save money. (I can't!)
4. His funny hair that goes in all directions.
5. He snores.

The things I LOVE about ROGER:

1. His cooking.
2. His honesty.
3. His openness.
4. His legs.
5. He avoids me when he swings his microphone!

The things I HATE about ROGER:

1. His Dippidy-Doo.
2. He's too concerned about his cars.
3. His mood when he wakes up in the morning.
4. Sometimes he swings that microphone too close!
5. He never has money when I try to borrow some.

The things I LOVE about PETE:

1. His sense of humour.
2. His songs.
3. The way he smashes his guitar. (It's Art!)
4. His sense of responsibility.
5. His patience with my insane antics.

The things I HATE about PETE:

1. Something he calls 'Creative Temperment.'
2. His driving.
3. He won't come out to 'loon about' the clubs all night.
4. Sometimes, he takes things too seriously.
5. He limits the amount of explosives I can handle!

The things I LOVE about KEITH:

1. His ability to enjoy life at all times.
2. His wild drumming and energy.
3. His complete lack of inhibitions.
4. He is never at a loss for witty comments.
5. He can turn on that innocent look when in trouble.

The things I HATE about KEITH:

1. His comments about my Dippidy Doo!
2. The way he treats the Bentley owned by him and John.
3. He is the world's most disorganized person with clothes.
4. He eats outrageous combinations of foods at one sitting.
5. He blares his record player at all hours of the night!

The things I LOVE about JOHN:

1. His ability to always stay cool about things.
2. He acts as moderator and never takes sides on arguments.
3. He spends more time trying to control his hair than I do!
4. He's writing some very good songs lately.
5. He doesn't groan too loudly at my bad jokes.

The things I HATE about JOHN:

1. When I'm upset about something, he stays unruffled!
2. His lack of attention to the Bentley (see Keith!).
3. He sometimes only growls (literally).
4. The sight of him in the morning (or of anyone!).
5. He won't admit that he fusses with his hair more than I do!

The things I LOVE about PETE:

1. His incredible talent.
2. He is totally unselfish when it comes to work.
3. He never holds grudges against anyone.
4. He can be the funniest person in the world.
5. He has an interest and knowledge in so many fields.

The things I HATE about PETE:

1. He does take things almost too seriously at times.
2. Can't get a word in edgewise when he's involved!
3. He has a knack of winning arguments—wish I did!
4. I can't think of anything else to hate about Pete.
5. I'll think of something else to hate tomorrow!

The things I LOVE about KEITH:

1. He's my best friend.
2. When I'm in a bad mood, he cheers me up.
3. We have the same sense of humour—sick!
4. His drum playing.
5. His wild ideas which keep life from being boring.

The things I HATE about KEITH:

1. He always buys the same clothes I do.
2. When I'm really in a bad mood, he makes it worse!
3. Sometimes, he destroys my possessions.
4. He always wants to stay up when I sleep.
5. His taste in food and drink.

The things I LOVE about ROGER:

1. His enthusiasm.
2. His beautiful, blond hair.
3. His generosity.
4. His singing.
5. Usually, his good nature.

The things I HATE about ROGER:

1. His ability to bring things up at the wrong time.
2. His fussiness about his hair.
3. Dippidy-Doo, too!
4. His interest in (ugh!) antiques.
5. His jangling bells and beads.

The things I LOVE about PETE:

1. His sense of humour.
2. His musical brainwaves.
3. The encouragement he gave me for songwriting.
4. His ability to talk to journalists all the time.
5. His neatness and organization.

The things I HATE about PETE:

1. His temper (that only lasts 5 minutes).
2. When he makes a mistake while we're playing MY songs.
3. His drive for perfection can be maddening.
4. His depression when things don't go well.
5. He eats without gaining weight! I gain.

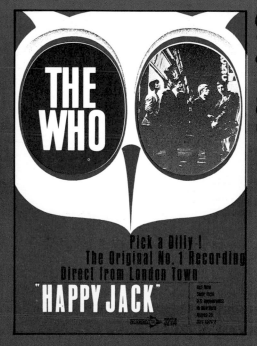

USA, 1967: Facing page sequence: On 'The Smothers Brothers Show' the whole of America saw the band create havoc, when Keith Moon secretly added extra flash powder to the special effects. The explosion at the end of *My Generation* was enormous. Pete temporarily lost his hearing and singed his hair, a fragment of flying cymbal embedded itself in Keith's leg, and show guest Bette Davis fainted into Mickey Rooney's arms.

They also undertook an exhausting five sets a day stint for the 'Murray the K' show. Stamp told them to smash up their equipment each time, and not worry about the cost, but at the same time he was rushing around to every musical supplier in New York, signing the band away for gear. Pete said, "We really worked the destruction bit down to a fine art in our spot. I developed a great thing where I hit myself on the head with my guitar and made me see stars, and I thought, 'that's nice'. At one time I noticed Keith throwing his big bass drum at me with the spikes protruding, and Roger hurling the stand mike at me from another direction. I made myself very thin, and the mike shattered to pieces in front of me, while the spike from the drum ripped my shirt down the back". Total destruction from the shows was: 22 mikes, five guitars, four speaker cabinets and a 16-piece drum kit.

Above right: The nearest the Who got to psychedelia.
Left: *Happy Jack,* the first US hit.

83

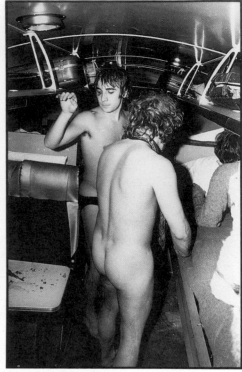

USA, 1967. At Monterey Eric Burdon came on to announce the Who: "I promise you, this group will destroy you in more ways than one".

Above centre: In an old plane, the package the Who, Herman's Hermits and the Blues Magoos toured for seven weeks. The rather 'straight' audience that the better known Herman attracted were simply unprepared for the Who's mayhem.

Right: On his birthday, Keith told the world that he was twenty-one, to get round the problem of underage drinking. He wasn't; he was twenty. The party Decca threw for him at the Holiday Inn in Flint Michigan resulted in wrecked cars, a broken tooth for Keith and a Holiday Inn life ban.

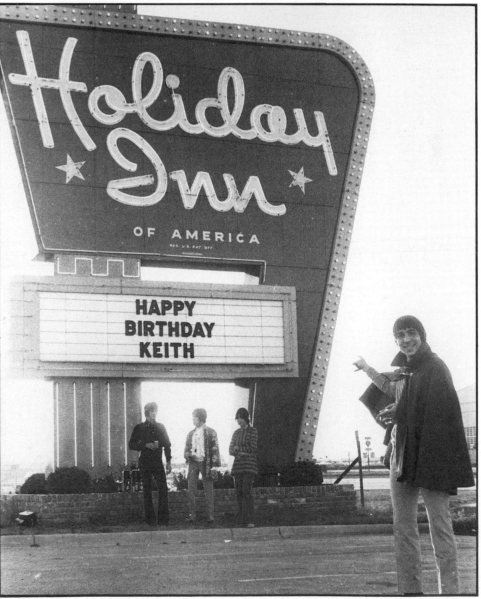

84

HERMANS
HERMITS
CONCERT

WED., AUG. 23, 8 P.M.

Starring

★ HERMANS
HERMITS

★ BLUES MAGOOS
★ THE WHO

Atwood Stadium

FLINT. MICH.

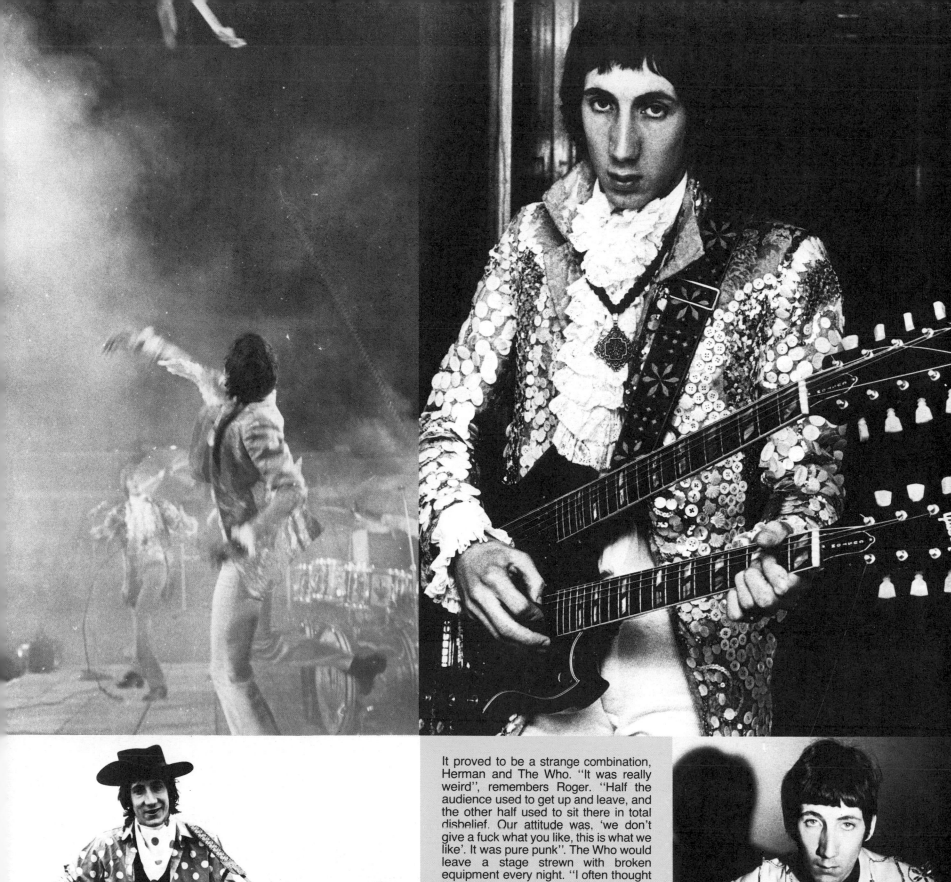

It proved to be a strange combination, Herman and The Who. "It was really weird", remembers Roger. "Half the audience used to get up and leave, and the other half used to sit there in total disbelief. Our attitude was, 'we don't give a fuck what you like, this is what we like'. It was pure punk". The Who would leave a stage strewn with broken equipment every night. "I often thought I'd hate to have to walk out there like Noone did, after all that damage and have to sing. Invariably there would be a bad sulphur smell and a lot of smoke about. He'd come on in his spotlessly clean white shirt and tie and do his sing song routine".

Right: Pete's flashing light jacket, specially made for the 'Murray The K' show. Eventually, it blew up.

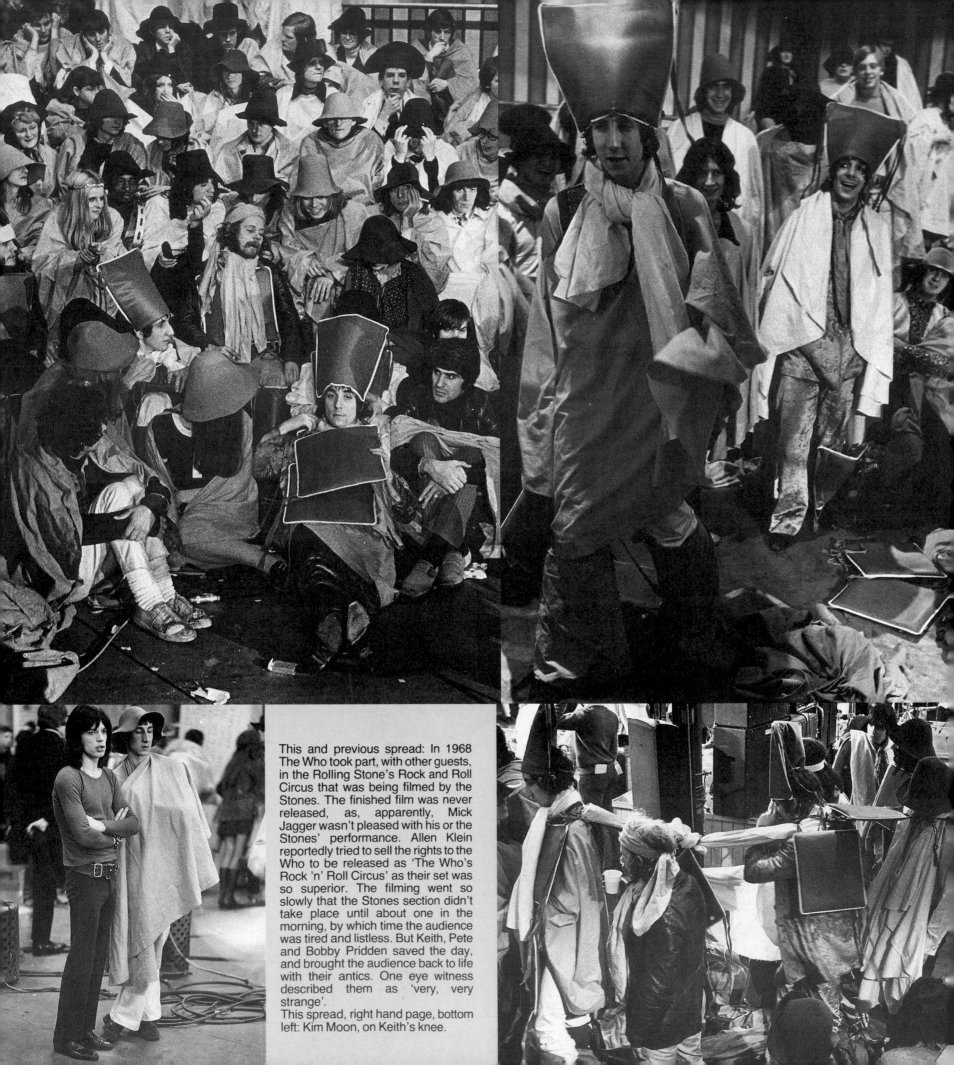

This and previous spread: In 1968 The Who took part, with other guests, in the Rolling Stone's Rock and Roll Circus that was being filmed by the Stones. The finished film was never released, as, apparently, Mick Jagger wasn't pleased with his or the Stones' performance. Allen Klein reportedly tried to sell the rights to the Who to be released as 'The Who's Rock 'n' Roll Circus' as their set was so superior. The filming went so slowly that the Stones section didn't take place until about one in the morning, by which time the audience was tired and listless. But Keith, Pete and Bobby Pridden saved the day, and brought the audience back to life with their antics. One eye witness described them as 'very, very strange'.

This spread, right hand page, bottom left: Kim Moon, on Keith's knee.

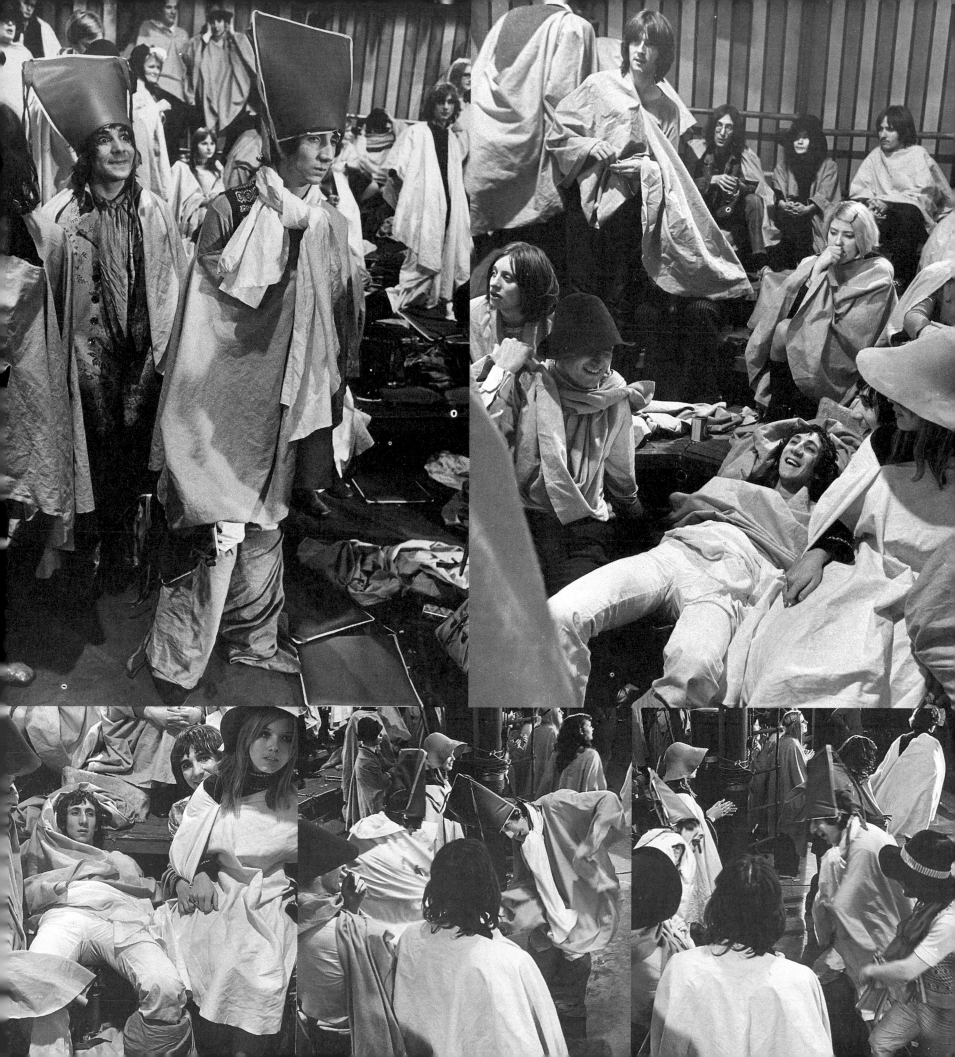

Empire Theatre - Liverpool
ONE NIGHT ONLY — TWO PERFORMANCES
Wednesday, 20th November at 6.15 and 8.35 p.m.

THE WHO

THE CRAZY WORLD OF ARTHUR BROWN

SPECIAL GUEST STARS

THE SMALL FACES

JOE COCKER AND THE GREASEBAND

THE MINDBENDERS

TICKETS: 15/-   12/6   10/6   7/6

Above: The Who did a short tour at the end of 1968. On the very last show of the tour, at the Empire Theatre in Liverpool, everybody on the tour came onstage to join in a twenty-minute version of *Magic Bus.* Keith Moon and Kenney Jones played together on the same drum kit.
Left: Keith with Joe Cocker, backstage at the Marquee.
Below: The Lyceum soon after the release of *Magic Bus.* Next to Pete is his wife, Karen.
Below right: The Lyceum again.

1968: *I Can See For Miles, Dogs* and *Magic Bus* had sold disappointingly in Britain, and the band desperately needed renewed chart success. They were forced into the studio to get what material they had of *Tommy* recorded, long before its final form was properly worked out: Chris Stamp remembers, "We had to go in and start, because we *had* to have records. At that time the Who were falling apart. We weren't going anywhere... we'd spent all the advances from record companies, and we had to pull this one off, to get anywhere near to making big money". It was, "one huge, once-and-for-all gamble".

Left: Promoting *Magic Bus* in Oxford Street, replete with models, clowns and animals.
Above: The much criticised US compilation album.
Below centre & right: In the UK they released *Dogs,* in the USA, *Call Me Lightning*.

THE WHO: 'DOGS' c/w 'CALL ME LIGHTNING' 604023

Look what they're saying about the new single by
THE WHO
"CALL ME LIGHTNING"

If you don't understand, don't worry... because You'll understand 'CALL ME LIGHTNING' is an immediate stone smash

DECCA

95

1969-1975

'Tommy'/Pop is out/New prestige/Huge tours/Management rifts/'Tommy' film

It is interesting to look back at the Who's career up to this point a few months before the release of *Tommy*. In England they had issued ten major singles plus three released by Decca from the first LP. One as the High Numbers, one to promote the cause of the Stones' drugs bust court case and the *Ready Steady Who* EP. Of the ten major singles all but the last three were chart successes. Their three albums all received good critical reviews. Each of the last two introducing some major new album pop concept. The band had toured extensively and in that respect were without doubt the hardest working group in England. However, the energy and time put into touring had been at the expense of their record output.

Their act had been incredibly expensive to maintain. The equipment bills and the lavish style of business that Kit carried on. Despite getting two huge advances when they renegotiated their contracts in '66, they were now back in debt. The group had somehow managed to stay together despite constant rows and fist fights, dissentions and periodic splits. Working on the *Tommy* album, which had taken up most of the latter half of 1968, they had found a new harmony between themselves and a spirit of co-operation had grown up in place of the previous outright contempt and competition.

They were all united in their belief in their new Rock Opera. This was the big gamble. If this didn't pay off then the future looked bleak and once again they were on the verge of breaking up.

In March of that year they released a single from the forthcoming album, *Pinball Wizard*. They announced that the forthcoming album, 'The Deaf, Dumb and Blind Boy' would now be called *Tommy* and released in a couple of months.

It was a period of intense activity for Pete. Firstly, *Tommy* was due to be premiered. Secondly, he was about to release the first single he'd produced by the group Thunderclap Newman which was made up of Pete's musical idol from art school days Andy Newman, Speedy Keene, and little Jimmy McCullough, an amazing Scottish 15-year-old guitarist. Kit Lambert wanted to call the group, 'My Favourite Freaks', but settled on Thunderclap Newman. Their single, *Something in the Air*, written by Speedy Keene became a hit on both sides of the Atlantic, a No. 1 in the UK. And thirdly, he became a father as his wife Karen, gave birth to a baby girl, whom they named Emma.

Pete told Richard Green of NME about the forthcoming album. "It's some of the best stuff I've ever written, equal to *My Generation*." He was very confident about the album. "I never set out to write anything as good as that, but it just happened. The LP can be taken as one of three things – a spiritual symbol, the life of a pop star, or a rock and roll album."

When *Tommy* was completed Roger explained, "The last six months – it's been like the rebirth of the Who. We've calmed down a lot. Before that all our energy had gone in trying to keep the group from splitting up. We still have our differences but we're much more harmonious."

Keith's drumming was brilliant. "I'm the best Keith Moon type drummer in the world."

Pete referred to the major change that had happened to the Who when he said, " . . . I don't call our music 'pop' any more" and went on to say that the best scene in England for the Who at that time were the colleges where the audiences seriously listen to music.

The first time *Tommy* was played to an audience was when they booked Ronnie Scott's jazz club in Soho for a

press reception to launch the album. They played the whole thing straight through at incredible volume to the amazed journalists. Pete first of all introduced the work and gave a small explanation of the story, "It's about a boy who is born normal, just like you and me. He is later raped by his uncle and gets turned on to LSD . . . " He said to applause that it was not sick "contrary to what one hears on Aunty BBC." This was a reference to BBC Radio's Tony Blackburn who described *Pinball Wizard* as sick. Pete's reply to a burst of

applause was, "I think Aunty is the sickest thing in this country." Chris Welch of Melody Maker said that twenty hours after the event his ears were still singing. He talked of the Who having calmed down. "Even if they have . . . they can still scare you. There were moments during *Tommy* when I had to clutch the table for support. I felt my stomach contracting and my head spinning, but we wanted more." There were two basic reactions. Many papers like the NME agreed with Auntie BBC and thought it was 'sick'. "Pretentiousness is too strong a word; maybe over-ambitious is the right term, but sick certainly does apply." The other reaction was summed up by the headline in Disc. WHO'S TOMMY – A MASTERPIECE. Disc said that it was "Probably the first significant attempt to use pop as a truly dramatic medium."

The biggest danger facing something as ambitious and serious as *Tommy* was that it would be seen at the very least as self-conscious. The Daily Mirror's pop columnist Don Short had called it 'pretentious'. In response to this, Pete surprisingly laughed and said, "He's dead bloody right, it is."

The album was recorded at IBC on eight-track and a lot of it today sounds a bit crude. Pete attempted with *Tommy* to bridge the gap between their stage act and their records. However, listening to the *Tommy* album is one thing, seeing the Who perform it live is a whole new ball game. I think that

the most exhilarating pop experience I've ever been exposed to was seeing the Who perform *Tommy* at the Isle of Wight festival.

The Who had now assembled the biggest and most perfected sound set-up ever and had developed a top road crew to operate it. It was pure power that assaulted you from that huge bank of speakers. (It was the first time I'd ever seen warnings about keeping 15' away from the speakers.) At the IOW Festival they launched into practically the whole of *Tommy*. No stopping for rests, just one number straight after the next. The whole opera must have taken over an hour. These were the same vicious, screwed up, spitting little mods that had done £18/12/6d damage to the Railway Hotel ceiling. Professionalism was the word that kept coming into my mind. Roger had acquired that magnificent male sexual image with his mane of curly hair and his flying fringed jacket. His skill at swinging mikes, hurling them 20 to 30 feet in the air and catching them just in time to sing the next verse was outstanding. *Tommy* had made Roger the frontman of the group. Keith was a show in himself, all the time keeping up a one-man spectacle hurling drumsticks in the air and catching them and pulling the most incredible faces. John's bass was fuller and faster than most group's lead, he kept the whole show together musically and visually. As John said, "If I didn't keep still and anchor the whole thing down, they'd all fly off into the air." Pete was a powerhouse to listen and watch. Jumping, leaping, twisting, swerving, swinging his arm like a rotor, punishing his guitar and forcing everything he could out of it. Pete said of that Isle of Wight show, " . . . the Who were totally and completely in control."

They'd just returned from an American tour where they started their shows with early singles and the mini-opera, then did *Tommy* from start to finish and ended with *My Generation* and "a great long drawn out boogie that included *Magic Bus*. The kids used to like the heavy metal but they didn't know quite what to make of *Tommy* and so people just used to sit very quietly and they would clap between numbers . . . Now halfway through a gig in Chicago all of a sudden everybody realized that something was working – I don't know quite what it was, but everybody all at the same time just stood up and stayed standing up. From that moment on they would stand up at the same point . . . It was the first time we'd created a theatrical device that worked every time . . . We really started to explore its potential and by the time we got round to that Isle of Wight we knew what worked and what you skipped over quickly. It was a great concert for us because we felt so in control of the situation. We were able to just come in, do it and not need to know anything about what was going on . . . we knew we were on to a good thing and it gave us such strength and confidence." Thus Townshend summed it up. One thing I didn't know at that time was that Keith had broken his foot in an accident at his home a week earlier. The only way he was able to play at the IOW was by having painkilling injections in both legs just before they went on.

Melody Maker called their performance, "An hour of electric rock at its most electrifying," claiming that Pete played "one of the best guitar solos in Who history on *Young Man Blues*." *Tommy* finally broke in the States for the Who. The reaction to it was incredibly positive. There was little talk of it being 'sick' although some record stores in New York refused to stock it. The group had left for an eight-week tour of the States shortly after the Ronnie Scott's reception taking in Boston, Detroit, Philadelphia, Pittsburgh, Chicago, Colombus Ohio, Syracuse, Washington

DC, Hartford, St. Louis and Cleveland. In the first two weeks of sales, *Tommy* sold over 100,000 copies in the States.

Shortly before the Isle of Wight, they had flown back to the States for Woodstock. They hated Woodstock. Roger told the New Yorker, "That was the worst gig we ever played. We waited in a field of mud for fourteen hours, sitting on some boards, doing nothing, and doing nothing is the most exhausting thing in the world. As a result we gave one of the worst shows we've ever done." Pete said, "From a human point of view it was great; three people died and two people were born and half a million people managed to get on together, but musically it was awful. Pete took Karen and his young baby daughter to Woodstock and couldn't cope with all the chaos and confusion. He says in Jonathon Cott's 'Beyond Deaf Dumb and Blind' "I immediately got into an incredible state and rejected everyone . . . And I was telling really nice people like Ritchie Havens to fuck off and things like that." He was spiked with acid and after the sixteen-hour wait to play wasn't particularly in tune with the peace and love vibes of the event. He had to clear the stage of photographers before they could play and kicked Abbie Hoffman off the front of the stage when he tried to make a political speech. . . . "he must have felt it for a couple of months after." The Who's act was saved by the sun. "*Tommy* wasn't getting to anyone . . . by this time I was just about awake, we were just listening to the music when all of a sudden, bang! The fucking sun comes up! It was just incredible. I really felt we didn't deserve it, in a way. We put out such bad vibes . . . and as we finished it was daytime. We walked off, got in the car, and went back to the hotel. It was fucking fantastic."

The Who's performance at the Fillmore West in June had been described as 'perhaps, the performance of their life'. They did an unprecedented five days at the Fillmore East in October. They returned to the States for a second tour later in the year and became the first group to play Anaheim stadium in California.

Opera News reported a show at the Fillmore East saying, "As with medieval Indian musicians their bodies expressed the sound of the music and, to a certain degree their libretto . . . though the tonal score never became all beat or noise, it failed to detail the emotions found in the libretto and lacked the musical originality of, say, the Beatles . . . unfortunately all my feelings on *Tommy* were overshadowed by its loudness. Three times as loud as 'Hair', ten times as loud as the fff in the 'Dies Irae' of the Verdi Requiem, *Tommy* passes the pain threshold. The Who may soon be asking 'What?'."

Leonard Bernstein praised *Tommy* and Life Magazine said, "Now Peter Townshend of the Who, British rock's toughest and most innovative group, has made the dream a reality with *Tommy*, a full length pop opera that for sheer power, invention and brilliance of performance outstrips anything that has ever come out of a rock recording studio." The New Yorker (Ellen Willis) said, "*Tommy* works both as a long coherent piece and as a collection of songs. Although rock opera is a dangerously pretentious concept, the album is neither arty nor boring, because each cut – except for one rather monotonous instrumental – is a short, self-contained, excellent pop song. *Pinball Wizard* is even more than excellent – it's one of the great rock songs of the decade."

At the time of the release, what was described as radio history was being made in the States with DJ's playing the whole album non-stop.

Tommy had not only bought the Who great prestige and finally the recognition that had eluded them throughout the sixties, it had given them unprecedented confidence, which was reflected in their stage playing. The feeling about the Who's live shows among critics and audiences alike was summed up after the group's September performance at the Fairfield Hall, Croydon, a hall noted for its outstanding acoustics. The show was the first time in England that the Who had played without a support group. They played for almost two and a half hours and included three-quarters of *Tommy*. The Melody Maker said, "Surely the Who are now the group against which all the others are to be judged" and their Alan Lewis described their performance as "The best live show I've ever seen by a group."

Performing *Tommy* on stage had given Roger a much needed major role on stage, he became the frontman, the centre of attraction, the focus of the stage act at last. He was Tommy. He created the archetypal macho rock singer, much

copied in the Seventies. Roger had an easily identifiable and very sexual image. Hi Fi magazine in the US wrote "Roger Daltrey, once the weakest link in the quartet, petulant off stage and on, and a mediocre vocalist to boot, has matured tremendously as a singer; his stage personality is now the equal of the Doors' Jim Morrison – controlled, angry, and most aggressively sexual." The Who spent the rest of the year performing *Tommy* either in its entirety or a good three-quarters of it all over the States.

John had said that he'd written *Cousin Kevin* to be sung very high so that Roger would have trouble singing it. *Cousin Kevin* is one of the better numbers from the work, however, it was dropped because it was so high to sing.

Pete was producing Thunderclap and looking for a follow up to their No. 1 single, *Something in the Air*. Roger was producing a group called Bent Frame. At the end of the year they announced that they would be playing at the home of British opera and ballet, the London Coliseum. Tickets for the show sold out in under an hour when they went on sale. The show was a two-hour spectacular similar to the highly successful Fairfield Hall show. It was a tremendous event as was their show at Bristol Hippodrome, where two smoke bombs were thrown on to the stage, one of them land-

ing in front of John Entwistle . . . As a spotlight swung up to illuminate the box from where it came, Roger stormed off stage. The culprit dropped his trousers and exposed his rear to the audience. Pete's wit saved the situation. "Did you see those pimples?" He said and they hurled themselves into *My Generation*. The smoke had affected Roger's throat, however, and Pete stopped the song before the end.

Kit Lambert and Chris Stamp had originally planned a glittering launch for *Tommy*. They wanted to premiere it in New York and Moscow at the leading opera houses. Chris Stamp attended dinners at the Russian Embassy to try to persuade them. "We wanted the headline, ROCK BREAKS THE IRON CURTAIN. They would play in Moscow then fly to the Metropolitan in New York or Sadlers Wells in London. "We spent months trying to get the Met. We were eventually offered Leningrad, we couldn't get Moscow, but by then it was too late." Nathan Weiss who had been the Beatles' American lawyer was negotiating for the Met. At first the director Rudolph Bing wasn't too keen on the idea, or as the New York Post put it, Bing turned a deaf ear to the whole project. But Weiss persisted and persuaded him to listen to a copy of the album which apparently impressed him.

Meanwhile *Tommy* had been performed at the London Coliseum to overwhelming acclaim. A tour of the major

European opera houses followed. Resistance to rock in these hallowed precincts was overcome by Kit Lambert pointing out that opera was originally for the people and only recently were opera houses taken over by the high-brow elite. They were usually subsidised by government arts councils and he argued "Why shouldn't the kids hear their kind of twentieth-century opera in these fabulous venues." Kit and Chris saw the rock opera as an extension of their own particular partnership. Kit was educated at an exclusive fee-paying public school. Chris was very working-class and from a state school in London's East End. His father was a docker. "We were like east and west" said Chris. "The two extremes and rock opera was like the two extremes rock and opera. The natural thing was to get an opera house tour and all the jive round it."

The European tour was very prestigious. They played at the Champs Elysees Theatre in Paris, the Royal Theatre of Copenhagen, the Cologne Opera House, the Hamburg State Opera House, the Berlin Opera House and the Amsterdam Concertgebouw. The three German dates were in aid of the Save the Children Fund and they were given a high ranking reception in their honour by President Heinemann and Chancellor Brandt of West Germany.

Tommy live – "I cannot exaggerate perfection"

A couple of months later they flew to New York to begin a tour that was to stagger audiences in nine cities. The tour began with two shows at the Metropolitan Opera House. After agreeing to pay the Met union double rates because they were bringing in their own equipment and taking out a huge insurance indemnity policy to cover crowd rowdiness, the shows went ahead, sandwiched on a Sunday between Aida and Turandot, the Met's summer productions. Tickets had sold out in an hour and there were still hundreds waiting outside in case there were cancellations. The two shows each held 4,000 spectators. It must have been the first time that the Metropolitan Opera House had the smell of pot smoke drifting around its gold chandeliers. After the Who had finished the Tommy section of the show the applause was deafening and prolonged. "We gotta carry on before you wear yourselves out" said Pete, and launched into *Summertime Blues* and *Shakin' all Over*. At the end he bashed his guitar on the stage and threw it into the audience. The standing ovation lasted 11 minutes for the first show and 14 minutes for the second. Rudolph Bing commented that he'd seen nothing like it since before the war in the days of grand opera.

At the beginning some kids kept shouting 'Louder, louder'. "It gets louder later" said Pete. He'd introduced it in these auspicious surroundings as 'Thomas, the rock opera'. Amid the thunderous applause after the first show just as they were going back out for the encore he turned to Kit Lambert and said "You really book us on some bum gigs man!" Pete returned at the end of the second house to explain that after two, two-hour shows in one night they were too tired to do an encore. He lost his temper, which though justified was a pity when some of the crowd began booing. He told them where to get off in very unoperatic terms and threw the mike into the audience. After the show, top Decca executives presented Pete, Roger, John and Keith with an award for *Tommy* album sales of 5 million dollars. An unusually bizarre sight backstage were the huge equipment crates stencilled with the WHO amid boxes of scenery labelled 'Traviata', 'Lucia' and 'Aida' and huge forests and cathedral domes and painted scenery.

There wasn't any audience trouble. Although T-shirts and jeans outnumbered dinner jackets by ten to one, the young crowd were well behaved. One usher said afterwards "The kids are much more polite than their parents." Press reaction was mostly favourable if not ecstatic. The New York Times ended its article on the show thus: "Awake, the forces of the future are no longer standing at the gates. They are inside."

The show at the Met was supposed to have been the last time that the Who played *Tommy*. They had been playing it in its entirety or thereabouts for the past year and were tired of it. However there was no way that they would be allowed not to continue. The Chicago Daily News commenting on the decision to drop the whole of *Tommy* from the act said " . . . It seemed to signal the end of an era. The Who had finally made it and could now behave like other giants and relax." However, when Pete announced at the Chicago show "Something we've done 40 or more times and swore never to perform on the stage again" there was such a great roar of anticipation and delight from the audience, it could only be quieted down by Keith standing up and shouting into the mike "It's a bloody opera! So sit down and shuddup!" The Chicago Tribune commented "I'll bet there wasn't a person in the Auditorium Theatre last night who won't tell you that this was probably the best concert Chicago has ever had. Even those that have seen Janis and Cocker and BS & T. In *Tommy* alone there were five, six, seven maybe eight standing ovations."

As they moved methodically across the country, the Who left a wake of mind-blown, disbelieving Who converts. In San Diego, San Francisco, Los Angeles (where they were the first group ever to play the Anaheim stadium to a 30,000 crowd), Dallas, Philadelphia, Cincinnatti, Cleveland, Chicago and Detroit, the press reviews were almost competing with themselves for superlatives to describe the Who live. The San Francisco Examiner: "They had just heard the finest two hour concert of contemporary music of their lives. They knew it. The Who knew it . . . Exaggeration? I cannot exaggerate perfection." The Maryland Democrat went even further: " . . . UNBELIEVABLE! REMARKABLE! OUTSTANDING! . . . or anything else you want to call better than the best was the Who concert at the Spectrum Philadelphia.' The San Francisco Chronicle eulogised, " . . . The Who show at Berkely Community Theatre was absolutely staggering in its emotional and musical power . . . writing about their music is something of an exercise in futility. It need not be explained to those who were there, it cannot be explained to those that were not. If a single word can sum it up, that word is 'shattering'."

The group were deliberately trying not to play huge stadium venues. Roger said the maximum for an audience would be 10,000 sometimes 15,000. Ralph Gleason of the SF Examiner said that other bands were going to have to do what the Who were doing, in this case at the Berkely Community Theatre, and " . . . find ways to play in smaller halls to avoid the audience-performer alienation of the Cow Palace type of things."

Woodstock, the Met shows and the subsequent tour were creating new interest in *Tommy*. Almost a year after it was released Chris Stamp and Kit Lambert approached Decca. Stamp recalls telling them "Fucking re-release it and do a big campaign on it." They did and it sold even better than when it had first been released. It went up to No. 4 in Billboard and stayed in the chart for about another year. That summer *Live at Leeds* also shot up the chart to get to No. 3 in the UK and No. 4 in the US. During the tour Pete was talking to Pete Rudge, their US tour manager, about the success of *Live at Leeds*. As both were from Britain they easily understood Pete's fairly common term "I heard it was going a bomb in New York" meaning it's going extremely well. However, they happened to be sitting on an Eastern Airlines plane waiting to take off from the runway at Memphis International Airport at the time of their conversation and a passing stewardess thought they were talking about a bomb on the plane. She told the pilot who radioed the control tower and the plane had to taxi to a secluded part of the airport where the 69 passengers were all taken off and searched along with all the luggage by police. An hour and 20 minutes later the plane left but Pete and Co were still being questioned by police and FBI representatives.

When they finally arrived at their destination, Atlanta, they found that their rooms booked at the hotel had been let to some Eastern Star ladies there for a convention. Further, the equipment truck with their 4-ton PA was stuck miles away. The very exhausted Who didn't start the concert at Memorial Auditorium until after midnight. However practically the whole 6,000 audience had stayed and waited.

Undoubtedly it was *Tommy* that achieved the US breakthrough for the Who. However the release of *Live At Leeds* was a masterstroke. Pete later said that as successful as *Tommy* was, it wasn't really the Who. *Live At Leeds* restored the balance. The Who weren't only a very intelligent and serious band, they also had 'balls'.

It seemed obvious to release a live album to follow up *Tommy* and the Who had never had one. They had recorded

every show from their American tour of autumn '69. "We thought that would be where we would get the best material" said Pete. "When we got back we had 80 hours of tape. I said "Fuck that. I'm not going to sit through 80 hours of live stuff, let's face it you'd get brainwashed." So we just scrapped the lot. We put it all on the bonfire to stop bootlegging. They booked the Pye records mobile which recorded them playing at Hull and Leeds Universities. The Who were the original heavy loud rock group. Heavy metal hadn't become a style of its own in the sixties. Anyway anyone who only heard the Who on record would have no conception of their live sound. *Leeds* became a major influence on all heavy metal bands of the seventies and eighties.

Pete talked about "trying to sophisticate our sound a little, make it a little less ear-rending . . . We haven't got any louder but our PA has got bigger. It's now 1500 watts and it just chucks it all out. That is what's deafening people. One of our troubles is Moon – he's so deafening. If we do a two and a half-hour show he just starts playing like a machine. I'm sure he puts out more watts than the rest of us put together. The post-*Tommy* Who were now superstars. *Tommy* had made them all very rich and bought them world-wide fame,

but it had also bought some unexpected problems. In the States, many people were aware of *Tommy*, but not of anything else by the group; they thought the group was named Tommy. They also had to try to release further albums in the wake of *Tommy's* monstrous success. Usually when an artist had an enormously successful album it meant the end of the rest of his career, as everything else paled into insignificance. Pete was determined that the Who would overcome this inbalance. "It was highly overrated, because it was rated where it shouldn't have been and it attempted to tell a story in rock music. I enjoyed making it very, very much. We were going down the drain – we needed challenging after putting out corny singles like *Dogs* and *Magic Bus*. Making *Tommy* really united the group and that was the good thing about it. The problem is that has elevated the Who to heights they haven't attained."

Pete explained how he saw their dilemma to the NME (Nick Logan) "*Tommy* was definitely a result of image building. I mean, I'd spent two years writing the thing but it was still more an image idea than a musical idea. And it was the whole thing of it being taken up in the States as a musical

masterpiece that threw us. From selling 1500 copies of *Who Sell Out*, right, we were suddenly selling 20 million, or whatever it was, of *Tommy*. It was ridiculous from the sublime. It had to have repercussions. Christ almighty, we thought, here we are being told we are musical geniuses and all we are is a bunch of scumbags. I mean we've always been respected as a group, right, but we've never among ourselves had the feeling of being a good musical band. We've always been a gimmicky band."

Pete was also completely fascinated by Meher Baba and longed to spend more time on Baba activities. He'd produced a disc magazine for the English Meher Baba association. A group of songwriters, musicians, writers, designers and poets who were all into Meher Baba had got together and produced a magazine of pictures, articles and poems by or about Meher Baba which accompanied a record. It was released in a limited edition of about 2,000 on Baba's birthday, February 25th, and called *Happy Birthday*. Ronnie Lane's solo version of *Evolution is included. Also* Pete's solo version of *The Seeker* and his dodgy rendition of Cole Porter's *Begin the Beguine*, which was one of Baba's favourite songs.

Pete's writing was now heavily influenced by his interest in mysticism. He told Rolling Stone magazine " . . . I'm still on a kind of self with a capital S trip, you know. It's a bit difficult, writing heavy when you really want to write light, or when you really want to write devotional, you know? It's like a period that a lot of other people have already gone through. I know the Beatles went through it, and quite possibly the Stones for a while . . . *The Seeker* is a bit like back-to-the-womb Who, not particularly good, but it's a nice side."

The Seeker combined tongue-in-cheek devotional lyrics with a heavy Who backing, but didn't make much impact on the charts. The post-*Tommy* Who had changed from being a singles band to an album band. This coincided with the growing importance and popularity of albums over singles in the seventies. It also reflected a more serious and less flippant Who style, although Pete at the time still said he preferred singles. "I got a much bigger buzz out of *I'm A Boy* reaching No. 1 than out of all the success of *Tommy*."

The group worked on their new album at Pete's home studio in Twickenham. "It's much better and it doesn't cost as much", commented John to the NME. "It cost thirty pounds an hour to hire a studio and we'd book it for say three till twelve, but we'd all arrive late, then sit about and by the time the pubs were open, we'd all go out for a drink."

Keith also liked recording at Pete's "We start at lunchtime and have a track finished by about five. If we record every day for a month or two, we'll have enough albums for the next thirty years. I always said we'd finished up coming on stage in our wheelchairs. By that time John'll be about twenty stone and he'll have to be hauled on stage like a piece of equipment. His arms will be all puffed up with two mandibles on the end that will clamp his guitar. Roger's hair will be down to his face like a curtain and it'll be shaped like the curtain at the West Ham Odeon, it'll go up to reveal an old cracked face."

John aired his feeling further on studio sessions, " . . . Recording bores me to death. I like the number the first time, but by the time you've done it again and again just to get one part right I get really fed up. We seem to take it in turns to do something wrong. We get the pattern of the song and the part you've got to play so firmly in your mind that when it comes to doing it, you don't concentrate properly and make a mistake. There's always one of us to sod it up."

Roger was married in October in 1970 to American Heather Taylor, after divorcing his first wife in 1968. John was planning to do a solo album of his own songs and Keith went and bought a pub in Chipping Norton, Oxfordshire called 'The Crown and Cushion'.

After their return from the States, the Who played at the second Isle of Wight festival. The huge fences surrounding the festival site were being ripped down in places by French anarchists who thought the festival should have been free. Pete defused the situation with his comment from the stage, "We come home and find ourselves playing to a load of bloody foreigners causing trouble." Keith had arrived at the festival site the day before and, with fellow conspirator, Viv Stanshall from the Bonzo's, kept up a perpetual round of mischief backstage like dropping egg yolks into the tea cups of the press. They became very close and Keith produced Viv's single *Suspicion* later that year. Among other jolly japes they took to wearing Nazi uniforms and clerical clothes and larking around the West End. Melody Maker labelled them "a dangerous duo".

The first 'ordinary' album/Keith at home

Pete was becoming very interested in 'getting a real performance vehicle for the Who that would be filmed.' Various articles began appearing in the music papers announcing special experimental concerts and filming by the Who at the Young Vic in South London. This was the beginning of 'Lifehouse'.

Pete had started writing a monthly half-page article for Melody Maker in 1970 and in a February 1971 instalment he talked at length about 'Lifehouse'. This and other longer pieces written at the time didn't clear up the mounting confusion. If anything, they added to it. The more in-depth the features became, the more the reader would feel as if they were falling into a huge hole. Pete at this time was very spiritually 'high'. He had boundless energy – even emanated a kind of light. His enthusiasm was contagious, but as willing as those who worked with him were to understand 'Lifehouse', they couldn't quite grasp Pete's very abstract, intellectual plans. As ideas, they were perfectly plausible but when Pete talked about turning such ambitious aspirations into a physical reality, he went beyond the comprehension of most people.

Pete's spiritual state was more than apparent in the press. One story was headed "CHANGE BY TAKING PEOPLE UP". "The power of rock music as a liberating force is completely untapped", Pete explained. "I've seen Who concerts where the vibrations were becoming so pure that I thought the world was just going to stop, the whole thing was becoming so unified. But you could never reach that state, because in the back of their minds everybody knew that the group were going to have to stop soon, or they'd got to get home or catch the last bus or something." Pete felt that if you could sustain this level of communication between performer and audience, they could become one. "We have invented the fantasy in our minds – the ideal – and now we want to make it happen for real. We want to hear the music we have dreamed about, see the harmony we have experienced temporarily in rock become permanent."

No doubt he had been reading from Inyat Khan's writings on music. However, the audience of "freaks and 13-year-old skinheads" that showed up at the unannounced concerts at the Young Vic, wasn't as ready for this. "If we had advertised the thing as a Who concert, we could have packed the fucking place for a year," Pete said later, "But we were opening the door and playing, waiting to see who came in. It was a disaster."

'Lifehouse' seemed to be a case where Pete was given free rein when he needed the restraint that someone like Kit could offer. The project became so complex, "I ended up getting very confused myself" said Pete. The main problem seemed to be getting his ideas over to the others. This was the most frustrating thing for Pete – and probably for everyone else involved. No-one was quite sure whether he had come up with the most brilliant rock concept to date, or simply gone off the deep end. Pete had expended so much time and energy in the project that he just couldn't let go. He had been to the University of Cambridge to work with an expert in electronic music, worked with scientists feeding astrological details, brain patterns, heart rates and other vital statistics into synthesizers- wrote four different scripts, about forty songs, and spent a fortune on lighting equipment, PA systems, playback machines and the like. Meanwhile Universal Pictures had put up a million dollars to finance a film of it all, and to add to Pete's frustration, Kit was trying to re-direct the money for a film version of *Tommy* behind his back.

It wasn't until a fews years later when he got some distance from it that even Pete was sure what 'Lifehouse' was about. He once attempted to explain it. "The essence of the storyline was a kind of futuristic scene. I now have realised that actually the basic idea was very derivative of '1984' and 'Fahrenheit 451' and a lot of the stuff in it has now been covered by 'Clockwork Orange' being made. It's a fantasy set at a time when rock 'n' roll didn't exist. The world was completely collapsing and the only experience that anybody ever had was through test tubes. They lived TV programmes, in a way. Everything was programmed. Under those circumstances a very, very, very old guru figure emerges and says 'I remember rock music. It was absolutely amazing – it really did something to people.' And he talked about a kind of nirvana people reached through listening to this type of music. The old man decides that he's going to try to set it up so that the effect can be experienced eternally. Everybody would be snapped out of their programmed environment through this rock and roll-induced liberated selflessness. Then I began to feel "Well, why just simulate it? Why not try and make it happen?" Thus the experiments at the Young Vic. "I was talking wildly about a six-month rock concert, hiring a theatre for it, and having a set audience with a closed house of maybe 2,000 people. I was going to write a theme for each individual, based on a chart that told everything about them. All these themes would be fed into a computer at the same moment, and it was all going to lead to one note. All these people's themes put together would equal one note – a kind of celestial cacophony. The fatal flaw, though, was getting obsessed with trying to make a fantasy a reality rather than letting the film speak for itself."

Eventually Pete had to let go of 'Lifehouse' for his own sake. "In the end it got to the point where people were saying 'It won't work. It won't work.' I said, 'Listen, not only will it work but I'll fucking do the film, I'll show you how it works. I'll actually put a concert together where people actually do start to transcend themselves.' A lot of the things I was talking about and claiming were pretty wild then, but now they're common knowledge – the fact that each individual, has a particular kind of electric frequency, that music is healing, and all that kind of stuff. And everybody has just been treating me as if I was some kind of loony and I think for a while I lost touch with reality. The self-control required to prevent my total nervous distintegration was absolutely unbelievable. I had the first nervous breakdown of my life. I'd spend a week explaining something to somebody and it'd be all very clear to me, then they'd go, 'Right. Okay. Now can you explain it again?' There were about fifty people involved and I didn't have the stamina to see it through." Apparently it wasn't just the 'Lifehouse' script that needed explaining John remembers, "That was the period when Pete was reading the dictionary. Said he was going to learn a new word every day – to extend his vocabulary, but he didn't really bother to learn the meanings of them. That was when everything for him was a 'traumatic experience' and me and Keith went out and bought dictionaries and looked up traumatic."

WHO CHARGED WITH ASSAULT ON POLICE IN STATES

NEW YORK, Tuesday. — Pete Townshend and Roger Daltry, of the Who, were charged with assaulting a plain-clothes policeman after an incident on the stage of Fillmore East last Friday (16).

They face a maximum penalty of a £420 fine or a year in jail. A court hearing has been set for May 27.

The police allege that patrolman Daniel Mulhearn went on stage to warn the audience of a fire in an adjoining building and was kicked and beaten.

According to theatre manager Kipp Cohen the audience already knew of the fire and "an orderly evacuation" was in progress when the officer jumped on stage.

Pete Townsend later told reporters: "We mistook the policeman for some kind of heckler. We very much regret the whole thing."

TOWNSHEND
'much regret'

Roger was a bit more sympathetic. "I mean, basically it just wasn't right that Pete should have had all that responsibility. It should have been put into the hands of someone who knew about the process of filmmaking. He was left to do it practically alone." It was Roger, as usual, who injected some sense of proportion to Pete's ideas with his down-to-earth and practical thinking – reminding Pete that they were in need of an album or a tour. After the 'Lifehouse' fiasco, Kit got the band to fly to New York and do some recording work. Some of the 'Lifehouse' material was salvaged for an album, the subsequent *Who's Next*. "It's a third of the songs and only really a tiny glimmer of the idea. When you listen to songs like *The Song Is Over*, Pete says "You are only literally hearing the end of the film." *Baba O'Riley* wasn't actually information on Meher Baba fed into a computer to produce an electronic musical representation, as Pete told some reporters at the time. He later explained that it was his "impression of what it might come out like" if they were to feed *any* individual's personal statistics into a computer linked to a synthesiser, a method which he was trying to perfect with 'Lifehouse'. (The O'Riley bit is named in honour of Terry Riley whose *Rainbow in Curved Air* originally sparked Pete's interest in electronic music back in art school.)

Behind Blue Eyes also fits into the story. "*Behind Blue Eyes* really is very off the wall because that was a song sung by the villain of the piece – the fact that he felt in the original story that he was forced into a position of being the villain whereas he felt he was a good guy." *Won't Get Fooled Again* was a sort of *We're Not Gonna Take It* from the people in the 'Lifehouse'. As Pete says, "The first verse sounds like a revolution song and the second like somebody getting tired of it. It's an anti-anti song. A song against the revolution because the revolution is only a revolution and a revolution is not going to change anything in the long run, and a lot of people are going to get hurt." Pete told one interviewer "I've never taken as heavy a political stand on anything as Dylan or Lennon, even, either musically or in things I've said or done in public. In fact, the most political thing I ever did was kick Abbie Hoffman off the stage at Woodstock."

At the time of its release none of the Who were particularly pleased with *Who's Next*. Roger thought the album, with the exception of a couple of tracks, was a bit weak for the Who. "I felt we'd lost one bollock," he said. It appeared to the group to be no more than a 'salvage job' of the 'Lifehouse' material. "It's not the world's best live album and it's not a rock opera," said Pete when it was released, "In fact, it's the Who's first *ordinary* album."

Tommy marked the beginning of the end of the Townshend-Lambert relationship and Kit's influence over the group waned considerably.

After *Tommy*, Kit still had more ideas for the group, "Concerts on the Moon", but according to Pete the group wanted to improve its sound. Something that had always suffered in the interests of their image building. Pete and Kit used to sit and plan ridiculous things like the Who playing at Covent Garden and the New York Metropolitan, never really believing they would actually achieve them. After *Tommy*, Kit was quite hurt by the group's attitude and went his own way. The group needed a different kind of record producer. As Chris Stamp put it "Kit was never a great ears producer. He wasn't into getting a perfect sound, didn't know about the best place to position the mikes and all that. He was a creative and intuitive 'ideas' producer."

Apart from their first LP *Who's Next* was the first album *not* to be produced by Kit Lambert. They had gone to New York with Kit to mix it, but as soon as they returned to England they began re-mixing it with Glyn Johns. Glyn Johns had been the engineer on many of their records, and inevitably, without Kit in the studio, Glyn ended up producing *Who's Next*. Pete explained to Sounds Magazine "Up to now Lambert has thoroughly produced all Who records, to the point of altering things in composition and influencing me in certain directions. At the same time he has his own particular kind of manipulation in the way of getting things he wants in the studio. When it finally got to *Tommy*, I think both of us – Kit and the group – realised that there was very little further we could go using that kind of relationship, and we figured we could go on using it hopefully in making the film 'Tommy'.

". . . Kit thoroughly understands the Who but we don't understand him at all, which puts us in a very difficult position. We knew that his pride was going to be hurt by us producing ourselves, but at the same time we knew that it was the only thing that could be done." The band, and especially Pete had grown to resent Kit regarding them as an outlet for *his* creative talents.

Playing *Who's Next* on stage presented the group with a few problems. Pete's keen interest on organ and synthesiser, so apparent on the album, meant that there was a hole left on stage. "It seems a pity that four guys can develop amazing empathy with incredible control over their music and can't have more at their disposal than guitars and a drum kit", said Pete to Disc Magazine. They planned to drop the keyboard part from *Won't Get Fooled Again* on stage as they found it very difficult playing to pre-recorded tapes." They had reached a point in their live act when they had no new material to play. They were trying to get away from playing *Tommy*, and *Live At Leeds* had robbed them of most of what was left of their stage act. "We were musically frustrated so we thought of augmenting the group with a keyboard player. But we thought we might lose the magic we've got as four individuals" said Pete. "We're still going to do some stuff with synthesisers but getting a keyboard player has been very tempting. One of the things wrong with that would be that we would be a different group to join. I wouldn't like to join the Who."

Keith bought Tara House in July, a strange modern house built in 22 acres of landscaped ground in Chertsey. He paid £65,000 for it and was the first of the Who to buy an expensive house. Pete had bought his house a few years before for £17,000 and although it was a beautiful Georgian house on the Thames in Twickenham, it wasn't the usual rock star mansion. Keith's house was typically Keith. It was built like five pyramids all on one level. The walls were mostly glass and in the centre was the main living room which was planned around a sunken conversation pit in the floor. It was very modern and functional and the perfect fun palace for Keith. He had a very expensive house-warming party with a firework display. Later that year Roger moved to a new mansion in Burwash selling his half-timbered cottage in Berkshire to Who production manager, John Wolff.

The Who went back to tour the States for the first time in over a year and took their new stage act playing nearly all of *Who's Next*. At Forest Hills in New York, they played to a total of 28,000 at two open air concerts in pouring rain. Outside a young usher was stabbed to death by a gate-crasher. The headlines in a NY paper read "YOUTH SLAIN AT ROCK CONCERT". Keith said it should have read "ROCK SLAIN AT YOUTH CONCERT". At Boston Music Hall they announced from the stage that they'd like to welcome an old friend and what appeared to be John Sebastian walked on the stage in his tie-die outfit. It turned out to be Keith Moon in disguise.

The big Who summer concert of 1971 was called the 'Goodbye Summer' concert held at the Oval cricket ground. It was held in aid of the victims of Bangladesh and was an all day open air affair with supporting acts, the Faces, Mott the Hoople and Lindisfarne.

At the concert John Entwistle was backstage showing off his new custom-built Cadillac. The car was extraordinary and he'd had it shipped from the States to England on the QE II. "They showed me this catalogue with all the extras you can have and I just chose what I wanted. It was over 20ft long, black with black tinted windows, two sun roofs, and a TV aerial. The back was like a Lincoln Continental with the spare tyre encased in the bodywork of the boot, only John's Cadillac had double spare wheels. The front grill was hand-made and there was a ridiculous looking hood-ornament which stood out about 20 inches. We sat inside to admire the television, fridge, three tape machines and bar, while sampling his three cognacs.

The Who gave an amazing performance at the Oval. It was the first time most of the 35,000 crowd had heard the new material from *Who's Next*. In keeping with the surroundings Keith played his drums with a cricket bat for part of show.

In November, the Who were booked to open the new Rainbow Theatre. London was incredibly short of good rock venues and the old Astoria Cinema, Finsbury Park, where the Beatles used to hold their Christmas shows, was being transformed into a major rock venue by John Morris from the Fillmore along with Joe's Lights. Pete said from the stage "You've got to like it, 'cos there's no other place to play." The Who were brought on stage at the end of a line of

ostrich-feathered high-kicking can-can girls.

Behind Blue Eyes was released in the States as a single and *Let's See Action* was released in Britain and the rest of Europe. Also about this time *Meaty, Beaty, Big and Bouncy* was issued. Although in Britain there had been various re-releases of early material this was the first time that all the singles had been available on one album. This was because the five-year contract with Decca had expired, and the early Shel Talmy produced material had reverted to the group.

The Who returned to the States for another tour in November and December of 1971. At the Forum in LA they broke the record for the fastest sell-out, beating both the Stones and the Beatles, when 18,000 tickets sold out in 90 minutes. The Who insisted that the first ten rows go to the general public and not to the usual music biz liggers.

All sorts of people would somehow end up staying at Tara, the home of Keith Moon which he shared with his wife, Kim. When I first met her, I recognised her as the girl that had tripped and emptied a glass of wine over me a week earlier at the Speakeasy nightclub. "Well, I'm very short sighted" she explained. Kim was apparently so myopic that she had been banned from both local supermarkets in

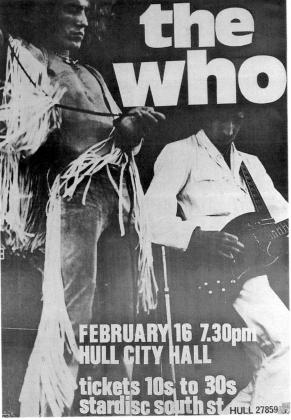

the who

**FEBRUARY 16 7.30pm
HULL CITY HALL**

**tickets 10s to 30s
stardisc south st** HULL 27859

Chertsey, because she kept walking into the displays of tins stacked neatly on the floor and knocking them over. She really was the sort of person that would start a conversation with a hat and coat hanging on a hat stand. A bit like a Mrs Magoo. She used to be a model. "Well I was more of a muddle than a model", she told me. Kim was like a combination between Marilyn Monroe and Mrs Magoo.

There used to be a section in the Readers Digest headed 'The Most Unforgettable Character I've Ever Met'. I think that, undoubtedly, Keith would have to be the one I would have chosen, and that probably applies to many of the people who met him. Keith really was like all the things that have ever been written about him, only more so. He was like a fictional far-fetched, rich young zany pop star character out of a B-movie. Living at Tara was like being in a Monkees TV show, only really funny.

I visited there once and ended up staying on and off for most of the next year. There was an element of fundamental confusion at Tara. Kim, Keith's wife, wanted it to be their home. As well as their daughter, Kim's mother, Joan and her 8-year-old brother Dermot also lived there. However, Keith as well as wanting it to be his home also wanted it to be his

play house. "I want to create a situation where there is a non-stop 24 hour party going on here," he explained. "So that whenever I return, I can walk in and just carry on from where I left off."

There were also two different Tara's. The one when Keith was there and the one when he wasn't. He spent lots of time away and then everyone settled down and relaxed and lived a fairly normal life. Usually, though, when Keith was home with time on his hands, the days were very hectic, funny, extravagant and neurotic. Keith was, of course, the inevitable sad clown. It was difficult to know the real Keith as he had so many different personalities. His excessive drinking and pill-taking didn't help either. When he came down, he was incredibly lonely and unhappy. Keith loved to be busy, to be active, to be the centre of attraction, to make people laugh.

He did of course make people laugh. But Keith wasn't just a loon, a prankster, a mere practical joker. He was genuinely witty and original. I've never known anyone to ever get in the last word with Keith. He's had comic battles of wits with some of the funniest people in show business, but he'd always top them with some devastatingly funny last line. I've even seen him so drunk that he's just about to pass out, but he'd stay conscious, just long enough to deliver some verbal gem before he collapsed.

Keith was also the great showman and show-off. Who else would hire a helicopter to go down to the local pub which was only at the end of his 300 yard drive?

There was often a certain nervousness about being with Keith. I remember one day we were in his local pub and it was unusually crowded and he couldn't get served. "Service bar steward, service!" he'd shout. "I know how to get some attention." Quick as a flash Keith was stripped naked and lying full length along the bar. The bar staff were used to Keith and were not particularly surprised, but served him immediately. On another occasion he got so bored with waiting, he jumped into his Rolls sped back to the house and returned with a shotgun which he fired up at the ceiling. The noise of the blast was tremendous and the whole place went deadly quiet afterwards with the whole pub, deafened and shocked, looking at us: "Excellent" said Keith as calm as ever, "That'll be three large Courvoisiers with American dry, two pints of best bitter and a bloody mary with no Worcester sauce please."

There was also a very tiresome side to Keith. He wouldn't know when to stop. You could be in a very posh restaurant and everything would have gone fine and everyone would think "We're going to get out of this one alright", but about ten minutes before everyone was due to leave, suddenly, without any warning, he would be lying stretched out and naked on the table smoking a cigarette from a cigarette holder, completely oblivious to everyone's protestations. Even after he'd made his point and it was becoming boring, he'd carry on or start something even more unsociable. He really didn't care at times.

On the other hand the guy that has his soup ruined by Keith using it to fill his fountain pen can tell everyone the next day at work that Keith Moon came up to his table at a restaurant and filled his pen from his soup bowl. He might also be sent over a bottle of champagne afterwards for his trouble. Keith himself noted "When you've got money, and you do the kind of things that I get up to, people laugh and say you're eccentric... which is a polite way of saying you're fucking mad."

Tara House was a fairly small house, but it was built in such a way that lots of things could go on at the same time without impinging on each other. It was similar in style to a hotel and maybe Keith felt more at home in this kind of environment. Kim used to say it was like living in an airport lounge.

Records played incessantly day and night. Keith's bedroom, the master bedroom would have his sound system, including two enormous Who speaker cabinets he'd got the roadies to rig up. He played continuous cassettes that ran for about an hour and a half and then cassettes that contained about two albums of music and played continuously 24 hours a day. Then there was the record player in the central sitting room. Joan, his mother-in-law, also had a player in her room, there was a radio and another cassette player in the kitchen and in the so-called study. This room was really the play area, decorated with professionally painted Marvel Comics murals, where all the booze was kept; this held a juke box.

A typical moment at Tara House would feature the Beatles playing in the bedroom, the Beach boys or Jan and Dean playing in the sitting room, and the Stones, the Who, Partridge Family, Slade or Gary Glitter on the juke box. Joan might be playing the Sound of Music or Frank Sinatra in her room. Walking around the place from room to room was a schizophrenic experience. Certain records would come into fashion and be played to death like Nilsson, or Sha-Na-Na, Townshend's *Who Come First*, or Keith's ultimate sound experience of the moment, the *Jan and Dean Anthology*, particularly the nauseating 'zany' side with the dubbed laughter and bad 'wacky' humour. Oddly, he also had a penchant for deafeningly loud exceprts from Swan Lake, which he would accompany with a tottering ballet routine.

Outside in the yard he had his collection of cars. At the time I frequented Tara, he had thirteen vehicles, crashed six and acquired two. He had *three* Rolls-Royces, Keith loved Rolls-Royces. They were the ultimate in status and comfort and if he hadn't been restrained he would have spent every penny he'd earned on buying up old Rolls'. He had a Rolls Corniche convertible, which he used as his everyday transport, his original 1953 bright lilac Silver Cloud Mark 3 with a TV aerial on top, and a 1962 Rolls Phantom 5. He also had what was supposed to be the fastest car on the road at that time, an AC Cobra together with a Ferrari, a Morgan, a Jaguar E-type, a Chrysler Hot-rod and a 1937 Chrysler Wimbledon Limousine that he was restoring, plus a Mercedes 350 SL and a Cortina Estate for his mum-in-law. Add to this his electric milk-float, his hovercraft and a white horse that was too pot-bellied to be ridden and you have the Moon transport fleet.

Keith couldn't drive himself and didn't hold a licence. He had a driver, the long-suffering Dougal Butler. However, Keith did go out driving every now and again and more often than not he dented whatever he was in. Pete explained once that he simply didn't know how to steer a car, he just couldn't do it. Keith drove some of the cars around his little driveway. He crashed the Hot-rod, the Morgan and the Mercedes while I was there, in the space of two days. He had this amazing indestructible quality. The cars would all be twisted and dented and Keith would always just walk away laughing mischievously and rubbing his hands. One evening, about eight of us had been to a local club and were on the way home. Six of us got in the Mercedes and Keith and his friend whom he had invited to try out the AC Cobra, followed behind. We were driving down some narrow, winding little roads, when Keith apparently had urged his friend to 'put his foot down'. He duly obliged, but the car was so powerful that it just leapt off the road and went sailing right through a hedge into a ploughed field, where it continued to lunge about until it came to a halt in the middle of a ditch. We all ran across the fields and fences, through barbed wire – getting badly cut – to see what had happened. The car was a write off, all twisted and torn and pouring out steam. Keith and his friend were standing there completely unhurt. "I say, dear boy, any room in the Merc? We've had a bit of a prang", asked Keith grinning away. The six of us were covered in cuts and bruises, but Keith hadn't a mark on him.

Keith himself was aware of his apparent imperviousness to injury. "You can't really plan anything, and I suppose that's one of the reasons why I don't often hurt myself. I never ever consider *I* might actually sustain an injury. If I did, then I'd probably get hurt. Now if I had some kind of morbid death wish, I never would have survived any of those times when I've crashed my cars. I suppose it's luck, and the fact that I never think anything could happen to me."

His hotel smashing is, of course, legendary. One estimate has put the cost to him of all his hotel work at £150,000, but it is difficult to know the truth, as so many Keith Moon stories have been embroidered and exaggerated. There was a time when he carried a hatchet around in his suitcase, ready for prospective sites. In Saskatoon in Canada, Keith is reported to have chopped the bed, the cupboard, the chairs and the TV into small bits of firewood. He looked upon it as a creative achievement. After one particular bout of room wrecking Keith stood back surveying the scene, and in all seriousness turned to the people that had come to see it and said "I really think this is my best yet." Keith always owned up to everything and paid for it. "Hotels know what they are in for when they let me stay. They don't lose anything, I always pay." Very often he had to pay way over the top.

Because of Moon, many hotels won't allow the Who to stay. On one British tour the group were returning to London, but were running late and decided to meet up at a hotel on the way back and stay the night. They hadn't booked and the first to arrive were Pete and Roger. The manager at first refused because they had stayed there before and Keith had caused a bit of trouble. They were persuading him and reassuring him that it would be alright. "I was so exhausted that I just wanted to fall down to sleep", recalled Pete, "But we had to placate this hotel manager." Finally the manager was just about to agree to letting them have rooms when Keith walked in dressed up as a wasp complete with net wings and wearing flying goggles and a band around his head to which was attached a stick with a small propellor whirling around. When the manager saw this grinning black and yellow wasp going "Bzzzzz Bzzzzz", he had a fit and threw them all out. They slept in the cars in the car park. Very often Keith would leave a room exactly as he had found it. Well

The Who
11.8.
Freitag, 11. August 1972
Frankfurt, 21 Uhr
Festhalle,
(Messegelände)
in concert

not exactly. He would have carefully unscrewed everything so that when the next guest used anything it would collapse.

Keith's drinking is almost as legendary as his drum playing, his hotel smashing, his car crashing or his humour. Life at Tara revolved around the bar in the study and the local pub. Tara was like a sort of trap. You would stay the night. In the morning or whenever people were awakened, you'd be aroused with a large gin and tonic or a Joan Collins, which was Keith's mother-in-law's own specially lethal version of a Tom Collins. What were considered light drinks were imbibed during the day. Gin, vodka, Pimms, beer alternating between the pub and the house. After six o'clock, though, it was serious drinking. This was a hangover from Joan's days on a tea plantation in British India. Joan would switch from gin to Bells or Teachers whisky and Keith would switch from beer, or whatever, to Cognac. The problem was that the days were one long blur. Each hangover was hidden with yet more gin breakfasts in bed and so another round of semi-tired silliness would start.

Most people who visited the house would get drawn into this form of alholic mayhem. We developed a running plot for a mock adventure story entitled 'Escape from Tara', which involved plans to tunnel out of the grounds, only to be caught and sentenced to two large gin and tonics. Every couple of days the soberest person would drive the 300 yards to the local pub to stock up. If Keith's Speakeasy bar bills alone came to a staggering £500-£600 a month, he must have been responsible for a good 10% of the total sales of that pub. Part of that was accounted for by grateful hangers-on, for sure, but still Keith regarded himself as a connoisseur of his chosen art. Once Moon had complained that he had been served the wrong brandy. As the drink had been doused in ginger ale the barman pleaded that Keith had no way of knowing. This was a dangerous move. Keith promptly ordered that a measure of each available cognac be poured out and topped up with Coca Cola. Then, taking a sip from each, he reeled off a list of names: "Remy Martin VSOP, Courvoisier, Martell, Hine, Hennessey XO." All perfect.

Keith used to spend money faster than it was being printed. Although the Who had all become very rich and were already dollar millionaires, Keith always spent more than he had. Every now and then somebody from Track Records would come out to Tara and explain to Keith the position and that he couldn't keep buying cars and things. After one such visit, Keith declared that he was completely bankrupt and would probably go to prison and that they'd have to have an economy drive. He turned off the heating for the house first of all. It got miserably cold, but Keith never noticed as he spent most of the day in bed playing records. When Kim and Joan returned from shopping he went mad, holding up tins of food and saying that they couldn't afford to buy food anymore. He went to amazing extremes with his economy drive, turning off all unnecessary lights, insisting that all empty bottles be returned and the deposit money collected, he even came close to threatening to ration the supply of booze. This went on for about four days and then he returned from opening a clothes shop somewhere locally really excited about a diamond studded watch strap that he'd bought for £600 and describing the suit that he'd liked in the shop that he'd ordered six of. The economy drive was never mentioned again, he was a bit annoyed and puzzled that the house was so cold and that there wasn't anything to eat. This pattern became a regular thrice yearly feature with Keith.

Although Keith's excessive spending was often ludicrous (as when he devised a £35,000 plan to build a swimming pool with underwater bar), the rest of the band tolerated the situation, although he was using their money. There wasn't much else they could do really. They didn't want Keith to go bankrupt or be in a position where he wasn't a member of the band. There was only one Keith Moon and the spending habits and costly lunacy all came in the same package as the incredible drumming. They were stuck with the situation and just kept bailing him out. Also Keith was *the* outrageous pop-star. If the press wanted to denounce the decadent lifestyle of pop-stars they would usually cite Keith's. It was all part of his Moon the Loon, over-the-top-image. In a way, Pop needs a Keith Moon to act as everyone's release. We can't all behave like that, so he does it for us.

Keith was very much loved by nearly everybody that knew him. He was so lively and funny and mischievous that it was difficult not to like him. Of course he had a darker side. He could be incredibly insensitive at times. His treatment of the long-suffering Kim could be downright cruel. She was as patient and understanding with Keith as was humanly possible, but he would never let her know what he was doing, he would pick up other girls at clubs and sometimes even bring them back to Tara. He could be totally unreasonable and self-centred. Kim preferred it when he led his own life and let her get on with hers.

The Monkees TV Show lifestyle at Tara tended to wear thin after a time. Kim and the rest of the household found it difficult to find Keith funny anymore. He wanted a home life and a wife and child but not at the expense of anything else. He wanted to show them off really. Kim was very beautiful and was very shy and feminine. Everybody took to her straight away, but she was a very private person and devoted herself to bringing up Mandy. Coping with Keith was proving too much even for her.

Keith went off later that year to act in the 'That'll Be The Day' film that was being shot on location in the Isle of Wight. At the same time, Pete and John both released solo albums. Pete's wasn't really a true solo album. The *Happy Birthday*

Meher Baba album that Pete had contributed to was being bootlegged in the States. It was selling in great quantities for as much as $15 a copy. A second 2000 limited edition Meher Baba album had been released in January and had also been bootlegged because of the Townshend tracks. Pete's American record company were worried about so much of his stuff being bootlegged, that they wanted to officially release the next Baba album. They offered him a dollar per album royalties and were going to press about 3,000 copies. Hearing how generous they were going to be, Pete suggested they go all out and do a fully professional album, with all the royalties going to Meher Baba charities. It wasn't really Pete's solo album, as it just contained various songs written for Baba projects and also material written and sung by others, such as Ronnie Lane from the Faces and Pete's friend and songwriter Billy Nicholls. The clever title *Who Came Frist* worked particularly well with the cover picture of Pete standing on a floor of eggs. It was thought up between Pete and cover photographer Graham Hughes, Roger Daltrey's cousin.

John's album was a proper solo effort, his second, and like Pete's album, *Whistle Rymes* featured John on other intruments, in addition to the bass. Circus magazine said, "It makes sense that two members of the finest rock band in the world are as strong separately as they are together." However, while Pete's album received an overwhelming proportion of rave reviews, those of John's album were very mixed. Album sales reflected the same preference. Criticism of John's album that the lyrics were a bit grotesque, and in some cases, tasteless, bought the reply from John, "Let's face it, it makes a change from love songs . . . I started realising that was no proper outlet for my songs because the Who were more or less based on Pete's style of writing and Roger sang Pete's compositions best. I'd written my music for me to sing really."

Pete also had his reasons: "I think what I hope to achieve through this album is that people will realise that Pete Townshend being a Baba lover is as much a part of his work as anything else." John looked back over the period of solo activity: "Pete's done his Meher Baba album, Keith's got his film, and Roger's been planting potatoes on his farm."

Tommy orchestrated and a new studio

Lou Reizner's version of *Tommy* played by the London Symphony Orchestra brought the four members of the Who together in what was really a non-Who project. Originally, Rod Stewart had been asked to play the role of Tommy, but he refused, admitting that there were just too many lyrics to learn. Pete then suggested that Roger himself would be perfect. Reizner hadn't considered Daltrey because he thought Roger, like the rest of the Who, had had enough of it. However, Roger was delighted, "It's part of me. I was only too glad to do it. I could never get tired of it." Pete went along to most of the recording sessions and made himself available to Reizner, but as usual he was drawn into it and got more involved than he originally intended. Roger and Rod Stewart, who took the less taxing part of 'pinball champ', both urged Lou Reizner to do some live performances of *Tommy* with the LSO. They planned to do two shows at the Rainbow Theatre – it had been banned from The Royal Albert Hall. Pete had also been worried that if Rod Stewart had been Tommy, there would have been inevitable comparisons between his interpretation and Roger's. The Who's version of *Tommy* had been so rushed towards the end of the recording period that the vocals weren't perfect. So Pete felt it would be good to give Roger the chance to do them afresh. "Plus the undeniable fact that as a singer, Roger has improved a fantastic amount."

Originally Lou Reizner had intended to use both classical and rock singers. He then thought it would be better with just rock singers, reasoning that they would fuse better with the symphony orchestra. Pete hadn't liked the idea of using an all-star cast and thought it would be distracting. But Pete's role was just advisory: "Normally I wouldn't have got drawn into it, but because Lou Reizner's such a persuasive fellow, I just found myself getting involved. It's simply a matter of me coming along to the sessions, listening to what's happening, and then approving the various tracks. I've got no control over anything anyway."

The orchestral scoring and arranging for the LSO *Tommy*

was by Wil Malone, except for *1921, Amazing Journey, Eyesight To The Blind* and *Uncle Ernie*, which were all done by Big Jim Sullivan. The all-star cast included Rod Stewart, who sang *Pinball Wizard*, probably the most difficult song to sing on the album, Maggie Ball, Stevie Winwood, Merry Clayton, Sandy Denny, Graham Bell, Ringo Star, Richie Havens, Richard Harris plus Pete, John, Keith and of course Roger.

Reizner's version of *Tommy* follows the same story-line as the Who's, however, he did try to clarify some of the inconsistencies in the story. "The one discrepancy I tried to clarify once and for all was at the very beginning, when young Tommy witnesses the murder of the lover," Reizner told the NME at the time of the album's release, over three years after the original. Wil Malone, the arranger, had pointed out to him that when Tommy's mother and father sing 'You didn't hear it/You didn't see it/You won't say nothing to no one ever in your life,' Tommy replies 'I heard it/I saw it.' "But on the Who's record you don't see this written in the text or the libretto. In fact you can hardly hear him sing these very important words – which as it happens hold the key to the whole story explaining the reason why Tommy was suddenly struck deaf, dumb and blind." Surprisingly, the orchestrated version of *Tommy* was very well

received. The NME devoted an entire two-page spread to the album calling it "A milestone in contemporary music" and the "best rock concept album ever made." Chris Charlesworth in MM said that "Townshend's masterpiece has finally got the treatment it deserves with an all-star cast, a full symphony orchestra and a presentation that ranks among the best in the history of rock music."

The two performances staged at the Rainbow were equally praised. What was quite remarkable about the Rainbow shows was that the 200 artists, singers, musicians, soloists and technicians were assembled and rehearsed in one week.

The Rainbow shows caused considerable hysteria. The shows were in aid of the 'Stars Organisation For Spastics'. BBC radio news programmes talked about the fact that Paul McCartney had to pay £1,000 for five tickets. Indeed, tickets were fetching the highest prices ever for any show in Great Britain. The show was great until Rod Stewart came on to do *Pinball Wizard* and tried to steal the show. Rod might have tried to steal the show but he failed miserably. If anyone came out with flying colours it was Roger. Roy Carr, having slammed Stewart's performance in NME opined: "When reviewing the album . . . I said of Roger Daltrey's performance that he was unquestionably the star . . . With supreme

confidence he turns in a sensitive performance so striking in its brilliance and grasp of the complexities of Tommy's personality that if Oscars were awarded to rock then Daltrey would surely secure the accolade for the best-recorded vocal performance of the year."

Pete had been rather useless as the narrator and was probably suffering from severe stage fright and forgot his lines during *Sally Simpson*. John was also slightly self-conscious but handled his contribution – *Cousin Kevin* – quite well. Keith dressed in grubby underwear and a pair of old trouser legs cut off at the knee held up with string suspenders and nothing else under his old flasher's raincoat had the audience in hysterics. The NME said, "As the fiddling pervert he was the epitome of warped depravity, to the extent that you could all but smell him."

Tommy, which had begun to be such a millstone around Pete's neck, had been Roger's finest hour. The two Rainbow shows raised about £10,000 for charity. Pete realised sometime afterwards that he shouldn't have been involved; the Who should have kept an eye on it as far as they were allowed to but not been too publicly associated with the whole pantomime of live performance.

About this time, Peter would usually finish off an evening's recording with a drink or a dance at a nightclub, usually the Speakeasy, a terribly dark, overpriced and claustrophobic little club that was the main drinking haunt of the rock business, until it closed in the mid seventies. I was with him on some of these occasions. Usually Pete would walk straight in and head for the dance floor and just bop nonstop for about 30 minutes. On one occasion I remember he asked the D-J to play Derek and the Dominoes' *Layla* five times during the course of the night, and was sitting at his table talking about Eric Clapton not having left his house for nearly two years and what a loss it was to rock and so on. He was very concerned about the situation. It didn't come as such a surprise later when I heard that Pete was trying to help Eric out and get him to regain his self-confidence and play again live.

Bobby Pridden the Who's sound man lived near Eric and involved Pete. Eric had got very hung-up on drugs and hadn't played live for a long time. He had been asked to do a concert by his father-in-law Lord Harlech, and had told Pete that he'd do it if Pete did it with him. Pete rang around for some musicians to help out – Steve Winwood was interested but tied up in the States – Ronnie Wood offered his help and his studio that he'd just had built in his new house, The Wick, in Richmond.

On the first day of rehearsals they met a drummer called Jim Carstine, who had been playing with the Crickets, and he sat in. The original line-up was to have been Ron Wood on bass and Pete on second rhythm. The final line up for the two Rainbow Theatre shows was Eric and Ronnie as dual lead guitarists, Pete on rhythm guitar, Steve Winwood keyboards, Rick Gretch bass with Jim Capaldi and Jim Carstine both on percussion.

Pete was very anxious on the drive to the show. He thought that Eric might not turn up. The whole thing had been arranged so loosely that almost anything could go wrong. Backstage before the concert everybody but Eric had arrived and changed and was sitting around nervously drinking. As time went on, the thought that he wasn't going to show up returned. "We should have sent somebody to get him," Pete had said, "I should have gone and picked him up myself." Ronnie Wood thought that he'd got a last minute attack of nerves as his 'phone was off the hook. They debated whether to try and do a show without Eric in the hope that he might show up later. The thought of announcing a cancellation and arranging to give back the money was in the promoter's worried mind. The place was packed and two of the Beatles and their wives were sitting in the first few rows as well as Elton John and half the biggest names in rock. All of a sudden Eric walked in with his driver. "Sorry I'm late." Eric explained that Alice, his wife, had had to sew in a V-shaped patch at the back of his white suit trousers, as he'd put on weight and couldn't get into them. They nervously walked on stage and began with a rather shaky version of *Layla*. Then straight into *Badge*. The audience loved it. Eric's solos were a joy and it was during his blues solos that one could see why Pete had gone to all the trouble of arranging the thing.

Apart from helping out friends, Pete was also involved with writing the next Who album. Pete felt he needed the creative input of Kit Lambert once again. He explained to Melody Maker in February 1973 that although he had no difficulty writing songs, "I cannot write a strong plot."

The Who were having major problems with their studio work, because they couldn't find a studio sound they liked. "We tried everywhere, test recorded at every studio but nothing came of it," Pete told the MM. "At Advision we spent hours getting a sound down. After we had finished recording, Kit Lambert turned around to the engineer and said, "That'll do for a demo." They decided that they would have to build a studio of their own. They found a disused church in Battersea that was for sale for only £15,000. They quickly bought it up and formed their own company called Ramport. They put their road manager John Wolff, known as Wiggy because he is bald and used to wear a wig, in charge and the four group members were all equal shareholders. This company would handle all the Who's affairs from then on in terms of holding and spending their money, dealing with the equipment and so on. Ramport was also to finance and build the Who's own recording studio. It was to be the first purpose-built quadrophonic studio in Britain.

Meanwhile Pete had been writing and recording demos in his home studio for *Quadrophenia*. He explained to me one day at his house that he was going to write an all-embracing story of the group that would at the same time as reviewing their mod past, free them from it completely. He felt that they were too involved with their own legend and their mod connections and he wanted to cut this connection so they could search for new directions. While waiting for their Ramport studios to be built both Roger and John did solo sessions. Roger released his first solo album recorded in his own home studio at Burwash in Sussex titled simply *Daltrey*. It had a soft focus cover portrait picture by his cousin Graham Hughes, which was reprinted as the record centre on the British copies.

The recording was completed in five weeks during January and February. Most of the songs were written by Dave Courtney and Leo Sayer specially for Roger. He released *Giving It All Away* as a single in May, a month after the release of the album. The album was well received by the critics and it was agreed that it was good for Roger to use his voice for ballads and non-Who stuff. Disc commented, "A fresh original album that extends Daltrey way beyond anything he's ever done with the Who." Roger denied the obvious suggestions that he was making a solo album because the Who were splitting up: "I couldn't touch any rock and roll on the record because I can't do that any better than I can with the Who . . . I feel that if I did a live show, I would be betraying the Who. The stage part of me belongs to the Who." Roger's singing of other people's songs gave him much more scope as a vocalist. "When I get back to singing with the group, it can only help them. It was nice to get out of the group environment for a change and learn more about singing." He also said in an interview with NME that he thought Pete would be only too pleased if the album wasn't successful, Pete, meanwhile, talked about the paranoia in the group being reversed because of the possibility of Roger going off and being a superstar," . . . which he could do very easily in the wake of something like *Tommy*."

In June, John released his third solo album, *Rigor Mortis Sets In*. He had formed a new band called Rigor Mortis. The cover was typical Entwistle black humour and showed a coffin. Inside was a photograph of a grave stone with the inscription "Rock 'N' Roll 1950–00 Never Really Passed Away Just Ran Out Of Time."

They decided to start the new album at Ramport studios even though it wasn't finished. They were determined that Ramport was going to be a top rate studio and had been dissatisfied with the control room, so had ripped out all their work and were rebuilding it. The studio itself, however, was finished. So they brought in Ronnie Lane's mobile, parked it outside, and ran cables out from the studios across the pavement and into the mobile, which was used as the control room. A video camera gave the engineer, Ron Nevison, a view of the studio and two way mike link-ups were installed for communication. Ron Nevison had never worked on a major album before, but was brought in because he had built the equipment into Ronnie's mobile originally. Typi-

cally, Pete was trying to record the most ambitious and complex album of their careers in a studio that was still being built, without a producer and in quadrophonic sound, a medium that had not yet been perfected.

Ronnie's mobile was 8-track, so the first thing that happened was that over the first weekend Ron Nevison and his partner Chris Fawcus worked day and night to change it to 16-track. By Monday's session they had a 16-track control room.

Pete had already made highly finished demo tapes and those that were on 8-track were transferred to 16 at Olympic Studios and actually used for the sessions.

Ron Nevison explains, "Pete's demos had him playing pianos, synthesisers, all guitars and drums plus some sound effects. It was silly to try and redo it, so the demos were used to work to and as they overdubbed parts they wiped Pete's originals. They added John's bass and Keith's drums and wiped off Pete's demo bass and drum tracks. The pianos and synthesisers remained." Two tracks had been recorded a year ealier by Glyn Johns at Stargroves using the Rolling Stones mobile. They were *Is It In My Head?* and *Love Reign*

O'er Me. A whole team of builders, electricians and carpenters were working away at Ramport studios under John Wolff's direction during the whole time *Quadrophenia* was being recorded. Every time the group stopped they would carry on putting in the air-conditioning or acoustic ceiling tiles. The album was supposed to be recorded in what was thought to be the next big technical revolution of the music industry – quadrophonic sound. "We spent a lot of time preparing for quadrophonic mixing," recalled Ron Nevison. They thought that by the time the album was finished the recording industry would have sorted out the problems of quadrophonic albums, but MCA records hadn't even made up their minds which of the many competing systems around they were going to go with. "We had various encoding and decoding machines sent over from the States, and we tried a lot of things but then we gave up. Quadrophonic simply wasn't ready for *Quadrophenia*."

While recording *Drowned* there was a summer thunderstorm and cloupburst and with about 10 inches of water the studio started getting flooded. The piano booth filled up

while Nicky Hopkins was playing. Everyone was so into the track that they just continued recording. Ron Nevison outside in the mobile didn't even know anything was happening until he saw the blue flashing lights in the street of the fire engines that had been called to pump it out.

A lack of response for *Quadrophenia*

The group politics and the division between them, particularly Roger and the management, had reached a point of no return. There had been allegations about mismanagement and large sums of money that were unaccounted for. Roger had put an auditor into the management company to see where the money had gone to and it looked likely that legal proceedings between the group and their managers would be started.

Pete was really unhappy about the situation and at first defended Kit and Chris to me. "What does it matter if a million has gone astray. If we spend all our time and energy checking up on every penny we've made, we'll have none left to put into the band." Pete saw that there was a danger of the group doing less and less work and spending their time looking after their money and becoming "Fucking investment brokers." Pete could afford to be big and generous because as the composer of most of the group's material including the hugely successful *Tommy* and *Who's Next*, he was a lot richer than the rest of the group. Yet his point was that Kit Lambert was needed to help produce the group's future albums and to come up with creative management. Just because money wasn't properly accounted for they shouldn't break up the working relationship they had that had enabled them to earn that money in the first place. Kit and Chris were also 'very out of it' and Roger particularly felt they were not doing their job properly anymore. For their part, Chris and Kit felt that it was petty to expect them to be involved in the minutiae of day-to-day management when they had set up a management team under them that was handling it perfectly well anayway.

By the time the *Quadrophenia* sessions started even Pete had lost patience with Kit Lambert. "I had backed him up, talked the band into letting him produce, fought Glyn Johns on his behalf, and he let me down. He didn't turn up and he left me holding the baby for the production which was bloody difficult." *Quadrophenia* was a monumental recording task. It was a long double album that needed lots of complicated over-dubs and sound effects. Fortunately everyone was working at their best. Keith's drumming was consistently brilliant and John simply threw himself into the project. The recording of his own three solo albums had made him very experienced in the studio. Roger too, was now the total professional and came in and did the vocals without any trouble. Nevison remembers " . . . very much a couple of takes and he has it." Although, on two tracks Roger sang so loudly that he blew up the mikes.

The various sound effects had to be recorded as there were hardly any available in stereo, all the FX libraries being mono. Pete and his driver, Rod, did much of the recording for the effects. Rod bribed a train driver with £5 to blow his whistle as he was leaving Waterloo station – strictly against British Rail regulations – for the beginning of *5.15*. Pete drove down to Cornwall and Ron Nevison towed the mobile there to record the sea, wading along the shore, flocks of mallard ducks taking off and so on. Nevison was stopped and questioned by the police when he was trying to secretly record crowd noises at Speaker's Corner in Hyde Park. He sent his girlfriend to ask the brass band on the Kensington Gardens bandstand to play a Souza march which he recorded with his hidden Nagra. The famous BBC newsreader voice of John Curle was recorded at Ramport and put through a synthesiser to simulate a radio.

The final climatictic note involved Keith playing lots of percussion instruments. Nevison remembers the session. "There was this big note at the end and we got all these percussion things out for Keith – loads of 'em and there was only one take, and in one fell swoop Keith wrecked everything. He didn't know what to hit and Pete was going 'Just hit everything' so he did. He got the tubular bells and dumped them over into everything else. There was this incredible crash. And if I hadn't recorded it everything would have been destroyed, and even though I'd recorded it I wasn't sure at the time. I thought Oh my God how can I use that. If you listen to it, it's just sheer destruction and it worked perfectly." In his recording notes issued to the press Pete writes, "*Love Reign O'er Me* closes the album with a traditional Who ending. We smashed the whole bloody lot."

Pete used another of his studios – "I'm a man of many studios" at his cottage in Goring-on-Thames to mix the album. This was a lengthy task. I got a 'phone call from him while he was doing this, asking if I could help sort out the cover project. He brought photographer Ethan Russell over from the States to take pictures for the cover and inside booklet. As Ethan was American, he didn't really understand about mods or the whole sixties mod lifestyle. The Who's crew and lots of ex-mods had all been offering opinions and advice, but they all disagreed with each other and Pete thought a lot of their memories of mod fashions "highly dubious". Ethan had been over for about six weeks and nothing had yet been resolved and a shot had yet to be taken. I hadn't been a mod, but as Pete said that I'd gone through that whole period with the band observing it all and I would probably remember the fashions and things. The first thing I did was to go down to the local pub and pick up Lydon Kirby from the floor and sober him up. Lyndon had been a dedicated scooter mod and still had a good memory for the all important details. He became main mod adviser. Ethan had picked out some kids that lived in the same street as Ramport studios on Battersea to be models for the project. The photo sessions took about five weeks. We took all the models down to Brighton and stayed at the Grand Hotel, where we photographed the bellboy and so on. After some acrimony, Ethan lost the actual cover shot on the album to Daltrey's cousin, Graham Hughes.

The 44-page booklet of Ethan's black and white pictures that was part of the *Quadrophenia* package was to illustrate in a literal way the story of Jimmy. Pete felt it was good to look at, but it just further mystified an already confused American public. The record was released firstly in the US in October. It concerned a young mod kid disillusioned with it all. A story of adolescent spiritual search, Jimmy is 'quadrophrenic', he has a four-way personality split. Each personality represents one of the Who and each one has a major theme in the music. Roger's theme was, *Helpless Dancer*. John's theme was *Doctor Jimmy (Is It Me?)*, Pete's was *Love Reign O'er Me* and Keith's was *Bell Boy*. The release of *Quadrophenia* was the first Who activity in a long time. People were wondering whether the group were drifting apart because Pete's Clapton concert, Roger and John's solo albums and Keith's film work. Their previous album, *Who's Next*, had been two years before.

Although much of *Quadrophenia* was Pete Townshend's personal responsibility he did comment on John's contribution: "The real surprise for me was the amount of energy he put into it. John's always been as much a quiet one in the studio as he is on stage. He worked like 14 hours at a stretch on each number, multi-tracking horns."

John himself was quoted as saying, "*Quadrophenia* was the first time I really let myself go on playing bass. I played very easy on it."

Townshend, probably *the* most important British rock writer, had once again bared his soul and laid his balls on the line. *Quadrophenia* is a mammoth work much more in the mainstream of rock than was *Tommy*. Circus magazine's review read, "It's about time; The Who fell into a gaping hole of Calcutta with *Tommy*, and I never thought that they'd emerge unscathed. Yet here they are with a hot one, plenty of rhythm guitar à la *Baby Don't You Do It* and Keith Moon is at last recorded on a fine piece of music. Entwistle plays loud clean and well . . . Daltrey sounds like himself but stronger. Pete's always Pete and *Quadrophenia's* almost as good as the Who writing about being horny."

Yet, surprisingly, *Quadrophenia* wasn't acclaimed as a work of genius. After its initial impact, it failed to build in stature and popularity unlike *Tommy* or even *Who's Next*. Creem magazine talked about it being the most intelligent and important album of the year. "But", the writer continued, "I like the New York Dolls more. But they are an artifact. *Quadrophenia* is alive, and it is deep, and it grows on you which is why it takes three months to be able to hear it . . . " The following year a writer in the New Yorker commenting on the Who being ten years old, wrote that although *Quadrophenia* was conceptually brilliant and rewarded careful listening "I still find myself approaching it more as a cultural monument than as a pleasure." A major rock work like *Quadrophenia* had to compete with the Wombles and Bay City Rollers. The album was due to be released in October in the States and November in Britain.

However, there were a number of delays and the band began playing it on stage before the audiences had heard it. This was a major mistake. They had only allowed two days for rehearsing *Quadrophenia* for live performances, the first of which turned into a catastrophe. Roger was angry that Pete and Bobby Pridden arrived late because they had been recording tapes. After a short while Roger went to leave and Pete objected. "Well I've been waiting here all day," insisted Roger. "Well I've been working six fucking weeks solid on this album," came back Pete. They got into an argument and according to Roger, "Pete was in one of his moods and was picking on everybody. After a while he lost his temper and the next thing I knew I had this guitar over me head." Remembers Roger, "Don't treat me like one of the crew," he yelled to Pete. "So all the roadies jump up and lean on me – they know what I'm like. They're holding me back, and he's spitting at me and yelling at the roadies, 'Let him go! Let him go! I'll fucking have him. So they let me go and he threw two punches. They went either side of my head, boom boom. And of course he was completely off balance." Roger punched Pete on the chin knocking him unconscious. "His feet actually came off the ground when I hit him." Pete was rushed by ambulance to hospital, and when he was

eventually revived, was suffering from loss of memory. "I lost my memory for a long time, and because of that day I had lots of problems and amnesia attacks for a long time afterwards."

Pete introduced *Quadrophenia* from the stage at the beginning of November at the Manchester King's Hall by saying, "Now we'd like to do something from the forthcoming album. We're still finding our way with it. We were expecting the album to be out and in your possession by now, but of course it isn't" Being a double album and having such an extensive cover with a 44-page booklet attached had caused production delays. Because the audience hadn't heard it and because its story wasn't too easily discernable from the songs, Pete gave it a short introduction. "This album doesn't need too much explanation 'cause it's about everybody here I'm sure . . . it's about a young screwed-up, frustrated idiotic teenager. Like us. Well, I feel like a teenager – watch this." Pete promptly did a series of cartwheels and acrobatics on stage.

Originally, playing *Quadrophenia* live involved over 20 guitar changes. They dropped five numbers for the Manchester show. At Newcastle, however, on the next night it all went to pieces, and when one of the tapes came in too early Pete finally snapped. He dragged Bobby Pridden over the sound desk and knocked over an amp. "And then he came round and pulled everything apart, all the tape machines, smashed up weeks of work," recalled Bobby. "I just walked off stage and out of the fire exit. I said, 'That's it, I've had enough, I'm off'." John Wolff and Bill Curbishley went after Bobby and persuaded him to return. After raging about the dressing room for over half an hour Pete came back and they carried on playing old hits, and at the end of the show Pete smashed his guitar to pieces for old times sake.

The next day Bobby Pridden had to salvage and reassemble the equipment. "We had no money and I had to buy a guitar out of my own pocket to keep the flag flying. And the old chap (Pete) is on the phone, 'Do you need a hand down there Bob?' I understand it, if I didn't, I wouldn't have been with them all those years."

The *Quadrophenia* section of the shows left the audiences completely unmoved. The difference between the early part of the shows, the middle *Quadrophenia* section and the final part were clear. It just wasn't getting across. Worse still, the audience would sit quietly, patiently listening to the new work, but as soon as they played anything from *Tommy*, the whole place would erupt into ecstasy.

There were also problems with the very complicated tape playbacks. The synthesiser tracks and sound effects all had to be cued and played at the right time in sequence with everything else. The band had to play at the pre-recorded tempo of the tapes. It was the most complex stage playing ever attempted. Keith had a lot of difficulty playing like that. By the time they opened their US tour, in the Cow Palace at San Francisco, Roger announced to the audience, "We'd like to carry on our present act with our new album, or parts of it. We've had a few problems and we've cut a few songs out. We'll do what's comfortable to play. Anyway, written by Pete Townshend, featuring a lot of effects – Good God! – *Quadrophenia*!" This was the first Who concert in America for two years. There had been the highest demand for tickets ever known in San Francisco.

It was a very important tour for the Who and was to prove crucial in its long term effect. After the *Quadrophenia* segment Roger said, "For you who've come on the first night of the tour – *Won't Get Fooled Again*!" They played a great version of this stage favourite, but during the synthesiser break, the drums stopped and Keith slumped over his drum kit. While the others tried to bring Keith round, Pete spoke to the audience, "We're going to try and revive our drummer by punching him in the stomach and giving him a custard enema." It became obvious that Keith was out cold and they took him off stage and revived him in the shower. "I think he's gone and eaten something he shouldn't have eaten . . . it's your form of food," Pete explained to the audience: "The 'orrible truth is that without him we're not a group, and, er, you'll have to fucking wait!" Half an hour later the group were back on stage with a revived Keith on drums. "He's still a bit sort of dodgy but he'll be alright now," Keith shouted out. "Couldn't be better!" However, after a couple of numbers he passed out again. Keith had been drinking with two girls before the show and somebody had spiked their drinks with monkey tranquilizer. They were taken to hospital and apparently one of the girls very nearly died from it. Onstage the band were in a quandry. Pete told Rolling Stone, "I had just been getting warmed up at that point: I'd felt closed up, like I couldn't let anything out. I didn't want to stop playing." He announced from the stage, "Can anybody play the drums? I mean somebody good." A young guy in the audience called Scott Halpin made his way onstage and played with them the final three numbers, *Smokestack Lightning, Spoonful* and *Naked Eyes*. Afterwards Roger praised his playing, "None of the papers picked it up, but he was good."

By the next concert at the Forum in Los Angeles, Keith was back in shape. After playing *Drowned*, Roger announced, "Here's a geezer that gets drowned every night and it isn't in water, Mr. Keith Moon." Keith stood up to acknowledge the cheers of the LA crowd, "Thank you Atlanta," he said. "The next song is for all those people that bought the bootleg of Entwistle, 'Live at the Whiskey A-Go-Go'; *Won't Get Fooled Again*!"

They continued to have technical difficulties with *Quadrophenia* on stage and they also met the same lack of response wherever they played it. Roger thought that it needed to be explained to the audience and would attempt a running commentary about each number. "In a couple of months when everyone knows the album, we won't have to explain," he figured. Roger's explanations got longer and longer, so much so that Entwistle couldn't stand it any longer and interrupted Roger with a determined, "Fuck it!"

A month later in London at the Edmonton Sundown Pete himself began to explain the story only to be interrupted by the audience shouting, "We know it!" Roger explained why they'd reduced the *Quadrophenia* portion of the show even further, "We started off playing it all, actually, and it went down bloody awful. So this is what's left . . . we only play what's good to play on stage."

I think their inability to put across *Quadrophenia* at the time had a profound effect on Pete. Its failure to take off as a major album shook him. He had put a lot into the album and staked the Who's future on its being able to allow them to stop having to play *Tommy* and the sixties stuff on stage. Nevertheless the album was voted 2nd best album of the year in the NME poll and quickly became a million seller.

"Every Who album has been a step forward," Pete said after the first American tour, "I wonder whether the step needs to be such a monumental one." He knew that the Who weren't going to have an opportunity to record another album for a long time as most of their time for the next year was to be taken up with filming or doing the music for Ken Russell's film version of *Tommy*.

Pete hadn't wanted to get particularly heavily involved with the making of the 'Tommy' film. He'd been on a transatlantic flight the year before and Robert Stigwood told him about the film arrangements. Stigwood asked him to be the musical director. Pete said he couldn't fit it in. Stigwood said that there would be a $100,000 fee for the position. Pete looked doubtful and Stigwood countered, "Make it £100,000 then." In the end it seemed that there wasn't anybody else that could do it but Pete. The money was immaterial. Considering the incredible amount of work involved, the changes, the recording, Russell's frequent need for new bits of music and additional songs, and the enormous amount of time it took, the fee was probably nowhere near enough. Pete fatalistically accepted that once again he was going to get drawn in on a Tommy project. "I quite liked the opportunity of having a bash at the music again, I felt it had been short changed the first time. The only thing was I went right over the top, trying to like improve it and show that some of the compositions were good and because they had been short-changed by the original production, I tended to *over*-produce – loads and loads of synthesiser on everything. I wouldn't let anything go by without covering it with synthesiser and lots of clever introductions to cross-themes and things like that. In other words all those overdubs that we were denied on the first album, I was making up for on the 'Tommy' film."

Pete had taken on an enormous workload, recording sessions, mixing, rewriting. Tracks had to be timed to the second for dubbing and synchronising with the film. One day I went round to his house with a reel of very rare film of Meher Baba that somebody in America had sent in answer to requests from Pete. They had sent it to me to give to him. His wife Karen and his secretary Judi were sitting downstairs and said, "Take it up to him, he's in the studio." When I went in, he was surrounded by miles of recording tapes and synthesisers and equipment. The sound was deafening and he was completely engrossed in the work. When he saw me in the studio, he looked startled and shouted, "What the fuck are you doing here? PISS OFF! GO ON FUCK OFF OUT OF IT!!" Sensing my presence wasn't entirely welcome, I put the reel of film down and left. That evening, Pete called to apologize, "When I'm in my studio and working on something like this, which is so intense and complex I can't stand to be disturbed. It's such a personal thing. It's like being interrupted in the middle of masturbating."

I remember being on the location of the 'Tommy' film at Southsea and Hayling Island and Pete coming down during filming. He seemed incredibly down and unhappy, which I thought was very strange as the whole procedure, at least to me, was exciting and interesting. In one way he was pleased and flattered, because the film would be very prestigeous for him and make lots of money if it was successful. But he thought that the band had just got over the *Tommy* hysteria and worked it out of their act then they were slap bang in the middle of it again.

The trouble with Townshend is that he is far too honest and open about his life. He had very high ideals and sets impossibly difficult standards for himself. Pete somehow hadn't allowed success, fame and wealth to change his life drastically. He hadn't let himself get hung up on drugs. He'd given them up in the late sixties when not only the physical and psychological damage was brought home to him, but also the spiritual harm. "I gave them up and became an alcoholic," he used to joke.

In an article about him in Sounds magazine in 1974 he was described by film producer David Puttnam as "Someone who has managed to retain an extraordinary degree of purity. He's the exception that proves the rule, because he's managed to keep his reception to other people's ideas and because he tries things where most other rock stars are just in their rut, terrified of being laughed off if they try something different and fail . . ." The article continued, "Pete Townshend has stayed involved, where a lot of big names get rather sniffy about the newer pop groups, he will put in a good word for anyone he thinks is a good cause, anyone from the Sweet to Kilburn and the High Roads."

With reference to the post-*Tommy* era, Pete told Zig-Zag magazine, ". . . Up to that point we really had been our own bosses and then we weren't anymore. *Tommy* and America, the great consumer nation, took us over and said, 'There are 50 million kids that wanna see you perform; what are you

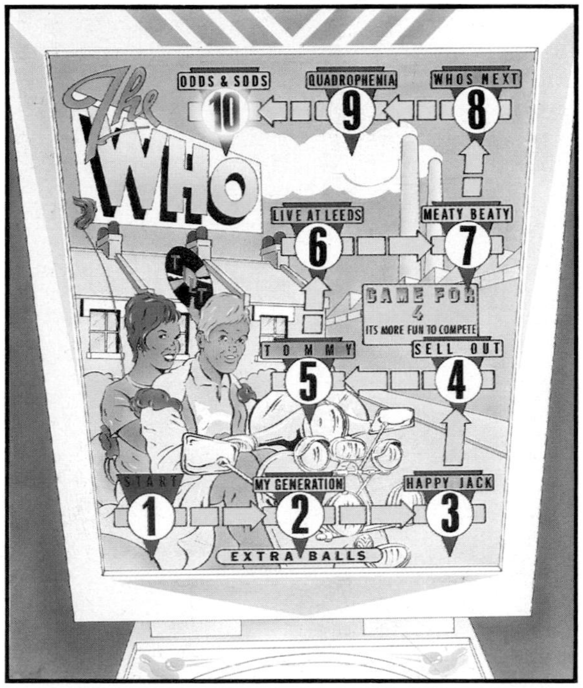

gonna do about it – are you gonna stay in Twickenham and work on your next album, or get your arse over there?' So you get your arse over there and you get involved in the standing ovation and interviews, the 19-page Rolling Stone articles, the presentation of the gold albums, you know, blah, blah, blah, and that all takes two years to get out of the way and then you realise that it's gonna take another two years to work on the thing."

The Who were also trying to carry on without Kit and Chris as creative managers. Roger tried to keep an eye on the finances and got fed up with being fobbed off. He also complained that Kit and Chris were simply not managing the band. They weren't around much. After *Tommy*, both Kit and Chris had started taking large amounts of cocaine and were drinking heavily. The cocaine led to other drugs and soon they were using everything that was around. However, they *had* set up an organisation that was handling the band competently. "They *were* being managed," maintained Chris Stamp. "There was an office, there was Bill Curbishley, there was Mike Shaw, there was Vernon Brewer, there were accountants, there was anybody they needed. And Pete Rudge was looking after America. They were covered worldwide tax-wise, art direction, creative – any way you like. So, you know, it was a mad charge." Stamp's point was that Roger eventually wanted to take on Bill Curbishley as manager when Bill Curbishley was there nine-to-five every day anyway. He doesn't deny he and Kit were heavily into drugs. "So however out of it we were, and we were out of it – we were fucking out to lunch – no doubt about that, there was no need to be around anyway. All you had to come up with was the one great tour idea, the one great album idea, and that was all that was needed."

Chris also put the unaccounted-for money into perspective from his viewpoint. "The lawyer sort of said, it wasn't as if you didn't look after that money, what we hadn't done, we hadn't meticulous accountants, you know. And it hadn't really gone missing. I mean loads of people like Moonie used to grab a big bundle of cash, so did Townshend, so did Entwistle, so did Daltrey, right? None of it had actually gone missing – it just wasn't on the books. You know there was a ton of drugs money, booze money and madness money, and that's where it went. And over ten years – TEN YEARS – there were millions of dollars that had gone missing – this was years of madness on the road, smashed cars and paid off chicks and so on. Anyone in rock 'n' roll knew that, but the lawyers had a case." At this stage Pete sided with Kit and Chris. He was worried that the group might be cutting off their nose to spite their face and he wanted Kit's creative contribution to the group to continue.

Pete and Roger disagreed about the management problem. Roger was all for getting rid of Kit and Chris and was backed up by John. Pete and Keith were against the split. These two had always been closer to them anyway. The Track records and Who management office was being run on a day to day basis by Bill Curbishley and Pete Rudge. Bill had been brought in in 1971, because he was an old friend of Chris Stamp's. According to Bill, he saw early on that some of the contracts that they had could be improved upon. Pete Rudge went over to the States and Kit and Chris were arranging a European tour. "I went to Lambert and said, 'Look I've been looking at these Italian deals and I think I can get more money.' He was doing a sixty/forty deal and I said, 'We can do a ninety/ten deal.' Lambert said, 'Yes, but that is without guarantees, you've got to get the bird in the hand.' I disagreed and told him that I'd talked to all the promoters, and I was sure we could sell out all the shows. Europe was a bit of an unknown quantity. Anyway, I took the bull by the horns and went and did the deals I wanted without any guarantees for ninety/ten because I'd heard gossip in the business that other people were on ninety/ten deals." Curbishley earned the Who band vast amounts of extra cash on the tour. 'And then I was really in amongst it. I was intrigued by it all, recording contracts, deals, promotions, touring, the lot. I just threw myself into it."

Kit and Chris/ The 'Tommy' film

Kit and Chris were without doubt the most creative pop managers in Britain in the sixties, and although they got some pretty good deals, (soon after *Tommy* they signed an 8-album deal for $750,000 per album) which was considered very good at the time, they weren't the best of business brains. Curbishley, however, soon built up quite a reputation for getting the best possible terms. When Roger brought his solo album into the office to play it to Kit and Chris, according to Curbishley, "They told him it was a lump of crap. And he went crazy, he threw it up in the air, he cried and he kicked it down the street and he went fucking mad, you know." Bill thought that they were worried that if Roger had any solo success it would hurt the Who. "But it didn't matter about them pandering to Townshend all the time. What they didn't realise was that if Roger had any success at all it would give him confidence. Townshend had all the confidence because he was the songwriter and the genius and everything. All Daltrey needed was self-confidence. They used to bash away at his confidence all the time. He doesn't need too much confidence, because he can be cocky; but he needed enough and, anyway, this was a good album."

Soon afterwards, Roger called Bill Curbishley and asked him to put out the album and he would pay Bill the management money. Bill Curbishley became Roger's personal manager as a result of this.

The management situation dragged on and deteriorated. One incident that Bill remembers was when the Who needed money to pay for all the work at Ramport studios. "I did a rough calculation with our accountant, John Field, and I went to Kit and Chris and said, 'Look you owe the band about 70 or 80 thousand pounds you know, you have to pay it.' This was just before Kit Lambert was leaving to go to Venice where he'd bought a palace. Kit said, 'Oh we'll give them thirty' and wrote out a cheque. But before going to Venice the next morning he put a stop on the cheque." According to Bill this move even upset Pete. "Townshend went fucking mad, so did Daltrey because they wanted money in Ramport. Kit was going off his head and after that it all started blowing up."

During the recording of *Quadrophenia*, Roger was upset because Kit wasn't in the studio. Chris Stamp remembers that semi-hostile period: "Kit said that there was no point in him sitting in the studio for ten hours, and I mean Pete understood. I would come in and the session would start at say, four o'clock and Kit would arrive at seven. I mean all that was happening was that the engineer was getting the sound balance. There was no need for Kit to be there, right? And he would have arranged for a fantastic French chef or something to show up at ten o'clock with some incredible food and some decent wine or something. Kit used to do things like that. Why should he be there when they were tuning up? It was this fucking clocking in and clocking out mentality which was really such bullshit."

However, there was no doubt that Kit was getting himself into a state and not facing up to his commitments around this time. It was during the *Quadrophenia* recording sessions that the split between the band and management became very apparent.

Pete had hoped that Kit would have been able to do what he had done before, even if he wouldn't have been able to produce the album properly and that was "to interfere in the right way as it were, and we wouldn't have ended up with the sort of rumbustuous undynamic backing tracks that we had. I mean, Ron Nevison was engineering and he was the only objective foil that we had while we were working on a track." After a while the conflict was brought to a head when Roger made an ultimatum, either the band got rid of Kit and Chris as managers or he would leave the group. Pete reluctantly agreed. The management had according to Chris Stamp offered to resign. "Kit and I said to the group, 'Listen, we'll pack it in. We'll have a party and that will be all sweet and nice, right.' And that was not accepted by the Who. A year later we were issued with a fucking writ from their lawyer, you know."

Eventually, Roger, John and Pete instituted proceedings against Kit and Chris on the grounds of mismanagement. Bill Curbishley remembers "The thing that really ignited Pete in the end was when he found a vast amount of his publishing money was gone from America." Keith wouldn't join the action against Kit and Chris. Stamp remembers, "Keith almost represented Lambert and Stamp. He said, 'Of course that money went missing because we blew it all on the road and everything.'"

They took time off from the set of "Tommy" to play five nights at Madison Square Gardens, where Pete lost his spontaneity and subsequently his nerve. He told Nik Cohn in a later interview, "In all the years that I had been with the Who, I'd never once had to force myself. All the leaping and guitar smashing even. I'd done it a thousand times, it was always totally natural. And then on the first night at the Garden, I suddenly lost it. I didn't know what I was doing there, stuck on stage in front of all those people. I had no instinct left; I had to make every move from memory. So I looked down into the front row and there were all these kids squealing, 'Jump, Pete, jump, jump, jump.' As if I was Pavlov's dog or some performing seal. And I panicked and I was lost. It was the most incredible feeling, after twenty years or whatever, more than half my life, to suddenly go blank. The other three shows I was terrified, I got smashed, or I couldn't have gone on." Roger later referred to these gigs and said that "The group were running on three cylinders."

In April Pete had done a charity solo performance to raise money for a school bus for the Camden Square Community Play Centre. Apart from playing at Baba gatherings, this was the first time he'd ever played in public without the rest of the group. I'd watched Pete play at various Meher Baba meetings and so on, usually singing with acoustic guitar and he'd been absolutely superb. Without doubt, some of his best singing and playing was accomplished at these small functions.

The Roundhouse solo gig started out as a small gesture to help out a charity, but grew into some kind of all-important rock event. As the date got nearer a flood of telephone calls and telexes about it came from the States and people were preparing to fly over for it. "I did that after the 'Tommy' film recording sessions so I was still pretty shattered. I'd just overcommitted again, I think. I'd said to Lisa Streiker who was one of the singers on the 'Tommy' film, 'Oh yeah, I'll do the Roundhouse for you,' and I thought it was going to be a very small thing but it turned out to be bloody massive. And people were ringing me up and saying, 'I hear you're doing a solo gig at the Roundhouse' and I thought, 'Hold on, this is getting out of control,' and I started to work seven days a week before the gig trying to get material together to make it better, so that by the time I came to do the gig, I'd actually been doing it for about a week before up in my studio."

When I met Pete on the day of his solo concert he was as white as a sheet. "I couldn't believe how nervous I was," he said years later. He told me that he hadn't been able to eat for the last three days. But despite nerves and a drunken

heckler, the gig was successful. Possibly the nervousness that Pete experienced at his solo concert was one of the factors that kept him in the group rather than go solo. The same applied to Roger who suddenly found how lonely it could be singing solo on TV without the rest of the group.

The Who provided the big rock event for that year when they headlined a one day rock festival at Charlton football ground in South London. It was the first time a soccer stadium had been used as a rock venue and was probably inspired by the Who's use of the Oval cricket ground in 1971. The event was criticised for being too big and the day too long. The support bands were Humble Pie, Lou Reed, Maggie Bell, Lindisfarne, Montrose and Bad Company. The BBC filmed the Who for a 50 minute special that was to be shown later in the year. There were many complaints about the overcrowding and bottle throwing in the crowd in the rock press afterwards, but the consensus of opinion was that the whole long painful process was justified by the Who's act.

The show came during the filming of 'Tommy.' Ken Russell was planning to build a raised walkway all around the grounds so that when Roger sang *I'm Free* he could run

around it while being filmed and it could be used in the final film. However the idea was scrapped at the last moment. Roger had been working really hard on the set of 'Tommy' during most of 1974. Roger seemed to be the natural choice for the part of Tommy, although David Essex was at first going to do it. The rest of the casting was not so simple. Pete wanted Tiny Tim for the Pinball Wizard originally. "I imagined it would sound really great on a hundred ukeleles." He wanted Arthur Brown for the doctor, Cleo Laine or Georgia Brown as the mother or even Joan Baez. Mick Jagger was considered for lots of parts and Bowie was approached to be either the Pinball Wizard or the Acid Queen. Lou Reed was also considered for the Acid Queen. Keith Moon was at first going to have a much bigger part and be more villainous, but much of that was rewritten so that the lover, played by Oliver Reed, did all of it. Keith as the lecherous Uncle Ernie ended up just as the stooge of the lover. Keith wasn't happy about this when he found out and threatened to walk out.

The main actors were to be big name stars like Ann Margret, Oliver Reed and Jack Nicholson. These and Elton John were all names that Stigwood wanted. He realised that 'Tommy' could appeal to a much wider audience than just rock fans. Pete felt that 'Tommy' should be allowed to become public domain, and whoever wanted to do whatever they wished with it, could. "With Ken Russell I was prepared to make concessions and compromise some points in order to have Ken make his alterations – it just meant another evolution in the concept. I told him I didn't care if he altered all the words if he needed to." I asked Pete in a book he and I compiled at the time of Ken Russell's film called 'The Story of Tommy' whether it had occurred to him that the original *Tommy* rock concept had been made into a Mary Poppins and that maybe Who fans would think that he'd sold out. "It's occurred to me, yes. I think to a great degree you've got to live with the fact that it *has* been sold out. It's just that it should have been sold out sooner."

Pete and Kit and Chris had wanted a film of 'Tommy' made soon after the original album had been released. The fact that it took five years before it was filmed reflects much on the state of the British film industry on the one hand and the haphazard state of the Who's affairs on the other. Their attempts to film not only *Tommy*, but Lifehouse and *Quadrophenia*, which they wanted to shoot at the same time as making the album, were all frustrated. This had a severe effect on the Who's career in the early seventies and was a major contribution to Pete Townshend's disillusionment with being in the band.

Filming was set for 12 weeks with a budget of $2,000,000. By the time it was over the schedule had been extended to 22 weeks and the budget stretched to $4,000,000. It could be argued that 'Tommy' was really the first ever true rock movie. It was certainly the first (and probably the last) film to have a quintaphonic soundtrack (basically quadrophonic with an extra speaker for vocals behind the screen). The film was excellent for Roger and vice versa. As Jon Landau in an otherwise uncomplimentary put-down of the film wrote in Rolling Stone, ". . . Roger Daltrey, in the major part of Tommy, makes a sensational screen debut. He comes off as a natural, at ease in front of the camera, remarkably unselfconscious."

Russell signed up Daltrey long before the film had finished to star in his next production 'Lisztomania'. Of course, Roger was much more familiar with Tommy than anyone else on the set but he was new to acting. He told Barbara Charone in Crawdaddy: "My idea of acting is never to act, just go and fucking do it. I really went in at the deep end on this one. I'd never been in a fucking school play. And there I was on the third day on the set, Ann-Margaret, Jack Nicholson, and ME! And I thought 'What the fuck am I doing here – scumbag Daltrey?'"

The sheer over-indulgence and deliberate excess of the film shocked and delighted most critics in the non-rock press. Typical was Jay Cocks of Time magazine who wrote: "(Russell's) unceasing visual imagination gives the movie an exhilarating boldness, a rush of real excitement." Though the rock press was divided over the film's virtues it certainly stands up well against Pink Floyd's *The Wall*, released eight years later in 1982. The 'Tommy' film was a huge box-office success in both Britain and America.

"What I feel is very important about *Tommy* is that as a band it was our first departure from something that wasn't the same old pilled-up adolescent brand of music". — Pete.

Top left and right: Rehearsals for *Tommy* in South London.
Right: A very early *Tommy* cover rough. Pete had originally written a song, *Glow Girl*, about a baby girl born on board a crashing plane. It contained the line: "It's a girl, Mrs. Walker, it's a girl".

Pete Townshend starts a revolution—
WHO 'BRAIN' PLANS BIG POP OPERA

SMALL FACES LP OUT IN MARCH

PETE TOWNSHEND: an impromptu dance of glee

Tackling the most serious project of their lives

Tommy broke new ground as the first real concept album. It finally brought The Who great prestige, which had eluded them for years, and gave them unprecedented confidence. With its release, Pete said, ''I don't call our music 'pop' anymore''.
Left: Roger adopts the *Tommy* look; long curly hair and fringed jacket.
Below: *Tommy* is played for the first time to the press at Ronnie Scott's club in London. The Melody Maker reported: ''The Who were hair-raising... Surely (they) are now the group against which all others are judged. The best live show I've ever seen by a group''.

Is this man sick?

'PINBALL WIZARD' STORM: BACK PAGE

WHO'S SICK OPERA

THE WHO: TOMMY (Track stereo 613 013/4; 75s 1d)

I REALLY was looking forward to this "pop opera," which has occupied Pete Townshend's mind for so long. Really I was. But what a disappointment, even though I tip it for the NME. LP charts.

Admittedly the idea is original, even though other groups seem to be jumping on the bandwagon now, but it doesn't come off. Running for over an hour, it goes on and on and isn't totally representative of the Who; maybe it's time for a change in style, but if this is it, I long for a return to the old days.

Beautifully packaged in a tri-fold

"roots music." Or down-home-country-music as opposed to big-

WHO'S PETE—SICK OR TRUTHFUL?

I HOPE the public will not be conned into keeping quiet about "Tommy," by that much over-used phrase "sickness is in the mind of the listener" Pete Townshend crawls neatly out of the sick category, by using this phrase in reference to

Who's 'Tommy'—a masterpiece

THE NEW LPs

THE WHO "Tommy," It's A Boy; 1921; Amazing Journey; Sparks; The Hawker; Christmas; Cousin Kevin; The Acid Queen; Do You Think It's Alright; Fiddle About; Pinball Wizard; There's A Doctor; Go To The Mirror; Tommy Can ... h The Mirror; Sensation; Melodic Cure;

BRILLIANT WHO

PINBALL Wizard (Track) I gather, from what Pete Townshend has been telling me, that this is one of the tracks of the group's forthcoming LP telling ...

TIMEBOX

BAKED Jam Roll I ... (Dream) I ...

An extremely tasteful pop opera

AMERICA CALLING

Who's 'Tommy' success

... in Los Angeles last week, but they kept ... seem to San Francisco

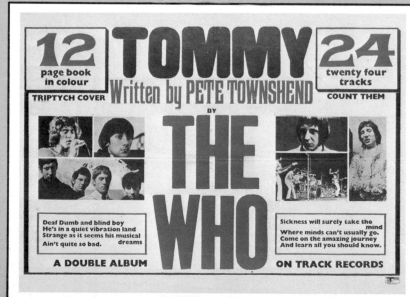

WHO TAKES 'TOMMY' TO EUROPEAN OPERA HOUSES

Who storm New York

TOMMY
LES GRANDS
BALLETS CANADIENS

Rock Opera Gets Ovation at Met

Met Goes 'Longhair' For Young

Rock Opera Stirs 4,000 At Staid Met

BY MARY CAMPBELL
Associated Press

Who and 'Tommy' – million dollar U.S success

June 1970: The Who played *Tommy* twice at the Met in New York, the home of American opera. Staged between 'Aida' and 'Turandot' on a Sunday afternoon, each show attracted 4,000 people with many locked out. At the end Townshend smashed his guitar and hurled it into the audience. The standing ovations lasted eleven and fourteen minutes respectively. Right: One of Pete's famous leaps during *Tommy* at the Albert Hall in London.

Summer 1971: *Who's Next*. The first album *not* to be produced by Kit Lambert, whose influence on the band was waning considerably.

Above: The original idea for the album sleeve, dropped after one use in an ad.
Below: An out-take from the final version. The plinth was spotted on tour.

Above and right: The band performed *Who's Next* (with suitable gestures – see right) at the opening of London's newest rock venue, The Rainbow. Pete said from the stage: ''You've got to like it, 'cos there's no other place to play!''
Facing Page: The 'Fêtes Des Humanités', put on by the French Communist party.

WHO LAUNCH LONDON ROCK CENTRE

theatre and plan to turn it into Britain's first permanent concert hall with the accent on rock.

Morris, asked about restrictions on audience behaviour replied: "I think audiences are changing. People these days tend want to sit down and listen if they want.

Townshend to back Clapton at Rainbow

The Who sell-out in L.A.

from JACOBA ATLAS
in Los Angeles

Who retain title at Oval

WHO GO HEAVY

Who carrying three tons of equipment on American tour

Riots over Who tickets

RIOTS broke out in Glasgow at the weekend amongst 6,000 fans attempting to secure tickets for the Who's concert

Top left: During 1971 Pete Townshend continued a long-standing association with Thunderclap Newman (with glasses) by producing his album, *Hollywood Dream*.

Above: Townshend was also responsible for getting Eric Clapton back on stage in 1972 after a long flirtation with drugs. Booked at the Rainbow for two shows, Clapton very nearly didn't show up. At the very last minute, he strolled in, explaining that his wife had to sew a 'v' into his trousers, as he'd put on weight.

Below: Pete's solo, Meher Baba-inspired album *Who Came First,* released in November 1972.

Top left: Roger married Heather Taylor.

Top right: Reversion to a mod look, taken for the booklet given away with *Quadrophenia*.

Bottom right: *The Real Me*, taken from *Quadrophenia,* and released in the USA in January 1974. The picture is made up from parts of each of the group members' faces.

THE WHO
THE RELAY
(Peter Townshend)
Produced By Glyn Johns And The Who. Recorded in England.
THE WHO

NEW SINGLE B/W WASPMAN (Keith Moon)   Decca 33041

Can you see
"The Real Me"
Can you
The Who

MCA RECORDS

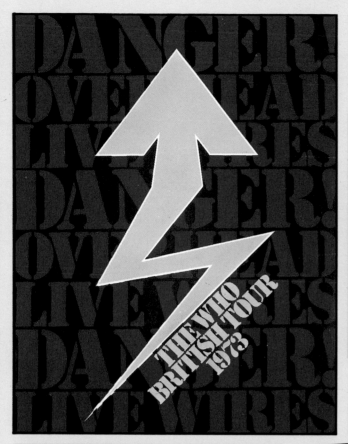

Michael Alfandary for John Smith Productions Ltd presents

the Who

AND FRIENDS

LOU REED | HUMBLE PIE

BAD·COMPANY

LINDISFARNE

DAVE·MASON

THE LUCKY WHO SIGN!

SATURDAY 18 MAY

SUMMER OF '74
CHARLTON ATHLETIC F.C.

Ken Russell's *'Tommy'* film, was shot for a budget of $4,000,000 and was the first film to have a 'quintaphonic' soundtrack.
It was a great boost particularly to Daltrey's career, who was described as making 'a sensational screen debut'.
Far left: Pete with Eric Clapton (left) and 'Pinball Wizard', Elton John.
Centre Sequence: Stills from 'Tommy'.

CERTIFICATE
OF
NOMINATION
FOR
AWARD

Be it known that
Peter Townshend
was nominated for an
ACADEMY AWARD OF MERIT
for outstanding achievement
Adapted Music Score
"TOMMY"

This judgment being rendered with reference to Motion Pictures
first regularly exhibited in the Los Angeles district
during the year ending December 31, 1975.

THE
ACADEMY
OF
MOTION
PICTURE
ARTS
AND
SCIENCES

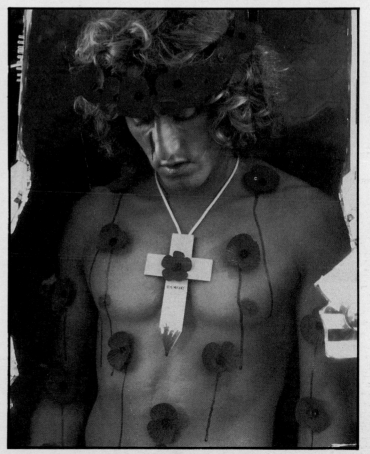

1975-1978

Wealth/Pete's domination/Splits/In a rut/Solo projects/Death of Keith

'Tommy' undoubtedly made the four members of the Who vast amounts of money and certainly widened their appeal, but whether it was wise to have undertaken the film, in view of the perilous state of their rock career is questionable. Had the same amount of energy gone into another album and some sort of live event or even a world tour, who knows what the Who would have come up with. However, they had been trying to move into films for some time and one of the reasons why Pete, for instance, was so keen to get into films was that he'd come to hate touring. "I love playing live, but I can't take all the rest that goes with it." I first realised Pete's dread of touring when I happened to call at his house one day before he was due to leave for a tour. He was so agitated and depressed. I asked him if he was excited at the prospect and he replied that he really didn't want to go. He was also worried that the effects that touring had on him might wreck his marriage. The long suffering and eternally patient Kim Moon had finally run out of patience and left Keith. Pete was very aware of the pressures of the life that rock stardom brings and the inevitable marriage break-ups.

He was unhappy with the way the band was going, with the management hassles and with him carrying the can generally. "I was unwilling really to carry the band to the extent that the band seemed to want me to carry them," he says now looking back on that period. "I think that everybody was, like, behind me, but I think they also felt I was a bit megalomaniacal about the whole thing, and really I was just working under pressure. If I got involved in a project that I was sure would work, like *Quadrophenia* or Lifehouse or things like that, I got fed up with trying to explain it to people that couldn't understand. So I said, 'If I can't explain it, I'm sure that I can do it and then they'll understand it.' That's what happened with *Quadrophenia*. I thought, fuck it, I'm not gonna go through that Lifehouse thing again. I'm gonna do it all myself and then they'll see that it will work." His position as producer, however, altered the balance and working relationship of the band. "And that, again, was something which I think I suffered from and the band suffered from, because it put me into a corner. It meant that somebody in the band was taking a lot of the bad raps that normally Kit Lambert or Glyn Johns would take. If somebody wasn't happy with the bass sound it was my fault or if the mix wasn't right, it was my fault."

It's difficult for people outside the band to realise just how bad communication between the members of the band is. Apart from touring and recording, they hardly ever see each other. Group meetings are few and far between and very often don't really resolve anything. The band members simply hardly ever sit down and talk things out with each other. The band themselves are aware of the situation yet nothing ever seems to resolve it." One day in 1981 as he was walking into the office of Keith Altham, their publicist, Pete met Roger who was just leaving. They exchanged greetings and talked a bit about the snow the country was experiencing and Pete asked Roger whether he had come up to London in his helicopter and then they each said goodbye and parted after 5 minutes. This was the first time they'd seen each other in months and Pete was prompted to ask Keith Altham, "Do you think that counts as a group meeting?"

So it's probably not that surprising that Pete unloaded his doubts and frustrations about the band not to the group, but in interviews with the rock press. He did two extensive interviews, one with Steve Peacock of Sounds Magazine in April of 1975, and the other with Roy Carr of the NME seven weeks later, which was reprinted in October in Creem Magazine in the USA. In Sounds Pete talked about how

awful he found the Madison Square Gardens and French gigs the Who had done the year before. "I don't think I've been so deeply depressed in all of my life . . . Roger just had to carry the show. I felt like a complete caricature of myself." He talked of the band splitting, each member being so involved in solo projects but added, "But once we're in the studio, once we're recording, it's inevitable that we'll go on the road afterwards, and then we'll see just what has hap-

pened to this group in the last two years." He went much further in the NME interview. He talked about feeling too old to be on stage at times; "Because to some extent the Who have become a golden oldies band and that's the bloody problem." Pete said that part of the depression he felt the last time they gigged was because "I honestly felt that the Who were going on stage every night and, for the sake of a few die-hard fans, copying what the Who used to be. However, if we restricted our gigs to performing songs we'd just written yesterday and ignored all the old material, then I'm positive that we'd really narrow down our audience tremendously." Pete also laid into the hard-core New York Who fans that he so disliked at Madison Square; "The kids pay us for a good time, yet nowadays people don't really want to get involved. Audiences are very much like the kids in Tommy's Holiday Camp, they want something without working for it."

(In one respect this last statement illustrates how completely out of touch Pete was with Who fans. The stories of Who fans travelling thousands of miles for a concert, queueing in line in wintry conditions throughout the night and

selling off possessions to attend Who concerts are common. Even in Britain, the sheer torture experienced by the kids standing waiting at the chronically overcrowded Charlton Festival (despite the promoter's promise to limit attendance to 50,000) with poorly organised food stalls and inadequate toilets and having to dodge flying bottles and beer cans for a whole day to see the Who suggests that they *are* working for whatever they get.)

"We would have been recording the new album much earlier were it not for the fact that Roger is making another film with Ken Russell. Roger chose to make the film and John wanted to tour with his own band the Ox, so I've been working on tracks for my next solo album. Invariably what will happen is that once we all get into the studio, I'll think 'Oh fuck it,' and I'll play Roger, John and Keith the tracks I've been keeping for my own album and they'll pick the best. So as long as the Who exists, I'll never get the pick of my own material . . . and that's what I dream of." He always gave the band the first pick of his best material, leaving the rejects for any solo work he might do. ". . . If the Who ever broke up because the material was sub-standard then I'd really kick myself," he added.

The separate solo projects that each member of the band were engaged in made their coming together in the studio more difficult than usual. Keith was now living in the States and the other three in Britain. Pete at the time of his NME interview (May '75) hadn't seen Keith for nine months. However, all the non-Who activity of the other members relieved the pressure on Pete as main songwriter. ". . . I don't put pressures on them," he claimed, "I don't say we've got to get into the studio this very minute because I've got these songs that I've gotta get off my chest. It's always the other way around. They always rush up to me and insist that we've got to cut a new album and get back on the road."

After getting all his worries and frustrations about rock music in general, and the Who in particular, firmly off his chest in the NME, the dirty linen was washed again in public through the pages of the same magazine when a few weeks later, Roger replied in an interview with Tony Tyler. This was also reprinted in Creem, the month after they had run the Townshend one. Roger spared nothing while answering Pete's initial outburst. The interview was supposed to be about the new album, *Who By Numbers*, as it was conducted just after the sessions had been completed and Roger was waiting to hear the final mixes. However, he doesn't dwell on the album for long. "I never read such a load of bullshit in all my life" he begins, "he's talked himself up his own ass. And there are quite a lot of disillusioned and disenchanted kids about now . . . my main criticism was the generalisation of saying the Who were bad." Roger didn't mince his words; "I think we've had a few gigs where Townshend was bad . . . and I'll go on record as saying that." It was strange that the group had just spent a long time working in the studios together since Pete's first interview, yet here is Roger, continuing the row in full public view. They probably never mentioned it face to face. What *would* the rock press do without the Who?

"Also in the studio there's not a lot of room for a group because it's becoming more and more dominated by Pete," Roger continued. "John seems to do all right at it – but every suggestion *I* make I just get laughed at." Prompted by the interviewer, Roger poured out *his* problems and frustrations with the group. ". . . I don't want to be in a group with anybody else, although, if I could choose three friends to go about with, it wouldn't be those three . . . I've always felt a bit of a misfit in the Who." Roger then loses his temper when reminded of Pete's earlier remarks. "The naivety of that is that the last few bad gigs the Who did were in my opinion – apart from his head trip – bad, because they were out boozing and balling all night. And by the time it got to the show at night they were *physically incapable of doing a good show*. So . . . put that in your pipe and smoke it . . . don't talk to me about booze because I've never been onstage drunk in the last seven years, Mr. Townshend!" Roger too talks of the imminent break-up of the Who and points out that "one of the sad things is that Pete and I aren't ever gonna be able to communicate."

"Ageing music for the ageing young"

The Who didn't break up and that was very significant. This wasn't simply another time when the Who haven't broken up. They've been not breaking up regularly since they started. At one of the 'Tommy' premiers Pete remembers the best moment being when he and John and Keith were all drinking at the bar and Keith said had the others heard that they'd broken up; "It's in all the papers."

It is actually remarkable that a band like the Who have stayed together for so long. It's true that the friction in the band has always provided its energy, as Roger said on the eve of their British tour at the end of that year. "In a way, it's been a creative driving force. Anyway, the Who have always slagged each other off in public, that kind of thing has wrecked other groups, but not us." He described it as a 'back to basics' tour. "We've all decided to own up musically. We're a first class rock and roll band playing first class rock and roll. This is the start of the Who getting back together." However, when asked if it was the end of all the mayhem in the band he answered, ". . . if word gets round that we've mellowed to the extent that we *never* fight, those rumours about the band breaking up might have some foundation."

In fact it might have been a good time for the band to have parted, or at least for Pete to have used the material he had written for a solo album. Pete, looking back now, regrets that he didn't stop playing in the Who at this period when he first felt that he should. All the talk about each member of the Who needing the talents of the other and their affinity for each other is, of course, true, but the main reason they have stayed together is for money. Quite simply, in the sixties they were in such debt that they could hardly break up and the only way out seemed to be as the Who. And all their individual solo projects, even if successful, simply weren't in the same league as the Who. John lost about £75,000 on his Ox tour and album and Keith's solo album didn't sell too well either. Roger's solo career was more successful but was partly due to his identification with the role of Tommy in the public eye.

However, by 1975 they were all millionaires and sufficiently famous individually to extend their solo careers. Certainly, Pete should have got his more personal songs out of his system and even Roger thought that it would be good for Pete to do a solo album: ". . . He would get some of the musical frustrations out, which he can't accomplish with the Who, because he can do fucking incredible stuff that the Who'll *never* do. They just haven't got that sort of scope."

The Who album that was released in 1975, The Who By Numbers was in many ways a Pete Townshend solo. Some of the songs were very personal, reflecting some of his deeply felt frustrations. In *However Much I Booze*, a song which Roger wouldn't sing as it was so personal, Pete sings the line: "I see myself on TV, I'm a faker, a paper clown/It's clear to all my friends that I habitually lie/I'll just bring them down/I claim proneness to exaggeration/But the truth lies in my frustration/But however much I booze/There ain't no way out." Although Who By Numbers appeared a very subjective album for Pete, the material was all chosen by the rest of the band from a selection of demos brought in by Pete. It's probably one of those Who albums where many tracks almost sound better on the original Townshend demos than on the finished album. The cover was one of John Entwistle's drawings of the group in dots. It was regarded as a weak album for the Who. What people politely called a transitional album. Nowadays it is more respected, and Roger, in fact, looks upon it as his favourite.

One of the main differences between this and previous Who albums is the emphasis on lyrics more than on melody.

That is why it seemed such a personal album, and many thought it heralded Pete's departure from the group. Roy Carr in the NME went further. "If I didn't know better, I could have easily construed this LP as the grand gesture – Townshend's suicide note." The Who started their first English tour in two years with a concert at a new venue at Bingley in Staffordshire. The Evening News predictably spoke of rumours that it would be their last tour. The two Bingley concerts, their first live appearance since Charlton a year and a half before, attracted 16,000 kids. Ever ready to confound a rumour, the Who did get back to their devastating best and demand for tickets was exceptionally high. The tour promoters reported that 75,000 plus were expected to see the group at 11 dates in 5 cities. Barbara Charone reviewing the first show said, "What makes the Who great is the sense of danger that permeates each concert, the knowledge that any minute chaos could break out." She explained that that moment had arrived during the playing of The Punk and The Godfather. "Townshend, obviously irritated, stopped in the middle of the song. '. . . I can't hear Keith!' he screams out, forgetting momentarily the 8,000 observers. After the song he apologizes: 'Keith says I made him look

like a cunt. I'm sorry.' "

Charone continued: "The first couple of rows scream out, 'Teenage wasteland' with fists held high . . . tonight the Who were beyond superlative description. Brilliant was even an understatement." During the tour their aircraft was delayed by fog at Glasgow airport. After driving to another Scottish airport at Prestwick to try for another flight and having no luck, Keith lost his temper and assaulted and broke a BEA ticket computer, for which he was arrested. He spent the night in the cells and was fined £60 at Ayr Sheriff's Court. A lawyer for Moon pleaded that, "Owing to the strains of his profession he is perhaps a little less patient than other people would be." Keith claimed that the night he spent in the cells at Ayr police station was "the best night's sleep I've had in years," and caught up with the rest of the group in Leicester in a specially chartered plane.

The climax of the tour was three nights at Wembley. During *I'm Free* a young kid in a white T-shirt felt-tipped with Who slogans dived off the 20ft high balcony. As Charles Shaar Murray wrote in NME, "He shimmered out of nowhere and vaulted straight over the edge." He summed up Wembley: ". . . There ain't no finer sight in all of rock and

roll than the Who doing *Pinball Wizard*. The power of the stage show is a testament to the power of the Who." Derek Jewel in The Sunday Times didn't agree: ". . . musically in fact the show was indifferent. . . . Like flies in aspic the Who are trapped playing ageing music for the ageing young . . ." Sounds almost like Pete talking.

The tour had one or two of the hotel excesses associated with the Who. Penny Valentine reported overhearing in a hotel lobby, ". . . Aren't they silly, I mean they're not kids anymore and they only have to pay for it. What good does it do?" Curbishley apparently was worried that Keith was getting old, "I distinctly saw him test his weight on the chandelier before he swung on it."

One reporter wrote: "It's hard to tell who did what, but the results are: one bedroom door smashed in; one whole floor flooded; one girl found naked in the hall at dawn covered in shaving foam."

However it was their on-stage activities that mattered and that re-established their reputation in the eyes of rock purists. Philip Norman writing in The Times said, ". . . It was Russell's film of their opera Tommy, which transformed that most honest and uncompromised band into the undreamt heights of empty glitter and pretence. Yet, somehow, they came back."

A 19-date tour of the States followed, starting at Houston on November 20th. This tour was the first time they used their $36,000 lasers in the act and the first time lasers had been used in a rock show anywhere. They were employed during the Tommy section which had been re-introduced and consistently brought the house down. The band seemed to be saying, "Well, there might have been a ballet and an orchestral version and now a very overblown glittering film, but for all the Who fans, here's the real thing; five numbers of the live, never-to-be-beaten rock version." The Providence Sunday Journal accurately wrote, "None of the attempts to dramatize or film Tommy has ever come close to matching the simple wonder of the Who's stage performance."

On this tour, they were the first rock group to play the Pontiac Stadium in Detroit. They played to 78,000, the largest crowd to hear an indoor rock concert in Detroit's history. They had 14 tons of equipment and used 72 speakers. The show took over $600,000 and the tour in all grossed over $3 million, of which the group's share was £1,589,097. Unfortunately, the support group they brought over to the States, the reggae band Toots and the Maytalls were treated abominably by Who audiences throughout the tour and often couldn't complete their set because of booing and missile throwing.

I arranged to meet up with the band in New York prior to their last concert in Philadelphia. When I came out of La Guardia airport, there was a uniformed man paging me and I was comfortably whisked away in a big black Cadillac limousine to the Navarro Hotel on Central Park South. The Who were all booked into different hotels. Pete was at the Pierre, John at the Plaza and Keith at the Barbizon Plaza. They are all virtually next door to each other on Central Park South. Roger was at a hotel several blocks away. Again, the realms of ludicrous fantasy loom up. They are all under assumed names. Pete was registered as Sherlock Holmes, Keith as Moriarty, Bobby Priddon as Dr. Watson and so on. In the Pierre I had to ask if either Mr. Sherlock Holmes or Dr. Watson were still in their rooms. However, the clerk seemed to take it all in his stride.

The tour was not without unfavourable critics either. Dave Marsh in Rolling Stone, in an article headed, "The Who: Losing the spark after a generation,' based on the opening night, criticised Keith and Roger and thought that the band had played for too long. Richard Cromalin in Phonograph Record also attacked Roger, ". . . he seemed to be separated from the rest of the band, isolated in his cell of Adonis poses."

They finished the year with three triumphant concerts at the London Hammersmith Odeon. Once again, there was a record application for tickets. Roger had meanwhile become involved with the 'Free George Davis Campaign' that was being waged in London. George Davis was a cab driver who had been jailed for his alleged part in an armed robbery. However, it was widely believed in the East End of London, where he came from that he had been 'framed' by the police. A very determined and effective campaign of graffiti and publicity stunts to free him had been carried on by his supporters. Roger added his support and wore a 'Free George Davis' T-shirt for the Hammersmith shows, thus ensuring stacks of free publicity in the national and rock press.

Roger had had quite a year. 1975 saw the premiere of two films in which he starred and the release of his second solo album, plus the 'Lisztomania' and 'Tommy' soundtracks and of course the Who album. He was also offered a lot of money by Viva magazine to pose in the nude for a centrefold, but turned it down.

The Who continued touring practically throughout 1976, off and on. In late February, they did dates in Munich, Zurich and Paris and spent three quarters of March touring the States again. In May they played Colmar and Lyon in France and began their 'Who Put the Boot In' tour of London, Glasgow and Swansea football grounds beginning with their second Charlton football ground concert. In August, they did a mini-tour of Washington, DC, Jacksonville and Miami and they finished the year in October with an 11-date tour of the States and Canada. This was to be the last tour the band would ever do with Keith as drummer.

One reason why the band were doing so much touring was that all their royalties and money had been stopped because of the situation between the band and Track Records. Soon after the band had started litigation against their managers, Chris Stamp and Kit Lambert's lawyers had frozen all the money that was being handled by the company. The group had been managed by Bill Curbishley and Pete Rudge between them while the dispute was going on. However, at the end of the 1975 US tour, Bill went to see Pete in his suite at the Pierre to try to change this situation, as he felt there were a lot of problems and that various people in the Who organisation were working against him. "There's a problem between me and Rudge that is not going to be resolved," Bill told Pete. "You've got a choice, you either have me or you have him. I am not going to do the job with anybody else, and that's the way it stands." Pete didn't want to decide between Rudge and Curbishley, rather that they should continue together. Pete felt that he was being forced by Bill, who was supported by Roger, into taking sides. According to Bill, "He tried to get us back together again, tried to resolve it, but there was no way it was going to be resolved because I didn't trust Pete Rudge any more." So Bill Curbishley took over the running of the band, although at this time Kit and Chris were still legally their managers. The March 1976 American tour was the last one to be arranged by Pete Rudge's Sir Promotions. Pete Rudge reluctantly disassociated himself from the Who after that and concentrated more on his work with the Stones. Bill informed the band that while the legal action was going on, the only way the band was going to survive was, ". . . to get out there and tour." The relationship between the band and Kit and Chris was in its terminal stages.

Kit was apparently spending more and more of his time at his palace in Venice with young boys. His business dealings were getting erratic and confused. He was also getting very paranoid and was convinced that Chris Stamp was trying to cheat him. According to Bill Curbishley, Robert Stigwood wouldn't deal with Kit on the 'Tommy' film. Chris Stamp had an 'executive producer' tag, and Bill was involved as Roger's manager, but Kit, who had originally conceived of the Who recording a rock opera and had written the first film script way back in 1968, didn't even get a screen credit. All the time that the film was being shot, there was all sorts of trouble between the interested parties. "It got really crazy with Kit sending strange telexes all the time, saying he wanted his money from the film in gold and things," remembers Bill.

Bill and his wife Jackie hadn't realised the extent that Kit and Chris were into drugs. Bill remembers that Chris had problems negotiating with Stigwood on the 'Tommy' film because of his heroin and cocaine habits. "We were so naive at the time, we didn't know. But one day Chris collapsed while he was trying to pull out the cork from a bottle of wine and had to be rushed to hospital. Bill had earlier left Track and was working on his own in a little office in Bond Street, although Track sent his pay cheque around every week, which he tore up and returned. Then Chris involved me on the 'Tommy' negotiations. He said 'Will you come and help me on this film?' "

Bill was offered a percentage by Chris Stamp, but the agreement he drew up never got signed. "I was going through a terrible period then, because I thought I was getting used all the time. I can't disassociate myself from the film, because I've got to promote Roger. Stigwood's got me running everywhere, I'm the only one that they trust at RSO, I'm the only one who can get things done, as the other two are zonked out of it, and I ain't even got a contract."

According to Bill, Chris was trying to get Kit certified at this time, and when Bill's percentage was eventually cut down by Chris, he severed his connections with them for good. Sometime after this, Bill remembers Pete calling him and asking him about managing the band. At first Bill refused. Jackie, Bill's wife remembers, "Bill was busy with Roger and Golden Earring and he said to Pete, 'Well I don't know, as far as I'm concerned you've already got management and you've not actually broken with it.' There was definitely friction between Townshend and Bill for no real reason, apart from the fact that Townshend was Kit's man and I don't think he had really accepted that Kit had gone completely bananas." Bill adds, "Townshend also resented the fact that it was all falling down around his ears – that management situation."

It wasn't until May 1976 that Bill was officially appointed as manager of the Who. As soon as he was appointed, Bill began re-negotiating their deals. He soon upped most deals by three or four percentage points and generally negotiated

much more favourable terms and conditions for the band. Years earlier when Curbishley was working for Track, he had to negotiate with Polydor simply on trust. "I had to negotiate the *Quadrophenia* contract with John Fruin who was the then managing director on a handshake, because the band wouldn't sign the contract." Bill says the band were so paranoid that they wouldn't sign anything, because it was between Track and Polydor. "Fruin said, 'You owe us four albums, are you going to confirm that?' I said: 'All I can give you is a handshake John.' I had a great relationship with him and we did the deal on a handshake, and we did every subsequent album on handshakes. We gave them *Quadrophenia, Who By Numbers, Odds and Sods*, all on handshakes."

At the time of the management upheavals, Kit and Chris had just signed a 19-year lease for a vast office for Track Records. Track's business was dwindling and all their income was being held up by the litigation; whatever Kit and Chris did get went to pay for their solicitors, the staff's wages, the office rent and so on. Soon they were fairly broke. Stamp remembers, "And it came down to it that the staff had left except Mike Shaw, you know, in this great big office." After some time Kit had built up a £56,000 overdraft. The lease of his mother's house was in the bank as collateral against this loan. Chris Stamp tells the story thus: "It really affected him, in case they were going to reclaim – not his house – but his mother's. So Kit being Kit was very clever. He found this very ancient court called the Court of Protection. He got an old friend from Oxford to be the signatory for him. So he went into court. Once he was in the court, the bank couldn't touch him, couldn't touch his mother's place." Chris explains the Court of Protection as "Suppose you've got an 85 year old woman who's got ten million pounds. This court is so that some 18 year old gigolo can't come along and fuck her to death and take it all. That's the basis of it, to protect people from themselves."

Chris explained that Kit's scheme was viable providing the person under whose care he is, did what he wanted. It worked for some time, but after some months the woman he'd asked to collaborate in the scheme had left her husband and met and married a Russian Count and took to using Kit's palace in Venice. Eventually, Kit was reduced to living on £5 a day. "It was hell, he was like on a fiver a day. Somebody like Kit, who was used to the best, on a fiver a day."

Chris Stamp pulled a final 'scam' for Kit. "I went down to the bank with him and one of our accountants who used to work at Track and still had some old Track Records cheque books. And we went there at twenty to two, we knew that the manager and assistant would be out, right, and all they had to refer to was the files and the two signatures of Lambert and Stamp, right? There was seven and a half grand in the account and we signed and the assistants couldn't do anything. It was our money and there was no manager to refer to who knew about the court and knew about the action. So it was all very much timed and we put two cheques through – one for four and one for three and a half – got the cash and ran to the nearest boozer for the share out."

The court that had Kit under their protection hauled Chris Stamp up before them. "I nearly got locked up for doing it. They said, 'You knew it should have gone through the court,' and I said, 'Well, I just saw the guy living in a wardrobe – I mean he was living in a tiny room in a transient hotel run by Pakistanis in Earls Court.' " *Even* £7,500 wouldn't last very long with Kit and he was usually very hard-up, relying on handouts from people.

Dubious financial dealings

The management change had been initiated and fuelled by Roger. Roger was always 'looking out' for the Who. It was Roger that cared about the details and percentages and didn't share Pete and Keith's social intimacy with Kit and Chris. He didn't much like Kit. Chris Stamp thinks Roger built up lots of resentment against criticism. "Kit telling him about not singing right and him taking it personally instead of as a sort of professional direction."

The Who had always been dominated by Pete. Roger's influence was minimal, but he'd grown to accept it. However, with his identification in the public eye with the character of Tommy, and his success on the London Symphony Orchestra version and his successful first solo album, Roger had grown in confidence and performance and was speaking out more. He told Hit Parader in 1976, "They have been nonconstructive, and, in a way, it's almost worse than having no management. And I've been into Townshend about it, and it finally came to a head with some things that went down between them and John during John's tour with *The Ox*." According to Roger, John was going to sign a solo deal with an American record company when Kit called Allison saying he was going to sue John if he signed with anyone else. "So I phoned up Pete and said, 'Look, Pete, if we don't get rid of this fucking lot, I'm not going to record another Who album, because if they're going to get their slice of it, no fucking way.' Because the Who don't shit on anyone. The Who's not the kind of band that deserves that shit . . . It's in litigation now. I can't say what areas we've been screwed in, but it's a nasty situation. Townshend wants out of it, but he don't want to be the one to do it, because he feels he owes them something."

Looking back on that episode, Roger seems dubious about some of the financial dealings going on. They did a record deal and came and told us our share was something like $520,000.55 cents. I thought that was a bloody strange figure – fifty-five cents? They were on a straight 30%. And I went and got a copy of the record deal. I tried to tell the group what was happening and they didn't believe me, none of them. We rectified the deal but we still didn't get rid of Kit. I didn't mind, because, although we didn't get on, I liked Kit. I love Kit and I miss him very much. Then we did some tours and they were in the dressing rooms all the time but weren't interested in the band at all. They were just ligging. Getting stoned while we were working our asses off and I hate carrying anyone around. They'd show up out of their brains after a gig. I'd ask them what they thought of the show and they'd say, 'Oh, I didn't see it.' It went on and on and on . . . Apart from the record deal, I don't think they were responsible for what happened. I don't think they were in control of it in a way or tried to steal that money. The tax things were all so far behind. It was such a mess. We would've had to leave England, which I think would've been the end of us anyway." Pete, initially, did not want to confront the problem, but eventually had to admit that something was amiss, and as Roger continues, "Once Pete said he wanted them out, of course, it was easy. But I had to fight for like five years to get them out."

Pete discussed the whole problem with a business friend, explaining that he thought the real problems were between Roger and himself. He was advised simply: "Let Roger win."

In a long self-analytical article he wrote for Rolling Stone in 1977, Pete looked back over his virtual domination of the group. "I had always been the helmsman of the Who. Roger, Keith, John and our management always had plenty to say in the group's affairs, but, because I wrote the majority of songs, they were inexorably tied up in my feelings, emotions and directions. I took the band over when they asked me to write for them in 1964 in order to pass the Decca audition, and used them as a mouthpiece, hitting out at anyone who tried to have a say in what the group said (mainly Roger) and then grumbling when they didn't appreciate my dictatorship. Roger often sang songs I'd written that he didn't care for with complete commitment, and I took him for granted. I said what I wanted to say, often ignoring or being terribly patronising about the rest of the group's suggestions, then sulked when they didn't worship me for making life financially viable." He added, "Kit Lambert went through the same process; he did great work for the Who, not realising that we were satisfied that he should be thanked, credited and presumably made to feel quite happy by his royalty cheque each month."

Pete admitted in this article, which was written just after the management litigation had been settled, "I had resisted Roger for many years in his justifiable revolution against our managers." He ends the paragraph with what I think is an enormous understatement. "As for Kit and Chris, my feelings now can be summed up concisely: I miss them."

The Who started their year of touring in Europe. Keith was voted 'Best Drummer in the World' in the French rock magazine 'Best' for the ninth year in succession. He announced from the stage, "I'd like to thank you for voting me again, for the ninth year running, the best drummer in the world. You've got taste, Paris, you've got class, France. And now, true to my modest self, I'd like to do a number which features me . . ." The rest of the band tell him they are doing *Behind Blue Eyes*. "Oh, it would appear I've been voted down, so I'd like to announce, *Behind Blue Eyes*."

Keith was in good spirits and later that night announced, "We'd like to do something that Pete wrote several years ago that since has been made into lots of things – sterling, dollars, pounds, yen. This is something called, *Tommy!*" A week later, they opened their US tour with a show in Boston. Keith was very ill with influenza and during the opening number, *I Can't Explain* was struggling all the way. They went into *Substitute* and he collapsed on the drumkit. Pete announced, "I think we've got a little bit of a problem, folks, Keith Moon is in very bad shape." The crowd thought it was Keith larking around so Roger told them it wasn't bullshit. Pete announced from the stage, " . . . what difference does it make, he ain't here so we're gonna go and try to work something out."

After a hurried meeting with the promoter backstage they agreed that the show would have to be cancelled and that they would reschedule it later in the tour when Keith was better. Roger came back on stage to announce the news to a very disappointed audience that had only heard two songs and were now booing. " . . . We'll make it up. Nobody wants to play more than the 'oo – I'll tell you that now, but we don't want to kill Keith Moon, right?"

They arranged to return at the end of the tour and also had to postpone the next night's show at Madison Square Garden until the following day. They also had to reschedule shows in St. Paul and Denver. At the beginning of the tour, Pete Rudge had sent memos to PR's and promoters asking them to keep booze out of Keith's dressing rooms and hotel rooms. Dougal, Keith's driver/minder, was trying to keep him away from alcohol and ensure that no money was ever in Keith's wallet.

Keith was not really in a fit state to tour. He was drinking far too much and popping too many pills of various sorts. Officially, the Boston gig had been cancelled due to Keith's influenza. However, he had taken too many Mandrax, because he was so nervous about the tour, especially the first night. The rest of the group were not happy about Keith. Jackie Curbishley remembers, "Roger wanted Keith out of the band. He was adamant. He wanted him thrown out. And so did John. The three of them were going to get him in a caravan and give him a right going-over, verbally lash him. Moon was in no fit state to stand it; he would have probably thrown himself out of the window or something." Jackie thought that Keith's problems were more than just drink and drugs. "He was like a child, it seemed to be affecting him

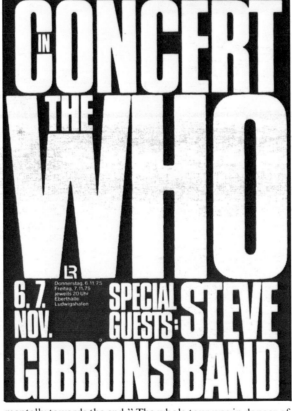

mentally towards the end." The whole tour was in danger of being cancelled. "Anyway, it ended up with Pete going into the caravan with him on his own and talking to him. He straightened himself up for the rest of that tour." Roger later said, "I got really close to Moonie on that tour, 'cos he was really ill after that Boston one and nobody went up to see him. I did, 'cos he couldn't get out of bed. It came to me in the night – I'd always felt there was something really worrying him – he's kicking himself over his marriage. He really loved Kim, and that was just after the big ding-dong with her. He was on self-destruct. I went and saw him and I said, 'I think you're trying to punish yourself over your marriage' and he was broken up, in tears. He hadn't seen Kim and his daughter for two years, and I said, 'Why don't you go round and see her? It's never as bad once you've seen 'em,' and he went round as soon as he got back off the tour and he was a lot better."

Their concern for the welfare of their fans didn't seem to extend to London. It was surprising that after the misery inflicted on the fans at the first Charlton concert in 1974, the Who hadn't learned anything, and staged another in 1976. This was the first of three mammoth shows in England,

Scotland and Wales called, 'The Who Put The Boot In' tour.

The numbers were again supposed to be restricted to 50,000, but because of thousands of very professional ticket forgeries the police decided that all ticket holders would be allowed in; consequently, the stadium was once again packed out with between 60,000 and 70,000 kids. It poured with rain all day and everyone was soaked. The whole tour was a massive operation involving eight artic trucks to transport the sound system around. Apart from the 30 tons of equipment, there was a specially designed stage, special trains laid on by British Rail and over 200 ground personnel at the shows. The Charlton gig was observed by a helicopter, which was trying to count the number of kids for the Greater London Council, who issued the licence for the concert dependent upon crowd numbers and volume. Their limits on both were exceeded as were many of their other conditions. At Charlton, the Who officially got the title of the world's loudest rock and roll band and were entered in the 'Guinness Book of Records'. They were measured at 120 decibels – roughly equivalent to a jet at 200 yards.

Although loud, the sound was clear and sharp. The sound system specially built for the show by Tasco, and costing £7,000 just for that night alone, had never before been used in England. The long throw bass speakers ensured that even people at the back got high quality sound. Barbara Charone summed up the whole affair in her article: "Charlton was one of those infrequent moments that happen in rock 'n' roll. Charlton *was* ugly and seedy, wet and dirty. Stripped of any surface glamour, Charlton was the supreme test. How many other bands could make 50,000 kids forget that they'd been standing in a steady downpour for over five hours?"

At the climax of *Listening to You* all the £100,000 lights including the huge arc lights set up behind the group, facing out into the audience, were switched on, and the effect from this simple piece of theatrics produced one of rock's greatest and most climactic moments. Charlton was reported in the press as an 'orgy of violence'. The police later said this phrase was exaggerated. The reported 300 injured was a bit far fetched. In fact 30 people were taken to hospital, seven with head injuries, two with drink injuries and the rest with cuts and bruises.

However, at the Scottish gig, the second on this three festival tour, there was little if any violence. Apart that is from Keith Moon and the winner of the 'Help Keith Moon Smash up the Giant Organ From The Tommy Film' competition run by the Scottish Daily Express, both laying into the film prop and demolishing it. The third festival at Swansea reportedly didn't have the magic that Charlton had had. Swansea was to be the last concert that Keith Moon played before a paying audience in Britain.

They flew to the States in August to do a mini-tour of four dates, two in DC, one in Jacksonville and the last in Miami. Keith wasn't at all well on this tour. A couple of days after the Miami show, he was taken away from the Fontainbleau Hotel, after having wrecked his room and being found sitting in the middle of the room, talking (some reports said, shouting), to himself. Bill Curbishley had him put under psychiatric observation. In the Hollywood (Florida) Memorial Hospital where he stayed for eight days, it was diagnosed as extreme exhaustion. Before the Fall tour of America, Keith 'dried out' in a health club in LA. "It was terrible," Keith told the London Evening News, "Grapefruit, then gymnastics, then tennis, then grapefruit, then volleyball, a boiled egg, a sauna, massage and collapse. I've never felt so ill in my whole life."

The tour included a Bill Graham promotion at Oakland with the Grateful Dead. Jerry Garcia had told Bill Graham that he'd always wanted to play with the Who and Graham mentioned it to Bill Curbishley, who agreed to the package. The show was advertised with huge signs fixed behind eight airplanes that flew around San Francisco. The shows failed to sell out, but still pulled in 49,000 on the Saturday and 43,000 on the Sunday. After the Sunday show, Bill Graham was in the dressing room pleading for the Who to do an encore. The kids wouldn't go until they got one and had applauded for 20 minutes. He eventually persuaded them by bribing them with a full set of Fillmore posters each. They dedicated *Shaking All Over* to the Grateful Dead and their fans.

The public attitude towards the two bands was succinctly highlighted in Phonograph Record: "Nobody considers the historical implication of any Dead lyric the way they do, 'The simple things you see are all complicated' . . . But every time a greedy, excited crowd screams 20 minutes for an encore they never get, you know the Who have scored one more victory over the changing tastes in rock 'n' roll."

Touring with Keith was becoming even more of a problem for the band. He was so erratic, playing brilliantly most nights but others leaving everyone wondering whether he was going to be able to get to the stage, let alone play. Tom Wright remembered in the sixties Keith being paralytically drunk before a show: "He was real real drunk, out of it. And I was real disgusted about something and I said, 'Fuck it man, I'm just gonna get this guy up there and then *he* can deal with it.' And I carried him, and it was real awkward walking with him 'cos he was like a dead weight, and I got him just right behind the drums and kinda shoved him through the curtains and balanced him on the drum stool. And he just sat at the fucking drums like he'd just got up in the morning, picked up the sticks and didn't miss a note."

After Oakland, they played Portland and Seattle. These were the last gigs Keith played in the States. They travelled on to Canada for some dates and ended the tour at the Maple Leaf Gardens in Toronto on 21st October. He did do two gigs in 1978 for 'The Kids Are Alright' film, though they were not general Who concerts open to the public, so Toronto was Keith's last Who gig proper. He was on form and drumming well. Roger introduced him as "The hotel manager's nightmare – the indestructable Keith Moon!" Keith introduced *Behind Blue Eyes*, for which number he leaves the stage as it has no drumming until the second part: "Good evening and thank you for attending. Well, as most of you abstained from singing on the last number – I intend to do the same on this one – just for spite." Later he introduced the Tommy selection, "I now present for your edification and delight – presented by the original artistes: by the original composer; the original bass player; the original singer; and the original drummist . . . Ladies and Gentlemen, *Tommy*." Pete closed that show by smashing his guitar at the end of *Won't Get Fooled Again*.

The band didn't work at all the following year. One of the problems was that Keith was permanently living in the States while the other three and the management were still in England. With the money from the 'Tommy' film they bought a large share in Shepperton film studios with the intention of turning it into a film and rock complex. The huge studio buildings were empty for long periods because of the decline in the British film industry. The Who wanted to move into film production themselves. Pete had asked Chris Stamp and Nik Cohn to write a screenplay for *Quadrophenia* and the band were planning to produce a film retrospective of their career. They had grand plans of renting out buildings to record companies, recording studios and perhaps building a hotel there for visiting rock bands to stay, especially as Shepperton was so near to Heathrow Airport. The idea would be a sort of rock/music/film industry complex where bands could stay, rehearse, record, store their equipment, and eat and drink in a rock business atmosphere. Some music business companies did move to offices inside the studio grounds, but the completed vision of the Who has never really been given a chance because the four individual members lost interest very quickly. (To an extent Shepperton has been a white elephant. It serves as a home for the equipment hire company that the Who set up for their road crew, ML Executives.) The Who had built up the biggest and finest collection of sound equipment of any band in the world, but were touring less and less. This expensive equipment, plus their top road crew were very much in demand by other bands, so they set up ML Executives to hire out the equipment when they weren't using it. ML added more equipment and also bought a fleet of specially adapted trailer trucks and a fleet of luxury coaches with beds, TV, showers and so on for groups to tour in.

During 1977 Daltrey produced his third solo album, *One of the Boys*. John played bass and also on it were Jimmy McCulloch, Rod Argent, Alvin Lee, and Hank Marvin from the Shadows. Pete did a solo album in partnership with his old friend Ronnie Lane. Ronnie had been having a patchy time since leaving the Faces. His *Ronnie Lane's Passing Show*, although a brave idea and fitting perfectly the gypsy lifestyle he and his then wife Kate loved, lost a considerable amount of money. He had recently gone into the studios with the reformed Small Faces, but hadn't liked what they were doing and had walked out of the sessions. Pete suggested they do the joint album when Ronnie approached him for help. Also on the sessions were Eric Clapton, John Bundrick (Rabbit), Peter Honetvan and Charlie Watts, who although not credited played the drums on *My Baby Gives It Away*. It's a strange album and was much praised by the critics. One of the tracks, *Street in the City*, was described by Trouser Press as "a groundbreaker . . . utterly unlike anything he's (Townshend's) ever done before . . . the effect is totally chilling."

Pete welcomed the British new wave in music that surfaced in 1976. He'd been predicting it for years and was starting to give up hope that music would change, so when it erupted on the scene, he was quite relieved. He knew that if rock music was to be healthy at all, a new generation with their own energy and values had to take over. More than anyone else in a similar position Pete kept in close contact with the whole punk/new wave movement. It rekindled his interest in the music in the charts. The Who were the original

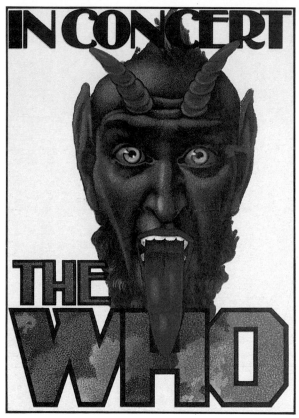

punk band anyway, and Pete, in particular, was responsible for many of the lyrics that they liked. Nearly all punk bands included an early sixties Who song in their repertoire, an honour not given to any other established rock band. After a chance meeting between a very drunken Pete at the Speakeasy with two of the Sex Pistols, they told the NME that they held a very high opinion of him. Paul Cook said, "He thinks he's past it, but he ain't really, he's still great." And Steve Jones agreed; "He was a really great geezer, even though he was, like, paralytic."

Pete thought that with the Sex Pistols, the Who could hand over their self-appointed responsibility as the guardians of rock. What surprised him was that they weren't interested and further that *they* were depressed at the thought of the Who breaking up. Pete had been spending the last few days in very tough negotiations for a new song publishing deal with David Platz and Alan Klein. He was so deflated and exhausted by it all that he'd gone and got drunk. He was at the Speakeasy to hear John Otway. When he met the two Pistols he started unloading his problems onto them. "I was telling Paul Cook about the shit that I'd been through and the Who were fucking finished and everything was

finished and rock 'n' roll was finished, if this was what it was down to. They were the only band that had a chance. And they had to pick up the fucking banner. I was preachin' at 'em and preachin' at 'em. . . . And they weren't interested in rock ideals. I mean all they were into was going round the world and making money and fucking birds. . . . Paul Cook said to me, 'The Who aren't gonna break up are they? . . . We really like the Who . . . Be a drag if they broke up!' "

Pete wrote *Who Are You?* about that particular night. He left the club and staggered around London falling into a doorway drunk. As it says in the song, a policeman recognised him and said that if he could get up on his feet and walk, he wouldn't run him in.

"Rock is not work, it's fun"

At this time Pete immersed himself completely in running a new Meher Baba centre near Richmond. He had bought the building and dedicated it to Meher Baba. It was named Meher Baba Oceanic, later known as 'Oceanic'. It had a fairly large theatre with a stage and film screen and a small control room at the back. The theatre could be used for plays, films, as a recording studio and so on. He had his own personal office upstairs with his private secretary and there were rooms for guests, two kitchens and a room set aside for Meher Baba meetings.

Pete's intentions were highly laudable. He had high hopes for the project and was very ambitious. He even had the cash to back all his grand schemes and was doing so. However, he never really saw things through to the end. He was constantly initiating new ideas and projects but in a few days or weeks, his mind would have raced ahead to something new and he'd be changing everything again. He'd have builders in to alter the place, pull down a wall and then erect another somewhere else. A few weeks after the paint was dry he'd have the new wall taken down and the place altered again. At first there were facilities for filming and editing, then it was video, then it was recording. Pete was like a rich kid with too many toys.

The place was supposed to be an English Baba centre, but apart from Pete's secretary, it was, for the first year or so, full of Americans. Many were very sycophantic and I fully expected one day to see the photographs of Baba on the walls replaced by those of Pete. Pete was only trying to give people the opportunity and the facilities to carry out their own creative Baba projects.

He also set up a number of companies under the banner of 'Eel Pie Ltd'. I was staggered at the stupidity of some of the people Pete had given key jobs. By mistake, the tape would be wiped off a day's recording session, or a video film would be ruined because somebody forgot some vital function. The whole place was deadly amateur but with the budgets of professionals.

Many people took advantage of his idealistic good nature; not that they were calculating, but, in the main, they were just inept and hopelessly disorganised – someone would quite gladly spend all day in a company car looking for a box of staples. The Baba Centre evolved just like one of Baba's parables. It became far removed from having any real feeling of love surrounding it, as mountains of expensive technology seemed to amass itself. The incongruous combination of recording studio and Baba workshop under one roof was a typical, badly thought-out move by Pete. The whole place seemed to be a reflection of his own confused state of mind at that time.

Pete decided that he wouldn't do any more touring with the band after the '76 U.S. tour. Pete was unhappy that their live act was still based mostly on their earlier material, and that the last two albums had been practically disregarded on stage. The diverging paths of the Who on album, and the Who on stage were now clear to see. Pete's writing had become more sophisticated. He was writing more for the head and heart, rather than just for the gut.

Pete first talked about 'not touring' in Trouser Press Magazine in April 1978: "I've always tried to make sure there was material that would work live and it's never been used. *Quadrophenia* and *Who By Numbers* had a lot of raunchy material that never got on stage. All that seemed to work was a couple of old singles, the stuff from *Tommy*, a few rock and roll numbers and finish. That was the act we went out and did again and again and again. That was the act that we were acclaimed for. That was the list. And really it wasn't a list, it wasn't an act, it wasn't a group, it wasn't anything. It was a fucking celebration of our history. I'm fed up with doing it. I'm as much of a Who freak as any other Who freak, and I like what the band has done. I don't think there's anything as exciting as going into *My Generation* and seeing people go crazy, but after a while it's automatic, it's like being the Queen. People wave and shout just because you're there, they don't really care what you're doing. I've ceased trying to analyze that. I think that in itself it's a wonderful thing, but in the end, for somebody like myself, when you realise the price you have to pay emotionally – with your family and with everything else – to actually go and hawk your body on the road for six weeks at a stretch, twice a year in the USA, I don't think it really gets the right results anymore."

Pete thought that despite the huge success of the live shows the band was in a rut. " . . . I mean as far as stage material goes Keith has actually had a list of numbers printed on one side of his drums. That's the list that we use. It hasn't been altered for the last two years."

Pete had told Bill Curbishley that he was going to leave the band. He thought that was the only way he could stop the pattern of firstly recording, and then when a subsequent tour was booked, "I, like a puppy with a Pavlov bell ringing in my head, will get on the airplane and go."

However, Pete described the next group meeting; "I said, listen, I'm not up to doing any more tours etc. etc. Roger said, 'I feel the same way'. John's face fell because John loves touring." It was a huge surprise and a relief for Pete to hear that Roger, who is always trying to get the Who on the road and can only relate when the band is playing live, and Keith, who, according to legend, is like a fish out of cognac when not touring, went along with him. "Keith is a funny guy. On the outside he's all brash and confident, but when he goes onstage to a Who concert he's often sick as he climbs up the stairs. Sick with fright."

Pete found Roger's attitude unexpectedly sympathetic. " . . . It was amazing because he felt the same way I did. I couldn't really believe it . . . I didn't expect him to be quite so sympathetic. Not only to me as a human being, but on his own account. He felt very similarly to the way I did." Whether Pete remembered the meeting accurately or Roger had altered his position is not clear, but the very next day, Roger told Trouser Press, "I can't wait to get back on stage." He went on, "Every time I get out on a stage I want to go back. That's what rock's about, 'specially the 'oo. I mean, Pete has had problems with his ears, it's true, but we all want to go back." He added, "We'll work on him."

Pete wanted the band to continue making albums, but also get into films. "We are probably the only group in the world capable of being both a rock 'n' roll band and capable of raising $7 million to make a film by snapping our fingers."

In 1980 Pete in an interview with the Daily Mirror, talking about touring said, "Rock's not work, it's fun. A bloody great picnic from start to finish. The champagne starts flowing the minute we get on Concorde, and it doesn't stop until we get back. Meanwhile Karen is at home. It's not much fun being Mrs Pete Townshend."

John Entwistle was going to make plans to go on the road with other musicians like Joe Walsh, in case the Who didn't tour anymore. He would still be part of the band and involved in recording and writing. Roger had another part in a not too brilliant British film 'The Legacy', which was released late in November. Roger's performance was called 'oafish' in the NME, while Record Mirror called the film, " . . . one of the most unrelentingly silly films ever made."

Roger also worked hard at being a family man and running his farm estate in Sussex. Moves were in hand to turn the book 'McVicar', the story of a jailed armed robber, into a filmscript for Roger to star in. In 1978 the Who were involved in the production of two major films. The first was a film documentary history of the Who, 'The Kids Are Alright', and the second was the long awaited film version of *Quadrophenia*. Chris Stamp and Nik Cohn had failed to come up with a screenplay. Eventually Pete approached Bill Curbishley and asked Bill to get the film off the ground. Bill wasted no time. He called Roy Baird, who had been associate producer on 'Lisztomania'. Various directors were con-

sidered, including Nick Roeg, who did 'The Man Who Fell to Earth' and Alan Parker who had done 'Bugsy Malone' and went on to do 'Fame'. "Ken Russell 'phoned up as well", remembers Curbishley. Ken Russell had been very anxious to do 'Quadrophenia' just after finishing 'Tommy'. Eventually they picked Frank Roddam, "because I saw 'Dummy' and thought it was great," said Bill. 'Dummy' had been a TV documentary that Roddam had shot about a deaf prostitute which the BBC had refused to show.

Bill got the finance from their record company and had the whole deal tied up within eight weeks of Pete talking to him. The Who also put up the money for Jeff Stein, a 19 year old American Who fanatic, to compile a film history of the group. It was a rather strange decision, although typical of the Who to want a true fan to have some control over a documentary film on themselves rather than a professional documentary film maker who wouldn't have had the passion and fervour of a New York fan. Yet to let someone so young and inexperienced be the director was questionable. Undeterred, Jeff set about tracking down rare footage of Who film and video.

Also in that year, another group of Who fans, this time in England started amassing material for an exhibition devoted

to the band. Townshend attempted to finance the project by approaching different companies with the line, 'You've all made money out of the Who, how about giving something to the fans in return?' A number of generous donations were accepted, though one of £10,000 from Alan Klein, to fund the whole show, Pete, for old time's sake, pointedly turned down flat. The exhibition was held in a couple of rooms on the top floor of the Royal Academy of Art and was called Who's Who. It was an extraordinarily comprehensive collection, compiled by fans in their spare time of photographs, smashed guitars, records, newspaper cuttings, gold discs, letters, posters, badges, original manuscripts of lyrics and all the sort of things that fans hold precious. It proved a great success.

The group went into Ramport studios in December of 1977 to start work on their next album with producer Glyn Johns. Recording the album was to prove an arduous and frustrating experience. Keith was a major problem. Although he had moved back to England to live permanently once again, he was in bad shape and was drumming very badly. The very first day in the studios he totally destroyed his drum kit. "He walked straight through it and totally

wrote it off," remembers Jon Astley who was then the tape op. "Then he was in reception looking at a new notice board that had been fixed up. 'What's this notice board here?' he said and picked up a lighter that was on the desk and set light to the bottom of it. It started to flare up much to Moonie's delight. And everybody just stood there thinking, 'Shall I interfere, shall I interfere?' There were about 20 people watching it, but nobody dared move, wondering what he'd do next. He looked really wild and they weren't sure if he'd set on them or not." The whole thing was in flames and the ceiling tiles were starting to catch. Finally, Cy Langston, one of the Ramport engineers, rushed over with a fire extinguisher and put it out.

Endless problems with *Who Are You*

Keith, John and Pete were all drinking very heavily during the sessions; not just the usual Who tipple of cognac, they'd also developed a taste for vintage port, as Jon Astley recalls. "At about six o'clock the port would come out and they'd all start sitting around talking about the old days and telling jokes until it was time to go home. Glyn would often get really bored with the lack of progress and leave." The drinking affected Keith very heavily. He'd be drinking as soon as he arrived at the studios and carry on throughout the sessions. His drumming was very erratic. "He'd be very good for about ten minutes, then he'd go off the boil. Then he'd be hopeless for an hour or so. Then he'd be good again for a bit more, then lose it," said Astley.

Keith was normally incredibly consistent and easily had enough stamina to keep up a powerful rhythm throughout a long number, but he seemed to have lost it. He was flagging and losing count. They did take after take and were not getting very far. Although the drink and drugs affected his playing, living in LA hadn't helped him either. He'd been California Dreaming for two years. He'd put on a lot of weight and his sheer physical size slowed him down.

The studio also had a series of technical problems that delayed things further. They stopped for a month for Christmas. Soon after the sessions were underway again Pete cut his hand badly. Pete had been to visit his parents and they had all had quite a lot to drink. His parents had started an argument and Pete had tried to intervene. They were oblivious to him, and finally, in a fit of emotion, he smashed his hand through the window. As this only momentarily stopped them, he then rubbed his hand on the broken glass, which had the desired effect and his parents stopped their row and rushed him and his bleeding hand off to hospital. Pete's dramatic and theatrical gesture also effectively stopped him playing guitar for a month while the cuts healed.

Not to be outdone, Rabbit (John Bundrick) who was playing keyboards on a few of the tracks, broke his arm falling out of a taxi as he arrived at the studio door.

John Entwistle was virtually co-producer on the album according to Jon Astley. "He was in the studio every day and kept his eye on everything. When nothing else was happening he'd replace his bass part again."

Because of Pete's hearing problem, they had a special set of headphones made up with a cut-out box in the system. If the volume went over a certain level, they would cut out. Another problem for Pete was that the control room at Ramport is very loud. He had to stay out in the studio listening to playbacks through his headphones, while the rest of the group went into the control room to listen.

No sooner had they worked round the delay caused by Pete's slashed hand when Glyn and Roger fell out. They had been getting on top of one another and finally they had a fight. It was actually over a trivial little incident. Glyn was playing back a tape that Jon Astley had just brought in of synthesisers that Jon and Pete had recorded at Pete's Goring studio. According to Jon Astley, Glyn was saying how good it was and Roger leant over the control desk and asked if they could hear more bass. "More bass!" yelled Glyn. "It's only a rough mix!" They both lost their tempers and out in the corridor Roger punched Glyn. "Glyn came back into the control room almost in tears and Roger shot off at about 120 mph in his Ferrari," Astley remembers. Apparently, Roger returned about an hour later and they made it up. However, it was probably the last straw for Glyn, who had another commitment at that time to do Joan Armatrading's album. The Who sessions had been so delayed that he'd run out of time. Just before he left, he tried a new studio. Mickie Most had just finished building his RAK studios and Glyn moved the sessions to there.

The group realised that they would have to confront Keith about his condition. He'd been given a job doing public relations and publicity for their Shepperton studios and it had helped him a lot. With a job that was almost tailor made for somebody like him, Keith began slowly to pull himself together. However, he still wasn't turning up at the sessions regularly, and when he did, it was either too late or he still couldn't get his drumming together.

One evening they went for a meal in a restaurant around the corner from RAK. The group had been putting pressure on Keith and on this night Pete had a talk with him alone. He told him that if he didn't pull himself together he would be out of the group. This talk, accompanied by pressure from the others, had the desired effect. They moved back to Ramport and Keith did practically the entire drumming on the album in ten days. Usually the drums are the first thing to be recorded, but in this case they were mostly added at the last minute. Pete already had a simple guide track on his demos. Keith had the added task of playing to tracks that were already down. Jon Astley had by now taken over as producer of the album. He did, *New Song, Guitar and Pen* and *Sister Disco* and finished off various bits on the others. "When Keith is good, he's very good" he said. "When he has to play to a click-track he's absolutely spot on because he's had years of practice playing on stage through headphones to a count-in on *Baba O'Riley* and *Won't Get Fooled Again*." Keith had stopped drinking and was taking pills to help him over that and was generally trying to sort himself out.

Roger worked very hard on the album. "He was at his best when none of the others were there" adds Astley. "He was very responsive and professional." Pete at that time was the perfect middle-class suburban husband. "He would come in at about 2 o'clock in the afternoon and put his music on the music stand. 'This is what I've got to do today, Jon.' He'd play it and at 5 or 6 pm go home to dinner. Often he would have to leave to fetch the kids from school."

One of the numbers that they were recording, called *Choirboy* wasn't working out. Pete said that he'd get another demo together over the weekend at Goring and came in on the Monday with a 24-track demo of *Music Must Change*. Keith couldn't handle the drumming required for this track. "He was coming out of his good spell and anyway, it was in 6/8 time and Keith always had trouble with 6/8 time, so we didn't really try," remembers Astley.

Pete took the track back to Goring and recorded his footsteps. "The percussion on that track is Pete's footsteps and on good stereo you can hear his squeaky shoes as he paces around the floor" says John. "We added the sound of a milk bottle falling down some steps too, as though he'd kicked it."

Pete asked Glyn to mix the album and so he and Jon Astley mixed it at Olympic. However nobody was happy with the mix. Jon Astley remixed it at CTS studios to general approval and relief.

While remixing, Roger came back to the studios for his easiest recording session ever; just one line of five words. In order to get the single, *Who Are You* played on radio, Roger sang "Who the hell are you?", which was substituted for the original, "Who the fuck are you?" A couple of hundred were mixed with the cleaned-up lyric.

Keith's death had always been feared

Getting album covers together for such a democratic band as the Who has always had its problems. "It's murder – they never agree ever. It's a real pain" says Curbishley, adding, "Mind you, they never agree completely on anything." His wife and co-director, Jackie says, "There's always one that will not like the photo or something. It's even difficult on solo albums when there's only one person to consult."

They operated a rota system where each member of the group got a turn at an album and title. Roger had done *Odds and Sods*, and John had drawn *Who By Numbers* artwork himself ("The cheapest cover the Who have ever had," said John. "I only got £30 for it") and this time it was up to Keith. He came up with some very strange ideas but nothing much got done. As a last resort they just did the shot of them

standing in all the leads.

The *Who Are You* album sleeve is one of dullest album pics ever. Apparently, the record company was screaming for the album and so they had to just shoot anything. Many people find some significance in the fact that Keith is sitting in a chair marked NOT TO BE TAKEN AWAY. Originally, he was standing up, but they sat him there to try to hide his large stomach.

The single was released in July in Britain and August in the States. The album came out in both countries in August. *Who Are You* is a strange mixture. There are three John Entwistle tracks on it – he submitted seven demos. The rest are by Pete, and what is surprising is that given the time the album was released, it makes absolutely no concessions to punk rock, heavy metal or disco music at all. This is especially strange, given Pete's involvement and encouragement of young British punk groups. Quite the reverse. Although Pete's lyrics are very concerned with musical changes, the album heads off once again on a completely new direction. It is almost jazzy. On *Music Must Change* Pete plays jazz guitar and the influence of Wes Montgomery and Pat Martino can be detected. John provided the brass for this track.

The reviews for *Who Are You* were very mixed. Pete's introspection, which was found refreshing on *Who By Numbers*, was now considered tedious by some critics. Pete

was accused of sterility and of confusion, lameness and uncertainty. On the other hand this album was hailed in other quarters as the best Who album since *Tommy*, refreshing and optimistic. John Swenson writing in Circus magazine compared it favourably with *Who's Next*: "Townshend not only invented punk rock, he also invented its antidote, power pop . . . he challenges his contemporaries, his fame, his protegés and finally himself with the record." Most critics were united in their praise for Roger's singing, " . . . The performance of his life . . ." says Swenson. Michael Davis in Record Review magazine says of *Music Must Change*, " . . . The music here doesn't match the intensity of Roger's voice." Much rock-journalese was spouted in a search for the meaning of the new Who album. Pete seemed determined to bare his soul once more through the lyrics either obviously or through subtle clues.

On August 12th Pete Meaden, their former publicist and chief inspiration for their early mod image and High Numbers period, died in London. He apparently committed suicide. Pete Meaden had been managing the Steve Gibbons band along with Bill Curbishley. I had seen him some months before and had a drink with him. I'd always liked Pete Meaden and was quite upset, as he was clearly very unhappy and unsure of himself.

If the Who were very upset at Pete Meaden's death, they

were completely and utterly shattered a month later on September 7th when Keith died. He had been at a party at Peppermint Park restaurant in London before the premiere of 'The Buddy Holly Story', given by Paul McCartney who owns the copyright to Buddy Holly's songs. Keith had announced his engagement to his beautiful Swedish girlfriend Annette Walter-Lax, whom he'd been living with for the past two years. Keith often announced that he was going to marry, but most people present thought that he actually meant it this time. According to David Frost who was at the same table as Paul and Linda and Keith and Annette, Keith was relaxed and content and "really delightful company." He spent his last evening sipping white wine. They went to see the film, leaving after forty-five minutes to return to his flat in Curzon Place, where Keith watched 'The Abominable Dr Phibes' on video and had some supper. Sometime during the evening he took some pills and fell asleep with the video still running.

According to the story that Annette told to the Sunday Mirror, "He woke up early in the morning and said he was hungry again. I started moaning and complaining that it was inconsiderate of him to expect me to get up and cook another meal. 'If you don't like it, you can —— off !' he snapped. *Those were the last words he spoke to me.*" (Their italics).

Keith had been prescribed by his doctor the drug heminevrin, a sedative used to treat acute alcoholic withdrawal symptoms, and acute mania. These were Keith's two big problems; however, some medical opinion has it that Keith should never have been prescribed the drug unless he was under supervision in hospital and treatment shouldn't last more than six or seven days. Keith had been taking them for weeks.

Keith ate the steak that Annette had prepared and went back to sleep. He took another handful of sedatives. It had first been prescribed after he'd had an epileptic fit as a result of his withdrawal from alcohol. Keith had taken 32 tablets in all that night. The sedative can be affected by even a small amount of alcohol making it very dangerous.

Annette woke up the following afternoon at about 2 o'clock and found Keith dead. He was still in bed. She called his doctor immediately. At about 5 o'clock Jackie Curbishley, who had been trying to contact Keith all day to set up a group meeting, called again. "A man picked up the phone and said, 'What do you want?' I said, 'I want to speak to Keith.' And he said, 'I'm sorry you can't speak to Keith.' I got a bit irate, you know, and I said, 'Who am I speaking to?' He said, 'This is Doctor Dymond.' So I said, 'What's happened?' I told him who I was and he said, 'I suppose I can tell you. Keith is dead.' " Jackie was completely shocked and didn't know what to do. Dr. Dymond said to her, "Look, you are going to have the press on to you soon, because the ambulance men are on their way and the minute they get here they will phone the press. You should be prepared for it." Bill Curbishley was on his way back from a meeting with Polygram, negotiating for the Who's films. Jackie called the Who's publicist Keith Altham, and while the phone was ringing Keith Altham himself walked into her office.

Jackie called Pete and told him what had happened and asked if he could tell the other people concerned. Then Jackie and Altham and one temporary receptionist had to deal with the press. "We were there until midnight. The phones never stopped. There were calls from the States and all round the world." A car was sent to get Annette and she came to the Trinifold offices. "She was hysterical by then," remembers Jackie.

Pete called Roger, John, Kim, Keith's mum and so on. John was in the middle of an interview with two Irish journalists when his mother interrupted to say that there was an urgent phone call. "I went back and finished the interview, and when they were asking me questions about the Who's future I sort of broke down and said, 'Look I can't carry on with this interview because I've just heard that Keith has died.' " Roger was at home when he got Pete's call . . . "He just said, 'He's done it.' I said 'Done what?' He said 'Moon' and I knew." Coincidentally, Mama Cass had died in the same room four years earlier.

A couple of days after Keith's death I went to see Kim who had been living with ex-Faces keyboard player, Ian MacLagan. Mac was in the States and the press wouldn't leave Kim alone. There were two reporters from the Sunday

Mirror that kept calling at the house. After a while we thought that they had gone and had believed the story that I and Kim's friend had told them that she had gone to her father's place in the country. We hadn't seen them for about five hours. Kim wanted to go and see somebody, and I was going to give her a lift in my car which was parked around the corner. Her friend and myself left the house in Wandsworth High Street and walked around the area searching for any sign of their car. When we were satisfied that they had gone, we returned and waited for about half an hour and then left the house. About 15 seconds after leaving, their car appeared from nowhere and roared up the road. We ran round the corner, but they caught up with us and held this ridiculous interview while we were all running along the road. One photographer was running along backwards ahead of us taking pictures of Kim as he went. He said to me, "We don't want to harrass anyone or be a nuisance."

The question facing the Who, once they had tried to deal with the personal grief of Keith's relatives, was of course whether they should now break up or continue together as the Who. They put Annette up in Blakes hotel and gave her a weekly allowance.

Keith's death had always been feared. Any normal person would have been killed long ago if they had led the kind of life Keith had. The legend had grown that Keith was indestructible. "I think he actually believed himself indestructible," said John Entwistle, "I mean, I've seen him tumble down thirty stairs and get up as though nothing had happened and begin a conversation. He was quite shocked that he had broken a few bones over the past few years." Pete said, "Keith's death is something we expected for twenty years, but when it happens you just can't take it in. I'm very upset, I've lost a man I loved."

In the last few weeks Keith had been in good spirits, although physically out of shape. He had intended to tackle his weight problem. "He'd gone to seed and he wanted to get it back," noted Roger. "I went with him to see 'The Kids Are Alright' and he got so depressed. It must have been horrific for him. There was this young drummer, great looking kid, going bananas, who turns out at the end of the film, a fat old thing, falling off the drums, being held up. We were going to get a gym together at Shepperton."

"He was a bloody institution"

Radio stations all over America began playing tributes to Moon as soon as they heard of his death, and in England his passing was front page news. Many glowing tributes from both friends and critics about not only Keith Moon the drummer, but Keith Moon the eccentric personality, followed in the days after. The rock world was stunned. At the end of the Knebworth Festival, Todd Rundgren joined The Tubes onstage to play *Baba O'Riley* and *The Kids Are Alright*. Blondie's drummer, Clem Burke, kicked over his kit at the end of their show declaring, "That's for Keith Moon, the Greatest Drummer in the World."

At his peak he was drinking two bottles of cognac and several bottles of champagne a day. Jackie Curbishley remembered the day before his death Keith was in Trinifold's offices. "He was dressed in his riding get-up, like on the *Who Are You* album sleeve. He'd taken to wearing it most days. He also had on make-up which he also wore quite regularly for photo sessions and stuff. I said to Chris Chappell. 'Look Moon's been in and he's only drunk this much brandy.' I showed him the bottle. There was only about $\frac{1}{4}$ gone. He usually used to finished the whole bottle in an hour."

Keith had been in the office because he had wanted to buy a house for himself and Annette.

Keith had been entertaining people with his drumming and his perverse humour for as long as people could remember. John Schollar remembers when Keith tried to join his very first group, the Beachcombers: "At first we turned Keith away because he was too little to take into pubs, but he was so persistent, and after he'd auditioned he was so good, there was no way we weren't going to let him in. His dad came with him on his first few gigs to see that he didn't get up to mischief. When we used to do *Little Egypt* we used to carry Keith on in a basket and he'd do the talking intro bit dressed up in a fez."

Even before Keith joined The Who he was the ace clown. "He used to dress up in these pantomime horse and donkey outfits that somebody had pinched from an ice show at Wembley Arena", says Schollar, "He'd go everywhere in them, on the underground, up the escalators, everywhere. I remember once he tried to get on a bus dressed in the horse's outfit and the West Indian conductor wouldn't let him on. He was arguing with him through the slit in the costume, offering to pay double fare and everything. After one gig the Beachcombers played at Brize Norton American Air Force Base, the security on the gate searched our van and confiscated all the cheap packets of cigarettes that we'd bought in the PX. Keith was so angry that he stopped the van a little way outside the gates and put on the pantomime donkey outfit, went back and started charging the guard's hut. He kept ramming it and these GI's didn't know what was going on. They pulled guns on him and we had to drag him back to the van. They'd have shot him if he'd carried on."

Once in The Who, Keith soon built up his world-wide reputation as a hotel-wrecker. Tom Wright witnessed Keith's finest devastation on The Who's 1967 U.S. tour, soon after Keith had bought 1,000 fireworks in South Carolina.

When they reached New York Keith got to work with his cherry bombs blowing up doors at the Waldorf Astoria Hotel. The group were promptly thrown out and had to sleep on the bus all except Pete who was put up by a New York friend. It was also in New York at the Gorham hotel that Tom Wright had his most hair-raising experience with

Keith. They were staying there for a week. "Keith discovered that he could light these cherry bombs and just throw them out the window and it had just a stunning effect on the street life below. They would explode about ten feet up before they hit the ground. People were just screaming and yelling and guys were hitting the fucking sidewalk, not knowing what was going on. He had a room on the corner and he'd throw 'em out of one window – BOOM – then give it about a few minutes and when there was a whole new crowd he'd toss one out of the other into the other street. Boom." Tom was playing tapes in his room and thought that the noise was just cars backfiring. Unbeknown to anyone else, Keith was causing major disruption and panic in New York. Suddenly Tom heard a hammering on his door. "I opened the door and there was just like cops all the way down the hall. One guy was lying on the floor with a rifle pointed at my door and two guys up against the wall and the guy right in front of me had his gun straight out in both hands and was pointing it right in my face. 'What the hell is going on?' he said. 'Who's got the piece?' I said 'man everybody is peaceful here, no problem whatsoever.' They poured into my room and just did this whole thing. So I got on the 'phone to Keith's room. He wasn't there. They were now going off every once in a

while in the lobby and maybe the elevator and the manager was screeching 'This has got to stop!' The excitement level in my room with the Police and the manager and me scared to death – 'cause I had a whole load of smoke bombs and firecrackers in my room which were for the stage act, but they were illegal too – was just a perfect Keith Moon deal. He couldn't resist it. In the middle of all this he strolls in and shakes hands with all the cops and is real polite, you know, and talking like an English aristocrat and apologising and full of charm saying, he just thought they were like English fireworks and there'd been a misunderstanding. 'They are definitely not bangers ahahahaha! I threw it out of the window 'cause I was afraid it would go off in the room – not the kind of noise they make in England'." Well miraculously the cops had cooled down and it looked like we wouldn't have to go to jail. Keith got copies of Who albums and signed them all for the cops and hung around and they decided to let him go and split. The manager came back to my room after Keith and the cops had gone and started on 'Godammit this is terrible, where's that Chris Stamp? They told me blah blah blah.' Eventually I explained that Keith had mistaken cherry bombs for smoke bombs and we worked it all out with the police and it won't happen any more. The guy was in a state of shock and was wiping his brow and going 'Thank God, Thank You'."

Well, unbeknown to me Keith had used the bathroom and lit a cigarette and left a cherry bomb on top of the cigarette in the ashtray. A delay of about three minutes. I'm just assuring the manager that everything's under control and saying goodbye to him when BOOM! the room shook and it's like World War III and bits of pink bathroom curtain come flying into the room. The manager just turned white and ran down the hallway."

Keith carried on his running battle with hotel managers, much to the 'shocked' amusement and astonishment of the public. His driver, Dougal Butler, recounts a typical confrontation: "We flew into LA and moved into an extremely posh suite that Bob Dylan had just given up in the Beverly-Wiltshire Hotel. Keith went out and hired this huge hi-fi unit, which he used to play at full volume. The management went mad, 'cos all the millionaires and princes and that in the rooms around us kept complaining. It got so bad that one night while Keith was playing it they came in and cut off all his electricity by removing the fuses while he was in the bathroom. So Moonie promptly moved everything except the bed out into the hallway. He set up the table lamps, the table and chairs, the fridge, the telly, the sofa, the lot. And he went and pinched the fuse out of the fuse box for the lift. It was ridiculous. It's one of the most expensive hotels in America and the lift wasn't working! And Moonie was sitting there in his dressing gown in the hallway with his feet up on the coffee table, drinking Dom Perignon, watching telly with his hi-fi unit blaring out Jan and Dean. By the time the management turned up there was a crowd of outraged guests in evening wear round him. Moonie looked up and said 'You give me back my electricity and I'll give you back your lift'."

Dougal had worked for Keith on and off for seven years up until 1977, "I used to have to take two month breaks every now and then and anyway he used to sack me every five weeks or sometimes every half hour. I'd describe those seven years as 'totally unpredictable but amazing'. It was also absolutely exhausting. People don't realise that often we were more skint than rich. When we were living in Malibu we had to borrow milk from the next door to have a cup of tea. But then a couple of thousand dollars would come in and he'd blow it all in two days looning."

Keith was incredibly generous. One of the last things I remember was of him in this pub in Kings Road buying drinks for this old tramp. At the end of the night he swapped his solid gold Dunhill lighter for the tramp's old wick lighter."

Keith should ultimately be remembered as a professional musician. nearly every big name drummer recognized his genius, although his style was 'unconventional'. He once went along to Billy Cobham's drum clinic. After attacking the kit for almost half an hour, Cobham, who had been watching in silence, turned to Keith and said, "I don't know what it is you're doing, but whatever it is, just keep doing it."

Daltrey summed it all up when he said, "He was a bloody institution, he should have been nationalised!"

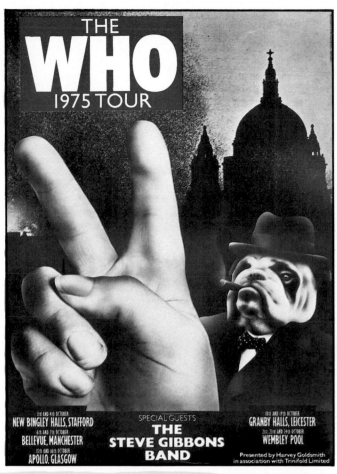

THE WHO 1975 TOUR

3rd and 4th October
NEW BINGLEY HALLS, STAFFORD
6th and 7th October
BELLEVUE, MANCHESTER
15th and 16th October
APOLLO, GLASGOW

SPECIAL GUESTS
THE STEVE GIBBONS BAND

18th and 19th October
GRANBY HALLS, LEICESTER
21st, 23rd and 24th October
WEMBLEY POOL

Presented by Harvey Goldsmith
in association with Trinifold Limited

Above: Oakland, California - 1976
Left: The logo for the 1975-76 US tour.
Below and Centre left: The 'Who Put The Boot In' tour in 1976 was climaxed by the overcrowding (over 20,000 forgeries were circulating - the extra fans were let in) and muddy squalor of Charlton. One reviewer said, "How many other bands could make 50,000 kids forget they'd been standing in a steady downpour for over five hours?"
Bottom left: Ken Russell signed Daltrey to play the lead in 'Lisztomania' after his success as 'Tommy'. The film was widely criticised.
Opposite: Philadephia Spectrum 1975.

The boot goes in — firmly

SOAKED, SUNBURNED — BUT IT WAS WORTH WHILE

Now Hear This II

The 'Oo make you deafer — official

WHO: Music conquers mud and blood

Loudest *Pop Group*

The amplification at *The Who* concert at Charlton Athletic Football Ground, London on 31 May 1976 provided by a Tasco P.A. System had a total power of 76,000 watts from eighty 800 W Crown D.C. 300 A Amplifiers and twenty 600 W Phase Linear 200's. The readings at 50 metres from the front of the sound system were 120 db. *Exposure to such noise levels causes PSH—Permanent Shift of Hearing or partial deafness.*

A KEN RUSSELL FILM STARRING ROGER DALTREY "LISZTOMANIA"

THE WHO
THE SENSATIONAL ALEX HARVEY BAND
LITTLE FEAT · OUTLAWS
STREETWALKERS

WHO PUT THE BOOT IN
AT CHARLTON ATHLETIC FOOTBALL CLUB LONDON 31st MAY
CELTIC FOOTBALL CLUB GLASGOW 5th JUNE
SWANSEA CITY FOOTBALL CLUB SWANSEA 12th JUNE

PRODUCED BY HARVEY GOLDSMITH ENTERTAINMENTS LTD. AND TRINIFOLD LTD

TICKETS £4 INC. VAT.

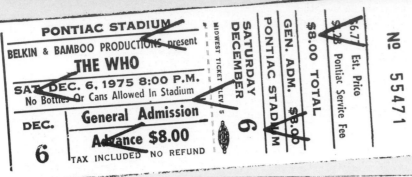

PONTIAC STADIUM
BELKIN & BAMBOO PRODUCTIONS present
THE WHO
SAT. DEC. 6, 1975 8:00 P.M.
No Bottles Or Cans Allowed In Stadium
DEC. | General Admission | 6
6 | Advance $8.00 |
TAX INCLUDED NO REFUND

No 55471

78,000 rock fans swarm to Pontiac Stadium show

Fans love 'Who': 78,000 jam stadium

Phenomenal Who just glorious

TENNESSEAN LIVING

Who's Energy Lifts Audience off Seats

Once, on tour, the Who chartered an ancient propeller-driven plane. The shake and noise was appalling — "Like bombing Berlin", As the commotion increased an extremely drunk Moon and Townshend stripped off completely and after a bout of naked dancing, during which Keith annoyed several people by offering them his groin, they made for piles of food stacked up in the kitchen at the back. They then ran straight through the curtain into the cockpit, and started pelting the pilots with the rolls. Lumps of ham and cheese and bread covered the pilots and controls, with crumbs fouling up different instruments, causing the plane to lurch violently. Amidst the hysteria Keith, had trouble getting into the toilet, and with people yelling at him to 'sit down', he simply tore the door off and sat down looking pleased with himself.

Right: The Pontiac-Stadium 1975.

Hailed as geniuses when we were a bunch of scum bags

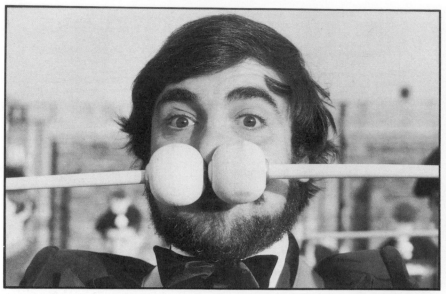

Mad Moon the door-blaster strikes again

WHAT THE Small Faces said, or didn't say, to that air stewardess in Australia recently pales into pure frolic beside the demoniac doings of the Mad Drummer, alias Keith Moon of The Who.

"He spent a night in New York blowing up hotel doors with dynamite, including the Waldorf Astoria," cribbed his Who colleague Pete Townsend. "Consequently, we all chucked out of a succession of hotels. The rest of the boys had to spend the night in the tour bus, but I was luckier. I went and stayed at some friends' flat."

WHO MOON (BLACK EYE, CUT LEG) TO STAY ON

KEITH MOON this week withdrew a threat to leave the Who. He said he hoped to rejoin the group for concerts after he has recovered from injuries sustained ...

BEACH BOYS WANT WHO'S KEITH MOON

It was learned this week that the Beach Boys have made an approach for Who's Keith Moon to join them on certain dates during the remainder of the year. Reason for the invitation is that regular drummer Dennis Wilson recently ...

Lobster in jail for Mad Moon

POP STAR Keith Moon, "wild man" drummer with The Who, has been on the rampage again—in style.

First he smashed ... airport—then he ... to his police cell from ...

PUB BANS MOON FOR SEX FROLIC

From John Hiscock in Los Angeles

ROCK star Keith Moon has been barred from a pub after a sexy frolic with a girl on the bar floor.

"The girl was on top of him," said landlord Phil Elwell. "They were simulating the act of intercourse. It was just too much.

"I told him to get out and come back when he learned to behave himself."

Moon and four friends

KEITH MOON—Barred

Would YOU live next door to Keith?

Moonstruck

THIS striking nor—

BEST DRUMMER
1. Keith Moon
2. Charlie Watts
3. Nigel Olsson
4. Carl Palmer

Keith Moon Hospitalized: 'I Felt Dizzy'

But he's out again. Be warned.

POP STAR'S

FLAT 'WAS

IN SHOCKING

STATE'

What hotels do now is book me into a room they're thinking of having redecorated'

MOON MADNESS TAKES OVER TINSELTOWN

L.A. was even a bit der than usual for lunatic Keith Moon, who hosted a birthday party for himself in Beverly Hills.

I'm Keith Moon what's your excuse?

"I destroy things that eventually destroy themselves. There's an art destruction. Some things look better with a few dents in them."

MOON THE LOON IS BUYING A HOTEL TO WRECK!

Pop drummer's smashing idea

KEITH MOON, the wild man of rock, who gets his kicks by wrecking luxury hotel rooms, plans to buy his own £100,000 hotel — so he can demolish it in peace.

BATTEUR PREFERE
					35,9 %
1	(2	3)	Keith Moon		8,5
2	(1	1)	Ginger Baker		5,4
3	(8	4)	Jon Hiseman		5,2
			Shrieve		4,6
					3,6

Fined drummer Moon asks a court: Will you take credit cards?

"I've always had the liberty to mess around, it's just the more famous you get, the more people write about it. I was saying 'bollocks' when I was six and nobody printed it". "I don't give a damn about a bloody Holiday Inn room; I book it and it's my home for the time I stay there. If I smash it to smithereens, I'll pay for it, — I always pay for the things I do.

Previous spread: Keith with Viv Stanshall and Oliver Reed. This page; Top right: With Stanshall again.
Centre left: Moon once threw a bottle at the wall in his London flat. It stayed there, so he framed it.
Facing page; Bottom left: Abusing an Australian reporter.
Third from left: With daughter Mandy.

IN CASE OF KEITH MOON BREAK THE GLASS

HOTEL

Keith, in Rolls, dropped in

All this and no driving licence

Moon owned and wrecked dozens of cars, from a milk cart to his favourite Rolls Royce Corniche convertible. While living in Malibu, California, his aide, Dougal Butler, recalls: "We were skint at the time. One day Moonie spots a reproduction Mercedes SS Excalibur, once owned by Liberace, which is covered in diamantes. When he was next due at the accountants he put on his Rommel hat, desert goggles. He walked in, demanded the $40,000 owing him, cashed the cheque and went to the car lot. After part-exchanging his Lincoln we had about $2,000 left. We were broke for months".

Top left: The study at 'Tara'.
Centre: With Alice Cooper.
Left: After driving into a pond, Keith saluted as the car went down.

Top left: Pete and Ronnie Lane recording the LP, *Rough Mix* (released in 1977).
Top right: Bill Curbishley takes his 20%. He was made official manager in 1976.
Left: Keith with Dougal Butler, his chauffeur and general life-saver: "I worked for 7 years, got sacked every week, sometimes every half-hour".
Right: John Entwistle's 1975 solo tour "cost me about $70.000, but it was worthwhile to me. It gave me self-confidence. The only thing I stay in the business for is playing live. If I'm not on tour within six months I get restless".
Facing page; Top: John's guitar collection; he usually has over 200.

BRUNEL UNIVERSITY S.U.
KINGSTON LANE UXBRIDGE **FRIDAY 17TH JAN.** LIC. BAR 8 TILL LATE

JOHN ENTWHISTLE'S
OX + SUPPORT
LIGHTS & SOUNDS

TKS. ADV. 70P ON DOOR 90P (INC. VAT) N.U.S & SOCIAL CLUB CARDS.
UNDERGROUND UXBRIDGE BUSES 207, 204, 223

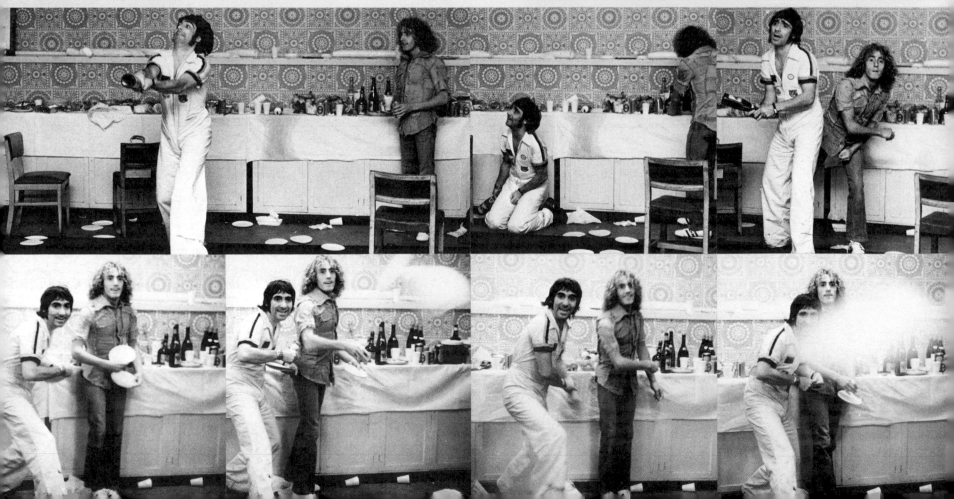

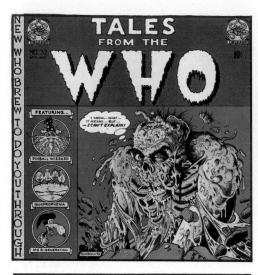

By 1977 the band was in a rut and there were rumours that they could break up. Pete talked about performing, which although highly successful, had become monotonous: "All that seemed to work was a couple of old singles, the stuff from *Tommy,* a few rock and roll numbers... it wasn't a list, it wasn't an act, it wasn't a group, it wasn't anything. It was a fucking celebration of our history... I mean, so far as stage material goes, Keith actually had a list of numbers printed on one side of his drums".

Above left and centre: Two Who bootlegs, featuring unofficial releases.
Right: Graham Hughes' award-winning cover for Roger's 1975 solo release, *Ride A Rock Horse.*

Left and top right: The Kilburn State in North London. This was Keith's penultimate live performance. His last was before an audience at Shepperton Studios, filmed for 'The Kids Are Alright'.
Above: The Who were voted 'Best Band' of 1976 by Rolling Stone magazine. Each member received a pair of red braces.

Who Are You, August 1978: A patchy album, for them that seemed to reflect the concern that the band had about their future. Fraught with difficulties in preparation (accidents and technical problems abounded) it paid little lip service to the punk revolution that was shaking the music business; even though it contained a song *Music Must Change*. Pete, suffering from acute hearing problems, had to record with headphones He'd been told by a doctor to "learn to lip read".

Left: A rejected 'cloning' idea for the cover.
Right: An out-take from the final version. Keith was eventually persuaded to sit down, to hide his paunch.

Who stunned by death of Keith Moon

The sudden death of Keith Moon could mean the end of the road for The Who — rated as one of the world's greatest rock and roll bands. Moon, who gave his age as 31 and boasted he had spent more than £200,000 paying for the damage he wreaked in hotels, planes and restaurants throughout the world, will be impossible to replace in the group.

He was "Moon the Loon" — the wild man of rock, hard

Vast overdose of sleep pills killed Moon

LONDON (AP) — Rock drummer Keith Moon cooked himself a steak breakfast, ate it in bed beside his beautiful Swedish fiancée, and then took a vast overdose of sleeping pills that killed him, a coroner's court heard Monday.

Westminster Coroner Gavin Thurston decided that the evidence did not justify a conclusion of suicide and returned an open verdict.

Pathologist Prof. Keith Simpson testified

MOON THE LOON IS DEAD

Riddle of 'drug overdose'
just hours after rock
drummer gets engaged

● *Loss of the Year:* No one really expected Who drummer Keith Moon to reach three score years and ten, but his sudden death in September was nevertheless a shock to the rock world. No one who ever experienced his inspired showmanship, or his practical jokes, or his warmth, or his drumming, will forget him.

Keith's death on September 7, 1978, was as ironic as it was tragic. After years of abusing himself to the general delight of others, he had shown signs of pulling himself out of a sharp decline. He'd stopped drinking and was taking medication to help him do so, and his drumming on *Who Are You,* which had been erratic in rehearsals was, in the end, superb. On the night before he died he had announced his engagement to his girlfriend of two years, Annette Walter-Lax. In the shock that followed, endless written and spoken tributes assaulted the public round the world. At the end of a Blondie concert, their drummer, Clem Burke, kicked over his drumkit shouting, "That's for Keith Moon, the greatest drummer in the World!"
Left; Series: Keith's last night in London, following the premiere of 'The Buddy Holly Story'.
Top left: Keith talking to the drummer who would replace him, Kenney Jones.
Centre left: With his Swedish fiancée, Annette, and David Frost, who said Keith had been "delightful company".
Bottom left: Chatting to Paul and Linda McCartney.
Centre right: Mrs. Moon and John.
Bottom right: The flowers sent by Roger.

1979-1982

Kenney Jones/Rejuvenation/Movies/Cincinnati/Pete's problems/Future

John and Pete had in fact discussed the possibility of a new drummer some time before Keith had died. John said, "Pete and I had foreseen the day when Keith would have an accident. He'd had a lot of accidents in which he'd been saved by a chauffeur or different members of the band and we talked about if we *did* get another drummer who it would be."

The last time I'd seen Keith was about a month before his death. He attended the opening reception of the 'Who's Who' exhibition with Annette. A few days later at another reception at this exhibition, I met up with Doug Sandom, the Detours' drummer. John had invited him along. Before Dougie left John signed a copy of the *Who Are You* album. When Dougie got home he read that John had written, "To Dougie – For Fuck's Sake Man. Where's your drumkit. We're desperate!"

Now that Keith had died the group were thrown into fresh turmoil. If they were going to split, now would be the time to do it. They were undecided for some time about their future and kept giving contradicting and confusing statements to the press.

Talking about Keith Pete said: "It's sad but I don't think Keith was a happy person. I suppose he should have been – he had success, money, a girlfriend – but he wasn't. At times I saw him very depressed. I think that what he missed was a really close friend. Of course he was very close to me and the others in the band and to his friends like Ringo and Harry Nilsson. But in a way he felt that even to us he had to keep performing. If he was ever really desperate, really depressed, I don't think he felt he could talk to us. We were his heroes and he had to carry on the act with us."

Pete talked of the band's loss, "We have lost our great comedian, our supreme melodramatist, the man who, apart from being the most unpredictable and spontaneous drummer in rock, would have set himself alight if he thought it would make the audience laugh or jump out of their seats . . . We are more determined than ever to carry on, and we want the spirit of the group to which Keith contributed so much to go on . . . although no human being can ever take his place."

Even before the band announced that they were going to carry on, dozens of drummers had called to say that they wanted to join or would just like to help out for the time being. John Entwistle, who shortly after Keith's death had to go to the States for work on the soundtrack for the 'Kids Are Alright' film remembered that everywhere he went he would meet drummers offering their services. "It got to the point where I couldn't even go into a club or restaurant without the guy at the next table drumming away with his cutlery waiting to be discovered."

At first Roger was adamant that the band shouldn't get a new drummer. "There's no question of us simply finding another drummer because it can't be done. It wouldn't be the same. Keith was the best drummer in the world. A hundred others could not replace him." He wanted the group to use different session drummers for different things. Pete wanted to take the opportunity of the band being re-aligned to bring in another guitarist and a keyboard player. There was also the question of whether the band was going to play live gigs and tour. What would that do to Pete's hearing problem and what strain would it impose on his private life? He issued a statement after having a meeting with Roger. "We are not tied to being the Who any more, but we could be back for concerts at Christmas with three new musicians." He pointed out that this was different to a full tour, "My days of dragging my body around the world on tour are over. I hate

touring." John had wanted Kenney Jones to join the band almost immediately. Pete too thought that Kenney was the obvious choice. He had been doing session work for them recently on the Tommy film soundtrack and of all drummers on those sessions he was the one whose playing worked best with Pete and John. The band had known Kenney since the days when he was in the Small Faces when they were both mod bands. John and Kenney had been friends since then.

Pete had hinted at a change of name along with the three new members he wanted to join. Eventually they agreed that they did need a new drummer as part of the band and that they should stay as the Who. A spokesman told the press, "After all, what would they call themselves – The Noo'Oo?"

There were differences of opinion over whether Kenney should be a full member of the Who or on some different

But Who are You?

THE WHO rock star Pete Townshend went to the world premiere of Quadrophenia, the film based on his group's album, last night. And got stopped at the door.

As he arrived at London's Plaza One cinema in Lower Regent Street the commissionaire demanded to see his ticket. Silently, the unrecognised star produced the ticket and went in to join a star-studded audience.

kind of contract. Roger with some justification pointed out that the band had been running for fifteen years and Kenney was joining after they'd made it. However, he was outvoted and Kenney became an equal partner. Most decisions in the Who are decided by voting. Each of the band has one vote and Bill Curbishley also has one vote. If Kenney hadn't been made a full member there could have been endless deadlocks. Curbishley said, "I didn't want any stalemates or anything. Time was too short."

Once they had officially endorsed Kenney, Roger told a journalist, "The 'Oo is a group again. Kenney is now a quarter of the 'Oo, and if one journalist says we are not the same without Keith, then I'll personally break his legs . . ."

Keith's death, in a way, saved the Who from withering away. It made them face up to their future squarely. Pete

said in an interview about three months afterwards, "To be blunt about it, Keith's death has opened a lot of doors for us. After fifteen years I was scared we were getting in a rut. From a group point of view, it has already had some positive effects. The Who were going round in circles. What I wanted to do with the last album was to smash the group to bits, because we were becoming cardboard cut-outs of ourselves. Well Keith's death put a stop to that. Everything has changed. Suddenly our reputation is on the line and nothing is certain. Kenney Jones is the new drummer, but he's not a replacement for Keith, because the old Who is dead and buried."

Kenney Jones had been about to join a new band being arranged by Glyn Johns. The band was to be an Anglo-American six piece called Lazy Racer.

Lazy Racer were rehearsing to go to Nassau to record an album. They had been offered a very good record deal that Kenney had just been about to sign. When Bill telephoned, Kenney suggested they had lunch and talked about it. "I had lunch with Bill and Pete the next day and didn't say yes or no at first, but after talking with Pete for two hours I agreed. After all it's where I come from anyway, as opposed to playing in a band with three Americans and two other English people."

Kenney had his own style of drumming, very different from Keith's. He had to set about learning all the Who numbers that he was likely to have to play on stage. He sat down to listen to various Who records to familiarise himself with the songs. "It's hard to learn just by listening because the music will probably change on live gigs anyway. Even the live tapes of the band I've got vary. The best thing I can do is stay myself, and wait for the proper rehearsals, and it'll all come out."

During 1979, Kenney's first year with the band, they seemed to be constantly in the headlines. The music press called it "The Year Of The Who". Much of the work that had occupied them for the past 18 months came to fruition.

Who Are You was becoming their biggest and fastest-selling album. This was partly because it was the last album on which Keith played.

After the British Punk explosion, came the Mod revival. During 1979 the sixties mod cult had been the inspiration for a new generation's fashions and lifestyle. Kids that weren't born when the first mods posed and strutted about the original Carnaby Street, were busy hunting down original mod clothes in secondhand shops and buying parkas from Army surplus stores. The Who, a couple of years before labelled both the originators of punk and 'boring old farts', were now the 'in' group for the young 15 year old new mods. Who graffiti appeared everywhere. The words 'THE WHO' in a circle with an arrow coming out of the O, was spray painted onto walls, bridges, toilets, underground stations, buses, advertising hoardings. Thousands of young kids had the Who logo painted onto the backs of their parkas and had 'Who' embroidered patches sewn onto their clothes plus hundreds of Who badges.

Early in the year came the debut in London's West End of a stage production of *Tommy*. Pete had been asked to go and see a production that was on at the Queen's Theatre in Hornchurch, Essex. The show was getting rave reviews and Pete went along one night and was very impressed by it. He suggested that they should try to get it put on in the West End.

Despite mixed reviews, particularly of the lead Allan Love ("a Daltrey clone") many people thought it was excellent and it did roaring business for a while.

Whatever criticism there may have been of the 'Tommy'

stage show premiere, the first night party afterwards will never be forgotten. The producers had hired the Sundown night club and discotheque for the occasion. After eating from the buffet and having a few drinks, the cabaret started, introduced by a disc jockey sitting on a raised dais. There was a snake charmer and fire eater, who got Pete to do an Eastern dance with her on the floor. Then there was a group of about ten bare-chested black boys, whose dancing was so good that apart from arousing all the women, it inhibited anyone else from wanting to dance later. Then the DJ introduced Commander Bill Cody with a Western sharp-shooting act. After performing some lasso tricks, his assistant set up a number of balloons on a partition. Commander Cody was going to shoot these balloons whilst facing the other way. He aimed by looking in a small mirror fixed to his rifle. The DJ announced through the P.A., "This trick is very dangerous and it cannot start until everyone has got out of the way and sat down. Please clear the area and sit down. This is very dangerous and somebody could get hurt." He went on until the firing area was cleared. Commander Cody fired a couple of times and hit the first few balloons. Then he missed a couple of times. What nobody realised was that although the DJ had cleared the area, he was still standing in the direction of firing himself up on his record dais. When he started spluttering through the mike, "I've been hit! I've been hit!", those that did hear him above the noise thought it was part of the act. His warning that somebody could get hurt had been prophetic. He was hurt. Eventually someone noticed that he was lying on the ground bleeding. The act was quickly stopped as the DJ, unbeknown to most people was taken backstage and an ambulance called. I had a table at the edge of the dance floor so could observe it all quite clearly. The floor was filling up with smoke which we all assumed was either one of the disco's 'effects' or was part of the next act. However, it got a bit heavy and a few people started complaining. Word then went round that there was a fire. Apparently, backstage, one of the lassos had got caught up with the bucket of liquid used by the fire eater. The bucket had been tipped up and caught alight. Not only that, but the three giant python snakes had all escaped from their baskets. Word now went round that there were escaped snakes somewhere in the dark club. This soon overcame any inhibitions about dancing as the dance floor was slightly less dim than the rest of the club. I decided to take my drink and explore rather than be crushed to death by a python at my table. I met up with the snake charmer girl looking very upset on the stairs. She told me that one of her snakes had been killed in the fire and that the others were burnt. I advised her to sue and continued my walk.

The Felliniesque scene inside the club now included about twenty firemen dancing with all the attractive girls on the dance floor. They were still dressed in their uniforms with bright yellow plastic over-trousers and helmets. Outside the whole of Charing Cross Road was blocked off as masses of fire engines and police vans were all over the street, all with their blue lights flashing. The fire had been put out, although they were checking the entire premises. The smoke had been almost cleared by reversing the air-conditioning. The DJ, on the other hand, was badly injured. He'd been taken to the Intensive Care unit at the Middlesex Hospital, where he underwent a ten-hour operation to remove a bullet from his spine.

When I left the place was still full of dancing, drinking firemen chatting up the girls. To cap it all Pete Townshend claims he stumbled across two firemen making love to each other in a dark corner.

At the end of 1978, John Entwistle's new year resolution was to "Get Pete Townshend back on the road with the Who – dead or alive."

Pete hadn't got in an extra guitarist as he'd intended, but he had included 'Rabbit' on keyboards. The new line-up set two weeks aside for rehearsing so that Kenny, Rabbit and the band could get used to playing together. Unfortunately, the Easter holidays came in the middle and they didn't start until 2 o'clock and ended at 6, so Kenney really only had a few hours to learn how to play one of the most demanding sets in rock, as well as learn all their new numbers. They knew, however, as soon as they began playing with Kenney, that it was going to work. No one could drum like Keith, a brilliant show drummer whose style was somewhere between Buddy Rich and Animal from the Muppets; his weakness, though, was that keeping time was always a problem. With Kenney's style, both Pete and John were released to an extent from that part of their playing. They were going to have one final rehearsal at the Rainbow Theatre before going to France, but Roger wanted them to play a gig for Londoners. He told Pete, "It was the band's London fans that got them off the ground in the first place, so it was only right to play for them before going to Cannes."

An announcement was made on London's Capital Radio that the surprise 'last minute' gig was to take place and that tickets would be on sale only from the Rainbow box-office from 10 a.m. The following morning, the day before the concert, a large crowd had gathered outside the Rainbow by six in the morning and the tickets all went within three-quarters of an hour.

Backstage were some of the Sex Pistols, Phil Collins, Mick Jagger and the usual 'liggers'. Roger had cut his hair short, and wore a black leather bomber jacket. His new tough, mean image was for his coming role in 'McVicar'.

The audience was packed at the front with young teenage mods, but also there were plenty of punks and Who freaks around. Melody Maker reported, " . . . Five shadowy figures loped onstage at 8.35 and cut into a wilful, almost irreverent execution of *Substitute* that had the entire audience on its feet from the first bar. No one sat down for the next two hours." The Who's sound system was incredible. The best and clearest sound ever heard at the Rainbow.

Kenney came across as a powerful hard driving stayer. At one point Pete and Rabbit started playing too fast during *Who Are You*, but the MM tells, " . . . they were conducted back to the correct tempo by Jones' assertive right hand." They ended their report, "Relatively adventurous arrangements of material both obscure and well-worn, irresistably urgent treatments of their simpler stuff, and a new found enthusiasm for performance suggest that the new Who might prove to be even better than the old Who."

The Rainbow had only been in front of 3,000 or so people. Fréjus, in the South of France, was their first sizeable gig with Kenney and Rabbit. It was by all accounts a triumph, so much so that as soon as the first show to 8,000 fans, packed into the open air Roman amphitheatre, had finished, the band agreed to do another the following night, although this clashed with the showing of their own film, 'The Kids Are Alright'.

Roger told the huddle of reporters that had flown to the South of France for the film festival, "You should have heard our second show at Fréjus – it would make a great bootleg – it probably has!"

Pete got on better with Kit and welcomed having him around. After Fréjus Pete told reporters "Kit Lambert has just spent fifteen minutes telling me what's wrong with the Who – and he was right."

Despite the euphoria of their shows with Kenney, Pete was still reluctant to get involved with touring. "To be honest I don't have much urge to go out and work. I lost that years ago. I've always been bullied into touring by the rest of the group, the fans and management. I enjoy it once I'm up there, but I suppose I'm a bit like a tired old bull that has to be lifted on to a cow. It's quite fun when you're up there, but it seems such a lot of effort."

Pete gave a deeper insight into his feelings about touring. "I wouldn't shed any tears at all if last night's show hadn't happened. I'd still be here. I'd still be a happy man. I loved it. It was great and the crowd were great and it was a good show. But I didn't need it. Ten years ago I couldn't have lived without it, and that's the distinction."

"I'm not bitter anymore" - Townshend

After seeing himself in 'The Kids Are Alright', Pete said of himself, "I've seen a cynical, bitter little prat up there talking." He then added, "I'm not bitter any more . . . "

The 'Kids Are Alright' was the film that had been compiled by American Who fan Jeff Stein. Stein had initially put together a 17 minute short and he showed this to the Who. According to Stein, "I've never seen such a reaction. Pete was on the floor banging his head. He and Keith were hysterical. Pete started hitting Keith when he saw the Smothers Brothers TV show where Keith blew up the drum-kit, 'That's where I lost me fuckin' hearing! You did it! That's when it all started!' Roger's wife was laughing so hard she knocked over the coffee table in the screening room . . . That's when they were convinced the movie was worth doing. It amused them, so they considered there must be an audience for it. They're always their harshest critics."

They gave Jeff the go-ahead. A budget of $250,000 was set. Jeff Stein advised them, "Don't get taken for a ride, put up your own money." They did put up their own money – the film eventually ran up bills of over $2,000,000. It also took an incredibly long time to complete. Roger expressed his doubts about Jeff's experience as a director to Circus Weekly just before the film's completion. "The last time I saw it I didn't like it at all. It was so unfinished I can't really say. But I must be honest and say it needed to go a long way. And one of the problems is that Jeff Stein is an amateur. Films need direction and one of the things I don't like about it was that it didn't have any."

Although a professional film maker could probably have completed the film in less time and for less money and returned all the unused material, it simply wouldn't have been a Who fan's film. The 'Kids Are Alright' isn't a public relations exercise and it doesn't necessarily show the Who in their best light. It's a very honest film, as befits the only band left from the sixties still with their credentials 90% intact. It probably needed the fanatical devotion and dedication of one bitten by the Who bug.

The Who's management and Jeff and Kevin Stein fell out over the film. The management and Roger wanted to know the whereabouts of much of the very valuable material collected for the film which disappeared or wasn't returned, and some kind of litigation between the two parties seemed likely.

John Entwistle sorted out all the various soundtracks and flew to LA, where he supervised the Dolby sound dub. Unlike most rock films where the so-called 'live' soundtrack has been beefed-up by overdubs, they kept the soundtrack totally authentic.

The film also served as a tribute to Keith. After his death there was no suggestion of adding more footage of Keith. In fact, they were a bit worried about some of the scenes and wanted to take them out, though technically it was already too late. Pete viewed the final cut two days after Keith's death and so found it very sad and moving. However as NME commented about the film, " . . . one is left thinking just how much fun he (Keith) had when he was alive . . . it communicates Moon's zest for life . . . " The film attracted a huge crowd of over 4,000 outside the cinema in London for its British premiere and was very well received by the critics. Three months later saw the British premiere of their second film venture, 'Quadrophenia'. It was released much later in the States. 'Quadrophenia' is simply, as Newsweek noted, " . . . a damn good movie . . . " Franc Roddam, an unknown director, had created one of the most realistic and entertaining films about adolescence ever to come from the British film industry. The timing of the film, released as it was in the middle of the growing mod revival in England, was perfect.

It became a huge box-office success in Britain. The main problem the film had was being virtually incomprehensible to the American audiences. The fast speaking cockney dialect was difficult for many Americans to understand and mods and rockers had no counterparts in the States. However, the LA Times noted, "Despite its British setting, 'Quadrophenia' evokes the universal feelings of teen emotions with a depth seldom captured on the screen."

In September, the Who hit New York for five sell-out concerts at Madison Square Gardens. The volume of mail requesting tickets for the 100,000 seats set an all time record for the Gardens. Scalpers (ticket touts in England) sold seats for $100 each. New York became Who crazy for a week. Prior to these shows the Who did two shows at the Capitol Theatre in New Jersey. All seven shows were a phenomenal success. The band liked the small "smokey and smelly" venue, "a real rock 'n' roll joint" Pete said from the stage on the first night, "Good 'ere innit? I wish we could play this sort of place all the time." Then added, "Excepting weekends . . . *We* picked these dates. Being the superstar motherfucking comrades that we are we could've ended up playing great big shit'oles."

Time magazine in an article headed 'A New Triumph for The Who' said: "The Who still play for the kids, an audience that has nothing to do with age. These kids are anyone for whom rock 'n' roll is far from entertainment and closer to a matter of life and death."

Before conquering New York they played London's huge Wembley Stadium, famous venue of British soccer's Cup-Final. It was a national Bank holiday in August.

The place was packed to the legal limit – 77,000 fans. Supports were Nils Lofgren, the Stranglers, and AC/DC. The Who were rather mediocre, despite Roger and John's efforts, but it wasn't for any want of trying on behalf of the Who fans, who ecstatically cheered every move to the point of near-hysteria. The sound system was of incredibly high quality, but simply not loud enough. The conservative Greater London Council (GLC), who controlled licences granted for events such as this, were not known for their support for rock music, although they spent thousands on subsidising opera. They had probably set a limit on the maximum volume. John Wolff, a leading expert on lasers in Britain, had arranged to create 'a massive pyramid of light' over the open air Stadium for the finale. GLC officers had approved the lights at a dress rehearsal three days previously but after a few minutes of them being used in the show, GLC officers waiting at the side of the stage ordered them to be switched off. "It was absolutely pathetic and almost ruined the finale of the show," complained the Who's press agent Keith Altham afterwards. "It was explained to the GLC beforehand in the most simple and schoolboyish terms that the lighting was perfectly safe." Apparently there was a slip up and one of the lasers 'momentarily' flashed on to the audience. The GLC officials said "When they were shone into the audience's eyes it was obvious they had to be stopped since this could be a significant health hazard. We didn't want to spoil anybody's fun, but clearly lasers have to be controlled very carefully."

Pete had been asked to help out with a fund raising gig for the 'Rock Against Racism' organisation that utilised rock groups to combat the growing racism amongst skinheads and others. Pete supplied the equipment and lighting for the event and formed a group with Kenney Jones, Rabbit, Peter Hope Evans on harmonica and black bassist Tony Butler to play at the event held at the Rainbow Theatre. Misty also played as did the Ruts and the Pop Group. The gig was called 'Southall Kids Are Innocent'. The Clash played a similar gig the next day and the two shows raised £5,185, which went towards the legal costs of the kids arrested at the demonstration against racism in the London borough of Southall.

The first show of the next US tour was in Detroit at the 4,600 seater Masonic Auditorium. It had been added to the front of the tour for ardent Who fans, who didn't like the huge Pontiac Silverdrome that the band were to play later in the tour, and it was also part of the love affair the Who have with Detroit. "You, or your mothers and fathers broke our first record in Detroit," Pete told the cheering crowd. The show was a warm-up for the tour but it was also the band's tribute to the place that had put *I Can't Explain* into its local charts fourteen years earlier.

When the band broke into the first few chords of *Substitute* to open the tour, the great roar from the crowd and the energy coming up to the stage from that relatively small audience was overwhelming. I soon realised that American Who fans are totally different to their British counterparts. In Britain, despite the loyalty of the fans, there isn't the sheer energy in the audiences that there is in the States and consequently the band reflect that in their playing. I was becoming very critical of the band in England, but the shows on this tour amazed me. It's difficult to be objective when you see so many shows. Certainly there were bad nights, but when they were good, they were probably the best there is. In Britain, the audiences are ultra-critical and it's almost as if the Who have to pass a test each time they play. In the States, the kids are more determined to enjoy the occasion rather than sit in judgement and give points at the end. At the same time, of course, the UK had undergone the Punk revolution and any old established band, if not openly villified, were held in deep suspicion.

Scalpers had sold tickets for the Masonic show at between $100–$150 a seat. I thought the show was phenomenal, as did all the reviewers. The Detroit Free Press explained the crowd's reaction: "Even after 2¼ incredible hours, the crowd was not satisfied. Roaring chants of 'Who, Who, Who . . . ' forced the band back onstage for a 15 minute version of *Dancing in the Streets*, which was followed

by *Young Man Blues* . . . That still wasn't enough, and Townshend came back, pleading apologetically with the crowd for a reprieve, grinning and exhorting the crowd to think 'positive', the Who will be back."

On tour, a distinct pattern emerges. Roger mostly goes his own way. He doesn't smoke or drink and is keen on sports. One of the five limousines that make up the Who's convoy is always kept strictly 'no smoking' for Roger. Smoke affects his throat and so he avoids smokers wherever possible. As Roger needs a full eight hours sleep, he doesn't get very involved with any late night parties, or outings to clubs or discos, and so, subsequently, he starts to live different hours to the rest of the group. Pete, Kenney and John, on this tour and the two 1980 US tours, would party quite a bit. John and Kenney were nearly always in the hotel bar or arranging to go to clubs on the days off and they both try to make up for Roger's non drinking. There was a rumour going around that Kenney was once seen without a glass in his hand, but no one could substantiate it.

On this particular tour Roger more than the others seemed to be the butt of everyone's jokes. Probably because he wasn't around much, but also partly due to his health food fads, his extreme caution with his money, and his inability to relax. He had a masseuse on tour to massage him after shows. Roger was always worried about some aspect of the tour. Very often, he was completely justified and he is, in fact, the only member of the band that is constantly thinking about the tour and its problems. A typical joke about Roger's 'tightness' came one night when the band were late for leaving the dressing room to go on stage. One of the crew said, "I'll get them on stage" and shouted out, "Roger! Someone's dropped a $50 bill on stage!" One day I'd got into Roger's limo along with Bill Curbishley and a few others, when Roger complained to Bill that he was getting a bit fed up with all the references to him being tight. There was a bit of an awkward silence and then Bill said: "But Roger, you *are* tight."

On the other hand, if Roger thought that somebody had worked very hard and he genuinely thought they deserved a reward, he could be very generous.

Roger had an absolute obsession for tea. Doug Clark his personal assistant usually wore a tea shirt with the words, "Cup of tea Doug?" printed on the front. This was Roger's favourite saying and Doug had to brew tea for Roger at the oddest moments. Roger had a British electric kettle, specially adapted for American voltages so that he could make tea in his hotel rooms. Making tea properly is an art, but in the States, a tea bag dumped in a cup of hot water is considered teamaking. Roger always had to have it made correctly by Doug and often sent Doug to make a cup of tea half way through a live performance. There were various nicknames for Roger; 'Dip' which comes from the sixties when he used to use Dippity Doo to set his hair. He was also called 'The Duchess' because of his hair style about the 1967 era. 'Sid' and 'Tarzan' were more recent names, 'Tarzan' because of his keep fit and exercising. The story went that while recording in Monserrat he used to swing from tree to tree to get to the studio from the beach.

Eleven people die at Cincinatti

The other major passion on that tour was Space Invaders. Pete was addicted, and we were constantly looking out for machines. We nearly missed every flight that took off from an airport that had one in the coffee shop. When we arrived in one new town, before he'd even got his cases brought up, Pete was on the phone to the lobby asking about Space Invaders machines. He even got Yellow Pages and rung around all the bars to discover if any had one. In one town the Who security were not happy at the thought of Pete and I going off on a bar crawl for Space Invaders.

John, Kenney and Pete were all having problems with their marriages during this period. John had fallen in love with Max, a girl from the Rainbow in LA and she had joined the tour. Pete was very unhappy at this time. The first night in New York I'd found him lying on the floor, half drunk with his ear pressed against his stereo cassette player which was turned up full and blaring out *Private Life* from the then unreleased Pretenders album.

Touring is incredibly hectic. The only constants are aeroplanes, airports, limousines and hotel rooms. Each person on the tour is given a book of information about the tour. Information about the size of the venue, the hotel, the limousines, the distance from the hotel to the venue, the times of flights, times for leaving, for having baggage picked up, what restaurants, clubs, music stores, discos, health clubs there are in each town and what special things have been arranged, record company presentations or welcoming parties and so on.

On most days off, the tendency is to sit in the hotel room and watch TV.

At the December 3rd Cincinnatti concert, instead of leaving with the band and most of the entourage for the sound check in the afternoon I decided to try to catch up on some sleep. I finally left after 8 o'clock. As the limo pulled into the backstage area, there was a huge fire truck and some ambulances parked there and a policeman waved the car away. We drove down the street then returned and were waved into the backstage area. I thought that the presence of the fire truck might possibly be a standard precaution taken by American cities when running a large concert. I met up with an old friend who'd driven over to see the show from Fort Jennings, Russ Schlagbaum who used to work for the Faces. Russ and I decided to go out into the auditorium to see the show from there instead of standing at the side of the stage. We went up to the top tier of the auditorium and wandered around the outside corridor. I saw several firemen rush past the kids and assumed that there was a small fire somewhere. I thought that I could see and smell smoke.

After a while I saw more police and paramedics rushing about and through the glass doors to the outside saw police, paramedics and firemen and spotlights and lots of activity. I asked a woman usher whether there had been a fire. She noticed my official Who Tour plastic pass. "Don't you people know what's happened here tonight – fifteen people have been killed." I was surprised, but for some reason didn't believe her. I thought that perhaps there had been a couple of heart attacks and a drug OD, and that the ushers had exaggerated the whole thing. We spotted a group of officials looking very clean-cut and worried, accompanied by top police officers and firemen inspecting the place and I knew that something was seriously wrong. I asked another uniformed usher why there were so many police and officials present. He told me that eleven people had been killed. Another elderly usher told me, almost with pride, "Didn't you know? History has been made here tonight. The whole world will know about this in the morning."

I still wasn't clear about what had happened at that concert, but a little later I passed a huge pile of shoes and jackets, scarves and bags. I actually shivered at the sight of it.

Back on stage Bill Curbishley was standing behind a stack of amps. "I've just heard about what happened" I told him. He said that the group didn't know or many other people for that matter and we should keep it quiet as he intended to tell the group as soon as they came off.

Bill hadn't known anything about the tragedy until the band were into their fifth or sixth number. The promoter came and told him that there had been two deaths. A little later he said that it had been four deaths. Bill remembers, "As we were going through the show, the supposed overdoses were mounting up. Then I learned what really happened." There had been a suggestion that the show should be called off. Bill pointed out that the worst thing that the authorities could do would be to stop the show. "If you are going to tell nineteen thousand kids that some of them are dead outside, you are not going to have a chance to clean up the Plaza and you'll chance a riot inside." The Fire Chief totally agreed. They were still treating people outside. It is not yet clear what happened, but it appears that because of the first-come-first-served basis of General Admission seating, a large crowd had already formed outside the Riverfront Coliseum by 1.30 in the afternoon. By 6.30 it had grown to around 8,000 and there were only 25 police on duty to control it. It was already getting out of hand as those at the back were pushing forward and appeals to the police to do something were ignored. People were falling down in the crush and getting trampled. However when the doors were opened it appears that only two or four were opened out of sixteen. The authorities afterwards claimed that more doors were opened, but eyewitnesses denied it vehemently. The kids who died were squeezed by the enormous crush of the crowd and simply couldn't breathe. The crowd trampled over bodies that had dropped to the ground while being caught in the surge to get in through the few open doors. All this time ticket takers inside insisted on seeing people's tickets.

The Cincinnatti Enquirer next day reported a 'Stampede' and the Dayton Ohio Journal Herald reported one of the doormen as saying, "First, they threw a bottle through a window in the door (about two minutes before the gates were to open). Then they pushed through the hole making it bigger. Three or four of us tried to hold them back . . . They carried in one boy and laid him on a table and he died . . ."

The same newspaper quoted an eyewitness who said he'd tried to revive three of the victims; "People just didn't seem to care. They could see the people all piled up and they still tried to climb over them just to get in." However, kids in the crowd refuted the media suggestions of a stampede. Rolling Stone reported one of them getting angry at the word 'stampede', " . . . because to him it was a concentration of too many people in too small a space with nowhere to go but forward . . ."

Hardly anyone in the audience knew what had happened. Bill Curbishley spoke to the band in the tune-up room when they came off in the interval before the encore. "Something very serious has happened. I would like you to go straight back on and do your encore and make it short. Then come off and come back in here and I will explain it all to you."

Bill told them not to stop and talk to anyone but come straight back. Pete gave a nervous little laugh and lit a cigarette and they decided on which numbers they would play for an encore and went back on stage.

In the dressing room afterwards the atmosphere was understandably heavy and intense. The table of food laid out was hardly touched and no guests came back this night. People talked quietly in small groups about what had happened. Mostly people were stunned and silent. After a while we started discussing it, but still weren't sure of the facts. Bill had been told that there were ten deaths and I had heard eleven or fifteen. The group were in shock. We seemed to stay in that room for hours.

Roger was visibly upset and said that it was the end of the tour and later talked of it being the finish of the Who. The talk went round and round, everybody searching for some explanation but no-one finding any. Everybody was totally drained and empty and drifted out to the cars to return to the hotel. The promoter had wanted the band to leave the city that night. Roger also thought that the band should fly out.

Back at the hotel there were already press and TV

KRUNCH!
THWAAAK!
BLAM!
KAPOW!

The Kids Are Alright
THE WHO

The double album from their film, including unreleased live material and 20 page colour booklet.

Film released through Brent Walker Film Distribution Limited.   Album & Cassette

cameras at the door. Everybody went up to their rooms. Outside the suite that Pete and I shared there were two large security guys stationed to keep out the press who were wandering around trying to find out who was where. After some time John Entwistle phoned round and got everybody into his room. It was a time to be together. Some of the people there were still in shock and just sat silently, others had talked it all out of themselves earlier and were feeling empty. The tragedy was hardly mentioned, although still at the back of everybody's mind. The TV was on and it was from that that we learnt what had really happened. John had realised that nobody could just go to their room and sleep and the gathering in his room worked in calming everybody down and giving everyone a chance to be together and get things more into perspective in their own minds.

The next morning I woke up at about 6.30 a.m. and turned on the TV. The names and addresses and ages of the victims were being flashed up on the screen on caption cards. I lay in bed crying at all this. The hotel was full of pressmen and TV crews. I went with one of our party to get

some breakfast and newspapers and immediately bumped into three reporters from Time magazine who were wandering about looking for someone to interview.

A call came through that some of us were to meet in Bill's room at a certain time and be packed to leave. The corridor outside Bill's room was packed with about thirty reporters and the band had given a short press conference. We all left and walked to the elevator. Somehow Kenney had been left behind. I went back through the throng and got Kenney and literally pulled him through the crowd into the lift. He was transfixed and didn't know what to do. The situation was bizarre. Pete, Roger, John, Kenney, Rabbit, Bill and a couple of others were standing in the elevator waiting to descend, but facing them were about six reporters, a film cameraman and a photographer who was clicking away the whole time. The group were in shock and nbody did anything for about two minutes. The elevator doors couldn't close with so many people in it. Bill Curbishley then said, "This is fucking ridiculous. Will the press please get out." After a number of requests they all got out and the elevator descended to the basement. Surrounded by hotel security guards, the whole party was led by the hotel manager through the laundry room and the kitchens, past surprised cooks and along various long passages past the garbage bins to a back parking lot where a couple of cars were waiting. We shot out of the hotel and missed the mass of TV crews that were set up facing the front entrance.

A TV crew followed the group on to the scheduled flight to Buffalo, but were refused permission by the airline to film interviews on board. At the other end another pack of TV cameras were waiting for the group to disembark but they left the plane by a special ramp straight into their car which had pulled up next to the plane.

The next two rock concerts at Riverside Coliseum were cancelled. When the next rock group, ZZ Top, played there in 1980, all 16 doors were opened.

The band had decided to continue with the rest of the tour that morning. The mayor of Providence, Rhode Island, had ordered the cancellation of the Who concert there, but the tour continued almost as planned except for some understandable over-reaction with regard to security. At many of the concerts there were hundreds of police and security people. In some places, even if a kid stood up to applaud, a uniformed official would threaten him. On arrival at one auditorium the police had dogs trained on the crowd of a few hundred waiting around the stage door as the Who entered. At Buffalo, Roger announced from the stage, "You all heard what happened yesterday, there's nothing we can do, we feel totally shattered, but life goes on. We all lost a lot of family yesterday. This show's for them."

Press people had flown in from Britain and all over the world to Buffalo. It was almost like a trial, yet the whole show went off perfectly and the crowd were magnificent, possibly the best audience of the whole tour.

Backstage, before the show, it had been very tense. The promoters had provided amongst other things a Space Invaders machine which helped take Pete's mind off things and calm him down. The promoter was quite relieved that the Who hadn't cancelled and I easily persuaded him to give us a Space Invaders machine. At each gig it would be set up in the hospitality room and Pete would challenge the roadies to games. However, if it was therapeutic for Pete, it was the opposite for Roger. He hated the noise and it was agreed that at the end of the tour he would be allowed to smash it up with an axe.

Three days after the tragedy at Cincinnatti, the band played a second show in the huge Pontiac Silverdrome in Detroit which was another festival seating event. There were plenty of doors open to get in but the crush of fans inside was frightening. The stewards were doing the best they could to pull kids out from the front of the audience where they were being squashed. It had all the makings of another disaster. Roger appealed to the crowd to take a step back at the start of the show and repeated it five minutes later. Pete also appealed to the crowd, "It would actually be great if you could ease off the pressure on the front here, 'coz even though we're only playing half the hall there's still 46,000 people and there's probably 20,000 on the floor. If something happened tonight we just fucking couldn't be able to face ourselves ever again. So please. If you could ease off at the back."

The pressures of touring made it impossible for the Who people to dwell for long on what had happened at Cincinnatti. The next show was in Chicago where the show was linked up by video to ten cinemas around the city. They showed the film version of *Tommy* as a first feature, then switched over to watch the live video simulcast of the Who concert. It was the first time that something like it had been tried and Bill Curbishley was very nervous. If everything went well it could provide a way for the group to play to a huge audience without having to play a vast impersonal stadium. In two of the cinemas the equipment wasn't working and they were upset about disappointing audiences. Curbishley remembers, "I thought, if anyone even sprains an ankle, let alone smashes the windows, it is going to be headlines all across America, you know, 'Another Who Riot!' If someone cut a finger, it would be 'Fan Nearly Bleeds to Death!' "

On the night of the show, Bill went around each of the cinemas. The two problem cinemas each sorted out their technical difficulties minutes before going 'on air'. Curbishley regards the Chicago simulcast as one of his most fulfilling moments, "It worked and the kids were really getting off on it. I was really nervous, but the minute they were on the stage, it was great."

Around this time, I got a very interesting insight into the casualness of rock finances. Bill mentioned the name of somebody connected with Chicago. "He owes me a bundle in royalties that he's never paid. I wish you'd have a go at getting it, Bill. He's had it for years," Pete said, matter-of-factly. The fact that such a huge sum of money could have been almost forgotten was incredible. Largish cash sums are certainly used daily and with amazing results, to oil the wheels of the tour. Nearly any problem encountered along the way can be solved by offering a large tip to somebody. It's amazing how many restaurants, bars, hotel room services etc. that have closed or are out of certain things can suddenly accommodate you at the sight of a $50 bill. One night Pete and I and a friend from San Francisco, Geoff Gilbert, decided to go to Myrtle beach in S. Carolina to the Baba centre there, for a break and a much needed rest. It was too late to catch a plane, so I thumbed through the yellow pages and called around to hire a plane. I negotiated a Lear Jet to take us from Philadelphia to Myrtle Beach and then to pick us up and take us to Washington in time for the show two days later. With a cash discount it came to about $5,000. I collected about $7,000 cash from the tour accountant, but as we were going to a club beforehand I had to put it in my shoe for safe keeping. I spent the whole time at the club with one leg about an inch higher than the other as I danced around with this $7,000 wad in my shoe.

We had to find the plane at a deserted airfield in the middle of the night and before we set off I had to count out the cash for the pilot. It seemed so strange paying for a private Lear jet as though it were a taxi. Once paid for however, the jet was ours and Pete told them to take off vertically. Pete had experienced this before and warned us to be ready. As soon as the jet had taken off, the pilot pulled the stick back and we climbed almost vertically up to 40,000 feet. It was so exciting that asked if they would land and take off again but they couldn't. After spending so much time and $5,000 arranging to get to South Carolina, Pete never set foot in the Baba Centre. He spent the whole time trying to catch up on sleep in the Myrtle Beach Hilton a half a mile up the coast from the Baba centre.

Nearly every concert on the 1979 tour was first rate. Kenney was proving that he could handle the hottest seat in rock with no trouble. The addition of Rabbit had enabled them to play material from *Quadrophenia* with lots of piano and organ. Pete would also make a point of introducing Rabbit each night and making sure that he was given the credit he was due. It was difficult to see Rabbit on stage as he was hidden behind all his instruments at the side of the stage and rarely had any lights on him. He was often mixed so low on the PA that it was impossible to hear him. Pete had wanted a keyboard player in the group and would have been happy to have included Rabbit at that time, but the others hadn't agreed. Roger, particularly, had wanted the Who to stay as a three piece after Keith's death and wasn't happy with having a permanent drummer, let alone a fifth member

of the band. Roger is always aware of the public image of the band and with maintaining as much as possible the essential Who line-up.

The horn section, Reg Brooks on trombone, Dick Parry on saxophone and Dave Caswell on trumpet were brought in on about a third of the numbers, and the line-up, although not liked by all Who fans, was more what Pete wanted. Complicated numbers like *Music Must Change*, which would have been impossible to play live with a three instrument line-up were possible and worked very well. It meant that they could perform three songs from their last album plus three or four from *Quadrophenia* as well as all their early classics and stuff from *Tommy*.

The Who finished the year playing one of the Concerts For The People Of Kampuchea at London's Hammersmith Odeon and a drunken and very funny Pete returned on the last night of the Kampuchea concerts to play in Paul McCartney's Rockestra along with eighteen other rock stars who were all (excepting Pete much to Paul's annoyance) wearing gold lamé top hats and tails.

Pete began 1980 by finishing off his solo album. During this period instead of returning to his home each night he moved into a flat in London's Kings Road. He was boozing

This guitar has seconds to live.

The double album from their film, including unreleased live material and 20 page colour booklet.

The Kids Are Alright
THE WHO

Film released through Brent Walker Film Distribution Limited.

heavily and regularly showing up at nightclubs and gigs of the newer groups around London. He turned up at a Clash gig in Brighton and at Joe Strummers invitation and with a guitar borrowed from Mick Jones, he got up on stage and played with them for part of the gig.

The second leg of the three part tour of North America began in Vancouver in April and continued down the West Coast to San Francisco and then through the midwest back to Toronto.

Pete's solo LP, *Empty Glass*, was released in England the day the tour started but held back until a few days after it had finished in North America. The album was originally going to be called 'Animal' or 'Sacred Animal' but because of the Floyd album called *Animals* and other doubts it was renamed. Pete's singing on *I Am An Animal* is the best he'd ever done and Chris Thomas, the producer, had generally enticed vastly superior vocals out of Pete. Another innovative number on this album, *And I Moved* was originally written for Bette Midler; ". . . I listened to it last night . . . and I thought it was like an admission of homosexual tendencies . . . " commented Pete in an interview to NME which was reprinted in Trouser Press. "One of the purest pieces of Schoolboy poetry I've ever written."

Empty Glass was really Pete's first solo album. *Who Came First* was simply a compilation of Baba songs and demos released to counter bootlegs. *Rough Mix* was just a release while the band was in limbo. This time he said, "I just decided to offer everything to the project that's going on at the time . . . I don't want to deny myself Who material because that's what I am." Many of the numbers wouldn't have had the same impact if they were done by the Who as they were very personal. The title track, with its its Sufi-like imagery, was sparked-off by Ecclesiastes; "It really reminded me a lot of Persian Sufi poetry, that it's only in desperation that you become spiritually open . . . Spirituality for me is about the asking, not the answers. I still find it a very romantic proposition, that you hold up an empty glass and say, 'Right. If you're there, fill it.' The glass is empty because you have emptied it. *You* were in it originally. That's why it's only when you're at your lowest ebb, when you believe yourself to be nothing, when you believe yourself to be worthless, when you're in a state of futility, that you produce an empty glass."

Pete's admission that his life was a mess, and the album's mixture of spirituality, carnal knowledge and boozing was a true reflection of what he was undergoing at that time.

Chris Welch, reporting in Musicians Only on a party given in Pete's honour at the time of the release of *Empty Glass*, tells of Pete's reaction to being asked if he'd go on the road with the musicians from the album and play live gigs. " . . . He shook his head and the haunted look seemed to pass over his face once more as he muttered under his breath about his fear of losing his hearing. His children gathered around him and tugged at him to go home while fans descended for copies of their album to be autographed." Chris Welch continued with unusual compassion for a rock journalist; "Townshend has given much to rock music and deserves our respect. He should not allow himself to be torn apart on the battlefield of youth culture . . . He should disengage from vexation, seek the comforts of home, reside in the bosom of his loved ones . . ."

However, Pete spoke about wanting to live in the centre of London being near the nightclubs and "living from day to day and from show to show and album to album."

He told Charles Shaar Murray of the NME, "See, I'm very heavily into Meher Baba, but I also drink like a fish. I'm still not the most honest person in the world. It's difficult, but I do at least know what's happening to me. I accept that there is a larger reason for me being alive than just being a rock star.

"It's not just because I need something to hang onto that I believe in God. If all there was as a pinnacle of human achievement was what I achieved, then there's not enough . . . To many people it would be a dream come true, and to me it's my childhood dream come true, but it's still not enough. It's not high enough and it's not pure enough.

"I'm not there yet, and that's what life is about; having to aspire. You have to aim higher, and if you're going to aspire to anything you might as well aspire to the universe as opposed to aspiring to the house next door, or to someone's tits."

Pete's problems/A plan for the Future

Pete's drinking problems and his marital problems were getting worse. He had always been capable of taking very large quantities of alcohol before he actually appeared drunk, and he never considered that he had any particularly serious drinking problem. However that's precisely what he had and it wasn't helping him face up to his problems. On a visit to New York, the husband of a friend of his persuaded him to take cocaine. Unbelievably, considering his public anti-drug stance taken in the past, Pete succumbed and started using it regularly from then on. On the final part of the North American tour which began with shows in San Diego and seven shows in LA, his coke and boozing habits had quite an effect on his performance. Occasionally he would play brilliantly, and bootlegs of many shows from this tour contain Townshend guitar solos which are among the best he's every played. More often, however, Pete would be so 'out of it' on stage that he would start to wander off on his own, jamming away at the end of numbers that the other three had thought had finished. Many of these guitar solos added on the end of numbers were 'strange'. They would catch Roger out and he would be left in the middle of the stage marking time and wondering what was happening. To a certain extent, I suspected that Pete would do this simply to wind Roger up, but many nights he just selfishly played away totally ignoring the other three. An eye-witness report of one of the LA shows appeared in the 'Who Magazine,' a Who fazine: "Pete appeared a bit more groggy than usual . . . *Drowned* seemed to go on forever. I thought it was finally over and Pete went into yet another guitar solo. The rest of the band looked at each other as if to say, 'Wah? This isn't the way we played it in rehearsal.' Roger's expression often said 'What the fuck is he doing?' All they could do was try to follow along. Pete seemed to enjoy taking charge. When the song finally finished Kenney fell off the back of his drumkit with exhaustion . . ."

Pete was also taking a great deal of amphetimines to get him through the tour. However, it would mean that he would talk his head off after a show backstage. He was always the last to leave. One night he spoke for hours to some fans, who couldn't believe their luck at getting backstage and having Pete talk to them. Eventually, even they were exhausted by him and left. After talking about everything to everybody, there wasn't anybody remaining as it was about three in the morning. There was only our bodyguard, a driver and myself left. But Pete ended up talking for another hour to the cleaners as they seemed prepared to listen.

Usually, backstage and at the hotel afterwards, Pete was the centre of attraction. He could be very very funny at times, but when he was drugged and drunk, he was usually stumbling and mumbling around spilling drinks, and although he held court every night much to the amusement and entertainment of everybody, he wasn't always witty or clever. Nobody had the nerve to tell him what a fool he was making of himself; indeed it would have been difficult to try to. Pete didn't give a damn what he looked like anyway. He didn't really want to be on the road although he loved being on stage.

Even if somebody was concerned, they didn't want to kill the golden goose. Roger, however, didn't like Pete's 'jerking off' on stage and let it be known that he thought Pete was becoming pathetic.

It's normal for rock bands to shove coke up their noses every 20 minutes, but Pete had always frowned upon it and been one of the few rock stars that had been at the top and kept his credibility by not getting involved in the whole camp, coke and limousine scene.

In the corner of the dressing room one night I tried to point out to him what he was doing to himself. The operative word *was* 'pathetic.' He tried to focus his glazed eyes as he chewed the inside of his mouth and said that he could 'handle it'. He replied that he was in control of the situation and knew what he was doing. "I don't wanna be a bloody wimp," he revealed. "It's alright for Keith. Why should he have all the glory?" Pete was clearly confused and lost. Every night when he sang *Drowned* he would ad-lib during the guitar solo lines like "I don't wanna die/I don't wanna die. I ain't scared of it, I just don't wanna die."

At night he would stay up talking and partying long after everyone had disappeared until he collapsed into bed or on to a sofa at about nine in the morning and it was remarkable that he could take so much booze and so little sleep without any major physical effects.

The last date on that tour was at the outdoor Toronto Exhibition Stadium in front of 75,000. It was a very hot day and the kids at the front had been waiting for seven hours for the Who. At one time the organisers sprayed a hose over the crowd to help keep them cool. The City of Toronto had failed in a bid to ban the concert in the Supreme Court a few days before.

After the show there was an end-of-tour party at a Toronto disco which went on all night. In the early hours of the morning the band left for New York to pick up Concorde and return to England.

We were all shattered as it had been a very hectic tour and we'd been partying all night. However, Pete's outrageous behaviour on this tour was yet to climax on the flight home. Concorde was kept waiting as our strange little party determinedly tried to 'wind down' or freshen up by drinking tea or bucks fizz and cognac in the New York Concorde

Lounge. On board, Pete was so 'out of it' and relieved that the tour had finished, that he just let go. There was a particularly attractive blonde stewardess on board and every time she passed by Pete would make a determined but drunken lunge from his window seat and try to grab her. Every so often, he would stand up and attempt speeches, often attacking his fellow passengers. "Ere we all are sitting 'ere travelling faster than a bullet in this supersonic rocket that I paid for with my fucking taxes . . ." and would quickly collapse. Then he took a liking to my meal and would scoop up a handful of lobster, chew it and start spitting out at everybody nearby. Bill and Jackie were in the seats across the aisle, but completely ignored Pete's antics and my appeals for assistance in keeping him under control. The pretty blonde stewardess was removed to work behind a curtain up the front of the plane and the passengers nearby were all moved away. The stewards, however, were all smiles and didn't seem to notice, even when I almost had him in a headlock. The head steward came up and asked if the pilot could have his autograph. Pete started to write it in his wobbly hand and then with a flourish circled the autograph. He went on circling it for about five minutes, so that it looked like a large spiral had been drawn

The Who

'LONG LIVE ROCK' A NEW SINGLE b/w 'MY WIFE' & 'I'M THE FACE'
'long live rock' is taken from the forthcoming film *The Kids Are Alright*
*Originally recorded when The Who were the High Numbers-a rare collectors item

on the page. The steward returned and was delighted, no doubt impressed at what an elaborate autograph Pete had. After leaving the Toronto party a kid in the street had presented him with a packet of cocaine. Pete threw the lot at his nose and it went all over him. Fellow passengers on Concorde probably thought that he had talcum powder all over his face and hair, not realizing that it was really $100 worth of cocaine. After apologizing to the passengers that had been moved and presenting them with free bottles of champagne for their troubles, I spoke to the head steward and suggested that perhaps a straight jacket might be in order. "Don't worry sir," he beamed. "We're not concerned over Mr. Townshend's behaviour. After all, he's our bread and butter." Roger and I were concerned about Pete returning to his family covered in spilt wine, brandy, cocaine and bits of food. Roger found a clean T-shirt in his bag, which I took for Pete to change into. Unfortunately, Pete tossed it out of the car window after we left the airport.

Kenney had complained to me during the tour that he didn't like touring while Pete's album was out. Roger and John were not happy too at the thought of the band working to help a solo album. *Empty Glass*, the first release on the

relaunched AKTO label, had been a big seller for a solo effort. It was selling much more than ever anticipated and had reached number eight in Billboard and was staying there. The second single released from it, *Let My Love Open The Door* had taken off and climbed well up the charts, and was one of a handful of singles to achieve over 1,000,000 airplays in the USA during 1980.

Earlier in the year, the group along with Bill Curbishley had flown back to Cincinnatti to give depositions in lawsuits arising out of the 1979 tragedy. The cross-examining went on for two days. One puzzling feature about this event was that as each member of the band was answering questions – through the window of the apartment opposite, were a number of naked women walking about. If it had been a subtle method of making them lose concentration nobody was complaining, except Bill Curbishley. "By the time they got round to me, there was just a nude bloke over there."

In the Spring, 'McVicar' starring Roger was premiered in London. Roger had been working with Bill Curbishley trying to get 'McVicar' off the ground for three years. Bill and Jackie Curbishley originally read part of bank robber John McVicar's life story in the Sunday Times while McVicar was still serving his 23 year sentence. They thought it would be good for Roger. It took some time to raise the money, but, by putting up the future profits from a soundtrack album which was supposed to be written and played by the Who as collateral, Polydor agreed to put up the money. In the event, Pete didn't write anything for it and the Who only played session parts. However the soundtrack album sold very well. The film received a lot of bad reviews in England but was still a number one box office success.

More tours were planned throughout 1981. An extensive 27 date British tour spread over two months was to be followed by a European tour. Bill Curbishley was also arranging their first Japanese tour which would be linked with dates in Australia. He also wanted to tour America again as soon as possible. The British tour was deliberately booked into very small venues around the country. Roger had said that he would only tour if it was in small places and if possible at weekends. As it turned out, many of the venues were too small for the Who whose equipment is designed for bigger halls and they had problems turning down the volume.

By the time the tour got to Cornwall early problems had been ironed out and the two shows to open the new Cornwall Coliseum were thought by the group to be among the best they'd played for years. However, the next concert, the first of three days at London's Rainbow to raise money for a charity for battered wives, was by most accounts a total debacle. Pete was pretty drunk and they were having technical problems. Roger explained, "My sound monitor blew up at the beginning of the set and after that I couldn't hear anything. So I was miserable and unhappy and I just wanted to walk off stage." He threw the mike into the back of the stage and at the end of the show threw down a second mike declaring "That's it! No encore" and stormed off stage followed by Kenney and John leaving Pete looking confused. Pete then started talking to the audience but was met with a lot of heckling. Members of the crew remember being embarrassed for Pete, though they did eventually return for an encore. The London Times observed, " . . . the preponderance of extended codas, slackly improvised at Townshend's behest, spoiled the flow," or as John Entwistle put it, "He kept boogying off on his own."

The London Evening Standard's pop gossip column was expanded the next night so that writer John Blake could report from 'behind the scenes' about the show. The article, headlined 'The Who At War', talked about the Who coming close to battering one another. "Personally I think that last night Townshend and Daltrey behaved like a couple of spoilt brats." But after describing what he thought was a 'chaotic' show, Blake added, " . . . despite the tantrums, the show proved that the Who at their worst are still better than the vast majority of bands at their best . . . They are far too precious to be destroyed by one silly evening."

The next night Pete was still drunk, but the show was a great improvement. They later dropped two of their new numbers from the set and brought back some of the surefire winners.

Later Pete admitted that he was completely 'pissed'

when he went on stage at the first Rainbow gig and had thought it was a great gig and thoroughly enjoyed himself and only at the end did he realise that the rest of the band and a lot of the audience thought it was lousy.

Halfway through the tour he said that at the very beginning the gigs were different and new. They did five new numbers "They didn't go down very well but they were different and I preferred them. I think we must do what we do and give the audience the chance to accept it or reject it. If we just keep doing the same numbers we'll never know if anything new would have been accepted." He thought everyone was obsessed with running order and things. He would like them to play all the new material, how they wanted, and see what happened.

The British tour continued on its' erratic way. The gigs were patchy and the band were completely unpredictable. After the gigs, Pete, Kenney, John, and their friends and some of the crew would stay up drinking or clubbing all night. Pete usually stayed up looning until the next morning. The Manchester gig was full of young mods, and, much to their delight, Pete accidentally smashed one of his guitars and walked off at the end, dragging the remains by the strap. The crowd sang 'Happy Birthday' to Roger. A 4ft square cake had been baked for Roger's birthday backstage, but five seconds after it was presented, Roger and about half a dozen others were completely covered in it. Roger was in a great mood. Besides it being his birthday, he had a new-born son, Jamie.

Towards the end of the tour, they released a Single, *You Better, You Bet,* and in March released the *Face Dances* album. As they were using a new drummer and making their first record for a new company, they wanted to use a new producer. They brought in an American, Bill Szymczyk. The Who wanted him to use Ramport Studios, but he chose Odyssey. None of the band were happy with the album. Roger says that you could feel on *Face Dances* that the band wasn't a *band.* Looking back, Pete agreed that the band weren't working together. "The chemistry was wrong and it wasn't just Bill Szymczyk." Apparently, the band never heard the tracks played back on the main speakers at Odyssey, only on the small playback speakers where it sounded alright. Pete went to Florida and pointed out to Szymczyk that the bass wasn't typical of John, and a few other things which were to be put right. John later commented, "If we'd been there to mix it, it might have been a bit better, but I don't think it was actually on the tape anyway." When Kenney was given his early copy of the album to approve the pressing quality, he handed it straight back to Bill Curbishley's assistant, Chris Chappell, declaring, "I didn't like the mix, so why should I like the pressing?" Despite The Who's misgivings, the album immediately sold well. In the US both album and single went to number one in Billboard's rock charts. In England, it was beaten to the number one position by Adam and the Ants, which sold *nine* more copies.

The Who were at a very low ebb at this point. They had an album out that they didn't like, they had a mediocre video, and did a lacklustre TV appearance on BBC's 'Top of the Pops'. They were just about to finish what had been quite an unhappy tour, despite the fact that the gigs were very exciting and dynamic. Pete was talking as though he had finished with the band. He told Bill Curbishley that he wouldn't do the European tour that was booked. However, Curbishley didn't cancel until the last moment in case Pete changed his mind. Tickets had already been on sale and sold out in some countries, so a massive refunding operation had to be set up. It was obvious that Pete couldn't carry on drinking and never sleeping, and Roger saw no point in doing a European tour with Pete in his condition. Pete also needed time to write and record his solo album. He wanted to spend more time with his family. The planned tours for that year left no time for anything else. "If touring is just getting up every night to play old favourites that I'd written out of my system years ago, then I don't want to do it." Pete's relationship with the band as the main songwriter was also weighing on him. He missed having somebody like Kit Lambert to play demos to, who acted as a buffer between him and the band. Halfway through *Face Dances* Pete explains, "I went and wrote four songs while everybody else was resting. When I played them nobody said anything, not a dicky bird. Eventually Rabbit said, 'I like such and such a song, that has some good bits in it.' He was trying to be positive because he was aware of this big pregnant silence. I just picked the tape up and walked out. I thought, 'I'm not breaking my back for these cunts.'"

The last date on the English tour was at the tiny Poole Arts Centre in Sussex. Rumours had been in all the papers that the Who were going to split and many people thought that this would be the final tour. Tickets were changing hands for up to £120. Pete and Roger were both in great moods, laughing on stage. It was a tremendous show and the audience, which numbered only 2,000, were wildly enthusiastic. A kid rushed onto the stage and half a dozen over-heavy bouncers made a grab for him. Roger, seeing what was happening, announced, "It's alright, he's with us. Leave him alone." And to prove it, Pete grabbed him and kissed him on the lips. Roger had requested that they bring back *See Me, Feel Me/Listening to You* to end the encore that night. I was taking pictures in the orchestra pit and towards the climax, which had the whole place in an ecstatic uproar, Pete saw me and raised his eyes upwards in a 'here we go again' look as he went through the 'Tommy motions'. Later at the stage door, a large crowd of fans waited, many in floods of tears, to thank the band and implore them not to break up.

The end of the tour party at the hotel soon got out of hand, with food and buckets of water being thrown around. Somebody swung from the chandelier and it came away from the ceiling. Curbishley warned the guests that The Who

wasn't necessarily paying all the damages. However, in the end, they did.

The Who did one more show that year, in Germany for European TV's 'Rockpalast' show. 'Rockpalast' was shown live in most European countries and heard on radio in even more. The Who were supposed to go through a camera rehearsal the day before but Roger's voice was cracking and he cut it short halfway through. "Somebody should tell him that this show is seen by eight million people," Pete said, underexaggerating for once. The show went out to over 50 million people.

After 'Rockpalast', the band took time off from Who activities for a while. Roger went home to play with his new son, Kenney bought a large house in Sussex for £180,000 to relax in, and Pete and John continued working on their solo albums.

John had been working on his album for quite some time with Joe Walsh and Joe Vitale. The Who and The Eagles had to come before solo projects, so it was difficult finding mutually convenient recording time. John says that he and Walsh only managed to spend two months together in the two years it took to make the album. Besides playing his usual bass guitar, John handled the synthesisers and piano on the album. "I was actually really pleased with the album," John said when *Too Late The Hero* finally came out in September 1981. I was stuck in the black humour bag for a long time. I felt very limited. Now the songs are humorous but not in the same way. Now I write songs about love, sex, and drugs, same as everybody else."

Meanwhile, Pete's solo album was also going very slowly. Progress could usually only be made on Mondays and Tuesdays after a weekend of rest. By Wednesday, he was already exhausted from his destructive nocturnal lifestyle. Producer Chris Thomas remembers one day talking to Pete at the mixing desk only to realise that Pete had been sitting at the controls fast asleep. Pete got stranger and stranger, dropped his friends, had gone in for a succession of unflattering haircuts, taken to wearing makeup ('Gay Whisper' and 'Sheer Genius'), and was 'generally weird'. Chris Thomas became alarmed that coke was ruining Pete's voice and told him in no uncertain terms that he should 'knock it on the head.' Talking about his degeneration became an almost full-time activity among Pete's associates and close friends. They were relieved when at one stage he was persuaded to take a couple of months rest. He stayed at his riverside country house alone, did some gardening and rowing, wrote some short stories, moderated his drinking, and completely cut out drugs. But after three weeks he was back, coked up to the eyeballs, twitching and shaking, and surrounded by the same old sycophants from the chic 'living dead' of clubland. After one late night at a club his driver couldn't find him and assumed he'd returned in a cab. Pete was, in fact, fast asleep on top of a pile of old rubble and bricks in a builder's skip in the next street.

Earlier that year he'd walked out of the Who tour in Austria and was discovered sleeping in the bear pit of the local zoo. He'd been cultivating his scruffy 'soccer hooligan' look for some time and behaving accordingly, but this was eventually replaced by his new smooth 'wimpy-camp' look as he began getting drawn into the English New Romantic movement.

Pete would often take Concorde to New York only to spend most of his time sleeping in some hotel suite. He got very friendly with Bowie, and once passed out in the cloakroom of Mick Jagger's Manhattan apartment after a night's drinking with Mick and Charlie. He ended a very costly trip to Paris to play on Elton John's album, by throwing up his champagne into the ice bucket in the restaurant of the exclusive Hotel Georges. About this time, Ray Davics announced from the stage in the middle of a Kinks concert in London, "We'd like to dedicate this song to Pete Townshend. We hear he's going through a bad time at the moment," and played *Nothing Left To Lose.* Comparisons were being made between Pete's lifestyle and that of Keith Moon, as Pete himself commented in hindsight, ". . . except I didn't have the constitution of Keith Moon, or the will to live of Keith Moon . . ." Like Keith, however, Pete was also running out of his nine lives.

Exactly two years and a day after Keith had died, Pete almost joined him. He visited one of his favourite clubs, the New Romantic 'Club For Heroes'. He'd been drinking with Steve Strange, Phil Lynott and Paul Weller. Later, when he visited the toilet, he was offered heroin, and being extremely intoxicated, accepted. No sooner had he taken it, than he passed out. The club didn't want a sleeping drunk in the toilet, so a huge six foot bouncer carried Pete over his shoulder through the club to his car outside. Pete's driver, Paul Bonnick, was used to driving Pete home slumped over the back seat. But this time he noticed that Pete's lips had turned blue. He stopped and felt Pete's pulse. "It was very weak, but racing." He thought he should take him to a doctor, but two others in the car were worried that some story would appear in the papers if they did. Pete's driver brushed this aside, "If we don't hurry, he might kick it," and rushed him to the nearest hospital. The first person Paul saw inside was a nurse. He explained, "I've got someone outside in a very bad way, and I think he's dying." Paul noticed how calm she stayed as she arranged for people to bring him in. "Then she went to the car, and as soon as she saw Pete she acted really quickly. Pete by now had turned completely blue. She said, 'Quick, we haven't got much time!' and ripped his shirt open and began to pound his chest." Pete was rushed from the car into the hospital and onto a life support machine. The nurse and the hospital's prompt action only just saved his life. Apparently, the hospital knew as soon as they saw Pete that he had taken heroin. They also knew who he was, but kept it confidential. This experience obviously shook him, and he went into an alcohol clinic for five days to dry out but it was four months before he went for a complete cure in California.

Apart from Pete's health, another stumbling block to the band's future was Roger's criticism of Kenney's recent performances. Pete and John totally refuted Roger's stance. However, Pete recalls, "When Kenney went through the initial stages of his divorce, he 'fell to bits'. When we were recording *Face Dances* he was playing very stiffly. He was running to the phone every fucking five minutes. I mean, one day even *I* exploded. He went out to answer a phone call and we were just about to do the take and he came back and he was shaking. It was just stupid."

Some close observers of the band thought that not only Kenney, but Pete *and* Roger were not up to their best on the 1981 British tour. Only Rabbit and John were consistent, and John was often far too loud. Roger persisted with his criticism but, as usual with the Who, nothing happened for several months. Eventually, Bill called a meeting at his house to discuss the group's future. The meeting began at two in the afternoon and went on until one the next morning. Roger again brought up the fact that he wasn't happy with Kenney. Although met by total disagreement, Roger forced the issue. "This happens a lot with Rog," Pete explained some time after, "because he tends to create ultimatums, and it's very difficult to back down when you've given somebody an ultimatum." Bill knew the meeting was going to be tense and had laid on some very fine wine from his cellar. "He was trying some kind of managerial stroke to create an atmosphere where the air would be cleared."

However, at nine o'clock Pete left. "I walked out on that meeting because it just seemed to be getting nowhere. Kenney was just sitting there taking insults, and really the only reason why he wasn't getting up and walking out was 'cos he couldn't afford to. I felt that that was wrong, that it was humiliating for him, and I didn't want to be a part of that, and I just said that John's and my reaction would be to try and keep the group together. Roger took that as a kind of a choice to stick with Kenney rather than with him. What John and I felt was if Roger wasn't gonna work for the group there wouldn't *be* a group, but that it was worth stating that we did have allegiances both ways. But there was no way that we were gonna be forced to make a choice." For a long time, Roger figured that he'd been thrown out of the band.

Pete and Roger had another meeting at Bill's house several weeks later. The usual positions were reversed. This time Roger didn't want to go out on the road, but Pete thought they should. At first Pete thought that the situation was his opportunity to get out of the band, but for some reason he changed his mind. They agreed at that meeting that they'd do two more albums, tour the States in the summer of 1982, and perhaps disolve the Who in two years time.

Pete began 1982 by going for his four week drug withdrawal program in Los Angeles. When he returned he began living with his family again for the first time in months.

In March, Roger released a solo album of greatest hits called *Best Bits* in America and Europe, but not in England. The album contained three new tracks. At the same time, Roger was working on his next solo album of 'pop songs', which was being produced by Jon Astley and Phil Chapmann. They flew to Montserrat in April, taking along singer/songwriter Billy Nicholls to provide backing vocals. Nicholls remembers Roger saying to him, "What this album really needs is a *Bridge Over Troubled Water*. Can you write one while we're here, Bill?' Roger had flu for the first couple of weeks and lost his voice, so they didn't get much recording done. When he returned, Roger opened his new eleven-acre trout farm and fishery that he had excavated himself on his farm in Burwash, which proved to be an immediate success.

At the annual Ivor Novello Awards presentation, the Who were each given a special award for 'services to the rock industry'. Bill accepted on behalf of Keith Moon, saying: "I don't know where he is at the moment, but I'm sure I'll get a bill for the damages."

Pete's solo album, *All The Best Cowboys Have Chinese Eyes* was finally released in June. It had taken a long time due to several problems. "Originally, I did a series of experiments, basically just rhythm tracks with poetry over the top," Pete explains, "When I took the first tracks to New York and played them for the record company, you would have paid money to have seen their faces! They said, 'Leave it to the

avant-garde'. Bowie was with me at the time and he said I should just go ahead and do it, what do the record companies know, anyway. But I came back and rewrote half the album. 'Cos there's little point in sitting and writing material, and getting obsessed with whatever you choose to get obsessed with, and then have nobody to listen. I was going to do a videodisc type scripted film to go with the record, which was going to be called 'Bilder von Lily' (German for "Pictures of Lily"), but it was abandoned halfway through." Pete had practically the whole recording process videoed for use in future promos. However, nobody kept an eye on this project and in the end the whole sixty hours of video, rumoured to have cost £70,000, was rejected, and another had to be hastily put together.

Pete's Eel Pie group of companies had run into financial problems, as he found out when he went to buy a £130,000 mixing desk for his Twickenham studio. He discovered that not only was there no money for the desk, but they were also over half a million pounds in debt. He explained, "I was caught in an incredible cleft stick: I'd not wanted to blow the money I had on mansions or Rolls Royces or homes in LA, because I thought it was much better to create jobs or put the

money into something which helps other people create, and to accept that this was part of my responsibility. But then I was unable to follow it through, either because I was so fucked up, or distracted, or simply not here. Also, the people I'd appointed to do the work thought there was an endless supply of money. I suddenly realised that after all the sneering I'd done about Apple, the same thing was happening to me."

Suddenly Pete was nearly bankrupt and had to deal with his bankers." . . . they wanted my bollocks, despite the fact that I'd put every personal penny I had into the company. They wanted my house, my recording contract – they wanted me to sign to them, and they would sign me to my record label." Pete considered declaring himself bankrupt and retiring to France but decided to fight back. "I'll beat the bastards at their own game. I'll come back from the dead and make some money."

Pete put in a hard-man accountant who cut down the staff of his companies from 37 to 17. He eventually sold off his bookshop in Richmond, The Magic Bus Bookshop, and closed down Eel Pie Sound, his PA hire company. His book publishing company had almost more staff than titles and

was cut back severely.

At about the same time as *Chinese Eyes* was released, Pete began giving a series of confessional interviews. Pete poured his heart out about the black two year period he had just emerged from. He claimed that he'd tried to use drugs as a replacement for drinking. "I just took anything I could lay my hands on, as a way of passing the time, really, because I hated the sensation of not being drunk." Looking back, he said, "I didn't feel that I was getting any real *help* from anywhere. I was getting gigs thrown at me. Bill's philosophy was that the best thing for me was to get me out on the road, treating me much like he treated Keith. John wouldn't know how to talk to me about what was going on, Kenney and I aren't yet close enough. Roger was really great a helluva lot of the time. He would come up and try and be matey and bring me out and talk to me. He would say, 'Listen. Stop the band if it'll keep you alive. It's not that important. You're the important one to me.' I mean, he was fantastic, but again, it was against a backdrop of the fact that we hadn't got a *real relationship* at that level." It was obvious Pete hadn't realised that for the last two years his condition had been the major preoccupation and worry of his friends, family, the band, and the management.

During the time Pete was at the drug cure clinic in California, Roger, John and Kenney had been working with Glyn Johns in his Sussex studio, trying to write material for the next Who album. Andy Fairweather-Low stood in on guitar for Pete. The band had been critical of Pete's songs on *Face Dances,* claiming they were too personal and not particularly Who-ish. After his 'miracle cure' Pete attended a meeting with the band at the studio. "I sat around with everybody and asked them, what do you want to fucking sing about? Tell me and I'll write the songs. It's a piece of piss! I've been writing songs for twenty years. D'you wanna sing about race riots? D'you wanna sing about the nuclear bomb? D'you wanna sing about soya bean diets? Tell me!" Pete established that there wasn't a whole lot of common ground between them. "However, we did find that we all cared very deeply about the planet, the people on it, about the threat to our children from nuclear war, or the increasing instability of our own country's politics." They agreed on a new approach: "We wanted to do something that was to do with life, that was real and hopefully a little easier to read than some of the songs on the last album which were very obtuse." He continued, "I'm more conscious now of trying to deliver the stuff which everybody in the band feels they can identify with. If I can't do it, nobody else can!" Writing the new songs and recording them went remarkably smoothly. They started recording in May. "It was pretty quick," recalls Pete, "more or less two days a track to completion. There are twelve tracks, so it was about twenty four days recording work and about another five or six days fiddling about mixing. I enjoyed it, because the way it came together was relaxed and unselfconscious. We just recorded twelve songs and those are on the record. We all know that if we carried on recording we'd get more tracks and we'd exclude some of the ones that are on the record, but we think it's more important to put this record out the way it is rather than waste time now trying to perfect it. We want it to go out as it is because it's natural. It wasn't just the time it took, it was also the atmosphere. It was almost like we had nothing to lose. I nearly lost everything that I had and so I'm glad to have what I've got. I feel very good about the band being just what they are."

The provisional title for the album was *It's Hard* and it was due for release in late August 1982. Bill Curbishley had planned two month-long tours of the States to coincide with the release of the album.

Roger's solo album, which had originally been titled *Pop Songs* and then *Pops In, Pops Up, Pops Out!,* was due for release in early '83. He had also been approached to star in a version of "The Beggar's Opera" directed by Jonathon Miller for British television sometime in 1983.

As for the future of the Who "the band will go on as long as we get a kick out of it and as long as we really feel that we're turning people on. We'll keep doing it as long as it works," Pete stated, "and as for our past, we've got a lot of history under our belts and we should stop thinking about it as something which is a pain in the arse, and start thinking about it as something which is of incredible value and really be proud of it and be pleased to have it."

WHO TO ADD JONES AND WANT ONE MORE

Jones moves in

KENNY JONES, formerly with the Small Faces, has now settled in as a member of the Who as the band continue their heavy work schedule into the New Year.

A Face in the Who

Who comeback plan

THE WHO are planning to make their stage comeback by playing a

The Who asked ex-Small Faces drummer, Kenney Jones, to join them as a fully-fledged member. Kenney, born on Sept. 16, 1948 in Stepney, East London, was an only child from working class parents; his dad was a lorry driver and his mum worked in a glass factory. Although his mum "could thump out a few East End tunes on the piano", the Joneses were not a musical family. They did, however, pay for his first drumkit, a £64 9s 9d white Olympic. (Kenney did his early practising on old biscuit tins with bits of wood). His first band was the Outcasts, formed with Ronnie Lane. They both progressed to the mod band, the Small Faces in 1966. From there he joined the Faces in 1970. A keen horserider, he came first in the 1976 Royal International Horseshow in London.

Right centre: The early Small Faces, l to r: Steve Marriott, Ronnie Lane, Kenney and Jimmy Winston.
Below: On the 1980 US tour with The Who.

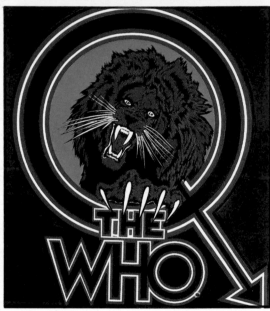

During 1979, Kenney's first year, the band seemed to be constantly in the headlines. Much of their previous 18 months work came to fruition. 'The Kids Are Alright' and 'Quadrophenia' were premiered, they played a sell-out concert at Wembley Stadium in the summer, and did five days at Madison Square Garden (their first US gigs for three years). With the mod revival in London, the words 'The Who' appeared spray-painted on walls everywhere.
Facing page; Left: At Shepperton. The first photo session with Kenney in the line-up.
This page; Top left: At the Rainbow (Kenney's first gig).

1979: The Year of The Who

SURPRISE FIRST GIG FOR THE WHO

All-night ticket queue for The Who

'Quadrophenia' completed

PRINCIPAL PHOTOGRAPHY for The Who's 'Quadrophenia' has been

Clash, Pete Townshend against racism

THE WHO, whose return to rock has been slowly gathering momentum since Keith Moon's death, surprised their followers and the music business this week with the sudden announcement of a two-hour concert tonight (Wednesday) at London's Rainbow Theatre.

The band's return to live work with new drummer Kenny Jones was to have been next weekend at a large amphitheatre near Cannes as part of the promotion for their two forthcoming movies.

But late last week the Who suddenly decided their British fans deserved to see the first show, and the Rainbow gig was advertised on Monday.

The band had booked the

Who plan all-day Wembley gig . . .

PETE TOWNSHEND APPEARED SO SOME PEOPLE WON'T DISAPPEAR.

Daltrey gets a hairdo like McVicar

Left: John "Rabbit" Bundrick, keyboard player.
Bottom left: 'Rockestra' - the concert for Kampuchea. Included were: the late James Honeyman-Scott, John Bonham, Robert Plant, Denny Laine, Pete, Paul McCartney, Dave Edmunds, Ronnie Lane and Kenney (up top).
Below: Kenney and Pete – 'Rock Against Racism' gig, '79

THE CINCINNATI ENQUIRER

OHIO AND INDIANA FINAL/PRICE 20¢/HOME DELIVERY: $4.50 A MONTH

A GANNETT NEWSPAPER

Stampede Kills At Least 11 At Coliseum Rock Concert

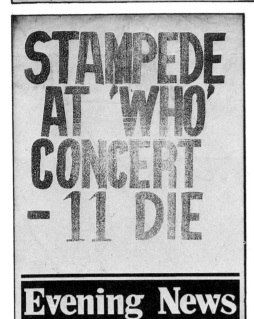

STAMPEDE AT 'WHO' CONCERT — 11 DIE

Evening News

OVERCOME — A young woman is carried to a fire rescue unit at the plaza level of Cincinnati's Riverfront Coliseum Monday night as a concert of the rock group The Who turned into a nightmare. Eleven concertgoers were killed and eight were injured seriously as a waiting crowd, thinking the concert had begun, surged toward the doors. (UPI)

Crowd, Thinking Concert Began, Trampled Its Own to Get in Hall

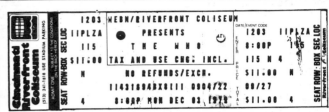

Monday, Dec. 3rd, 1979: The tragic events were unknown to the Who until they came off stage. The next morning they decided, after deliberation, to continue the tour. Roger announced from the stage at Buffalo: "You all heard what happened yesterday. We feel totally shattered... We lost a lot of family yesterday. This show's for them".
Below left: Paramedics try to help two of the victims.
Below right; L to R: Daltrey, Richard Barnes (the author), manager Bill Curbishley, Entwistle.

The Who are 'shattered'

DAILY RECORD, Thursday, December 6, 1979

Anguish of The Who

Why did it happen?

'They opened three doors. Everyone was pushing'

★★★

By Amos A. Kermisch and Thomas K. Diemer
Staff writers

List of fatalities

to the affluent suburb of Wyoming.

Raymond K. Schwertman, a doorman near the main entrance, said: 'They started to beat on the doors were open, but that only two turnstiles were operating There were too few ticket takers on hand.

chanting, "get back, get back," but the pushing continued and Eric ......, 16, lost sight of his 21-

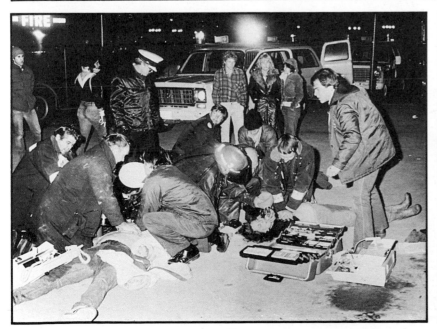

153

DECEMBER 17, 1979 $1.25

TIME
Rock's Outer Limits

New Pressure On Iran

THE WHO

Long Live Rock

THE WHO a new single

Throughout the excellent live performances of 1979 the addition of "Rabbit" on keyboards and a brass section enabled the band to play previously neglected material.

Top right: Two weeks after the Cincinnati tragedy, Time Magazine ran an unexpectedly complimentary cover story.
Below: Front and back of '79 British tour programme.
Right: The telegram informing the Who that they had been voted Best Band of 1979 in both Rolling Stone Reader's and Critics' Polls.
Following spread: Typical offstage larking about on the 1981 tours.

THE WHO

SUMMER OF '79

....and so to bed

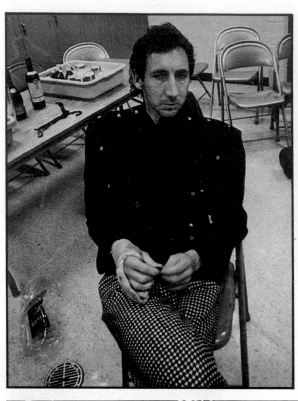

"ROCK NEEDN'T TURN YOU INTO AN IDIOT" – PETE TOWNSHEND

"I AM NOT A DRUG ADDICT AND I NEVER HAVE PARTIES.

Ageing rock star's shock revelations

'I don't matter. Roger doesn't matter. The Who don't matter . . . I just don't seem to care anymore. I just go out and play.'

THE PETE GOES ON

PETE TOWNSHEND

ON ATCO RECORDS AND TAPES

Pete was very unhappy about being on the road and was disillusioned with the Who in general. His solo album *Empty Glass* (released May 1980) was an admission that his life was in a mess.

Top right: Party at New York's Studio 54.
Right: Pete and young skinheads.
Below: Pete's all-important stage checklist taped to the back of his speaker cabinets. ('4711' is an Eau de cologne that he snorts between numbers).
Below right: Pete on Roger's massage apparatus.

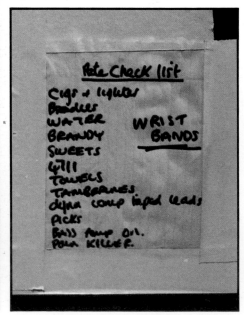

Pete Check list
Cigs + lighter
Bandies
WATER
BRANDY
SWEETS
4711
TOWELS
TAMBORINES
dyna comp imput leads
PICKS
Bass amp Oil
Pain Killer

WRIST BANDS

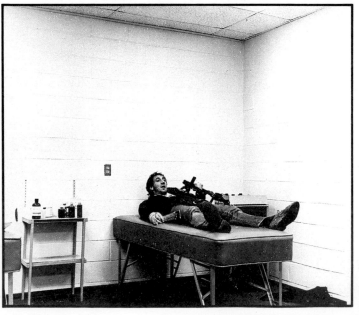

158

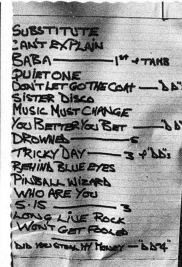

SUBSTITUTE
CAN'T EXPLAIN
BABA————— 1st & TAMB
QUIET ONE
DON'T LET GO THE COAT —— b b's
SISTER DISCO
MUSIC MUST CHANGE
YOU BETTER YOU BET —— b b's
DROWNED————— 5
TRICKY DAY—— 3 & bb's
BEHIND BLUE EYES
PINBALL WIZARD
WHO ARE YOU
5·15 ————— 3
LONG LIVE ROCK
WON'T GET FOOLED
DID YOU STEAL MY MONEY — b b 4"

The Who sign with Warner Bros.

AFTER FIFTEEN years with MCA Records, the Who have switched labels, signing a multialbum deal with Warner Bros. Records for a reported $12 million. Warners would neither confirm nor deny the $12 million figure, which only includes rights to U.S. and Canadian releases, but a spokesman for the label did call it a "big money deal."

by MCA under a one-album deal, and the *Quadrophenia* soundtrack came out on Polydor. It had been widely speculated that the Who would sign with Polydor, their label everywhere except the U.S. and Canada, but the band's asking price (which reportedly included a $5 million unrecoupable bonus) may have been too high. According to one source at Polydor, "It would have been nice to have them,

Apparently Mo Ostin, chairman of the board of Warners, was a big reason the group signed with that label. "Mo's been a Who fanatic for years," said one source. "He's always been keenly aware of them, and he's friends with Pete Townshend and their manager. When the group became available, he went after them." The Warners contract only includes rights to group albums; Townshend is

Top: Spring 1981 UK tour. Right: A young fan takes over on lead. Centre: Townshend at the Rainbow was out of it. As The Times observed "the preponderance of extended codas, slackly improvised at Townshend's behest, spoiled the flow," or as John put it, "He kept boogying off on his own."
Above: January 1980; a change of labels.
Below; centre: The band line-up with 'Rabbit'

Pop and Rock

1 (5) The Who Face Dances (Polydor)
2 (2) Adam and the Ants Kings of the Wild Frontier (CBS)
3 (1) Phil Collins Face Values (Virgin)
4 (8) Sky Sky 3 (Ariola)
5 (7) Status Quo Never Too Late (Vertigo)
6 (11) Stevie Wonder Hotter Than July (Motown)
7 (6) Spandau Ballet Journeys to

Face Dances, their first album with Kenney, was released in March 1981. None of the band were very pleased with it.
Opposite page; Top left: Roger and Kenney on kids' TV ('Tiswas').
Top right: John with album artwork.
Middle left: Pete joins Grateful Dead on German TV's 'Rockpalast'. Jerry Garcia told Musician Magazine, "The Who are one of the few truly important architects of rock 'n' roll. Townshend may be one of rock's rare authentic geniuses."
'McVicar', starring Roger, opened to mixed reviews in August 1980 in Britain and in late 1981 in the States.

Speeding rock star fined £100

ROCK star Roger Daltrey thought he was being chased by a jealous husband when police stopped him for speeding. Sevenoaks magistrates heard how The Who singer drove his Ferrari at 115 mph along the Sevenoaks bypass, chased by an unmarked police car. He was fined £100 and his licence was endorsed.

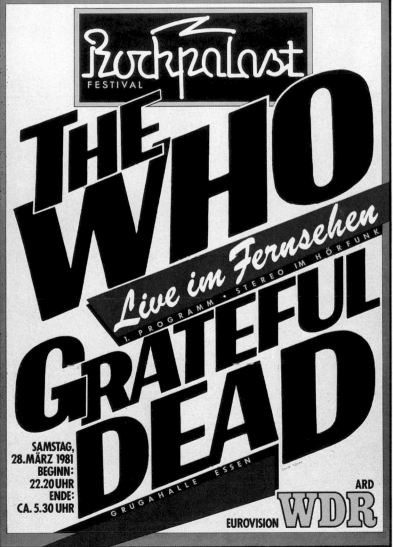

Kit falls to his death

KIT LAMBERT, 45, rock's most outrageous manager and the man who dis-

window to find a new cellophane-wrapped Bentley parked outside with a naked girl on the back seat.

imagination a languages, but ways versed

Death of 'genius' behind The Who

THE man who helped launch top rock group The Who has died.
Kit Lambert died in hospital after falling downstairs at his

The Who's lead guitarist Pete Townshend said yesterday: 'Without Kit there would probably not have been a Who.'

WHO MENTOR DIES

AFTER ACCIDENT

KIT LAMBERT, the man who turned The Who into one of the

behind the then outrageous antics of the band

Below: Kenney and Bill Wyman with Kit in 1979. Lambert, the svengali of the band in the sixties, died on April 7, 1981. After his phenomenal success as a manipulative manager and creative producer he "got bored" and felt he had done it all. He'd made a fortune and lost nearly all of it. Pete said, Without Kit there probably wouldn't have been a Who''.

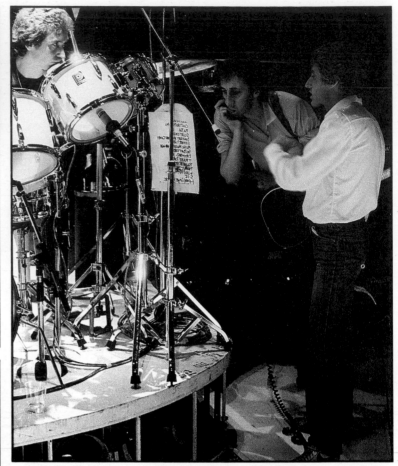

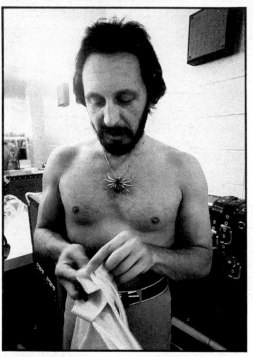

Top left: Backstage, UK tour 1981.

Top right: Roger generally arranges the song order once the numbers have been agreed upon.

Middle left: John and his portable wardrobe, 1980 US tour. On stage, John has two cycling water bottles (white wine and brandy) taped to his mike stand. Kenney has mineral water and cognac, while Roger prefers cups of tea and ice cream and yogurt for his throat.

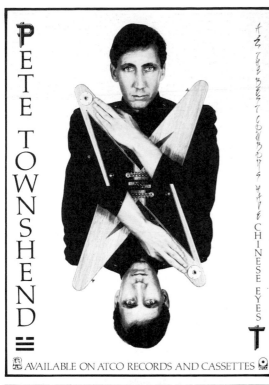

PETE TOWNSHEND

ALL THE BEST COWBOYS HAVE CHINESE EYES

AVAILABLE ON ATCO RECORDS AND CASSETTES

With the release of *Chinese Eyes,* in June 1982, Pete emerged from a black period: ''I hated the sensation of not being drunk''. After a 'miracle cure' the band discussed the next album. They had been critical of his ''personal and not particularly Who-ish'' *Face Dances* songs, ''so I sat around and asked them 'What do you want to fucking sing about? Tell me and I'll write the songs.''

Chinese Eyes; Top: The poster, and recording with Chris Thomas at Air Studios. Middle right: The video.
Above & Left: Working on the cover for the 1982 album.

John and Roger also put out solo albums during 1981/82. John recorded *Too Late The Hero* with Joe Walsh and Joe Vitale and released it in September 1981, ''It's the first album I've done that I'm really pleased with''. Roger released *Best Bits,* a compilation, in March 1982. In early 1982 Pete explained his and the new reborn Who's philosophy, ''I nearly lost everything that I had and so I'm glad to have what I've got. I feel very good about the band being just what they are. We found we all cared deeply about the planet and the people on it; there is an urgency now to do something revolutionary or at least something to do with real life''.

Opposite page: Bottom pics: Pete and John's photo sessions.

All Who songs written by Pete Townshend unless otherwise stated.
All entries UK and USA unless otherwise stated.

Singles

(UK) A. I'M THE FACE (Pete Meaden)/
B. ZOOT SUIT (Pete Meaden)
Fontana. Rel: Jul 3, '64.
Produced by Chris Parmeinter and Pete Meaden.

(UK) A. I CAN'T EXPLAIN
B. BALD HEADED WOMAN (Talmy)
Brunswick. Rel: Jan 15, '65.
(US) Decca. Rel: Feb '65.
Produced by Shel Talmy.

A. ANYWAY, ANYHOW, ANYWHERE
(Townshend, Daltrey) First version/
(UK) B. DADDY ROLLING STONE (Derek Martin)
Brunswick. Rel: May 21, '65.
(US) B. ANYTIME YOU WANT ME (Regovay-Mimms)
Decca. Rel: May '65.
Produced by Shel Talmy.

A. MY GENERATION First version/
B. (UK) SHOUT AND SHIMMY (James Brown)
Brunswick. Rel: Nov 5, '65.
B. (US) OUT IN THE STREET
Decca. Rel: Oct '65.
Produced by Shel Talmy.

A. SUBSTITUTE First version/
B. (UK) CIRCLES Second version
Reaction. Rel: Mar 4, '66.
B. (US) WALTZ FOR A PIG (Butcher)
ATCO. Rel: Mar '66.
Produced by The Who.

(UK) A. SUBSTITUTE First version/
B. INSTANT PARTY
Actually second version of 'Circles'
Reaction. Rel: Mar 4, '66.

(UK) A. A LEGAL MATTER/
B. INSTANT PARTY
First version of 'Circles'
Brunswick. Rel: Mar 11, '66.
Produced by Shel Talmy.

(UK) A. SUBSTITUTE First version/
B. WALTZ FOR A PIG (Harry Butcher)
Reaction. Rel: Mar 15, '66.

A. THE KIDS ARE ALRIGHT
B. (UK) THE OX (Townshend, Moon, Entwistle, Nicky Hopkins)
Brunswick. Rel: Aug 12, '66.
B. (US) A LEGAL MATTER
Decca. Rel: July, '66.
Produced by Shel Talmy.

A. I'M A BOY
(UK) B. IN THE CITY (Moon, Entwistle)
Reaction. Rel: Aug 26, '66.
(US) B. IN THE CITY
Decca. Rel: Dec '66.
Produced by Kit Lambert.

(UK) READY, STEADY, WHO! (EP)
Reaction. Rel: Nov 11, '66.
Producer Francis Hitching.

(UK) A. LA LA LA LIES
B. THE GOOD'S GONE
Brunswick. Rel: Nov 11, '66.
Produced by Shel Talmy.

A. HAPPY JACK
(UK) B. I'VE BEEN AWAY (Entwistle)
Reaction. Rel: Dec 3, '66.
(US) B. WHISKEY MAN (Entwistle)
Decca. Rel: Mar '67.
Produced by Kit Lambert.

A. PICTURES OF LILY
B. DOCTOR, DOCTOR (Entwistle)
(UK) Track. Rel: April 22, '67.
Produced by Kit Lambert.
(US) Decca. Rel: June '67.
Produced by Kit Lambert and Chris Stamp.

(UK) A. THE LAST TIME (Jagger, Richards) (sic)/
B. UNDER MY THUMB (Jagger, Richards)
Track. Rel: June 30, '67.

A. I CAN SEE FOR MILES
(UK) B. SOMEONE'S COMING (Entwistle)
Track. Rel: October 4, '67.
Produced by Kit Lambert.

(US) B. MARY ANNE WITH THE SHAKY HANDS
Decca. Rel: Oct '67.
Produced by Lambert and Stamp.

(UK) A. CALL ME LIGHTNING
B. DR. JEKYLL & MR. HYDE (Entwistle)
Second version
Decca. Rel: Mar '68.
Produced by Lambert and Stamp.

(UK) A. DOGS
B. CALL ME LIGHTNING
Track. Rel: June '68.
Produced by Kit Lambert.

A. MAGIC BUS Short version /
B. (UK) DR. JEKYLL AND MR. HYDE (Entwistle)
Track. Rel: Sept 18, '68.
Produced by Kit Lambert.
B. (US) SOMEONE'S COMING (Entwistle)
Decca. Rel: July '68.
Produced by Lambert and Stamp.

A. PINBALL WIZARD
B. DOGS PART II (Moon, Towser, Jason)
(UK) Track. Rel: Mar 7, '69.
Produced by Kit Lambert.
(US) Decca. Rel: Mar '69.
Produced by 'Baron Lambert' and Stamp.

A. I'M FREE
(UK) B. 1921
Track. Rel: July '69.
(US) B. WE'RE NOT GONNA TAKE IT
Decca. Rel: July '69.
Produced by Lambert and Stamp.

(UK) A. GO TO THE MIRROR
B. SALLY SIMPSON
Track. Rel: July '69.
Produced by Kit Lambert.

(UK) A. THE ACID QUEEN
B. WE'RE NOT GONNA TAKE IT
Track. Rel: July '69.
Produced by Kit Lambert.

(UK) A. CHRISTMAS
B. OVERTURE
Track. Rel: July '69.
Produced by Kit Lambert.

A. THE SEEKER
B. HERE FOR MORE (Daltrey)
(UK) Track. Rel: Feb 13, '70.
Produced by The Who.
(US) Decca. Rel: April '70.
Produced by Lambert and Stamp.

A. SUMMERTIME BLUES (Cochran, Capehart)/
B. HEAVEN AND HELL (Entwistle)
(UK) Track. Rel: July 10, '70.
(US) Decca. Rel: July '70.
Produced by Lambert and Stamp.

A. SEE ME, FEEL ME
B. OVERTURE FROM TOMMY
(UK) Track. Rel: Oct 10, '70.
Produced by Kit Lambert.

(UK) TOMMY (EP)
Track. Rel: Nov '70.
Produced by Kit Lambert.

A. WON'T GET FOOLED AGAIN Edited version/
B. DON'T KNOW MYSELF
(UK) Track. Rel: June 25, '71.
Produced by Engineer Glyn Johns.
(US) Decca. Rel: July '71.
Produced by Lambert, Stamp and Kameron.

(UK) A. LET'S SEE ACTION
B. WHEN I WAS A BOY (Entwistle)
Track. Rel: Nov '71.

(US) A. BEHIND BLUE EYES
B. MY WIFE (Entwistle)
Decca. Rel: Nov '71.
Produced by The Who.
Executive Producer: Lambert, Stamp and Kameron.

A. JOIN TOGETHER
B. BABY DON'T YOU DO IT (Holland, Dozier, Holland)
(UK) Track. Rel: June '72.
(US) Decca. Rel: July '72.
Produced by The Who.

A. RELAY
B. WASPMAN (Moon)
(UK) Track. Rel: Nov '72.
(US) Track Decca. Rel: Nov '72.
Produced by The Who.

(UK) A. 5.15
B. WATER
Track. Rel: Sept '73.
Produced by The Who.

(US) A. LOVE, REIGN O'ER ME
B. WATER
Track MCA. Rel: Nov '73.
Produced by The Who.

(US) A. THE REAL ME Edited version
B. I'M ONE
Track MCA. Rel: Jan '74.
Executive Producer: Stamp, Kameron and Lambert.

(US) A. POSTCARD (Entwistle)/
B. PUT THE MONEY DOWN
Track MCA. Rel: Mar '74.
Produced by The Who.
Executive Producer: Glyn Johns.

A. SQUEEZE BOX
B. SUCCESS STORY (Entwistle)
(UK) Polydor. Rel: Jan 24, '76.
(US) MCA. Rel: Aug '75.
Produced by Glyn Johns.

(US) A. SLIP KID
B. DREAMING FROM THE WAIST
MCA. Rel: Aug '76.
Produced by Glyn Johns.

(UK) A. SUBSTITUTE First version
B. I'M A BOY Long version
PICTURES OF LILY
Polydor. Rel: Oct '76.
Produced by Kit Lambert.

A. WHO ARE YOU
B. HAD ENOUGH (Entwistle)
(UK) Polydor. Rel: July 14, '78.
(US) MCA. Rel: Aug '78.
Produced by Glyn Johns and Jon Astley.

(US) A. TRICK OF THE LIGHT (Edited)
B. 905 (Entwistle)
MCA. Rel: Dec '78.
Produced by Glyn Johns and Jon Astley.

A. LONG LIVE ROCK
B. I'M THE FACE (Pete Meaden)/
MY WIFE (Entwistle) Live
(UK) Polydor. Rel: April 1, '79.
(US) MCA. Rel: June '79.

A. 5.15
B. I'M ONE
(UK) Polydor. Rel: Sept '79.
(US) Polydor. Rel: Sept '79.
Produced by John Entwistle.

A. YOU BETTER YOU BET
B. THE QUIET ONE (Entwistle)
(UK) Polydor. Rel: Feb 27, '81.
(US) Warner Brothers. Rel: Mar '81.
Produced by Bill Szymczyk.

A. DON'T LET GO THE COAT
B. YOU (Entwistle)
(UK) Polydor. Rel: May 1, '81.
(US) Warner Brothers. Rel: June '81.
Produced by Bill Szymczyk.

Albums

(UK) MY GENERATION
Brunswick. Rel: Dec '65.
Produced by Shel Talmy.
Side One: 1. Out In The Street/2. I Don't Mind (Brown)/3. The Good's Gone/4. La La La Lies/5. Much Too Much/6. My Generation.
Side Two: 7. The Kids Are Alright/8. Please, Please, Please (Brown, Terry)/9. It's Not True/10. I'm A Man (McDaniel) Unedited version/11. A Legal Matter/12. The Ox (Townshend, Moon, Entwistle, Hopkins).

(US) THE WHO SINGS MY GENERATION
Decca. Rel: April '66.
Produced by Shel Talmy.
Side One: 1. Out In The Street/2. I Don't Mind (James Brown)/3. The Good's Gone/4. La La La Lies/5. Much Too Much/6. My Generation First version.
Side Two: 7. The Kids Are Alright Edited version/8. Please Please Please (Brown/Terry)/9. It's Not True/10. The Ox (PT, KM, JAE, Hopkins)/11. A Legal Matter/12. Instant Party.

(UK) A QUICK ONE
Reaction. Rel: Dec '66.
Produced by Kit Lambert.
Side One: Run, Run, Run Mono version/2. Boris The Spider (Entwistle)/3. I Need You (Moon)/4. Whiskey Man (Entwistle)/5. Heatwave (Holland, Dozier, Holland)/6. Cobwebs And Strange (Moon).
Side Two: 7. Don't Look Away/8. See My Way (Daltrey)/9. So Sad About Us/10. A Quick One While He's Away.

(US) HAPPY JACK
Decca. Rel: May '67.
Produced by Kit Lambert.
Side One: 1. Run, Run, Run/2. Boris The Spider (Entwistle)/3. I Need You (Moon)/4. Whiskey Man (Entwistle)/5. Cobwebs And Strange (Moon)/6. Happy Jack.
Side Two: 7. Don't Look Away/8. See My Way (Daltrey)/9. So Sad About Us/10. A Quick One While He's Away.

THE WHO SELL OUT
(UK) Track. Rel: Nov '67.
(US) Decca. Rel: Dec '67.
Produced by Kit Lambert.
Side One: 1. Armenia City In The Sky (Keene)/2. Heinz Baked Beans (Entwistle)/3. Mary Anne With The Shaky Hand. This version is different from the US single/4. Odorono/5. Tattoo/6. Our Love Was/7. I Can See For Miles.
Side Two: 8. Can't Reach You/9. Medac (Entwistle)/10. Relax/11. Silas Stingy (Entwistle)/12. Sunrise/13. Rael 1 and 2.

(US) MAGIC BUS – THE WHO ON TOUR
Decca. Rel: Sept '68.
Produced by Kit Lambert.

(UK) DIRECT HITS
Track. Rel: Nov '68.
Produced by Kit Lambert.

(UK) THE HOUSE THAT TRACK BUILT
Track. Rel: '69.

TOMMY (Double)
(UK) Track. Rel: May 23, '69.
(US) Decca. Rel: May '69.
Producer Kit Lambert.
Side One: 1. Overture/2. It's A Boy/3. 1921/4. Amazing Journey/5. Sparks/6. Eyesight For The Blind (Sonny Boy Williamson).
Side Two: 7. Christmas/8. Cousin Kevin (Entwistle)/9. The Acid Queen/10. Underture.
Side Three: 11. Do You Think It's Alright?/12. Fiddle About (Entwistle)/13. Pinball Wizard/14. There's A Doctor/15. Go To The Mirror!/16. Tommy Can You Hear Me?/17. Smash The Mirror/18. Sensation.
Side Four: 19. Miracle Cure/20. Sally Simpson/21. I'm Free/22. Welcome/23. Tommy's Holiday Camp (Moon)/24. We're Not Gonna Take It.

LIVE AT LEEDS
(UK) Track. Rel: May '70.
(US) Decca. Rel: May '70.
Produced by The Who.
Side One: 1. Young Man Blues (Mose Allison)/2. Substitute/3. Summertime Blues (Cochran, Capehart)/4. Shakin' All Over (Heath).
Side Two: 5. My Generation with 'Tommy Reprise'/6. Magic Bus.

WHO'S NEXT
(UK) Track. Rel: July '71.
(US) Decca. Rel: Aug '71.
Produced by The Who.
Side One: 1. Baba O'Riley. Who's studio version/2. Bargain/3. Love Ain't For Keeping/4. My Wife (Entwistle) Who's studio version/5. Song Is Over.
Side Two: 6. Getting In Tune/7. Going Mobile/8. Behind Blue Eyes/9. Won't Get Fooled Again. Long version.

MEATY, BEATY, BIG AND BOUNCY
(UK) Track. Rel: Oct '71.
Tracks 1, 2, 6, 8 and 10 produced by Shel Talmy.
Tracks 3, 4, 5, 9, 11, 12 and 14 produced by Kit Lambert.
Tracks 7 and 13 produced by The Who.
(US) Decca. Rel: Nov '71.
Side One: 1. I Can't Explain/2. The Kids Are Alright. Edited version/3. Happy Jack/4. I Can See For Miles. Stereo version/5. Pictures Of Lily/6. My Generation. First version/7. The Seeker.
Side Two: 8. Anyway Anyhow Anywhere (Townshend/Daltrey) First edition/9. Pinball Wizard/10. A Legal Matter/11. Boris The Spider (Entwistle)/12. The Magic Bus. Long studio version/13. Substitute. First version/14. I'm A Boy. Long version.

QUADROPHENIA
(UK) Track. Rel: Nov '73.
Produced by The Who (Pre-production: Pete Townshend, Kit Lambert) Tracks 9 and 17.
(US) MCA. Rel: Oct '73.
Produced by The Who (Pre-production: Townshend, Lambert).
Side One: 1. I Am The Sea/2. The Real Me/3. Quadrophenia/4. Cut My Hair/5. The Punk And The Godfather.
Side Two: 6. I'm One/7. The Dirty Jobs/8. Helpless Dancer/9. Is It In My Head/10. I've Had Enough.
Side Three: 11. 5.15/12. Sea And Sand/13. Drowned/14. Bell Boy.
Side Four: 15. Doctor Jimmy/16. The Rock/17. Love, Reign O'er Me.

A QUICK ONE/THE WHO SELL OUT (Double)
Track. Rel: June '74.
(US) MCA. Rel: Nov '74.
Produced by Kit Lambert.

ODDS AND SODS
(UK) Track. Rel: Oct '74.
Producers: The Who, Kit Lambert, Chris Parmeinter and Peter Meaden.
(US) MCA. Rel: Oct '74.
Side One: 1. Postcard (Entwistle)/2. Now I'm A Farmer/3. Put The Money Down/4. Little Billy/5. Too Much Of Anything/6. Glow Girl.
Side Two: 7. Pure And Easy/8. Faith In Something Bigger/9. I'm The Face (Meaden)/10. Naked Eye/11. Long Live Rock.

THE WHO BY NUMBERS
(UK) Polydor De Luxe. Rel: Oct '75.
(US) MCA. Rel: Oct '75.
Produced by Glyn Johns.
Side One: 1. Slip Kid. Long version./2. However Much I Booze/3. Squeeze Box/4. Dreaming From The Waist/5. Imagine A Man.
Side Two: 6. Success Story (Entwistle)/7. They Are All In Love/8. Blue Red And Grey/9. How Many Friends/10. In A Hand Or A Face.

(UK) THE STORY OF THE WHO (Double)
Polydor. Rel: Sept '76.

WHO ARE YOU
(UK) Polydor. Rel: Aug '78.
(US) MCA. Rel: Aug '79.
Produced by Glyn Johns and Jon Astley.
Side One: 1. New Song/2. Had Enough/3. 905 (Entwistle)/4. Sister Disco/5. Music Must Change.
Side Two: 6. Trick Of The Light (Entwistle)/7. Guitar And Pen/8. Love Is Coming Down/9. Who Are You. Unedited version.

THE KIDS ARE ALRIGHT (Double) Music from the movie soundtrack.
(UK) Polydor. Rel: June '79.
(US) MCA. Rel: June '79.

QUADROPHENIA (Double)
Music from the soundtrack of the film.
(UK) Polydor. Rel: Sept '79.
(US) Polydor. Rel: Sept '79.

LIVE AT LEEDS/WHO ARE YOU
Polydor. Rel: 1980.

FACE DANCES
(UK) Polydor. Rel: Mar '81.
(US) Warner Brothers. Rel: Mar '81.
Produced by Bill Szymczyk.
Side One: 1. You Better, You Bet. Long version/2. Don't Let Go The Coat/3. Cache Cache/4. The Quiet One/5. Did You Steal My Money?
Side Two: 6. How Can You Do It Alone?/7. Daily Records/8. You (Entwistle)/9. Another Tricky Day.

(UK) PHASES (A Nine LP Boxed Set)
Polydor. Rel: May '81.

(US) HOOLIGANS (Double)
MCA. Rel: Sept '81.

IT'S HARD (Title at time of going to press)
(UK) Polydor. Rel: Sept '82.
(US) Warner Brothers. Rel: Sept '82.
Produced by Glyn Johns.
Side One: 1. Athena/2. It's Your Turn (Entwistle)/3. Cooks County/4. Hard/5. Dangerous/6. Eminence Front.
Side Two: 7. I've Known No War/8. One Life's Enough/9. One At A Time (Entwistle)/10. Why Did I Fall For That/11. A Man Is A Man/12. Cry If You Want.

ENTWISTLE (Solo)

Albums

SMASH YOUR HEAD AGAINST THE WALL
(UK) Track. Rel: May '71.
(US) Decca. Rel: May '71.
Produced by John Entwistle.

WHISTLE RYMES
(UK) Track. Rel: Nov '72.
(US) Decca. Rel: Nov '72.
Produced by John Entwistle versus John Alcock.

(UK) RIGOR MORTIS SETS IN
(US) JOHN ENTWISTLE'S RIGOR MORTIS SETS IN
(UK) Track. Rel: June '73.
(US) MCA. Rel: June '73.
Produced by John Entwistle versus John Alcock.

JOHN ENTWISTLE'S OX: MAD DOG
(UK) Decca. Rel: Mar '75.
Produced by John Alcock versus John Entwistle.

TOO LATE THE HERO
(UK) WEA. Rel: Nov '81.
(US) ATCO. Rel: Sept '81.
Produced by Cy Langston, John Entwistle.

Singles

Songs by John Entwistle
I BELIEVE IN EVERTHING/MY SIZE (From 'Smash Your Head Against The Wall')
(UK) Track. Rel: May '71.
(US) Decca. Rel: May '71.

I WONDER/WHO CARES (From 'Whistle Rymes')
(US) Decca. Rel: Nov '72.

MADE IN JAPAN/HOUND DOG (From 'Rigor Mortis Sets In')
(UK) Track. Rel: June '73.

MADE IN JAPAN/ROLLER SKATE KATE (From 'Rigor Mortis Sets In')
(US) MCA. Rel: June '73.

MAD DOG/CELL NUMBER SEVEN (From 'Mad Dog')
(UK) Decca. Rel: Feb '75.

TOO LATE THE HERO/I'M COMING BACK (From 'Too Late The Hero')
(UK) WEA. Rel: Oct '81.

TOO LATE THE HERO/DANCING MASTER
(US) ATCO. Rel: Oct '81.

DALTREY (Solo)

Albums

DALTREY
(UK) Track.
(US) MCA. Rel: Apr '73.
Produced by Adam Faith and Dave Courtney.

RIDE A ROCK HORSE
(UK) Polydor
(US) MCA. Rel: June '75.
Produced by Russ Ballard.

LISZTOMANIA
(UK) A & M
(US) A & M Rel: '75
Produced by David Puttnam and Roy Baird
Executive Producers: Brian Lane and Bill Curbishley.

ONE OF THE BOYS
(UK) Polydor. Rel: May '77.
(US) MCA. Rel: June '77.
Produced by Dave Courtney & Tony Meehan.

McVICAR: Original Soundtrack of The Who film.
(UK) Polydor
(US) Polydor. Rel: June '80.
Produced by Jeff Wayne.

BEST BITS
(US) MCA. Rel: Mar '82.

Singles

GIVING IT ALL AWAY/THE WAY OF THE WORLD
(From 'Daltrey')
(UK) Track. Rel: May '73.
(US) MCA.

THINKING/THERE IS LOVE (From 'Daltrey')
(UK) Track. Rel: May '73.
(US) MCA.

IT'S A HARD LIFE/ONE MAN BAND (From 'Daltrey')
(UK) Track. Rel: May '73.

ONE MAN BAND/THE STORY SO FAR (From 'Daltrey')
Track.

COME AND GET YOUR LOVE/HEARTS RIGHT
(From 'Ride A Rock Horse')
(UK) Polydor.

GET YOUR LOVE/WORLD OVER (From 'Ride A Rock Horse')
(UK) Polydor.

WALKING THE DOG/PROUD (From 'Ride A Rock Horse')
(UK) Polydor. Rel: Aug 75

OCEANS AWAY/FEELING (From 'Ride A Rock Horse')
(US) MCA. Rel: Jan '76

ORPHEUS SONG /LOVE'S DREAM (From 'Lisztomania')
(UK) A&M.

LOVE'S DREAM /ORPHEUS SONG (From 'Lisztomania') (US) A&M.

WRITTEN ON THE WIND /DEAR JOHN (From 'One Of The Boys')
(UK) Polydor. Rel: May '77.

ONE OF THE BOYS/YOU PUT SOMETHING BETTER INSIDE ME (Egan /Rafferty) (From 'One Of The Boys')
(UK)Polydor. Rel: July '77.

SAY IT AIN'T SO, JOE/SATIN AND LACE (From 'One Of The Boys')

(STEVE GIBBONS TRACK)/ONE OF THE BOYS (From 'One Of The Boys')
(US) MCA.

AVENGING ANNIE/THE PRISONER (From 'One Of The Boys')
(US) MCA. Rel: Oct '77.

LEON/THE PRISONER (from: 'One Of The Boys')
(US) MCA. Rel: April '78.

FREE ME /McVICAR (From: 'McVicar')
(UK) Polydor. Rel: Jun '80.
(US) Polydor. Rel: Aug '80.

WITHOUT YOUR LOVE /ESCAPE PART 1 (From 'McVicar')
(US) Polydor. Rel: Oct '80.

WITHOUT YOUR LOVE/SAY IT AIN'T SO, JOE (From 'McVicar')
(US) Polydor. Rel: Oct '80.

WAITING FOR A FRIEND /BITTER AND TWISTED (From 'McVicar')
(US) Polydor.

WITHOUT YOUR LOVE/SAY IT AIN'T SO, JOE/FREE ME (From 'McVicar')
(UK) Polydor. Rel: Feb '81.

MOON (Solo)

Albums

TWO SIDES OF THE MOON
(UK) Polydor
(US) MCA.
(UK) Rel: May '75 (US) April '75.
Original produced by Mal Evans then: Skip Taylor and John Stronach.

Singles

DON'T WORRY BABY (First mix)/TOGETHER (From 'Two Sides Of The Moon')
(UK) Polydor.

DON'T WORRY BABY (First mix)/TEENAGE IDOL (First Mix) (From 'Two Sides Of The Moon')
(US) MCA. Rel: April '75

SOLID GOLD/MOVE OVER MISS L (From 'Two Sides Of The Moon')
(US) MCA. Rel: April '75

CRAZY LIKE A FOX/IN MY LIFE (From 'Two Sides Of The Moon')
(US) MCA. Rel: July '75

TOWNSHEND (Solo)

Albums

WHO CAME FIRST
(UK) Track.
(US) Decca. Rel: Oct 72.
Produced by Pete Townshend.

ROUGH MIX
(UK) Polydor.
(US) MCA.
Produced by Glyn Johns.

EMPTY GLASS
(UK) ATCO. Rel: 14 April '80.
(US) ATCO. Rel: 10 May '80.
Produced by Chris Thomas.

ALL THE BEST COWBOYS HAVE CHINESE EYES
(UK) ATCO.
(US) ATCO. Rel: May '82.
Produced by Chris Thomas.

SINGLES

FOREVER'S NO TIME AT ALL/THIS SONG IS GREEN (From 'Who Came First')
(UK) Track

MY BABY GIVES IT AWAY/LANE TRACK (From 'Rough Mix')
(US) MCA. Rel: Nov. '77.

STREET IN THE CITY/LANE TRACK (From 'Rough Mix')
(UK) Polydor Rel: Nov. '77.

KEEP ME TURNING/LANE TRACK (From 'Rough Mix')
(US) MCA. Rel: April '78.

ROUGH BOYS/AND I MOVED (From 'Empty Glass')
(UK) ATCO. Rel: May '80.

LET MY LOVE OPEN THE DOOR/AND I MOVED (From 'Empty Glass')
(US) ATCO. Rel: June '80.

LET MY LOVE OPEN THE DOOR/CLASSIFIED/GREY HOUND GIRL (From 'Empty Glass')
(UK) ATCO. Rel: June '80.

A LITTLE IS ENOUGH/CAT'S IN THE CUPBOARD (From 'Empty Glass')
(US) ATCO. Rel: Oct. '80.

KEEP ON WORKING/JOOLS AND JIM (From 'Empty Glass')
(UK) ATCO. Rel: Nov. '80.

ROUGH BOYS/JOOLS AND JIM (From 'Empty Glass')
(US) ATCO. Rel: Nov. '80.

JONES (Solo)

Single

READY OR NOT/WOMAN TROUBLE
(UK) GM Records Rel: Oct. '74.